Early Modern Aristotelianism and the Making of Philosophical Disciplines

Bloomsbury Studies in the Aristotelian Tradition

General Editor:
Marco Sgarbi, Università Ca' Foscari, Italy

Editorial Board:
Klaus Corcilius *(University of California, Berkeley, USA)*; Daniel Garber *(Princeton University, USA)*; Oliver Leaman *(University of Kentucky, USA)*; Anna Marmodoro *(University of Oxford, UK)*; Craig Martin *(Oakland University, USA)*; Carlo Natali *(Università Ca' Foscari, Italy)*; Riccardo Pozzo *(Consiglio Nazionale delle Ricerche, Rome, Italy)*; Renée Raphael *(University of California, Irvine, USA)*; Victor M. Salas *(Sacred Heart Major Seminary, USA)*; Leen Spruit *(Radboud University Nijmegen, The Netherlands)*.

Aristotle's influence throughout the history of philosophical thought has been immense and in recent years the study of Aristotelian philosophy has enjoyed a revival. However, Aristotelianism remains an incredibly polysemous concept, encapsulating many, often conflicting, definitions. *Bloomsbury Studies in the Aristotelian Tradition* responds to this need to define Aristotelianism and give rise to a clear characterization.

Investigating the influence and reception of Aristotle's thought from classical antiquity to contemporary philosophy from a wide range of perspectives, this series aims to reconstruct how philosophers have become acquainted with the tradition. The books in this series go beyond simply ascertaining that there are Aristotelian doctrines within the works of various thinkers in the history of philosophy, but seek to understand how they have received and elaborated Aristotle's thought, developing concepts into ideas that have become independent of him.

Bloomsbury Studies in the Aristotelian Tradition promotes new approaches to Aristotelian philosophy and its history. Giving special attention to the use of interdisciplinary methods and insights, books in this series will appeal to scholars working in the fields of philosophy, history and cultural studies.

Available titles:
A Political Philosophy of Conservatism, Ferenc Hörcher
Elijah Del Medigo and Paduan Aristotelianism, Michael Engel
Phantasia in Aristotle's Ethics, edited by Jakob Leth Fink
Pontano's Virtues, Matthias Roick
The Aftermath of Syllogism, edited by Marco Sgarbi and Matteo Cosci
The Reception of Aristotle's Poetics in the Italian Renaissance and Beyond, edited by Bryan Brazeau

Early Modern Aristotelianism and the Making of Philosophical Disciplines

Metaphysics, Ethics and Politics

Danilo Facca

BLOOMSBURY ACADEMIC
LONDON • NEW YORK • OXFORD • NEW DELHI • SYDNEY

BLOOMSBURY ACADEMIC
Bloomsbury Publishing Plc
50 Bedford Square, London, WC1B 3DP, UK
1385 Broadway, New York, NY 10018, USA
29 Earlsfort Terrace, Dublin 2, Ireland

BLOOMSBURY, BLOOMSBURY ACADEMIC and the Diana logo are trademarks of
Bloomsbury Publishing Plc

First published in Great Britain 2020
This paperback edition published in 2021

Copyright © Danilo Facca, 2020

Danilo Facca has asserted his right under the Copyright, Designs and
Patents Act, 1988, to be identified as Author of this work.

For legal purposes the Acknowledgements on pp. x–xi constitute an extension
of this copyright page.

Cover design: Catherine Wood
Cover image © The British Library https://www.bl.uk

All rights reserved. No part of this publication may be reproduced or transmitted
in any form or by any means, electronic or mechanical, including photocopying,
recording, or any information storage or retrieval system, without prior permission
in writing from the publishers.

Bloomsbury Publishing Plc does not have any control over, or responsibility for, any
third-party websites referred to or in this book. All internet addresses given in this
book were correct at the time of going to press. The author and publisher regret
any inconvenience caused if addresses have changed or sites have ceased to exist,
but can accept no responsibility for any such changes.

A catalogue record for this book is available from the British Library.

A catalog record for this book is available from the Library of Congress.

ISBN: HB: 978-1-3501-3021-0
PB: 978-1-3502-5144-1
ePDF: 978-1-3501-3022-7
eBook: 978-1-3501-3023-4

Series: Bloomsbury Studies in the Aristotelian Tradition

Typeset by RefineCatch Limited, Bungay, Suffolk

To find out more about our authors and books visit www.bloomsbury.com
and sign up for our newsletters.

Contents

Preface	vi
Acknowledgements	x

Part One Methodus

1. The Origins and Development of the 'Acroamatic–Exoteric' Distinction in the Late Renaissance ... 3

Part Two Theoria

2. The Historical Significance of the Ramist Critique of Metaphysics ... 33
3. Ernst Soner's Commentary on the *Metaphysics* and the Scholastic Tradition ... 55

Part Three Praxis

4. The Aristotelians and the New Science of Politics ... 93
5. Franz Tidike's *Disputatio de fato* and the Teaching of Moral Philosophy at the Toruń Gymnasium at the Turn of the Seventeenth Century ... 135

Conclusion	171
Notes	175
Bibliography	231
Index	245

Preface

This book was sparked by the encounter between two fairly heterogeneous areas of interest. The more specific strand relates to the teaching of philosophy in the Reformed universities and schools of Central-Eastern Europe (Germany and Poland), while the more general theme is the reception of Aristotle's philosophy in various historic contexts. Fortunately, the meeting point emerges quite simply from the fact that the philosophy taught in such schools was Aristotelian philosophy. I have sought to discover in what sense this adjective was understood in this historic framework. In the course of the research I had to narrow the field to a selected number of contexts and figures. As a result, I do not expect to be immune from the charge of arbitrariness or subjectivity. Nevertheless, on the strength of a not entirely ephemeral frequentation of the literary production of the academic circles in question, I am also tolerably convinced of having touched on important topics – important in the sense that they are representative of ideas that became consolidated at the time and persisted at length, exerting a significant influence on the minds of the political, religious and intellectual elites of the time. While the essays can be classified as case studies, I don't believe they are *arena sine calce*. Indeed, certain topics follow through from one chapter to another and various authors also reappear since all the texts are somehow interconnected.

More specifically, this work aims to document an intellectual process that reached its crux between the last decades of the sixteenth century and the early seventeenth. The process – the formation of philosophical disciplines on the basis of Aristotle's works – was particularly noticeable within the Reformed German-speaking area with its flowering of new model educational institutions. A question arises: how did it come about that a set of principles and doctrines derived from a body of ancient texts was rendered functional to a modern school system with its curricula and institutional rules? From the very start, Aristotle seemed to have a competitive advantage over Plato or other thinkers or schools for the role of authority in academic training, if for no other reason than that he was the author of recognized canonical texts identifying a series of fields of research and study. But this alone was not enough to create proper 'disciplines', that is, contents suitable to be taught by teachers and assimilated by learners in a methodically constructed educational system. To make Aristotle's texts and philosophy fitting to this task, they needed to undergo a process of selection, reworking and systematization that was far from easy or of certain outcome. This operation was also influenced by many external institutional and cultural factors: the contribution of humanism, Ramist innovations, confessional conditioning and control by early modern forms of political power. Ultimately, the initiative was carried out in the decades around the turn of the seventeenth century and was essentially the collective work of one generation, with many important figures, now little known, engaged both in the organization of schools or directly in teaching. As one might expect, the need to disciplinize philosophy triggered a profound and extensive reflection on the manner of conceiving the legacy of Aristotle, now seen as a master of method and of the arrangement of knowledge in specific branches. Through this, moreover, his authority (or legend) was reaffirmed in the new historical context, although this general conclusion needs to be articulated differently in the case of the various disciplines that we will examine (metaphysics, ethics and politics). On this last aspect of the issue, I allow myself a few general reflections.

Considering that the works and the authors I have addressed are inextricably linked to a specific period, geographical area and milieu, it would be imprudent to hazard the validity of any extrapolations beyond certain limits. Nevertheless, the temptation to have one's say about the nature of the Aristotelianism of the time persists, spurred also by the literature on the argument. From the seminal essays of Charles Schmitt in 1983[1] through to the more recent book by Craig Martin,[2] and between these an infinite number of studies ranging from panoramic to more specific, a literature of frequently excellent quality bears witness to the vitality of this area of research. All these works have stressed the difficulty of sketching a profile of Aristotelianism across the sixteenth and the seventeenth centuries. This conviction is based on the consensus that the point at issue is not merely a philosophical (and scientific) theory, nor a defined set of doctrines, nor even a series of principles and categories underpinning such doctrines. Nor is it merely a 'language', nor one or more methods, nor even a generic *Weltanschauung*. Kuhn's paradigm comes to mind: a term used to refer to a variety of forms and articulations of scientific and rational thought. In other words, something which can, each time, be all the things we have just listed and others. Moreover, coeval representatives of this intellectual phenomenon seldom come to our aid, since they generally had little interest in defining the metaphilosophical conditions and premises of their academic praxes.

Given the impossibility of arriving at oversimplified solutions, while also attempting to find some general key to reading and framing the phenomenon in question in broader historical contexts, I have to admit that I began to favour an idea that has been formulated with reference to Aristotelianism in general and not specifically to its Renaissance variant. This is the idea of treating Aristotelianism as an exegetic tradition,[3] namely an intellectual endeavour taking various forms (commentaries, syntheses, translations etc.) dependent on the existence of a corpus of writings attributed to a master of recognized authority. Here, the risk of a tritely nominalist or circular definition (Aristotelianism signifies the Aristotelians who comment on the books of Aristotle) is avoided if one admits that at the origin of this phenomenon there is a specific historic process which, crystallizing, became its core or even – Aristotelically speaking – its formal principle or its 'soul'. It is a question of the consolidation and the transmission, from one period to another and from one milieu to another, of the authority of Aristotle, obviously understood as a principle both entirely rational and entirely compatible with unrestrained research and with the advancement and free circulation of knowledge. Being Aristotelian – and this holds for the major and minor figures we shall meet in this book – signifies, first and foremost, taking the words of Aristotle on trust, sustained in this gesture by the generations of readers and interpreters (authoritative in their own right) who have done so before us. In the mid-1570s, when this trust had already been undermined from left and right (Patrizi, Ramus ...), Ottaviano Ferrari took it upon himself to restore it. Ferrari clarified that the most authentic Aristotle was to be sought, not so much in specific doctrines, as in a certain type of philosophical discourse – a 'method' – which was the very reason why a serious programme of academic education ought to be based on Aristotle. More than fifty years later, Hermann Conring expressed his concept of *auctoritas Aristotelis* (here it is not important whether it was truly his or rather what his listeners expected to hear; see Chapter 3), arguing that, when a subject was to be addressed, the Stagirite should be given the first word. After that, complete freedom: the discussion could take any direction whatsoever and arrive at who knows what unheard-of conclusions. The Philosopher was due a species of right to formulate the question, to suggest its terms *quos ultra citraque* ... and even to map out the theoretical traps that one had to watch out for. In this sense, being Aristotelian means something different from being Cartesian or Hegelian, if we understand the latter as the adherence to certain more or less systematic philosophical orientations.

The studies that follow seek to cast light on the reasons that led various leading figures in the academic world of the time, in that testing ground of modern intellectual culture represented by the universities of Reformed Germany, to adhere to the exegetic corpus and again give credit to the fascinating and difficult works contained in that corpus. At the same time, these essays will also show how, long before the advent of the scientific revolution and the seventeenth-century revolt against all tradition, even in academic circles trust in the authority of Aristotle was already being subject to stress, erosion,[4] even subversion,[5] to which academe reacted with varying effectiveness and divers outcomes.

Acknowledgements

This book has its origins in a research project funded by the Ministry of Science and Higher Education of the Republic of Poland addressing the presence of Aristotelizing orientations in Renaissance Poland.

In the first place, I should like to thank the young collaborators who worked on the project, often subtracting time and energy from the preparation of their doctorates, with whom I frequently discussed the topics dealt with here. For their patience, their acute and erudite information and observations, I therefore thank Dorota Dremierre, Ewa Kondracka, Anna Laskowska, Marcin Loch and Roberto Peressin.

I should also like to thank my colleagues in the Department of History of Modern Philosophy at the Polish Academy of Sciences. My conversations with Sławomir Mazurek, Przemysław Parszutowicz and Wojciech Starzyński illuminated for me many aspects of the history of early- and late-modern philosophy and also made me realize that no philosopher should be idolized, not even the Philosopher. A special thank you to dear Valentina Lepri: during the period in which I was working on this book I benefited from her constant support, both moral and intellectual.

I should also like to recall here my Polish mentors: Juliusz Domański and the recently passed away Zbigniew Ogonowski, and Lech Szczucki.

Several of the topics addressed in the book have been presented at seminars, conferences and congresses, both in Poland and abroad (including San Diego, Boston, Chicago, Wolfenbüttel, Olomouc, Zielona Góra, Trieste and Verona). I should like to thank all those who lent me their attention and helped me with their comments and criticisms.

A special thanks to Helen Cleary, as well as for the constant encouragement, for the great work of translation. Needless to say, I am solely responsible for any errors and shortcomings in the final text.

I would like to express my gratitude to Marco Sgarbi for having accepted this book in his series.

I would also recall here the courtesy and competence of the staff of various libraries, in particular the Biblioteka Narodowa in Warsaw, the Biblioteca Ambrosiana in Milan and the Herzog August Bibliothek of Wolfenbüttel.

My most grateful thought goes to my wife Anna and especially to our three children, Giulia, Karolina and Antoni. None of them will go on to deal with the history of philosophy, but I believe that I have convinced them that studying Aristotle, and the court of the Aristotelians spread over the globe, is an endeavour worthy of a free man.

Part One

Methodus

1

The Origins and Development of the 'Acroamatic–Exoteric' Distinction in the Late Renaissance

Là c'est la science, ici une sagesse facile et vulgaire[1]

Starting from the second half of the sixteenth century, in the rich production of school texts expounding Aristotelian philosophy as a model for secondary and university education, a motif appeared which, although not completely new in the history of the Peripatetic tradition, now returned with particular insistence. It relates to the distinction between the two forms of teaching adopted in the old Lyceum, the school that Aristotle founded and directed, dividing his path from that of the Academy of Plato and Plato's disciples. Of these two forms, one was designed for a wider audience and the other for a more select one. The method and ideological implications of this distinction have been discussed since antiquity without actually reaching shared conclusions. After remaining in the shadows during the Middle Ages, the theme was taken up by Renaissance exegetes and, over the fifteenth century and up to the late seventeenth, became one of the points to be clarified in advance in every exposition of a given subject *ad mentem Aristotelis*. Therefore, it is useful to explore the genesis of this discussion and some of its most interesting episodes, to shed light on what the 'exoteric' Aristotle meant in the academic philosophy of the late Renaissance, before moving on to observing in the subsequent chapters the work carried out by the 'Aristotelian' professors in the elaboration of certain individual disciplines or groups of disciplines deriving from the texts of the Stagirite and from the Peripatetic tradition,

The ancient debate

The expression *logoi exōterikoi*, signifying 'external' discourses, appears in several passages in the works of Aristotle[2] and automatically implies a related or opposite category of discourses that are not external. It is not immediately clear how the adjective is to be understood, and the issue had already been addressed by the ancient doxographers of Aristotle in an attempt to resolve it. The words of Cicero and Aulus Gellius are particularly relevant, especially as regards the Renaissance tradition we are dealing with here. In the fifth book of *De finibus*, Cicero has the Peripatetic Piso pronounce two orders of considerations. First (4, 9), in the natural philosophy the ancient Peripatetics, that is Aristotle and Theophrastus, made recourse not only to probable arguments but also to conclusive mathematical demonstrations. Second, and more importantly (5, 12), with specific regard to the question of what is the chief good for human beings, the Peripatetics themselves produced two distinct types of work characterized by different styles and approaches. The *exôterikon* genre was directed at a broader public (*populariter scriptum*), whereas the scholarly texts (*commentarii*) were composed in a more scrupulous, rigorous or precise manner (*limatius*). Gellius, then, in his *Noctes Atticae* (XX, 5), introduces the question with reference to the two types of lectures that Aristotle delivered in the Lyceum after his return to Athens, one in the morning and one in the afternoon/evening. Gellius also provides several important clarifications – albeit variously interpreted – about the contents, methods and recipients of the respective types of teaching, which it is useful to briefly recall.[3] He states that Aristotle conducted two types of reflections (*commentationes*) with his pupils, and transmitted two kinds of discipline (*artes*), classified respectively as *akroatika*, or 'acroamatic' and *exôterika*. The latter were conceived for training in rhetorical skills, subtlety of argument and knowledge of politics (*quae ad rhetoricas meditationes facultatemque argutiarum civiliumque rerum notitiam conducebant*). The former lessons dealt instead with a more profound and rigorous philosophy, related to the contemplation of nature and dialectic discussions (*in quibus philosophia remotior subtiliorque agitabatur quaeque ad naturae contemplationes disceptationesve dialecticas pertinebant*). Aristotle devoted the morning course to the acroamatic lessons, which were addressed to students specifically selected based on their natural gifts and zeal for study, as well as a certain level of preliminary knowledge (*eruditionis elementa*). The exoteric lessons were instead held at dusk (*vesperi*) and were open to all (*vulgo... sine dilectu*). Aristotle extended this division of the two types of course to his books too, again broken down into acroa(ma)tic and exoteric.[4]

Coming chronologically between Cicero and Gellius is the testimony of Plutarch (*Life of Alexander*, 7), who speaks of two forms of teaching delivered by Aristotle, in this case to Alexander alone. On the one hand, ethical and political doctrines (implicitly of lower level) and, on the other, more arcane and recondite teachings (*aporrhêtai kai bathuterai didaskaliai*), also referred to as *akroamatikai kai epoptikai*, that are transmitted orally and are initiatic, that is, are intended to be kept secret. Seeing that Alexander the Great has already been called into play, the second part of Chapter 5 of Book XX of Gellius' *Noctes* is also relevant. Here he reports the exchange of correspondence between Alexander and Aristotle, in which Alexander rebukes his master for having made his acroatic teachings public (*quod ... invulgasset*) by publishing them in books. In reply, Aristotle defends himself by clarifying that these acroatic books were 'made public and not made public' (*editos... non editos*), since they could effectively be understood (*cognobiles-xynetoi*) only by those who had already heard his lectures and they would be incomprehensible to anyone else.

These are the main sources on the matter. We shall return later to the ulterior evolutions and other aspects of this question in the ancient world, and more specifically to the interpretations of the Neoplatonist commentators. Now we wish to move on to the sixteenth century, when the revival in the circulation of Aristotle's works, finally, in their original language, brought this aspect of the 'Aristotle question' back into the limelight. As we shall see, while substantially reapplying solutions that had appeared in ancient times, the Renaissance speculation on this issue not only progressively reveals which image of Aristotle was in circulation, but also at times illustrates points of tangency with important aspects of the intellectual evolution of the time. This seems to make the reconstruction worthwhile.

Juan Ginés de Sepúlveda

The circulation of the Greek originals of Aristotle's works[5] rapidly raised a series of questions among the humanists and philosophers about the corpus, its overall composition, the form of individual works etc. If nothing else, these questions were triggered by comparison between the accepted arrangement of the works that was in general circulation and the list of works cited by Diogenes Laertius in Book V of his *Lives and Opinions of Eminent Philosophers*, also considering the accounts of Strabo and Plutarch on the fate of these works after their author's death.[6] It was in this context that, starting from the mid-sixteenth century, the question of how the expression *logoi exôterikoi*, 'exoteric discourses', should be understood began to emerge with a certain frequency. The first important contribution was made by the celebrated humanist and rhetorician Juan Ginés de Sepúlveda (1490–1573), who briefly took a stand on the topic in a *scholium* commenting his translation of Aristotle's *Politics*. Having reached Book III, Ch. 4 (corresponding to Ch. 6 in current editions), Sepúlveda explains that what in his translation are the *sermones externi* are simply all the various books and discourses other than those which Aristotle was currently engaged with,[7] while it is not true that this expression indicates a particular genre, as Plutarch and Cicero before him understood it, theorizing the existence of two distinct types: one popular and one more secret (*reconditior*). The term 'acroamatic', which Plutarch and Cicero use to refer to this second type, can, according to Sepúlveda, be explained by the fact that the texts of this category can be understood by the pupil only if he has previously been able to hear the explanation from the master's own mouth[8] (a clear reference to Aristotle's reply to Alexander in the correspondence transmitted by Gellius). The mistake made by Plutarch and Cicero in identifying two specific and opposite types of text, continues Sepúlveda, stems from over-interpretation of the expression *exôterikos*, again in the light of the exchange of missives between Alexander and Aristotle, where the acroamatic books are described as hard to access without preparation and particular acumen. This leads seamlessly to the conclusion that the 'exoteric' books are, by contrast, easier and more accessible. However, concludes Sepúlveda, this is not consistent with the genuinely Aristotelian use of the term since, on the contrary, he often applies 'exoteric' to extremely difficult discourses – for instance, in *Nicomachean Ethics I* with reference to what is discussed in *On the Soul*, or in *Eudemian Ethics I* with reference to the 'theological' wisdom of the *Metaphysics* – not to mention the fact that Laertius, who accurately catalogued all Aristotle's works, knows nothing of this division of the texts into genres. Finally, it is not true that 'acroamatic' signifies the contents of a 'more hidden philosophy' (*philosophia reconditior*); Aristotle uses this expression only for the *physikê akroasis*, where the reference is purely to the oral-auditory character of the transmission of contents, without the slightest connotation of secrecy.[9]

In a word, Sepúlveda's aim is to deflate the meaning of the term 'exoteric', which is to be understood simply as 'other', 'different from the matter in hand'. This pulls the rug from under the alleged existence in Aristotle of two levels of discourse: one easy and clear and the other difficult and deliberately obscure; in actual fact, the latter is Aristotle's characteristic stylistic trait in general. As Sepúlveda writes in the preface apropos the criteria used for his Latin translation,[10] it is inappropriate to render in plain and simple language a philosopher such as Aristotle who:

since he deals with obscure arguments that the majority are unfamiliar with, he perforce uses new terms that people are not accustomed to, which are unusual even for cultured persons. Moreover, as the ancients have frequently pointed out, at times he courts obscurity precisely so that philosophy will not be undervalued should the knowledge of the highest things be easily available to slow and lazy men. This is why he has deliberately made his discourses sources of controversy (*dubias*), since they can be understood in different ways.[11]

In other words, the difficulty of grasping Aristotle's teachings is not restricted to a particular genre of arguments or books: *all* Aristotle is difficult, since he addresses serious philosophical issues. Before *Politics*, Sepúlveda had tackled the Latin translation of Alexander of Aphrodisias' commentary on the *Metaphysics* (1527) and he championed a style of translation devoid of rhetorical flourishes and Ciceronian rotundities. Here he is probably alluding to his work as an intermediary for the elite educated in *humanae litterae* which he had frequented during his studies in Italy, especially alongside Pomponazzi. Only this elite, on condition that it was adequately prepared and assisted, could accede to such complex subjects as those dealt with in Aristotle's main treatises and taken up by his ancient and mediaeval commentators.

Francesco Patrizi, Giacomo Zabarella and Carlo Sigonio

The considerations contained in Volume I, Book VII of Francesco Patrizi's *Discussiones peripateticae* are of greater philosophical interest. This is a work of immense erudition and remarkable critical acumen, although the latter is frequently marred by the author's anti-Aristotelian prejudice. The *Discussiones* can indeed be seen as the *pars destruens* of the overall philosophical project of the Italo-Croatian. Patrizi's positive thought consists of a retrieval of the *prisca philosophia* tradition culminating in Plato – and above all in ancient and modern Neoplatonism – understood in turn in the light of Hermetic literature or of the spiritual theurgy of the *Chaldean Oracles*. As regards Aristotle, in his analyses Patrizi is very unlikely to omit or overlook important passages, either by the Stagirite himself or of the Peripatetic tradition or subsequent doxography. In the first place, he expands the investigation to other crucial terms of the matter in question: not just 'exoteric' or 'acroamatic' books (although, as Patrizi duly notes, this term never appears in Aristotle's texts) but also – in the Latin form of Greek words – *epoptici* (Plutarch's term), *encyclii* (of which more later) and *ecdedomeni*.[12] As a result, he provides a complete overview of the recurrence of these expressions in Aristotle and also of the opinions of his ancient readers and commentators on the matter.

It is also well to bear in mind the historiosophical schema within which Patrizi inserts the issue of the Aristotelian books, peculiar to him as a fervent supporter of a form of neo-Hermetic philosophical esotericism and, in principle, alien to the other participants in this debate. This is the idea that true wisdom has always had an initiatic, mysterious, non-public character. The most profound knowledge passed from Noah to the Armenians, the Chaldeans, the Magi, the Etruscans and the Egyptians to finally arrive at the Greeks, with whom in some way the golden chain was broken. The practice of concealing the mysteries of this philosophical-religious knowledge from the majority was in fact corrupted by the Greeks 'in search of (vain)glory'. It was they who introduced the malpractice of spreading the secret doctrines and – one might add – not without ambiguity: Orpheus by concealing them within the packaging of lovely stories, Pythagoras by enwrapping them in numerical speculations, and Plato by using both methods. In short: a saying and not saying until we come to Aristotle who, by now completely unfettered from the original *mos maiorum*, strips away all the veils from knowledge and quite simply makes it public, with a sole proviso. Aristotle indeed kept only a few books with him, opening these up only to the students of his school, while he published all the others; this is what led to the birth of the dichotomy between esoteric and exoteric works. This descending schema applied to history, in which perfection is found at the origin, followed by progressive degeneration, leaves no doubts as to Patrizi's opinion of Aristotle and his strategy of communication. It is significant that he insists on Alexander's reproof to Aristotle, and also on the guilty conscience implicit in the master's reply. Moreover, as can be deduced from myriad passages in the *Discussiones*, Aristotle did not always listen to his good conscience as he was driven by the craving for glory and the desire to prevail over his own master/rival Plato. We shall return to this point in the Conclusion. Meanwhile, we can observe how Patrizi systematically rejects all the different interpretations of the nature of the exoteric discourses provided by the ancients. Cicero was wrong (these books were written in order to be easily understood – *populariter scripti*), so was Plutarch (they are books on ethics and politics); Gellius was wrong (rhetorical and 'civil' works), so was Ammonius (the lost dialogues of Aristotle); Philoponus was wrong (works written for the broader public) and, finally, so was Simplicius (historical books and dialogues). For Patrizi the exoteric works are quite simply the books that Aristotle published while he was alive, irrespective of argument or literary form, while the 'esoteric' works are those that remained unpublished because their author – 'a man extremely eager of glory' (*vir gloriae cupidissimus*) – simply did not have time to revise and correct them for publication before he died.[13] For Patrizi, therefore, the essential dichotomy was between exoteric and esoteric: substantially connected with the former term are others such as *ecdedomenus* and *encyclius* and with the latter *acroamaticus*, *acousmaticus* and *epopticus*.[14] Consequently, Alexander's reproach to Aristotle in the famous letter was justified (and Aristotle's reply hypocritical). Incidentally, the text subject of the complaint was in all likelihood *On the World*: a treatise containing what the master had orally transmitted to the future ruler of the world regarding the providential order governing it. These were the 'compendium of oral secret doctrines' (*secretiores doctrinae acroamaticae per compendium*) which ought never to have been made public.[15]

Patrizi's solution to the question of Aristotle's books and his *sermones* appears rather trenchant, conditioned by his image of a philosopher willing to violate the custom of secrecy that had been proper to the sages since the dawn of time to indulge his narcissism. But what is possibly even more important in philosophical terms – as well as being destined to leave its mark on subsequent debate – is another distinction introduced at the end of the chapter that does not directly concern the texts or discourses. The starting point is a passage from the *Physics* (IV, 10, 217b, 29–32): 'now we must move on to address time. As regards this it is best first (*prôton*) to investigate by aporias (*diaporesai*), and also through exoteric discourses (*kai dia tôn exôterikôn logôn*), whether it belongs among the beings or among the non-beings; then (*eita*) [we must ask ourselves] what is its nature?' In this fragment, by placing the emphasis on the scansion 'first … then' Patrizi intends to demonstrate that Aristotle has in mind two methods, two modes of addressing the same argument. The one explicitly associated with the exoteric discourses is none other than the dialectic method of developing the two parts of a contradiction (arguing *ad utramque partem*, does time belong or not belong among beings?), which Patrizi also immediately defines as logical and probable. The type of investigation introduced after the *eita* 'then' clause is another thing entirely. This is a question about essence or nature and is therefore a philosophical investigation, a concept that is specified by the use of expressions such as 'demonstrative', 'scientific', 'proper to the intrinsic essence of things'.[16] And if we understand *exoteric* in the light of all the passages where Aristotle uses the term without reference to books or to *logoi*, we can see that its meaning is determined on the basis of the opposition with *proprius-intrinsecus-in genere*, hence identifying a dichotomy referable substantially to the argumentative or expositional procedures: namely, the methods. We shall see how fundamental developments were to stem from this point.

Returning to the subject of time, the simple question of whether it exists or not is indeed *extra rem*, 'exoteric', since unlike true philosophical inquiry it does not stem from the search for the discourse that defines its nature. Citing the Greek Neoplatonic commentators Philoponus and Simplicius, Patrizi then takes the next step of identifying acroamatic and demonstrative (*apodictic*) investigation, while qualifying dialectic investigation as 'based on probable opinions' (*ek endoxôn kai pithanôn*), and even 'empty' (*kenous*), precisely because it is unrelated to the specific essence and refers instead to an abstract and generic level. After the customary, detailed review of the Aristotelian passages confirming this interpretation, the conclusion is clear: 'We must therefore conclude that in this second meaning [that is relating to the method and not to the genre of the books] exoteric signifies extraneous, alien, vain, dialectical, logical, *endoxon* [according to opinion], *katholou* [general] as opposed to proper, intrinsic, essential, scientific, demonstrative, analytical, philosophical and given as true'.[17] What appears to be particularly important here is the juxtaposition of philosophical truth (or truth *tout court*) and scientific demonstration. In other words, what can be achieved syllogizing 'from specific principles' (*ex propriis principiis*), remaining within the realm of a particular science,[18] instead of starting from common opinions and general principles as dialectic does. I believe that Patrizi was the first to clearly formulate – with abundant references to Aristotle's texts (albeit read through Ammonius) – the opposition between exoteric and esoteric as deriving from different types of *ratiocinatio*, identifying the key concepts supporting it. Nevertheless, also important in Patrizi's *Discussiones* is the denigration of the second element of the opposition, since the divulgation of the mysteries was in itself censurable. Dialectic therefore, as opposed to demonstration, is at best an empty discourse, devoid of philosophical value, and at worst dangerous, since it entrusts gems of knowledge to those who can only misunderstand it.[19]

Here a brief reference should suffice to the further evolution of Patrizi's interpretation of Plato's and Aristotle's exoterism, as detected in certain texts in the appendix to the *Nova de universis philosophia*. Patrizi's target here is not so much divulgation as such, since – as he admitted – Plato too published his dialogues. The point is that the latter can be understood only in the light of a 'mystical' teaching (compatible with Christian revelation) known solely to the few. In other words, Plato's divulgation was all but fictitious. Aristotle did the exact opposite: in his secret, exoteric teaching he remained faithful to his master's doctrine, while the content he spread in the published works was thoroughly incompatible with that same doctrine (and consequently with Christian religion). The aim of these historiosophical speculations is plainly the establishment of a species of new scholasticism, founded on Platonic-Hermetic thought instead of Aristotle's.

It is interesting to compare this position with that which, in Patrizi's time and milieu – namely, mid-sixteenth-century Padua, where he studied with Tomitano and Genua – was the *doctrina communis* regarding the function of dialectic and its relation with the 'scientific' type of knowledge. The exposé furnished by Giacomo Zabarella in his *De natura logicae* on the relation between demonstrative-scientific knowledge and dialectic can be considered the canonical one.[20] It is held that in the Paduan school, which in this respect continued a trend present in Averroes and in Averroism, the doctrine of scientific demonstration expounded in Aristotle's *Posterior Analytics* acquired the value of a model of knowledge in general, while other forms were an approximation or somehow subordinate to it.[21] Indeed, in the same way as Averroes, Zabarella reveals the terms in which we are to understand that the *ars demonstrandi* contained in the *Posterior Analytics* is 'dominant and end' (*domina et finis*) in relation to the general ordering of the parts of Aristotle's logic. In short, from the perspective of logic as pure theory (*logica docens, doctrina*), it is the end of the general theory of the syllogism contained in the *Prior Analytics*; from the perspective of logic applied to philosophy (*logica utens*), that is to the search for the truth, the theory of demonstration comes after the elenchus, contained in the *Sophistical Refutations*, and after the dialectic of the *Topics*, since the latter envisages it and considers it as the culmination of their specific task.[22] The sense is that in philosophy, before demonstrating the truth, false opinions have to be removed and then 'the hypothesis has to be secured by probable arguments. These reasons are in fact straightforward and commonly accepted and generate in the mind a certain idea of what is to be demonstrated, preparing it to perceive the strength of the demonstration, which alone can generate firm knowledge'.[23] In other words, dialectic – in its dual confutational and positive role – is acknowledged as some sort of function preparatory to the real knowledge. This, as the Paduan professor too is stoutly convinced, continues to be the demonstrative syllogism that starts from true premises which are, above all, proper and specific to the subject on which the demonstration is conducted. The theory of demonstration of the *Posterior Analytics* was, moreover, the hub of Zabarella's interest, whereas he made no in-depth reflection on dialectics nor, indeed, an adequate exegesis of Aristotle's texts on the topic.

Remaining in Padua, to complete the context within which Patrizi's conceptions matured, it also seems useful to recall the ideas of Carlo Sigonio (1524–84), possibly the most illustrious and internationally renowned of the Padua professors, along with Zabarella. These ideas are found in his *De dialogo*,[24] a short, dense treatise that examines the literary form of the philosophical dialogue, its relation with the habitus of the dialectician and of the orator and also its relation with artistic imitation. Sigonio, who appears to defend an epistemically positive conception of dialectic, hence inspired more by the Aristotelian model than by the moderately sceptical one proposed by Cicero,[25] chances *en passant* upon the question of Aristotle's books/discourses. The solution he embraces is the one found in the preamble to the commentary on the *Categories* by Ammonius, a writer whom he places in the vanguard of this debate. As Sigonio argues, the fundamental difference between the writings of Aristotle is between those in which he speaks in first person (*autoprósôpa*) and those in which there are several *personae*, namely the dialogues. In the former, Aristotle addresses a reader of specialized preparation, whereas in the latter he addresses a cultivated but non-specialist public. In the former he makes use of the most unwavering and subtle arguments, whereas in the latter, being concerned more with public utility than with the truth in itself, he settles for simpler reasons.[26] This, therefore – treatises and dialogues – is the dichotomy that everyone was aware of (Cicero, Gellius, Plutarch, Alexander of Aphrodisias, Eustratius...), but it ought to be stressed that it rests upon a more fundamental dualism, that between individual mental discourse and external dialogue with an interlocutor. It is true, Sigonio continues, that the interpretations of the ancients diverge, but essentially only in the details. For some – Gellius and Plutarch – the exoteric/acroamatic distinction divides different subjects (respectively practical and theoretical). For others – Cicero, Eustratius and above all Alexander of Aphrodisias – the distinction lies in the different way of addressing the same subjects, on the assumption that Aristotle was in the habit of offering two expositions of the same question, one with a view to arriving at the truth and the other to arouse a given opinion in the audience. Furthermore, Gellius, Eustratius and Plutarch agree that the dichotomy applies not only to the written works, but also to the orally delivered courses, thus making a distinction between the listeners.[27] Beyond the details, however, the ancients, too, were fundamentally in agreement about the distinction between private discourse and dialogue with an interlocutor, so that it is surprising that nowadays many people insist on generically and tritely applying the term 'exoteric' to the commentaries written by Aristotle 'outside the present discourse' (*extra rem propositam*),[28] probably a polemic reference to Sepúlveda.

In actual fact, however, Sigonio does not intend his monologue/dialogue distinction in a purely formal sense, since according to him this distinction corresponds to a dichotomy in the recipients of the different types of discourse. As can be deduced from Simplicius' commentary *On the Heavens*, Sigonio continues, 'exoteric' is synonymous with 'encyclical', namely with a discourse destined to the 'expert multitude', as opposed to the 'acroamatic and syntagmatic', which is aimed at a narrower circle of specialists.[29] Thus, for Sigonio, Aristotle's dialogues are at the same time exoteric works, since in them he aimed to represent discussions about what is probable. None the less – and this is the crucial point – what is expounded in them is not without effect on the search for truth: correcting Lucian, who called dialogue the 'son of philosophy', Sigonio instead proposes declaring it to be the 'parent'. It is precisely dialogue that shows the path leading from opinion to intelligence, from the credible to the true.[30] This confirms the idea that, for Sigonio, dialectic, the habitus imitated by Aristotle in the dialogues, possesses a value auxiliary or preparatory to the actual philosophical (or scientific) investigation, so that he refuses to consider it an empty exercise. In this he is undoubtedly mindful of the indications explicitly theorized by Aristotle himself in the *Topics*[31] and put into practice by him on numerous occasions. And so we have, in a way, an evaluation of dialectic that is significantly more positive than that of Zabarella which, being focused on the value of scientific demonstrations from 'true' premises, failed to specify the contribution of dialectic to the search for truth.

Ottaviano Ferrari's *De sermonibus exotericis*

The standpoints examined so far are sustained by outstanding antiquarian erudition and also by meditated philosophical stances. They nevertheless seem somewhat improvised, since the question of classifying Aristotle's writings is addressed in treatises pivoting on other matters. Now, instead, we move on to delineate the ideas on this subject of the Milanese, Ottaviano Ferrari, a prominent figure in the northern Italian humanist milieu of the sixteenth century and a friend and correspondent of other famous humanists such as Pietro Vettori and Paolo Manuzio. Ferrari, who was born and died in Milan (1518–86), studied medicine and philosophy at Pavia, Padua and Pisa. He was a professor of philosophy (dialectics and rhetoric) at Pavia, then at the Scuola Canobbiana in Milan and, for a few years before his death, also in Padua. In Ferrari, antiquarian and philological interests (*De origine Romanorum*, 1589) went hand in hand with the study of Aristotle's texts, of which he owned several manuscripts, later incorporated into the collections of the Biblioteca Ambrosiana.[32] His *De sermonibus exotericis*,[33] which is the most important text among those we refer to, is in the form of a somewhat freely structured essay featuring various digressions followed by returns to the main topic. Ferrari was more famous in his lifetime as a teacher and philologist than as a writer, but the *De sermonibus*, as we shall see, brought him a certain posthumous repute. In this work the paradigmatic significance of the classification of Aristotle's books is openly declared, the issue being to establish what Aristotle himself – and not his numerous interpreters – meant by 'dialectical faculty'.[34] Ferrari's text is presented as a continuous narration, without divisions into chapters and without titles and subtitles. Added to this is a considerable ballast of erudition and the already-mentioned tendency to digress, so that it is not unfair to say that Ferrari's exposé does not make easy reading. Nevertheless, the general structure of his argument can be fairly clearly discerned.

The starting point is the confutation of Sepúlveda's theory, behind which Ferrari sees none other than St Thomas Aquinas. As we saw, this theory sustains that *logoi exôterikoi* is merely a generic expression indicating the discourses or writings that are outside, external or extraneous to the matter at hand. Consequently, just to give an example, for Sepúlveda the recurrence of this syntagma in the passage at the end of Book I of the *Nichomachean Ethics* (1102a 26–7) alludes simply to the three books of *On the Soul*, which are in effect 'external' to the ethical question. On the contrary, for Ferrari, since the expression refers to a *thematically qualified category* (*certo genere*) of discourses, it is to be understood as an allusion not to *On the Soul*, but to the *Eudemus*, namely a lost dialogue also dealing with the soul. The description offered in the latter of the soul as consisting of two elements – one of which submits to the reason while the other does not – differs from the tripartite breakdown in *On the Soul*, but resembles that adopted in the *Nicomachean Ethics*. Above all, Ferrari continues, it should be stressed that the approach of the *Eudemus* was of an exoteric type, being supported by 'probable' arguments, and hence opposed to those used by Aristotle in the *Nicomachean Ethics*.[35] It is true that Aristotle was in the habit of referring to other 'external' books, but he did so explicitly by using their titles or a specific and unequivocal appellation, as for instance in the *Politics* (VII, 13 1332a 18–22) when he refers to 'ethical discourses', namely the *Nicomachean Ethics*.[36] Finally, a third reason for dissent from Sepúlveda derives from the fact that the latter refers Aristotle's expression '*logoi kata philosophian*' to a single discipline – *sapientia* or metaphysics – rather than more generally to a set of disciplines characterized by a certain mode of argument.[37] Enough, therefore, to confute the trivializing interpretation of the Spanish humanist and to establish that Aristotle uses the term 'exoteric' to refer to a particular type of approach that is opposed to 'acroamatic' or 'philosophical', depending on the case. Put simply, this means that we are to expect from Aristotle exoteric works in a specific sense, namely featuring a certain type of method and composition.

This is substantially the end of the main critical section (others are found scattered here and there),[38] which is followed by the *pars construens*, expounding the details of this interpretation. The preface that precedes it tells us a lot about the context of the *De sermonibus* and also casts light on the popularity the work enjoyed with its German publishers. It is, in short, a complaint about the changes made in the procedures for the selection and recruitment of young people for higher education. Or rather, the absence of selection! Now that education is dispensed at the public cost – Ferrari complains – and the doors of the universities have practically been thrown open to all and sundry, regardless of age or aptitude, everyone is admitted to the temple of wisdom 'as long as they come to listen to our lectures'.[39] The *docendi consuetudo* of the ancients was quite another matter, proceeding through a careful assessment of the intellectual and moral capacities of the candidates before admitting them to school (*in ludum*). Here Ferrari returns to the Renaissance *topos* of the 'ancients' wisdom' (*sapientia veterum*), the genealogy of knowledge *ab illo tempore*, even though the sobriety of these references – in effect limited to the immediate precedents of the Stagirite without even calling the Chaldeans or Egyptians into play – differentiates them decisively from the complex sapiential genealogies of Steuco or Patrizi, to mention two of the most typical. All Ferrari says is that it was Pythagoras and his school that treated a fundamental nucleus of teachings as secret, available only to disciples, and that this use was then maintained by Plato and, substantially, by Aristotle who admitted only a handful of listeners.[40] In fact, unlike his master who famously disapproved of the transmission of philosophical thought in writing, Aristotle entrusted his most authentic teachings to books, putting them down in writing. But then he never circulated them, so that – like the works of Theophrastus – they ended up in the famous cellar of Neleus of Scepsis. Without going into the details of this well-known episode, it seems that the key point for Ferrari was the cunning and substantially fraudulent manner in which Tyrannion of Amisus took everything he wanted from Sulla's library, into which all this material had previously been incorporated. The Aristotelian documents pilfered by Tyrannion then provided the basis for the famous edition produced by Andronicus of Rhodes.[41] Aside from this original misdeed in the divulgation of

Aristotle's philosophy, considering the connections between Andronicus and Tyrannion and between Tyrannion and Cicero, the latter's account in *De finibus* V of the Peripatetic school, its scholarchs and, above all, the dual method adopted in the writings, and of the existence of the 'exoteric' texts is most likely derived from Andronicus himself and therefore very ancient and authoritative.[42] Hence the existence of these works is ultimately testified by Cicero himself.[43] The evidence of Strabo in Book XIII of the *Geography* proves more difficult to interpret, and even a man with the skill and knowledge of Pietro Vettori was unable to provide a convincing reading of it. Here it is useful to cite the literal translation provided by Ferrari; Strabo says that:

> 'Contigit autem Peripatetici antiqui post Theophrastum, cum omnino libros non haberent praeter pauculos maximeque exotericos, nihil ut possent re ipsa [*pragmatikôs*] philosophari sed proposita declamarent [*thesis lêkythizein*].'
> And so it happened that the ancient Peripatetics who came after Theophrastus, possessing only a few books mostly of an exoteric character, were not capable of philosophical investigation of the subject itself, but merely declaimed pre-established issues.[44]

Leaving aside the difficulty of interpreting the details of this text, what Ferrari in effect takes from it is a dichotomy between two modes of argument. One is 'philosophical' founded on the 'things themselves' conserved in the lost books of Aristotle and appearing again with Andronicus. The other consists of 'positing arguments/issues', namely a form of enunciation that appears to stand between dialectic (suggested by the term *thesis* [hypothesis, argument]) and rhetoric (suggested by *lêkythizein* [declaim]), which Ferrari believes is possibly that used by the rhetoricians and operates by 'developing the two horns of a dilemma according to probability' (*utramque in partem probabiliter ad eam declamare*).[45] This is, moreover, the type of dialectic that Cicero himself attributes to Aristotle in several places in his works. Ferrari concludes that, despite the opinion of Alexander of Aphrodisias who failed to understand Aristotle and attributed to him the idea that dialectic serves to discover the truth, Cicero's interpretation must be preferred, namely that this dialectic-rhetoric is valid merely as a 'practice or exercise'.[46] Precisely because the successors of Theophrastus at the helm of the Peripatetic school, from Strato of Lampsacus to Critolaus, did not have Aristotle's philosophical books and were therefore unaware of the method proper to philosophy, they restricted themselves to this type of rhetorical-dialectic dispute, which was a useful form of training but without pretensions about getting to the truth.[47] Clement of Alexandria is of a similar opinion; he considered that

Aristotle's works should be divided into two categories, each identified by a distinct method, and, at least on some occasions, Aristotle discussed the same subject using both methods.[48] However, where Ferrari finds the best confirmation and the most complete exposé of this interpretation is in the prologue to the commentary on the *Categories* by Ammonius, son of Hermeias (a Byzantine commentator who died in AD 523). Without going into details, his discussion can be summed up in the fundamental distinction between two types, irrespective of whether they are discourses or books:

> The first of these he [Ammonius] says is called *autoprósôpon* and also *akroamatikon*, because in them the teacher explaining the subject to someone else speaks alone to a sufficiently prepared listener; in this case the listener remains silent, neither asking questions nor replying. The other type of book, which is the opposite of the previous type, is called *dialogikon* and *exôterikon*, since the single author himself, identifying with other characters for the public utility, plays the parts of many.[49]

Therefore, the difference comes down to that between a continuous exposition and dialogues, the former destined to specialists and based on rigorous demonstrations, the latter 'for the common utility', based on reasoning that is easy for anyone to understand. These types of argument – and this is what Ferrari sees as the core of Ammonius' presentation – are none other than the two types of syllogism, respectively demonstrative/apodictic and dialectical. Proceeding, then, on the basis of this distinction, Ferrari adds that the books of metaphysics (*de sapientia*), natural philosophy and ethics-politics were written in a demonstrative manner, whereas the exoteric books are characterized by the opposite, dialectical method. Thus Ammonius is right (and Sepúlveda wrong again) and it must be said that the exoteric books are none other than the Dialogues, which is exactly what Cicero says too.[50]

At this point the pivot shifts from the question of the type of communication inherent in the respective texts to the nature of the *rationes* used in them. Here the matter appears to have been stated most clearly by Philoponus – not incidentally a pupil of Ammonius – again based on the opposition between exoteric and acroamatic/apodictic discourses. Here a partially new clarification emerges, namely the association of the exoteric discourses with reasoning that 'starts from what is probable and convincing', specifying that 'probable' is used to render what in the original is 'starting from the *endoxa* – *ex endoxôn*'.[51] The exoteric/acroamatic dichotomy is a fundamental structure derived from distinct methods of reasoning, and whether it refers to books or to discourses or lectures is ultimately irrelevant. The conclusion can be summarized in three points: 'first, exoteric discourses are structured starting from the probable; second, they are not demonstrative and are not addressed to prepared and rightful listeners; third, they are developed starting from what can convince the multitude'.[52]

Subsequent interpreters, from Simplicius to Eustratius, do not have a lot to add to this basic format, except for the introduction of the term *enkýklion* to designate a form of general, non-specialist culture. In practice this corresponds to *exôterikon*, an argument on which Ferrari had already written a short essay some years previously,[53] returning to it towards the end of *De sermonibus*.

Having settled his accounts with the ancients, Ferrari moves on to the *recentes ac novitii*, to two in particular whom he does not mention by name but says were inspired respectively by Aristotle and Plato. He contests the idea of the first that the exoteric books contained a *paedia*, a programme of education in all the disciplines which, precisely in view of its generality, had to proceed from 'universal causes'.[54] Ferrari counters by claiming that the authentic *paedia* displays the features of an empirical and sectorial instruction rather than one of a general kind. Consistently with both the epistemology of the *Posterior Analytics* and with the theory of the constitution of the habitus in the first books of the *Nicomachean Ethics*, it is a question of equipping the student to master the principles of the single, *specific* sciences in the theoretical field and the guidelines of virtuous actions in the practical field. It is essential therefore for Ferrari to argue that one has to speak of several '*paediae*',[55] each of them assisting apprehension of the 'appearances' from which the search for causes proceeds.[56] It seems that the meaning of this long section[57] is to present a concept of education as directly functional to the acquisition, not so much of a generic cultural background, as of particular branches of knowledge: the *scientiae*. Consequently, Ferrari concludes, it must be ruled out that Aristotle wrote the exoteric (i.e. non-specialist) books with a view to this type of instruction.[58]

The other opinion, derived from Plato, presents two theories. Ferrari is willing to accept the first: namely, the idea that the exoteric texts are none other than Aristotle's dialogues. He is much more reluctant to concur with the second, which holds that the salient characteristic of the dialogues is that of imitating a discussion among several speakers in the course of which their *mores* are revealed. Ferrari retorts that this may well be the style of Plato's dialogues, but certainly does not reflect the criterion used by Aristotle in writing his, namely by strictly and exclusively following the rules of dialectic.[59] The fact of the matter is that the theory of the dialogue as imitation is merely the umpteenth trivializing interpretation obscuring the issue at stake, which is of an epistemological and not an artistic-rhetorical nature. However, Ferrari's polemic with those who see in Aristotle's dialogues a form of imitation, such as that described in the *Poetics*,[60] is substantially merely a pretext for finally presenting his own views, unfettered by historiographical hypotheses, exegeses of exegeses and erudite digressions of all kinds. Here *De sermonibus exotericis* reaches its crux and, a few pages later, its conclusion. It is hence worth looking at in detail, because what is set forth here is the conceptual synthesis of Ferrari's entire discourse.

Ferrari: The 'analytical' pattern of the *paedia*

The starting point – echoing famous passages from the *Analytics* – is the consideration of two different types of *ratiocinatio*, one founded on the truth of the thing and the other on the opinion. True demonstrations are conducted from the former and dialectic reasonings from the latter.[61] Now the characteristics of the demonstrative reasoning have to be better clarified; here Aristotle himself comes to the rescue, since in the *Prior Analytics* he states that this hinges on attributes immanent to the thing (*propria et sua cuiusque rei* – *idia kai oikeia*). However, these are equivalent to the attributes inherent per se to a subject or, in other words, to those that constitute a *genus* (the *genos hypokeímenon*): the demonstration therefore takes place within the same genus and hinges on its essential (*kath'auta*) attributes, excluding the accidental ones (*symbebêkonta*). Put another way: the major and minor terms and the middle of the syllogism must belong to the same 'subject-genus'.[62] This is the conclusion in which Ferrari efficaciously – albeit not without prolixity – sums up his argument: 'So it is necessary that the demonstration starts from what is in the same genus and not outside it. From which it is also clear that consequences which derive truly from the subject itself are not only true but are also per se and are enclosed within the same genus not dispersed outside it.'[63] This is none other than the rule banning the 'transition to a different genus', seen here as the fundamental criterion identifying scientific disciplines.

And this is what Ferrari has to say about the exoteric discourses, in substance about the *ratiocinationes ex opinione*. The first sentence in this section sets forth equivalences of vast scope and – evidently – also somewhat dubious from an Aristotelian point of view: 'Now let's talk about what derives to a subject starting from opinion: this is the Greek *endoxa*, while in Latin they are called *probabilia*, namely the premises assumed by the dialecticians in their reasoning. These are what Aristotle frequently calls *communia*.'[64] It is immediately apparent that the characteristics Ferrari attributes to the endoxical premises – namely being *probable* and *common* – emerge in opposition to the attributes of demonstrative reasoning, respectively *truth* and *appropriateness/specificity*, although these do not emerge from the texts of Aristotle presented as support. Nevertheless, having taken up this track Ferrari pursues it consistently, seeking to further demonstrate that *communia* and *probabilia* coincide, but here too their juxtaposition seems to be postulated rather than convincingly argued. Indeed, a little further on, as instances of these *communia* he proposes terms and propositions such as 'non-being', 'divisible things' and 'the part is a measure of the whole'.[65] While it is easy to see that these are 'common' concepts, in the sense of being transgeneric, it is not yet very clear in what sense they can be seen as 'probable'. In any case, here at last is the long-sought solution to the enigma of the exoteric discourses: dialectic starts from probable *and* common premises, but this is tantamount to saying that it makes use of terms external to any specific genus. Thus, 'exoteric' signifies external in this sense, certainly not that of Sepúlveda. Moreover it is clear that this adjective is to be applied first and foremost to the arguments, to the *ratiocinationes*, and only by derivation to the books.[66] Finally, this is completed by what Ferrari adds in the following pages, namely that the dialectic discourses are actually dialectic *syllogisms*. In other words they are reasonings that start with a questioner asking an answerer to adopt and defend a theory of his free choice – hence the affirmation that this is a reasoning *ex opinione*. Aristotle called this procedure 'dialogue'[67] and used it as the basis for his literary *Dialogues*. But this is *toto coelo* different from the demonstrative process: he who questions does not demonstrate and he who demonstrates – which is the same as saying he who teaches a 'science' – does not ask questions. One may argue – Ferrari continues – that Aristotle alludes to a non-dialectic mode of questioning (called 'epistemonical', see *Post. An.*, I, 12, 77a 36–40), but it is actually the kind of interaction that occurs in the teaching process, when the teacher asks the learner to say which of the two alternatives of the contradiction is true (not to arbitrarily [*ex opinione*] choose one of them, which instead triggers the dialectic procedure). The sort of 'dialogue' alluded to here can be plainly deduced from a passage from Lucretius, cited by Ferrari as an example (*De rer. nat.*, IV, 912–14): let Memnius be a docile and attentive listener! on the basis of what he is taught, he will discern the true and the false.[68]

The rest of the book takes stock of what has been said. It seems interesting that Ferrari insists on the fact that the *communia* can be easily learnt, that is they are understood by everyone, so that dialectic is consonant with a more popular type of training, suitable for the *multitudo*.[69] Perhaps this explains the association of common and probable concepts, in the literal sense that they can easily be 'approved' by a listener (pupil) who is without rigorous preparation – either because he is only at the start of his education or because he lacks intellectual capacity to pursue it. This would confirm that Ferrari's perspective is always that of distinguishing models of education and study curricula different in aims and method. It is nevertheless clear that, precisely because he is a slave to his own contrastive logic, Ferrari goes too far and ends up distancing Aristotle too much from the letter and spirit of his works. For example, when he claims that dialectic, like *ex communibus* or *exoterici* reasonings, must settle for 'an unfirm notion' of its object, or that it can know only how things 'seem',[70] an idea that it would be hard to find in Aristotle. Instead, what ought to be recalled is the latter's defence of a scientific use of dialectic,[71] which for him is not as external to epistemic knowledge as Ferrari believes.

What conclusions can ultimately be drawn from the history of Aristotle's writings? As Ferrari rightly says we now find ourselves in a situation that is somehow the opposite of that of the first pupils of Aristotle and Theophrastus, since they had only the exoteric dialogues and we only the acroamatic writings, adding that this is why the current 'way of philosophizing' (*philosophandi ratio*) is completely overbalanced in favour of acroamatic teaching.[72] Ferrari appears to end up yearning for a restoration of the situation at the time of Andronicus and Cicero, when the exoteric works of Aristotle had not yet been lost and the acroamatic works had finally been brought back to light. Now that the dialogues have been definitively lost, through a careful reading of the ancient testimonies and the internal references in Aristotle's own works it is at least possible to retrieve the idea behind their composition and, with it, the antique model of education in its entirety. This was an arrangement in two tiers, one popular and one specialized. It is likely that Ferrari – aware of the danger of higher education being made indiscriminately accessible – also glimpsed in this model an answer to the challenges of the time. Hence, an articulated *paideia*, based primarily on the selection of intellects depending on their inclinations and capacities, albeit without excluding the less gifted from some form of education, as long as it is not mixed with that which provides access to true knowledge. The latter is based substantially on the indications of the *Posterior Analytics*, interpreted in the light of how Neoplatonic scholasticism (Ammonius, Philoponus) understood the concept of 'acroamatic'. These inspirations and interpretations led Ferrari to elaborate a paradigm of 'scientific discipline' to be understood as a teaching subject to be communicated through a demonstrative method. I think that the underlying intention of *De sermonibus exotericis* is to be understood in the light of this. It all started with the question of Aristotle's books – what one might call a matter of humanistic philology. It then expanded to methodological-epistemological issues (the cognitive status of dialectic), gradually extending to various other questions (the nature of the literary form of the dialogue, literary imitation, whether moral virtues can be taught etc.), without neglecting polemics with those who came to hand (Sepúlveda, Cavalcanti and sundry anonymous writers). As to the other work published by Ferrari, *De disciplina encyclio*, mentioned at the very end of the *De sermonibus*, it appears to pursue a different but complementary objective. In fact, in this essay of 1560 Ferrari argues against the idea – resulting, inter alia, from a mistaken interpretation of a passage of the *Epinomis* provided by Cicero – that all humanistic 'disciplines' are bound (*constrictae*) to each other by relations of derivation or subordination and that there is a 'mathematical' super-science that provides all the other sciences with their principles (Proclus). Ferrari replies that this logical relation occurs only in the case of 'subordinate' (*hypallêloi*) disciplines, for instance optics compared to geometry, although this situation cannot be generalized. As regards this 'science of sciences', if any, it is certainly not a science that is *inside* the other disciplines, as if it were their *ratio formalis*, but is rather *prior* to them, by virtue of its being concerned with primary substances. Here Ferrari makes a clear allusion to metaphysics, which he prefers to call *sapientia*, as in the *De sermonibus*. In the context of this anti-Neoplatonic argument Ferrari is able to clarify in pretty Aristotelian terms the role of dialectics as that which 'dominates' – not subordinates! – the other sciences.

Ferrari's model of education

All in all, for Ferrari it was a question of claiming the authority of Aristotle (and of Cicero) to legitimize a didactic practice based on an elitist and specialist concept of higher education. What we know of Ferrari's activity as a university lecturer fits with this defence of a two-tier model. In fact most of his career, twenty-two years in all, was spent in the Cannobian school in Milan, founded and maintained by a lavish private endowment but aimed at the furtherance of public education. From his funeral eulogy we learn that admission to his philosophy lectures, in which interpretation was based on an attentive analysis of the textual sources, was open only to a select few, or rather the majority were kept away.[73] *De sermonibus* (and the specular and shorter work, *De disciplina encyclio*) can therefore be read in the light of Ferrari's concern about the uncontrolled opening of higher education to an undistinguished public, and hence is a contribution to the debate on the accessibility of humanistic studies that engaged the whole of Europe. We can almost hear him say that there is knowledge that demands elite competence and qualities, obviously referring to an intellectual rather than a social elite.

The immediate success of *De sermonibus* is due precisely to this formulation of the issues in the terms characteristic of late humanist culture. In other words, a discussion of the *mens* of the Philosopher coming up from the philological and critical analysis of the texts, paying due attention to the Greek interpreters – as Greeks, i.e. as direct successors of Aristotle, rather than as Neoplatonists – and to the antique Latin writers. In this way Ferrari distanced himself from Patrizi and all speculations on the *prisca sapientia*, understood as knowledge transmitted through initiates and hinging on theological, or rather religious, subjects, drenched in Hermeticism, de facto neo-Gnosticism. Already in the *De disciplina encyclio* it can be noted how careful Ferrari was to circumscribe the object of theological knowledge to the first substances, and to deny the existence of universal knowledge or languages aimed at grasping an assumed profound ideal structure of the real. *De sermonibus exotericis* in turn expounds the features of an elite knowledge not connected with the intrinsic loftiness (depth) of the subjects addressed, but rather with their technical difficulty, which demands methodical instruments that are the exclusive prerogative of a selected audience.

Finally, another point should be stressed: in the model brought to light through the interpretation of Aristotle's mind, the one which – as I believe – Ferrari also proposed and defended, we can discern a transformation in the mode of conceiving humanist education as a whole. This was still a general *enkýklos paideia*, that is a unified cultural training obtained through the contribution of various individual disciplines. But this very 'communication' and 'kinship' (*communicatio* or *cognatio*) – as Cicero and Vitruvius called it – of the disciplines targeted at the overall education of the free man is, when all is said and done, a weak point, a criticality that has to be removed. And the removal consists in establishing a higher level in which the specialization is consolidated, a level of disciplines that are by definition separate from each other. While it is true, in a sense, that the 'encyclical' runs parallel to the 'acroamatic' – and we know that Aristotle addressed the same subjects with the two methods – nevertheless authentic disciplinary education begins only with the latter. Ferrari certainly provides arguments for those who consider that practical philosophy or natural philosophy or metaphysics (*sapientia*), in their most mature versions, are sectorial science, which I believe explains the success of his proposal in the philosophical milieu of the Central European school. But this is to move into a different sphere of issues and a later historical phase. We shall instead settle for reconstructing the beginning of what we might call Ferrari's passage to Germany.

Philipp Scherb and the *Clavis Philosophiae Peripateticae* of Melchior Goldast

As known, *De sermonibus exotericis* was destined to end up in the hands of the Swiss Philipp Scherb (1553–1605). That is, the man who imposed a 'pure' Aristotelian approach at the University of Altdorf, in competition with the Christian-Neoplatonic revisitation of Aristotle's philosophy proposed by the famous Nicolaus Taurellus. Scherb's sojourn in Italy at the end of the 1570s, at the universities of Bologna, Rome and Padua, played a fundamental role in the evolution of this approach. His use of Ferrari can be placed within the general process of creation of an Aristotelian standard in the German universities, with Altdorf in the lead, in response essentially to two needs. The first was to curb the spread of Ramism, opposing what was presented as a simple dialectical-rhetorical training with a complete curriculum that did not exclude civil philosophy, natural philosophy and, most importantly, metaphysics. Let us remember that the infiltration of Ramism in Altdorf was due to the activity of Johann Thomas Freige (Fregius, 1543–83), who succeeded the humanist Erythräus in the capacity of dean, remaining in office from 1576 to 1582, the year to which can be dated the Aristotelian turnaround.[74] The second was to prevent this role being filled by some version of the Hermetic or Neoplatonic or even Paracelsian *prisca philosophia*, in view of the substantial difficulty of fitting the latter into a framework of Christian philosophy.[75] Possibly the most curious aspect of this debate was the tendency to utilize sixteenth-century Italian materials – such as the 'new' philosophies of Patrizi, Telesio, Bruno and Piccolomini, later the rereading of Nizolio and Maioragio by Leibniz, a student at Altdorf – to produce syntheses to be employed in teaching at German universities of a strong Lutheran or Calvinist-Reformed character. Scherb may well have felt that Ferrari's proposal had certain advantages over the others. In the first place he expressed typically scholastic exigencies which, excluding confessional issues, were similar to those of the German universities. This is probably evidence of changes in the development of university education – and naturally in social relations – that were similar throughout Europe. Without having anything in common with the discussions for and against Ramus, the acrimony towards Ferrari displayed by a neo-Ciceronian, nominalist and anti-Aristotelian – in short, an Italian Ramus – such as Nizolio[76] could have been to Ferrari's credit in the eyes of the German adversaries of the Frenchman; for them Ferrari's definition of the technical characteristics of an elite education was bound to be of interest. In the second place, Ferrari finally clarified the way that Aristotle's *ratio docendi* could be rendered rigorous for all scholastic disciplines, physics and metaphysics included. This is in fact the meaning of his recourse to the determinations of the *Posterior Analytics*, and in particular the key principle of banning the confusion of genera, which was in turn to enjoy particular popularity in the Ramist discussions. Further, Ferrari's austere Aristotle did not arouse the problems of invasion of the field, so to speak, which the philosophical religion or religious philosophy of the *prisca sapientia* brought in its wake. Such an Aristotle did not seem particularly inclined to get mixed up with *de divinis* issues, being above all a master of rational procedures, of method and, if anything, of moral prudence. Even the most theological of his speculations – the metaphysical – was considered infinitely more prudent than the unbridled Hermetic-Neoplatonic doctrines which could say almost everything about God, in other words, decidedly too much. Lastly, a return to Aristotle, or rather a confirmation of him as the basis of the curriculum, was in continuity with the Reformation mainstream. The prestige of Aristotle in Germany had remained substantially intact through the first Melanchthonian phase, albeit restricted to ethical-political philosophy, a discipline to which Scherb too gave primary importance.

In sum, Ferrari had found the way to restore dignity and depth to a renewed neoclassical philosophy in step with the times without reducing it to an (empty) art of discourse, and also without the temptation to see acroamatic Aristotle as a representative of Neoplatonic knowledge. Among the various texts that can demonstrate Scherb's borrowing of Ferrari's motifs is a collection of theses *On the Differences Between Analytics and Dialectics*, dating to 1589 and directly related to his teaching activities.[77] Many of the issues addressed by Ferrari resurface here, such as the question of the exoteric books, that of the dialogue and the monologue, the interpretation of the ancient testimonies etc. However, the main theses reveal how Ferrari's convoluted discourse is substantially reduced to its logical-epistemological nucleus, namely to the differences between analytics and dialectics mentioned in the title. Of particular interest in this argument is the attempt to understand the Aristotelian notion of *endoxa*, despite the fact that they are confused with other notions (*legomena, phainomena*, ibid., prop. IIIL). The epistemic asymmetry between endoxical and scientific premises – root of the essential difference between dialectical and analytic procedures, only the latter being productive of true knowledge – is an observation highly characteristic of Scherb, albeit not exhaustively investigated in this *disputatio*. Dialectic, as Scherb's student maintains and the greatest of the commentators, Alexander and Averroes saw it, is nothing more than a preparation for philosophy (100), but the analytical method is its proper organ, its 'hand' (prop. CI). At any rate, without entering into details, it is interesting to look at one of the final propositions.

> 112. From this sketched image of Dialectic and Rhetoric delineated by the ancients it is easy to see the shipwreck of what had been excellently established in the Peripatetic school. Indeed, to say nothing of other doctrines which, in such a learned century, have slipped through our hands, let us rather consider how illustrious is that Dialectic which has recently been introduced by certain new savants. The first thing they sing victory over (O homeland, o Ilium!) is about having got rid of the *logos didaskalikôs*: thus, it is the teachers themselves who subvert the method of teaching, the scientists that of science, the philosophers that of philosophy. And in fact those who deny the demonstration [*apodixis*] also deny the proper logic of teaching [*logos tês didaskalias*], deny the philosophical principle [*philosophema*], deny the science of the real and finally deny the perfect definition, which differs from the Aristotelian *apodixis* only in the position of the terms.
>
> 113. So why then do we not openly profess the incomprehensibility [*akatalêpsia*] and not immediately withdraw to the camp of the Pyrrhonists? Why do not Naturalists, Physicians, Politicians and all those who attempt to give a definition of their art do the same, since no one is in possession of the real cause of anything?[78]

What I feel is significant here is that in Scherb's school Ramism, which is clearly alluded to, is not considered a merely neutral technical innovation in the field of teaching. Its significant and destructive implications both in philosophy and, above all, in the sectorial disciplines are pointed out. Scherb returned to this issue again in a famous text, which will be dealt with at another time (see Chapter 2).

Possibly the most remarkable aspect of this whole story is the fact that Ferrari's text was taken up again by Scherb's pupil and fellow-countryman Melchior Goldast (1578–1635). As we have seen before, Goldast published *De sermonibus exotericis* and *De disciplina encyclio* in Frankfurt, based on an exemplar in Scherb's library, prefacing the edition with a letter *De cryptica veterum philosophorum disciplina* dedicated to the 'Marburg philosopher Rudolph Goclenius'.[79] Here we cannot but refer to the most interesting and penetrating analysis of this publication by Martin Mulsow, which offers a convincing explanation of the oddities present already in the title page of the book. For instance, the redundancy of the title ('Peripatetic Aristotelian'), the ambiguity of the identity of the addressee of the prefatory *epistola* (Goclenius the Elder or the Younger?) and the deliberate error in the date (1506 instead of 1606). According to Mulsow, all this is to be seen as a strategy – not less contorted than subtle – whereby Goldast sought to legitimize at the University of Marburg – and thence possibly throughout Germany – a Hermetic-alchemist approach inspired by Bruno and Patrizi. This strategy was, moreover, crowned with a degree of success, albeit not lasting.[80] It can be assumed that the effect of this publication was to make Ferrari turn in his grave, and probably Scherb too. The first pages of the *epistola* do contain a polemic on the *mal français*, an attack against Ramism, then Goldast goes on to complain that the authentic Aristotle is the one transmitted in the 'arcanes' of the acroamatic books: the loss of the latter up to Andronicus' edition was the direct cause of the degeneration of philosophy into dialectic,[81] but this is definitely less important than Goldast's attempt to accredit a 'true' Aristotle who was a cryptic supporter of a sapiential philosophy not unlike that advocated by Patrizi, from whose *Discussiones peripateticae* (Book VI)[82] Goldast drew no few quotations. In short, Goldast makes fairly clear his adherence to the Renaissance Hermetic Neoplatonism that Scherb and Ferrari wished to keep at a distance, although, according to Goldast, Ferrari's rejection was less resolute. In any case, Goldast admits that he himself added things that had been surprisingly omitted (*praetermissa miror*) by Ferrari, Sigonio and Scherb in their observations about education.[83]

Remaining in Germany, an attempt to put things back in place and restore its original value to Ferrari's work after Goldast's misinterpretations, or rather manipulations, was made in an anthology of texts published in Frankfurt in 1614. The first part of the title, *Clavis philosophiae peripateticae*, clearly refers to Goldast's 1606 publication and everything points to this work being a polemical rejoinder to it.[84] The compiler of the anthology was Michael Piccart (1574–1620), another pupil of Philipp Scherb and his successor in the chair of philosophy at Altdorf. I think that the details of the construction of this work are significant. First, the title declares that the book was composed (*conscriptus*) by Scherb himself, banishing all doubt apropos its general inspiration. Second, the book is in two parts and the first of these is nothing less than a new edition of the *Quaestiones logicae* of the Pisa professor Flaminio Nobili (first edition, 1562), a text that presumably Scherb himself had made known in Altdorf after his *peregrinatio academica* in the Italian universities, including that of Pisa. Nobili's work is substantially centred on the doctrine of definition and its relation with demonstration, commenting and interpreting the contents of Book 2 of the

Posterior Analytics. The analogy with Goldast's *modus operandi* in the publication of an Italian work is obviously striking. It is almost as if Piccart wished to emphasize that their common master had not read only Ferrari's *De sermonibus exotericis*, or even that the latter was to be read in the light of Flamini's work. And if all this is true, in other words if Piccart's operation is specular, identical and opposite to that of Goldast, then the publication of Nobili's *Quaestiones* was none other than a recall to the true nucleus of Aristotelianism, that is the logical-methodological nucleus. The second part of the anthology consists of *disputationes* discussed at Altdorf while Scherb was their *Praeses*, and it is curious that the first of the series (pp. 11–34) is actually by Goldast; it concerns the distinction between the acroamatic and exoteric books and is substantially devoid of Hermetic-Neoplatonic emphases. Was this too another way of reminding Goldast of the true *communis doctrina* of Altdorf as taught by its founder? This is possibly the reason why (one year before Goldast's *Clavis*) Piccart published his famous *Isagoge in lectionem Aristotelis*, in which the ideas of Ferrari-Scherb are taken up and reworked.[85]

The neo-Hermetic and sapiential use of the exoteric/acroamatic distinction appears to be restricted to the Marburg episode, whereas the epistemological interpretation of it provided by Piccart seems to have had an ulterior reception over time. This is indeed the version found in the leading seventeenth-century representative of the University of Helmstedt, Hermann Conring. He was familiar with the ideas of Scherb and Piccart about Aristotle's acroamatic books, since he had written a kind of review (*iudicium*) of a text where these ideas were thoroughly expounded and discussed, the second edition of Piccart's work just mentioned.[86] Here the acroamatic method is essentially the one that permits legitimate generalizations starting from a solid empirical basis of observations, or that underlies a treatment of the subject for advanced students (see Chapter 3). This technical-methodical sense is also the one Leibniz appears to have assumed in his *Dissertatio praeliminaris* to the new 1670 edition of Nizolio's *De veriis principiis*. Interesting here is the association between 'exoteric' and 'philosophical/dogmatic' (in the sense of 'didactic'): philosophy argues, but does not provide 'demonstrations'. Even Leibniz continued to use the acroamatic/exoteric dichotomy in his major works, although clearly not without further elaboration.[87] If the proposed reconstruction is convincing, then it may be possible to come to some conclusions pertinent to the history of philosophy of the early modern period in Central Europe. With the *De sermonibus exotericis* there took shape at the end of the sixteenth century and beginning of the seventeenth a tendency to consider dialectic – substantially understood as it was presented by Cicero – as a species of second-rate logic that was of no use to scientific and philosophical knowledge. Despite their different roles and contexts, the task of both Ferrari and Scherb was to forestall the risk that humanist dialectics could in effect trigger a slide into a sceptical neo-sophistry, and the theory of demonstration expounded in the *Posterior Analytics* was to be the dam to stop the slide. The solution was therefore, so to speak, to remove dialectics from philosophy and bring it closer to – or assimilate it into – rhetoric, at the same time admitting its inadequacy in the quest for the truth. In effect, even outside Altdorf in the nascent *Schulphilosophie*, the exoteric-acroamatic distinction became a widespread *topos* that easily identified a pro-Aristotelian and anti-Ramist approach. Nevertheless, in this operation a price was paid in terms of consistency with the principles of Aristotelian philosophy as traditionally understood: dialectic tended to be reduced to an 'empty' discourse. Later it even came to be defined as mere 'logic of appearance', despite the fact that Aristotle had theorized in the *Topics* and applied in all his works the use of dialectic in philosophy and even in the sciences: namely, for knowledge of reality. Furthermore, the risk for the various distinct parts of philosophical inquiry was of a methodological falling into line with the sciences via the canonization of the demonstrative method, again in the teeth of Aristotelian theory and practice. It could be concluded that, together with the natural scholastic tendency to produce ready-to-use syntheses, this factor contributed to minimizing the critical-sapiential dimension of philosophy, transforming it instead into a 'demonstrated' and hence 'taught' knowledge. In a word: disciplined, a very far cry from the search for final causes advocated by Aristotle.[88]

Part Two

Theoria

2

The Historical Significance of the Ramist Critique of Metaphysics

Goldast's activity in Marburg is not the only, nor even the most important, episode of the resumption on German ground of the Italian discussions on the exoteric/acroamatic dichotomy. Historically more significant in this regard is the reflection of the neo-Aristotelian professors of the Lutheran University of Altdorf (Nuremberg), with Philipp Scherb at their head, a figure whom historians tend to mention more than study. We have already dwelt on its role in the previous chapter, when we saw that, starting with Scherb, the exoteric/acroamatic distinction was used by Aristotelians to emphasize their own superiority over the followers of Ramus: i.e. the teachers of a dialectic, possibly not devoid of some practical use, but certainly lacking the methodological foundations and scientific rigour that should be proper to academic disciplines. Starting from these historical premises and gravitating around metaphysics as the 'queen of sciences' taught at school, a debate was sparked among Aristotelian and Ramist scholars that soon involved other academic centres in the German Protestant area, such as Gdansk and Helmstedt. It was this debate that triggered the formation of the metaphysics of the first *Schulphilosophie*, with the compilation of systematic treatises with a fairly characteristic thematic structure. This chapter is dedicated to this outcome and deals with a history circumscribed to the last decades of the sixteenth and the early seventeenth century. On the other hand, speaking of metaphysics in the Aristotelian tradition still means considering a phenomenon of *longue durée*, whose appropriate context is a centuries-old exegetical tradition that spans different historical periods and different intellectual milieux. This is the context we refer to in examining a work that is in many ways singular: the commentary on Aristotle's *Metaphysics* by a student of Scherb, Ernst Soner. Based on this, in Chapter 3 we shall propose a partially new interpretation of the presence (or absence) of confessional motifs in Reformed academic metaphysics, at the same time providing an outline of the fundamental trends of metaphysics in the schools of the early seventeenth century.

The problem of Ramus's philosophical thought and his attack on metaphysics

As known, in the face of the spread of Petrus Ramus's ideas about dialectic, the reaction of the philosophers teaching in the German universities at the end of the sixteenth century was decisive in the formation of a Protestant metaphysics.[1] Nevertheless, there is an anomalous, if not paradoxical, aspect to this, as scholars are far from agreed about the extent to which the philosophical ideas behind Ramus's thought were either well-defined or alternative to those of Aristotle. The principal scholar of Ramus, Walter G. Ong, fails to credit him with the stuff of a solid and consistent thinker, whereas Nelly Bruyère discerns a constant Platonic inspiration underlying his concepts of method. Most scholars of Ramus and Ramism can be found between these two extremes.[2] Much has also been written about the Stoic or nominalist elements of his thought, and this is certainly not the place for further speculation on this point. In general, I subscribe to the idea that the key to the activity of the Regius professor lies in his reform of the aims and methods of higher and academic teaching, in which recourse to philosophical theories of one or other origin was fairly instrumental and in any case secondary. A recent reproposal of this approach by Howard Hotson is not (as in Ong) aimed at diminishing Ramus's value as a thinker but rather at recognizing the historic importance of his innovations.[3] However, even if Ramus failed to specify his own new philosophical thought, he had willy-nilly already struck a deadly blow to the old philosophy, polemizing against its coryphaeus Aristotle. In addition, by placing method at the core of his reform, Ramus also set the agenda for his interlocutors and opponents, who were thus challenged to clarify their own doctrine on the point. According to Leinsle,[4] one of the clarifications concerned the relation between the principles and methods of knowledge set forth by Aristotle in the *Analytics* and the status of metaphysics. The following pages address the response of the Aristotelians to this provocation.

A born polemicist and a master of provocation, Ramus rapidly realized that to promote his cause he needed to go straight to the heart of the matter, even at the risk of making serious enemies. Consequently he had no scruples about branding everything Aristotle had written as *commentitium* ('fictitious' or 'artificial', whatever that may mean)[5] or criticizing the hallowed tradition of teaching dialectic on the basis of the famous *Summulae logicales* written by Peter of Spain. Nor was he daunted by the criticisms that came pouring down on him from the Aristotelians. The volley was first launched from the Paris circles (Gouveia, Vimercato and Charpentier). It was then taken up in what was to prove the most fertile terrain for the expansion of Ramism: the German upper schools and universities, led by the attack of the Tübingen philosopher and theologian Jakob Schegk. Ramus's subsequent declarations of esteem for Aristotle cannot simply be taken at face value. This is not because they were not sincere. On the contrary, historians have noted the increasing presence of concepts directly derived from the *Organon* in the successive editions of the *Dialectica*. This point, for instance, has been stressed by Risse to show that Ramus's revision of his dialectic after 1555–6 can be interpreted as a sort of reconciliation with Aristotle.[6] Not to mention the fact that Ramus unabashedly resorted to the old humanist formula of the quest for a 'truer' Aristotle than the one being passed off by the scholastics. Moreover, as Freige observed, open and direct criticism of Aristotle by Ramus is sporadic, not to say that he explicitly (or if you prefer, blatantly) presented himself as a loyal follower of Aristotle in the *Petri Rami defensio pro Aristotele adversus Jacobum Schecium*, which closed the long-drawn-out controversy with the Tübingen theologian.[7] It is, rather, because – as his opponents easily demonstrated – taking as valid the Aristotle of Ramus, 'Socratized' or read through Cicero and above all bent to the need to reform the university curriculum meant paying a price in terms of lacunae and distortions that no Aristotelian would be willing to accept. It seems to me that this concern was justified. While it is true to say that the crux of Ramus's achievement lies in his reform of teaching rather than in his philosophy, it is equally clear that his innovations in dialectic and his suppression or marginalization of metaphysics could have serious philosophical implications. Hence the alleged conciliation with Aristotle's doctrine was a sort of precarious balance that could not last for long.

The most decisive argument in the clash between Ramus's followers and opponents was honed down over time to the question of the utility of metaphysics in the curricula, denied by the former and upheld by the latter. This issue became particularly prominent after the 1590s, following a distinct revival in the German universities of a discipline hitherto marginalized in the prevailing model of study still derived from Melanchthon. It is not necessary to dwell here on the causes and circumstances of this revival, which have already been authoritatively dealt with.[8] It is instead worth noting that Ramus himself had already been aware of the problem. In the *Scholae in liberales artes*[9] he had returned to one of the recurrent themes of the Renaissance debate on Aristotle – the history of his 'library' as recounted by Strabo and Plutarch – to argue that even in antiquity all the known texts were corrupt and deficient. Then, exempting Galen, whom he considered the last philosopher-logician to use his own head, he went on to accuse the subsequent Greek interpreters of paying lip service to Aristotle, that is, being servile towards him while actually propagating theories that had nothing to do with his.[10] Starting from Alexander of Aphrodisias, such interpreters had taken advantage of the chaotic state of Aristotle's writings to manipulate his thought and render it radically different from the original.[11] This led to the crystallization of the 'barbaric' logic which came to dominate the schools up to the present.[12] Nevertheless Ramus ends by claiming that, despite the historic distortions, the 'true' Aristotelian logic can none the less be retrieved by adhering strictly to the three fundamental laws of the method. He then invented the respective formulas for these: (*lex veritatis, lex iustitiae* and *lex sapientiae*), holding them to be Aristotle's true bequest, of which he intended to be the executor.[13] Ramus also returns to the question of Aristotle's 'obscurity', claiming that it was not intentional (*de industria*), as other interpreters stated, but the result of the Stagirite's difficulty in conforming his method of exposition to the famous 'three laws' that he himself had established in the *Posterior Analytics*.[14]

While in this text it is still possible to talk of Ramus as a reformer of Aristotelian philosophy, the situation changes in the *Scholae metaphysicae*, a sort of anti-commentary or polemical commentary on the *Metaphysics* conceived as a development of the *Scholae dialecticae*. A glance at the preface is enough to realize that the notion of a genuine Aristotle, subsequently corrupted by ill-informed and ill-intentioned interpreters, has been abandoned. Here, instead, the founder is held directly responsible for the error of having decided to invent a science such as metaphysics: 'a science different from logic that studies all causes, especially the first cause; or having as object being in so far as it is being and principally the first among beings'.[15] Perhaps, Ramus continues, Aristotle intended this science to comprise purely and solely logical contents but objectively, verging into theology, 'the philosopher erred defying the decrees of his very own philosophy'.[16] The explanation provided as to what led Aristotle to this violation, to create a completely 'other' science, borders on the psychological. Aristotle was impressed by the praise for dialectic that Plato put in the mouth of Socrates in the *Philebus* and in the *Republic* where, inter alia, it is claimed that in some way it puts us in contact with the divine. Taking these words too seriously and hence misunderstanding them, Aristotle felt himself challenged to create an authentic *scientia de divinis*, later called by various names among which that of metaphysics prevailed. So it is easy to understand which 'decrees' have been violated: they are none other than the three laws that Aristotle set as the foundations of his universal 'art' of logic. These indeed prohibit (1) admitting to a discipline propositions which are not universally true, that is at all times (*lex veritatis*); (2) admitting heterogeneous contents (*lex iustitiae*); and (3) altering the order of exposition which requires starting from the most general proposition (*lex sapientiae*). Indeed, the metaphysics sketched out by Aristotle, as well as leading to clearly false, or rather, impious,[17] conclusions (violation of law 1), also trespasses into another area, since it is actually a logic that claims the right to deal with real causes (violation of law 2) and, finally, cannot conceivably claim to be the most general discourse since it is dealing with a being or category of beings that are extremely specific, namely the immaterial substances or God (violation of law 3). The final effect of these methodological errors was that the Scholastics, following Aristotle, made metaphysics the 'pillar' of the Christian religion.[18]

Ramus resorted to an unusual psychological explanation for Aristotle's enterprise: a spirit of emulation as regards Plato. *Aemulatio* is a *vox media* that can have both a positive meaning as an honest spirit of competition and a negative connotation as envy. I think that it is the second meaning that is intended here and that Ramus has in mind a *topos* of Renaissance Aristotelianism that identified envy as the principal trait of Aristotle's attitude towards Plato. Suffice it to mention the most significant example of the systematic use of this interpretation: Patrizi's *Discussiones peripateticae*. Their author also believed most of the fourteen books of Aristotle's *Metaphysics* to belong to the domain of logic and to be extraneous to metaphysics itself, though Patrizi's Neoplatonic-Hermetic philosophy and his occasional role as a Catholic apologist obviously distinguish him from Ramus. And so, the genesis of metaphysics as a science would be explained by Aristotle's inferiority complex, his fear of not measuring up to Plato and Socrates. Or at the very least, by his anxiety to be the first to give systematic form to a discourse which the two great Athenian philosophers had only vaguely sketched out. Since this pseudo-science is the outcome of reprehensible impulses and logical errors present from the start, clearly there is no purified version that might be deserving of retrieval. It must simply be done away with, demonstrating that – apart from a few theological passages – the remainder of the fourteen books are merely camouflaged logic. At most they are doctrines that Aristotle had already expounded in the other treatises of the corpus, 'tautologically' repeated here under the new title of metaphysics. Ramus's stance therefore appears to imply the following theses: traditional metaphysics contains an illegitimate ('heterogeneous') part which is its theological component; traditional metaphysics also contains a legitimate, so to speak ontological, part which cannot however be distinguished from a universal method applied to commonplaces (*topica universalis*).

This is the metaphysics problem that Ramus bequeathed to his numerous and spirited followers. Actually, it was not immediately seen as a problem by the professors teaching the use of Ramist techniques for tackling analysis of the classical texts and organizing the knowledge derived therefrom. Indeed, they praised the combination of eloquence and wisdom fostered by the new method – or, as its detractors dubbed it, the easy 'Thessalian' (= that could be learnt quickly) method – designed to teach how to write and speak about any subject. But it did then become a problem when, from the last decade of the sixteenth century, metaphysics – that is the metaphysics of Aristotle and his Greek, Arab and Christian commentators – came back into fashion. At this point of the story, it was the turn of the neo-Aristotelians in the universities to call Ramist or Ramist-contaminated thought[19] to account. The *redde rationem*, that is, the evaluation of the premises and consequences of the abandonment of metaphysics, actually took place in a fairly short space of time between the last decade of the sixteenth century and the first of the seventeenth. Here I want to give three examples of the pro-Aristotelian and pro-metaphysical retaliation, referring to the anti-Ramist polemic of Cornelius Martini, Philipp Scherb and Bartholomäus Keckermann, representatives of three important centres of learning and influential thinkers in the seventeenth-century world of scholastic philosophy. For all three, the clash with Ramus and Ramism was an important phase at the beginning of their careers and actually decisive in their intellectual formation. I hope to demonstrate that, despite being differently articulated and focused on different aspects, the responses of all three to the adversary had many points in common. As a result, their shared polemic against Ramism succeeded in establishing certain fundamentals that remained a permanent acquisition of *scientia metaphysica* in the schools of Central Europe in the seventeenth century.

Philipp Scherb: The Aristotelian shift of the Altdorf school

One of the first decisive reactions to the spread of Ramism in Germany[20] from a representative of Aristotelian persuasion was contained in the *Dissertatio pro philosophia peripatetica adversus ramistas*[21] by Philipp Scherb, a figure we have already met and who plays an important role in our reconstructions. After learning the Aristotelian approach in Italy in the school of Pellegrini and Zabarella, among others, Scherb helped to introduce it at the *Hochschule* of Altdorf in the wake of a period of Ramist domination under the rectorship of Johann Thomas Freige.[22] Scherb's was one of the first and most significant attempts to translate neo-Aristotelian principles – largely related to the structure of knowledge in general and that of science in particular – into a programme of secondary and higher studies. He then presented this programme as a return to correct education following the mania of the *novatores* which was seen by him as a veritable intellectual disease[23] or as an explosion of would-be youthful irreverence towards recognized authorities.[24]

The *Dissertatio* was therefore a brief and efficacious exposé of the objections that a young professor educated in the Padua school could make to the rapidly spreading success of the Ramist method, also singling out Ramus in person at certain key moments, for instance, when Scherb calls into question the main argument provided by Ramus to support his asserted role as the reformer of true Aristotelianism, namely his fidelity to the *tres leges* synthesizing what Aristotle had to say about method. Obviously, Scherb demonstrates that Ramus's claim that his strategy lies on Aristotelian foundations is arbitrary. Take, for example, the first law, which requires that a science can only admit propositions that are necessarily true. An overall view of Aristotelian epistemology reveals something else entirely, given that Aristotle applies this rule *sic et simpliciter* at most only to mathematical sciences, while at the same time admitting various other sciences – both theoretical and practical – inherently characterized by a different, and hence lesser, degree of 'scientific precision' (*akribologia epistêmonikê*), precisely because their ontological sphere of reference is different: an implicit reference to the famous opening of Zabarella's *De natura logicae*.[25] The error is even more serious in the case of the second law, since here Ramus muddles up no less than four types of *per se* (*kath'hauto*) proposition distinguished by Aristotle. Here the consequences are far-reaching and closely related to the issue in question. It can indeed be noted that the second of the *per se* modes, when one predicates a property of a subject (such as 'passions', 'powers', 'activities' and 'dispositions' that belong exclusively to that subject while extraneous to the definition of its essence), is wrongfully extended by the Ramists in such a way that dialectic is used to address what ought instead to be *proper* to the sectorial sciences.[26] The consequence of this extension of the principle of homogeneity is that the art which is competent in the most general genus/category is also competent in the subordinate and highly specialized species and also in those that are related, opposite etc. Thus, for example, the logic that knows the movement genus will also know all its innumerable species, and then also the subject to which the movement is inherent, that is the 'natural body' genus, and hence, again, all the species of the same. In this way, the new logic envisaged by Ramus makes it possible to embrace natural philosophy in its entirety. And why not extend this procedure to first philosophy? Suffice it to know the genus 'one' and there you are:

> Dealing with the one and all the modes of unity and identity... is the concern of he who deals with the being, of which the one is like a passion (indeed in its broader sense the being does not have real passions, but being and one convert between each other). And so the science of the being and of all its subdivisions will be yours [O Ramist dialectician! DF]. But he who deals with the being will deal with the first being or God, as must be the case of terms deriving from a principal term, as certified by your very adversary Aristotle. And so you will also deal with God, and so theology too is yours. So, since axioms such as 'in any being either the affirmation or the negation is true', 'one must not affirm and deny the same thing at the same time' are inherent to your being, they too will be yours, that is the habitus that we call *nous* will be yours by right. And why stop there? The habitus that is called *sophia aplôs*, made up of intellect and science, that too will be attributed to you if even the ocean of causes scattered through the philosophy of Aristotle – as you express it – is also your domain. Have I not made you sufficiently happy? Do you still want more? I would dearly have wished by the same entitlement to make you the owner of the mathematical disciplines, but I think that at this point you have enough, and perhaps you are already beginning to wonder if the very size of your domain will not in the end threaten it with ruin.[27]

With irony no less insistent than that adopted by Ramus in his polemics, Scherb derides the claim that logic can take the place of metaphysics, generating the theoretical sciences of the Aristotelian system from its own substance in the manner – one might say – of Bacon's spiders. As he repeats further on, logic is only an instrument of knowledge and not knowledge in itself.[28] Its highest expression is the theory of demonstration, apodicticity, as a set of rules for constructing demonstrations on a delimited subject, and thus not even this is an 'architectonic' science that prevails over others[29] (a clear allusion to metaphysics) but indeed merely a tool. Nevertheless, starting from these dubious premises the Ramists – these new Stoics! (sometimes Scherb harshly and antonomastically addresses his imaginary adversary as 'Chrysippus') – are promising German youth the acquisition of a *rerum omnium cognitio* which is actually an illusion, instead of placing it on a par with the Spanish and the Italians through serious philosophical studies.[30] Finally Scherb discusses Ramus's accusation that metaphysics violates the third law, which requires that the discipline should be organized starting from the more general propositions. Indeed, according to Ramus and his followers, this seductive *sapientia* lacks precisely this attribute of generality, since in the book called *Metaphysics* all Aristotle did was pointlessly accumulate 'tautologies', that is subjects dealt with in previous more specific studies without adding anything new to what he had already said. Against this, Scherb defends Aristotle – in truth, not very convincingly – by observing that the same material (for instance, the nature of the human soul, the criticism of the theory of ideas, the theory of the four causes) may be included in several treatises in different ways and for different reasons. However, what Scherb himself fails to address here is what metaphysics specifically consists of and what its function as universal science consists of.

In short, Scherb's discussion revolves around the possibility of applying to metaphysics the laws of method delineated by Ramus. His strategy seems to consist of showing that Ramus's claim is illegitimate since, as he argues, metaphysics is not bound to submit to such laws. In this Scherb appears to diverge from the writers considered later. What he does instead share with other anti-Ramist and pro-Aristotelian polemicists is the need to distinguish between a 'real' science and a 'topical' universal art, which in effect capitalizes on the lessons of Paduan Aristotelianism. Zabarella's distinction between 'primary' and 'secondary' notions also appears implicit in various passages of the *Dissertatio*. In Scherb's interpretation this amounts to the distinction between, on the one hand true knowledge, calibrated on things themselves and restricted to a specific genre, and on the other the clash of different *endoxa*, 'common opinions'. The latter derive 'from our storeroom' (*ex nostro promptuario*), namely they are logical schemes originating in our minds and subsequently applied to the real world.[31]

In a word, Scherb is the first to say that the Ramists don't understand that the epistemic import of dialectic is intrinsically limited precisely because it does not deal with primary notions derived directly from things but with secondary ones, i.e. notions of notions or generalizations of notions. In general, then, we can say that Scherb's reaction, on the strength of the neo-Aristotelian ideas he had learnt in Italy, casts light on the difference between two perspectives. One is of philosophical-epistemological origin, based on consideration of the intellectual habitus commensurate with the type of reality (necessary or contingent) they are required to explain, and on logic as the tool, or rather series of tools, which such habitus employ on each occasion. The other is a didactic-centred perspective pivoting on the elaboration of disciplines, of arts, that is systems of rules and precepts related to the individual fields of knowledge, which nevertheless leaves substantially unresolved the problem of knowing how such systems relate to reality.

In conclusion I would like to stress another point. As mentioned, Scherb does not seem very convinced in defining the terms of the universality of metaphysics as opposed to the universality of Ramist logic-dialectic. And it's not difficult to see why. His own conception, influenced by the epistemological theories of his master, the late Zabarella,[32] is based on the distinction between apodicticity on the one hand and dialectic and other disciplines of discourse on the other, reflected in the distinction between Aristotle's acroamatic books and his exoteric books. This approach leads him to posit a stark antithesis between the apodictic method, aimed at discovering the truth but only within the scope of a limited genus, that is the object of a single science, and the dialectic method, which is not constricted by any limitation and is aimed not at the truth but at victory in the debate based on shared opinions.[33] These principles were to become the most characteristic and fundamental for the school of Altdorf. Nevertheless, however useful they may have been to counter the Ramist concept of dialectic as a universal art, it's hard to see what space they leave to dialectic conceived as a tool for seeking the truth. Dialectic in its classic version clearly possesses this quality, making it particularly applicable to metaphysical knowledge, which is characterized by its generality and cannot be restricted to a delimited ambit.[34] At the same time, attributing the function of a 'universal science' to metaphysics becomes problematic, given that in view of the premises this expression appears to be an oxymoron.

I would say, therefore, that Scherb's text is dominated by the critical aspects, whereas a consideration of the cognitive value of metaphysics and its link with dialectic, and of its position in relation to other sciences, is missing. Unlike his rival at Altdorf, Taurellus, Scherb did not publish works on metaphysics. Scherb's ideas on the subject can nevertheless be retrieved in what was written by his pupils Piccart and Soner, and can be traced back to the teachings of Tommaso Pellegrini, whereby metaphysics is entirely founded on the 'analogical' unity of its subject, making it possible to combine the explanation of the being in so far as it is being and that of the first being.[35] However, the link between these positive doctrines of Scherb's and his anti-Ramist polemic – based instead on the teachings of Zabarella – is not clear. A dual inspiration, then, while it did stimulate a veritable school of Aristotelians, at a purely theoretical level suffers perhaps from the absence of a final amalgamation.

The semi-Ramist Aristotelianism of Bartholomäus Keckermann

The conversion of the young Keckermann from Ramism to Aristotelianism in its Paduan version took place while he was still a student at Wittenberg at the beginning of the last decade of the sixteenth century. Philipp Scherb – and more precisely the reading of the *Adversus ramistas* – was apparently the initial and decisive factor in this change of heart.[36] This event in intellectual history has been excellently described, as have the reasons why the Aristotelian Keckermann has to be qualified as 'post-Ramist'.[37] Namely, because he grasped the importance of Ramus's reform of higher teaching and proposed to continue along the same path, albeit without getting bogged down in the polemical excesses and theoretical simplifications of his predecessor. The result was an impressive series of works and, above all, a disciplinary model refined over almost a decade of frenetic activity which left a lasting mark on university culture, and on the intellectual culture of the seventeenth century in general.[38] As regards the presence of metaphysics, understood here as a curricular discipline studied in the second year of the three-year philosophy cycle, the situation is somewhat peculiar. Keckermann was indeed extremely clear about championing its rehabilitation, within the framework of Zabarella's dichotomy of practical and theoretical disciplines, of which metaphysics was obviously the acme. Furthermore, Keckermann repeatedly considered its abandonment as one of the capital sins of Ramism. This omission indeed encapsulated all the theoretical flaws of the adversary theory, consisting of a series of absent or insufficient distinctions: between primary and logical, or secondary, notions, between the contingent and the necessary sphere in reality, between the appetitive-operative habitus and the noetic habitus in the human subject, and between analytical and synthetic method.[39] For example, in the introduction to the *Praecognita logica* Keckermann poses a series of provocative questions to Ramus and the Ramists, the first of which is clearly intended to lay bare the raw nerve of the metaphysics issue:

> Are disciplines to be formed only through a consideration of the species of things and not their genus? In other words, should we not build a discipline such that it deals with the thing, or being, as a thing, and then deals with what inheres in it in common with natural, mathematical and ethical things, and not as logical arguments, but as real and positive affections and modes, such as essence, existence, goodness, perfection, finiteness and the relation to the prime being or God and its dependency on Him?[40]

Here, we might say, a programme of metaphysics in two or three phases is sketched out: the being in general and its affections, the prime being – which shortly we shall find again, not much altered, in Cornelius Martini.

We are scarcely more illuminated in a later work, the *Praecognita philosophica*, where the polemic with Ramus – with a reference to his *Scholae metaphysicae* – is taken up and clarified in Chapter II of the first book (*De philosophiae partitione*).

According to Keckermann, Ramus inflicted 'mutilations' on the system of sciences, primarily the elimination of the *pars praecipua et maxime sublimis philosophiae contemplativae*. The charge of the futility of metaphysics is also to be rejected; suffice it to consider – retorts Keckermann – how widely basic metaphysical concepts are used in Trinitarian and sacramental theology.[41] The argument is that the Ramists have not understood the need for a *scientia universalis contemplativa* 'which deals in the most absolute and general manner with the thing or being in so far as it is thing or being', thus violating the principle they themselves uphold whereby in the *ordo doctrinae* one proceeds from the more general to the more special. This science, if admitted, would therefore comprise the supreme and most general principles, for which reason Aristotle was quite right to call it 'wisdom' precisely to distinguish it from other particular sciences.[42]

It is, however, also known that Keckermann himself composed a short treatise on metaphysics, which was one of the last things he wrote[43] and the first to be published after his death in 1609. But anyone looking in it for further exploration and substantial clarifications beyond what had been said *en passant* in the other works on metaphysics would be fairly disappointed. What can be said is that it confirms the impression that, for Keckermann, metaphysics is substantially theory of the being in general, from which the 'special' discourses are separate. Metaphysics, indeed, does not deal with God, who is 'above' the being[44] and not even with the immaterial substances which are the realm of 'pneumatology'.[45] Moreover, the doctrine expounded here is in reality reduced to a series of distinctions grouped around the principal substance–accident dichotomy, and where considerable space is devoted to the various articulations of the concept of *ordo* (Chapters V–XIV: where, incidentally, the relations anteriority/posteriority, universality/singularity, principle / what descends from the principle etc. are probably derived from the third part of Timpler's treatise on metaphysics).[46] There is also the constant warning not to confuse the metaphysical plane of this order, that is the real, with the logical which is its transposition into concepts, a danger which is particularly evident apropos the concept of cause.[47] So, once again here we find criticism of Ramist logic in the name of Aristotelian principles. Keckermann moreover declared that he saw his work in metaphysics as a support for theological studies – and, we might add, for dogmatic definitions and confessional controversy. And he also recommended works that were more thorough than his own which had this same objective, such as those of Timpler, Taurellus, Jakob Martini etc.[48] In a word, it is clear that, while on the one hand circumstances did not permit him to produce a consummate exposé of his metaphysics, nor can it be taken for granted that a doctrine of the being in all its ramifications that could expound the essential of Aristotle's metaphysics with the clarity of Ramus[49] was even on the cards. Keckermann had, in substance, already composed treatises on all the other disciplines – both 'instrumental' (logic, rhetoric) and practical (ethics, economics, politics) – leaving metaphysics until last. Despite being glorified by him as the 'primary part of the contemplative science', it was in effect treated as non-essential in the construction of the *corpus doctrinarum* which, thanks to the work of Johann Heinrich Alsted, was soon to acquire the features of a veritable encyclopaedia. Within this, metaphysics was effectively a discipline like the others, incapable of reclaiming its 'architectonic' role. In actual fact, Keckermann attributed this role – namely that of doctrine of the principles and rules for establishing an integral system of disciplines, which was recognized as the characteristic contribution of the Reformed universities to seventeenth-century culture[50] – to the logic that he had, not incidentally, elaborated prior to the composition of specific philosophical treatises. Therefore, Keckermann's legacy on the point we are concerned with remains ambiguous. In effect, on the one hand he opens up again to the science of being, to an extent going beyond the horizon defined by Melanchthon and the deriving tradition,[51] while on the other hand one could even get the impression that this defence of metaphysics, and with it his subscription to philosophical Aristotelianism, resided in the sphere of words rather than that of deeds.

In this same period, in the Lutheran ranks the overcoming of the Ramist deconstruction of metaphysics led to more consummate creations which were destined to remain vital at length.

Cornelius Martini and the Helmstedt dispute

The institutional context of the Academia Julia of Helmstedt, founded in 1576, had a direct influence on the terms of the debate under way between Ramists and Aristotelians. The statutes of the new university were indeed the result of a compromise between a Gnesio-Lutheran trend represented by Martin Chemnitz and a Melanchthonian (Phillipist) approach linked to the name of David Chytraeus. The point is that the predominance of Aristotle was anything but taken for granted, since he was a recommended authority only within the teaching of particular disciplines, such as natural sciences and ethics, while a specific teaching of metaphysics was not envisaged.[52] It was indeed only as time went on, and largely due to the action of Johannes Caselius (professor at Helmstedt from 1590) and of Cornelius Martini (professor of logic from 1592) that Aristotelianism came to prevail in the academy of Helmstedt, albeit in forms that were no longer Renaissance. Yet even in the last decade of the sixteenth century the game was still open and, effectively, to legitimize their activity the Ramists had only to demonstrate or declare the conformity of their teaching to the thought of Melanchthon, demonstrating at the same time that Aristotle himself, duly interpreted, could be assimilated to this model.[53] It is nevertheless true that at the end of the day the Ramist faction does not appear to have been successful, so that its teaching was never officially established, being at the utmost tolerated in private lessons.

And so in this period a group of Ramist and Philippo-Ramist *Privatdozenten* was formed with the intention of playing their cards openly with the Aristotelians, essentially in a bid for survival. A treatise by Anton Nothold has been chosen here to represent the positions of this group.[54] The *De Rameae institutionis principiis et natura logicae*[55] is a precise rejoinder in thirty-two chapters to the attacks on the new logic launched by Cornelius Martini, champion of the 'Zabarellists'. Nothold's strategy is to defend his loyalty to the Melanchthonian tradition, as reinvigorated by Ramus, with his commitment to constructing a *dialectic* that can yoke together wisdom and elegance and that has a demonstrably practical purpose.[56] Restricting the analysis to the point we are interested in here, the reduction of metaphysics to logic-dialectic is substantially sustained by Nothold through the notion that the latter, as taught by the Ramists, can be considered an *ars universalis* which hence assumes the prerogatives of metaphysics, thus rendering it useless. Dialectic is therefore an 'art', a system of teaching aimed at forming a *habitus* in the students,[57] and is universal, that is it pervades all being – it may be applied to any sort of being. In actual fact, according to Nothold, Aristotle's formula at the beginning of Book IV of the *Metaphysics* ('being in so far as it is being') is to be applied to the domain of logic-dialectic and not – as Aristotle and his commentators wanted – to a different science which there is no need for, as Plutarch too had argued in ancient times.[58] Grafted onto this point is the explanation of the way in which the formula 'in so far as' (*in quantum, quatenus, qua, ut, utut*) is to be understood, intended as the operator of the *modus considerandi* of the object posited in the first part of the formula. As known, this topic ended up becoming a *topos* that could not be avoided in any of these scholastic treatises.[59] So, Nothold rejects the notion that this is to be understood as *specificative*, namely leading to a reduction of the field of inquiry through a specific *ratio formalis*, arguing instead that it is to be considered *reduplicative*, entailing that it is to be understood as being in its maximum extension and without limitations.[60] Nothold goes on to argue that this way of understanding Aristotle is consistent with that of Aristotelian authorities such as Fonseca (as well as Toletus and, obviously, Melanchthon),[61] who supported a similar extensive interpretation with the notion of *ens commune*, and further that it is also supported by a tradition alluding to the *prisca sapientia* (conjuring up the Pythagoreans, Francesco Patrizi and even Hermes Trismegistus).[62] Thus the Dutchman had all that he needed to conclude that Ramist dialectic can do perfectly well without metaphysics. This is a self-styled *scientia realis*, since the need for universality posed by the Aristotelian formula *ens inquantum ens* is already satisfied by dialectic itself as, on reflection – Nothold insists – had already been admitted by a possibly not very consistent Aristotle.[63] To the objection that a logic conceived in this way would also take into consideration all the beings forged by imagination (*entia ficta*) and the non-beings,[64] the response is that it is precisely because of this extensively understood universality that logic can address 'subjects' such as purgatory or free will, namely: imaginary (or mental) beings invented by Papists and Pelagians.[65] Finally, he reiterates a line that the entire Ramist school was very attached to: the aim of dialectic is not so much the search for the truth, but the practical purpose of *bene disserere de omnibus rebus*.[66]

Cornelius Martini (1568–1621) is generally considered one of the first advocates of the reintroduction of metaphysics into Protestant Germany,[67] and in any case as the one who took the decisive step of making it into a discipline, giving unified form to a jumble of disjointed parts.[68] It was Johannes Caselius, a humanist by training and insufficiently versed in philosophy, who entrusted to him the task of opposing the Ramists at theoretical level, first by putting forward a different conception of dialectic[69] and then – as a logical corollary – by rejecting the negation of metaphysics. Martini first expounded his stances in the university courses he held at Helmstedt from 1597 to 1599, a synthesis of which was published without his authorization in 1605 by one of this students, the Danish physician, philosopher and theologian Caspar Bartholin, who in the introduction signed himself with the pen name Thrasibulus Philaletes.[70] Martini too set his hand to this material and constructed his own exposition of metaphysics in 1610, although it was not published until 1622, a year after his death.[71] It is worth noting that, according to Leinsle, this edition is less important than the one of 1605 for the history of Lutheran metaphysics, since the latter became immediately known thanks to the defence of Martini's main thesis provided by Arnisaeus in his *De constitutione et partibus metaphysicae tractatus* published in

1606.[72] Two *disputationes* published in 1604 and discussed under Martini's own supervision are also of help in view of their synthetic character, albeit in my opinion entirely conforming in terms of contents to the 1610 work with which they display numerous correspondences as regards vocabulary and turn of phrase.[73]

I will not enter into the relations between the first and second editions except to note that the 1610 version is almost entirely without the direct references to Ramus and his followers which were frequent in that of 1605,[74] and that Melanchthon too is mentioned much less. Remaining on the subject of the sources, as often observed the main novelty of the 1610 edition is the citations from Suarez' *Disputationes metaphysicae*,[75] supplementing the small handful of other late scholastic writers (De Vio, Javelli, Acquario, Fonseca and Pereira) who are Martini's true masters. I shall return to this point in greater detail. Instead, as regards the general exposition, an evolution can clearly be discerned in the 1610 work where the arrangement and discussion of the topics is much clearer and more consistent. This is partly due to the decision to expound only the final result of the various questions, without the respective debates between the antagonists, and the omission of the summary of Aristotle's *Metaphysics* (20-9) and the reduction of the transcendentals from six to four (a solution also upheld by Suarez). This synthesis of 1610 is therefore a mature composition in which the principal concepts are definitively formulated and past polemics are considered laid to rest. In a word, it appears to be the expression of a victory, which was in a sense what Martini did achieve in the battle with the Ramists, at least at institutional level.[76] But here I would like to propose the theory that this victory was won by Martini bearing clearly in mind the issues raised by the Ramists, who therefore functioned to a degree as catalysts in the process of formation of a neo-scholastic metaphysics, the need for which was widely felt in the early seventeenth century in the academic circles of Germany and central Europe. Clarification of this point will be based principally on the *Metaphysica* of 1610, with an examination of its main theses.

The assertion that metaphysical science is not superfluous naturally enough pivots upon the determination of an 'adequate object' for the same,[77] which is what ought to be concealed behind the formula *ens inquantum ens*. For Martini, immaterial substances such as God or other intelligences are not eligible candidates since they can be the object only of a particular science. This is where the fundamental distinction between the *modus considerandi* and the *res considerata* comes into play.[78] Consequently Martini has to return to the standard question of the meaning of *in quantum* or *quatenus*, whether it is to be understood as *specificative* or *reduplicative*. He emphasizes the linguistic ambiguities that have burdened this distinction since the time of Scotus, ultimately rendering it useless. However, according to Martini one thing has to be established: the *quatenus* expresses only essential attributions, i.e. those coextensive with the being (= *passio adaequata inhaerens per se primo*, as formulated in the *Disputatio metaphysica secunda*, thesis 44). If indeed 'theology' were the science sought, then being would not be considered in its full extension but only according to a particular *modus* or aspect, that is in so far as it is immaterial.[79] In that case, such a science would be deprived of the universal character it ought to exhibit.[80] Now, as Aristotle teaches in the *Posterior Analytics*, the subject of a science is what is demonstrated in that science 'by means of its own principles' (*per suas causas*), namely its essential attributes (*affectiones*)[81] and consequently the subject of metaphysics will be 'the real being and its affections', these latter being both the four simple transcendentals (*ens, unum, verum, bonum*)[82] and the disjunctive ones such as act/potency, necessary/contingent, identical/different, all of them being coextensive with being.[83]

The formal/objective distinction

In my opinion, the key point in the first part of Martini's exposition (the chapters *De subiecto metaphysicae* and *De conceptu entis*)[84] is the distinction between the formal and objective concepts of being which emerged in the Thomist school and was taken up by Tommaso De Vio.[85] Martini in effect offers a tripartite breakdown of the way in which an idea inheres to the intellect: through the mode of formal concept, i.e. the *expression* of an idea by the mind; through the objective mode, when a common nature is presented to the intellect as *object*; or finally, through the *obiective consequenter* mode. In this latter mode the *entia rationis* are present to the mind and 'are appropriate to things not based on their nature, but in so far as they are represented by the intellect or due to the fact that the intellect negotiates around them'.[86] He goes on to explain that the object of this negotiation is indeed the terms of logic-dialectic, such as 'subject', 'predicate' and 'middle term', which are applied to things, so to speak, from outside, 'in such a way that the intellect can easily dispose, compose with each other, distinguish and debate about them'.[87] It is not hard to discern here the distinction of Zabarella origin between primary and secondary notions, albeit restyled in the language of late scholasticism with the express purpose of using it to lay the foundations for the distinction between metaphysics, *scientia realis* the object of which is the *ens reale*, and dialectic, the art of discussion operating with 'consequent' notions – that is not primary, not founded *in reipsa* or *extra mentem*.

As regards the formal and the objective concepts of being, the object of metaphysics, Martini declares himself in favour of a single concept, distinct (*praecisus*) from the other particular objective concepts (e.g. being in so far as it is immaterial, in so far as it is mobile etc.), although its foundation is not so much in reality as in an operation of distinction made by the intellect. Moreover, this common concept is neither univocal nor equivocal but analogous, according to an 'intrinsic' form of analogy, as explained by Gaetano and further clarified by Suarez. This means that the same formal reason of being 'is not equally and indifferently attributed to the inferior beings, but in such an order that it is first found in an absolute manner in the substance, and then in the accidents in relation to the substance'.[88] This is the point at which Martini declares that it is 'as clear as day' that a science such as metaphysics must be admitted. Its object is what has just been described, the real being, as distinct from the being of reason or the accidental being,[89] a solution moreover that leans heavily on the one adopted in the famous *Disputationes* of Suarez.[90]

At this point the discussion can move on to the affections of this subject (*de affectionibus entis*), which are what metaphysical science must demonstrate starting from the subject itself. They are the transcendentals and other coextensive attributes coextended to the concept or real being or inherent to its *ratio formalis*. Here two points need to be made. The first is that these affections do not have their foundation in an objective concept but derive from an act of separation or identification (*praecisio*) performed by the intellect. This is the same as what happens in the operation of conceiving God. Despite the fact that He is *simplicissimus*, our mind produces a formal concept of Him, separating intellect from will, and both these attributes from essence.[91] In this way, apparently, Martini wishes the *affectiones entis* be based onto the *ratio formalis* of the being itself, that is to underscore that they are coessential to it. The second point is that metaphysics described in this way is an authentic science, which is able to provide demonstrations starting from the causes of its subject and ending with its affections. Obviously – Martini admits – this can arouse perplexities, since it seems unacceptable that a subject such as being in so far as it is being or God, the prime being, have causes. The solution is found by drawing on a long passage from Suarez' first *Disputatio*.[92] Here, the *doctor eximius et pius* resolves the problem by explaining that, in this case, we are speaking not of *existendi* causes but only of *cognoscendi* causes and that the procedure is justified by the limitations of the human intellect, which in this case produces demonstrations a priori, proceeding from one concept and passing to another concept implied by the first but distinct from it.

The disciplinization of metaphysics: Consequences and aftermaths

The 'short and methodical' *Metaphysica* of Cornelius Martini then continues for several hundred pages, completing the programmatic exposition of the individual and disjunctive affections, but what has been highlighted is sufficient for the present purposes. It seems to me that, with his reflections on the real being as the object of metaphysics, Martini has replied to all the main criticisms made by his adversaries. In the first place, the need for metaphysics to derive from the specificity of its object, the real being. At the same time, this object is the most universal there can be for the *scientiae reales* and it is understood that, if dialectic gives the impression of covering a greater extension, this is because it is only an art, a *disciplina instrumentalis*, which by its nature does not need to insist on any ambit of the being since it operates through 'secondary' notions. What we have then is the definition of a *scientia realis universalis* for which the decisive identifying factor is the exclusion of non-being, the being of reason and the fictitious being. Nevertheless, metaphysics also respects the 'scientific' criteria established by the Ramists in their three laws, and I believe that the first part of Martini's treatise can be read assuming that he intended to show his adversaries that he was not violating the criteria they had established. In fact, the *lex iustitiae* is safe, given that all the propositions of metaphysics display essential predicates (what in Scherb were of the first *per se* mode): the individual and disjunctive transcendentals hold for *every* being as such. And it can be noted that their inherence to the being is given a priori, being founded not on an objective concept but on a 'separation' (*praecisio*) of the intellect itself (if anything, it is the concepts of the Ramist *inventio* that are superimposed). And again, the *lex iustitiae* had been called in since the *Scholae metaphysicae* to denounce the state of Aristotelian metaphysics, which, according to Ramus, not only is consigned to a disarticulated text, but above all displays a *metabasis es allo genos*, from logic to theology. So, with the retrieval of the concept of being as analogic Martini reasserts that the *ratio* of the real being, comprising the affections, is *generically* shared by the entire chain of beings. He is convinced that the notion of 'intrinsic analogy of attribution' (*analogia attributionis intrinseca*) inherited from Javelli and De Vio perfectly fills this role, guaranteeing the unity *of genus* of the beings. Finally we have also seen how the requisite that the initial concept is also the most general (*lex sapientiae*) is complied with, since metaphysics starts from the *ratio entis realis* in so far as it is being, leaving until later the determination of the *species entis*. It seems useful to add to all this the emphasis on the scientific character of metaphysics as a source of knowledge, which Martini defended by resorting to a famous passage from Suarez. Is this not perhaps a rejoinder to Ramus's charge that the metaphysics of Aristotle, metaphysics in general, produces only sterile tautologies? Moreover, as mentioned above, the 1606 edition offers a summary of Aristotle's *Metaphysics*, compiled, I assume, in order to show its organic structure and, in response to Ramus's charges, the absence in it of repetitions.

In conclusion, if Leinsle is correct in saying that if Ramus did make a contribution to the history of philosophy it consisted of challenging the Aristotelians to explain what they considered as the method of philosophy and of metaphysics, then certainly Scherb, Keckermann and, above all, Cornelius Martini fit perfectly into this historiographic scheme. Of the three, however, it was primarily Martini who took up the challenge and brought consistently to light the theoretical inadequacies of the Ramist conceptions, skilfully combining scholastic, neo-scholastic and neo-Peripatetic (Zabarella's) notions. In this way, the Helmstedt professor cleared of all obstacles the path to a metaphysics that filled the role of *regina scientiarum* and ensured it epistemological and functional independence from theology. To a degree the same can be said of Scherb and his school, although it continued to conceive this science primarily as a commentary on the works of Aristotle. Keckermann, on the other hand, appears to be less sure on this point. He sees metaphysics first and foremost as a science functional to theology, in view of the clarification of many concepts that it works with (substance, person etc.), a trait that continued to characterize his successors.[93] I can see also affinities between the school of Altdorf (I am thinking, obviously, of Soner) and Martini apropos the question – much debated in contemporary historiography – of the unity of the subject of metaphysics,[94] or rather of the efforts that the thinkers of the time made to hold together general ontology and special sciences of immaterial substances, especially because, in both cases, the principle of *analogia entis* underlying this unity was energetically argued and defended. On the other hand, among Keckermann's successors – despite ritual references to the principle of analogy – the distinction between a general and a special metaphysics was accompanied in practice by the prevalence of the former and the marginalization of the latter. As an example we could mention Makowski's metaphysics, which expounds the being in general in the first book, the categorial being in the second and the doctrine of the immaterial soul in the third, while the latter topic was removed in the third edition of 1658. Or Alsted, who refers mainly to Zabarella, Suarez and Jakob Martini and also to Keckermann while splitting metaphysics into general and special, where special signifies the doctrine of categories. In his definitive encyclopaedic arrangement[95] the alleged *regina scientiarum* becomes a mere discipline like any other. This, however, relates to the subsequent fate of the teaching of metaphysics in the Central European academic world, which is not being dealt with here.[96] What instead has been focused here is the phase in which the Aristotelians countered the Ramist theories with their own philosophical concepts, revealing – at least in the three figures examined – a certain similarity in sources of inspiration, arguments and solutions. I feel that the most appropriate final consideration is this: following the polemic outlined above, which the Aristotelians conceived as curbing the spread of Ramism, there were no obstacles to metaphysics returning with full entitlement into the curricula of the universities of Central Europe in a form that comprised both the theoretical elaboration discussed earlier and the new didactic requirements. However, the impression we get from the entire affair is that the Ramist attacks on metaphysics in some way forced the Protestant Aristotelians to fight a rearguard battle. These skirmishes hardly bear comparison with the profound process of re-elaboration of metaphysics as a fundamental philosophical science which took place in the Catholic countries before and after the Council of Trent, with the fundamental contribution of the representatives of the various religious orders, with the Jesuits in the forefront. It seems as if the area to the north of the Alps was lagging behind and found itself in the position of having to chase after what had already been achieved in the south by the generation of Pereira, Fonseca, Suarez and Zabarella.[97] This delay was, at heart, the price that continued to be paid for Luther's rejection of metaphysics (and Aristotle) and Melanchthon's suspicion of a universal science of being superior to or different from the art of dialectic. Finally, and this is a trait less evident in the Lutheran writers but blatant in Keckermann, by dint of treating metaphysics as a 'science', in effect as a 'discipline' of study, and insisting on its formal systematic arrangement rather than its effective contents, or on the question of its object or subject and its method, these Aristotelians effectively refuted Ramus but remained on exactly his same level. What I mean to say is that these elaborations, often sophisticated and supported by extensive important philosophical and logical background reading but radically conditioned by their practical (didactic) ends, salvaged little or nothing of metaphysics' dimension of wisdom: the quest for the ultimate causes of reality and hence the most characteristic part of philosophy.[98]

3

Ernst Soner's Commentary on the *Metaphysics* and the Scholastic Tradition

Problems with a Socinian metaphysics

Historiography of the religious and philosophical movement named after Fausto Sozzini has at length been dominated by the tendency to stress an inconsistency – if not a fundamental contradiction – in the religious doctrine of Socinianism. On the one hand, in the absence of ulterior specifications human nature is mortal, a conclusion moreover consequent on the Alexandrist and/or Averroist exegesis of Aristotle's noological and psychological doctrines that Sozzini himself assimilated. Therefore, the immortality promoted in the New Testament is due solely to God's initiative through Jesus, precisely because He finds himself before an 'object', namely the human soul, unable on its own to surpass the boundaries of the natural world. This is the direction of the radical gnoseological empiricism of the Socinians. However, it clashes with the other Socinian principle, whereby human 'reason' is called upon to evaluate and receive this promise and hence, in some sense, measures up to a transcendental summons that appears to exceed the empirical dimension. As a result, a tension emerged among the Socinians between the naturalistic anthropology and the gnoseology implied by their concept of the nature of Christian doctrine. This was easily transposed into an opposition between rationalism and fideism that was hard to dialecticize, and was in fact resolved only in Deism or in eighteenth-century philosophy. Logically, if reason is understood as judgement bound to empirical evidence or to demonstration *methodo sillogistico peracta* – that is, restricted to knowledge of an immanent, worldly character – one can hardly expect such reason to confirm the plausibility of the promise of salvation. Therefore this plausibility has to be *believed*. If instead one attributes to human reason the capacity to accept the promise of the Gospel as *reasonable*, it would have to follow that human nature has a status different from that of other creatures living in nature. This then calls into question the Alexandrist premise whereby the superior faculties of the human being depended on the material *mixtiones*, appearing to reduce humanity to a natural dimension. The existence of such unresolved intellectual tensions has caused Siegfried Wollgast to say that Socinianism is just an imperfect stage of modern 'rationalism'.[1] From this perspective, the pivot of these contradictions – in addition obviously to the theory of the human soul, or more specifically the intellect – is metaphysics. In the conception of metaphysics introduced by Sozzini it can no longer fill its traditional role as a philosophic preamble to the contents of religious faith. For Sozzini, in fact, there is no *natural* knowledge of God.

Apropos metaphysics, the attention of scholars has been attracted by a work of considerable size and content: the commentary on Aristotle's *Metaphysics* by Ernst Soner (1572–1612). The famous professor of medicine and philosophy was one of the most prominent figures at the University of Altdorf around the turn of the century. Born in Nuremberg, after studying philosophy in Altdorf and obtaining his doctorate in medicine in Basel (1601), Soner travelled for several years, accompanying two young nobles from Nuremberg as tutor, and visited several Italian cities including Padua. In particular, however, we should recall his stay in Leiden, where he came into contact with the Socinian 'missionaries' from Poland. In 1605 he succeeded Scherb (apparently at his request) in the chair of philosophy and medicine which he held until his death. During his years of teaching at Altdorf, Soner was an active and secret propagator of the Socinian creed, but this became known only after his death. In June 1616 the writings of Soner and his group were publicly set on fire in the historic centre of Altdorf.[2]

Consistently with the premises just mentioned, historians such as Ogonowski and Wollgast have stressed the aporetic outcomes of this impressive labour of thought and exegesis. According to this account, the aporias already emerge to a degree in Soner himself, but then come to fruition in his pupil (and critic) Johann Crell, who demonstrated the inadequacy of Aristotle's metaphysics-theology (in the version inspired by certain late-Renaissance interpreters) to express the Christian and in general biblical concept of God.[3] Still moving within the terms of the Aristotelian philosophy of his time, Soner failed in his attempt to philosophically ground an acceptable Christian theology. Even the Aristotelizing theology formulated by Crell, at once in continuity with and reaction against Soner, ended in checkmate: an anthropomorphized Christian God, understood as an entity diffused in space and immersed in time, limited even in his capacity to see future contingents (with the deriving inconveniences for his providence). These characteristics were as difficult to admit as those

Soner derived from Cesalpino (pantheism, necessitarianism). The moral of this history of failures is that it was, primarily, the rationalist (humanist, optimist, neo-Pelagian) approach to theology that failed, which obviously could only fling open the doors to fideist or sceptical outcomes. As regards this, Wollgast refers to Von Harnack's *Dogmengeschichte*, whereby Socinianism weakened the link between religion and rational knowledge of the world. It was in this context that a last-ditch attempt to salvage a rational path for religion was made by trying to replace metaphysics – understood essentially as Platonism and expression of a strict and closed rationalism – with ethics. Since metaphysics could not be improved, it could at least be made more elastic by diluting it within an ethical discourse, more adequate in its ductility to express the relation between the world and its creator.[4] Thus, in the space of about twenty years, the debate between Soner, considered the founder of the Socinianism of Altdorf and author of a *gran commento* on the *Metaphysics*, and Crell, the mouthpiece of the theologians of Raków with his *De Deo et attributis eius*, celebrated the triumph swiftly followed by the collapse of an Aristotelian metaphysics of Cesalpino stamp, without any valid alternatives emerging. This result then weighed heavily on the fate of natural Socinian theology, destined to be easily overrun by the Cartesian and Deist concepts of the late seventeenth century, no longer engaged in seeking unnatural compromises between the God of the philosophers and that of Jesus. It is worth quoting the final gloss of Ogonowski's extensive analysis of Crell's *De Deo et attributis eius*:

> If we compare the positions presented above: that formulated by Soner with that presented by Crell on behalf of the Raków theologians, we see that they start from different premises and are diametrically opposed, although they result in very similar issues. In fact, they make it patently clear that the philosophers' God and the biblical-evangelical God of the Bible and the Gospels are absolutely antinomic ideas, i.e. ideas that cannot be made reciprocally consistent on the basis of rational reasoning. Indeed, if one proceeds from philosophical premises, the conflict with theology is inevitable. Vice versa, if theology is taken as the starting point, one inevitably has to abandon various concepts that are plainly evident and derive from philosophy. ... This fact was thoroughly understood and expressed by Pierre Bayle in his *Dictionnaire historique et critique*. The ascertainment of this state of affairs – which obviously not everyone admitted – played an important role in the subsequent evolution of religious ideas.[5]

Among the various convictions supporting these reconstructions I attach a certain weight to the notion that philosophical discourse, in this case that transmitted through the exegesis of Aristotle, enjoyed little or no independence from the confessional context in the sixteenth and seventeenth centuries. According to this perspective, Aristotle's philosophy, more or less revised in the light of recent interpretations, was used for the principal or sole purpose of illustrating and founding specifically Socinian doctrines. In the case in question, Soner's commentary on the *Metaphysics* was merely a phase in a fairly subtle project that utilized Aristotle's philosophy to defend theories typical of religious heterodoxy in Lutheran Altdorf. Even those who have not discerned crudely manipulative and crypto-propagandist intentions in Soner's commentary have seen it as an operation of integrating inherently heterogeneous elements – Socinian theology on the one hand and heterodox Aristotelianism on the other – implicitly admitting that the latter was instrumental to the religious ideology.[6] In actual fact, this premise was already at the base of the famous reconstruction of 'crypto-Socinianism' made in the eighteenth century by Georg Gustav Zeltner:[7] a strictly confessional reading of the intellectual movements operating in the University of Altdorf, grappling with the 'snake' or with the 'venom' spread by the followers of the Sienese exile. Indeed Zeltner starts his history precisely with Ernst Soner, relating his meetings in Holland with Socinians and Arminians and subsequently his undercover propaganda in Altdorf for a radical reform of religious dogmatics. This was fundamentally successful, since it appealed to many students, and was interrupted only by Soner's sudden and premature death in 1612. And it was Zeltner, too, who specifically mentioned the commentary on the *Metaphysics* as an element of this apologetics. To this end, he emphasized certain circumstances, such as the statement by Johann Paul Felwinger, who published the commentary in 1657, that he had omitted certain 'theological' contents of the work.[8] To confirm the crypto-Socinian nature of the commentary, Zeltner then cites letters from Soner's pupil, the Socinian Martin Ruar, who busied himself with repressing the imminent posthumous publication so as not to 'stir up a hornets' nest', implying that the theological content of the opinions expressed might cause scandal.[9]

If truth be told, when read filtering out Zeltner's blatantly confessional slant, what his words convey is not so much an image of Soner as a crypto-Socinian philosopher but rather a general atmosphere of suspicion, not to say hysteria, in the Lutheran world of Altdorf. It is likely that efforts to publish Soner's commentaries on the *Metaphysics* were already being made shortly after his death and it would appear that the person in charge of the initiative was Georg Richter (1592–1651), who in the 1620s became professor of law at Altdorf. However, despite being at an advanced stage of preparation, the publication fell through. The point is, indeed, that Ruar, in a letter to Richter, staunchly denies that Soner's Aristotelian hermeneutics reveals any compromise with Socinianism. Simply because he treated 'certain things in a more peripatetic than Christian' manner, Soner has been accused of wishing to subvert the dogmas of the faith, whereas it is a well-known fact – Ruar reiterates – that the purpose of the commentaries was purely of a hermeneutic-philosophical nature, aimed at revealing what Aristotle had to say about first causes, the supreme Being etc. And the fact is – contrary to what Zeltner opines – that Ruar's final recommendation is not to halt publication but rather to include in the edition a 'modest preface' that would disperse all doubts about Soner's real intentions, which were far removed from fostering any subtle religious propaganda through his work on Aristotle.[10]

A similar conclusion can be drawn from the other letter extensively cited by Zeltner, in which Ruar describes his 'transit' (Zeltner's term) to Socinianism following private discussions with Soner. Zeltner sees this letter as *sic et simpliciter* proof of Soner's subtle action of 'Photinian' propaganda from the very start of his philosophy teaching. However, what Ruar actually states in the letter is a different story. In the first place he declares that, as an interpreter of Aristotle, Soner was unrivalled, even though the spread of his fame was undermined by the fact that his disciples did not dare to publish his commentary for fear of renewing the accusations against him (which, as we have seen, Ruar argued were due solely to misunderstanding combined with malice). In the second place, since Ruar was interested only in philosophy, Soner invited him to reflect on 'somewhat higher things', namely on how a 'strict and manly piety' is necessary for eternal salvation. From what follows we realize that Soner means by this a piety corroborated by philosophical reasons, and had indeed convinced Ruar that, despite the common contempt for reason among (Lutheran) theologians, there was a harmony (*convenientia*) between the light of reason and the truth sent to us from heaven. Finally, after discussing with Soner – not without inner torment – some *logos katêchêtikos* of Gregory of Nyssa (a fourth-century polemic against the Arians) Ruar ends up resolving his doubts and now sees the justice of his master's religious doctrines.

As I see it, this account makes no reference to a neo-Aristotelian metaphysics oriented towards Soner's dogmatic-confessional choices. These appear only at the end of the account, when the master reveals himself, arousing Ruar's anxiety and finally bringing about an authentic conversion. The crucial role here is played by the sudden appearance of daring Antitrinitarian theories, those polemicized by Gregory of Nyssa, and the equally (to Ruar's eyes) surprising defence made by Soner. Instead, in the early stages of their alliance there was nothing to disturb or arouse the suspicions of the pupil who, on the contrary, was 'soothed' by the postulate advanced by Soner regarding the harmony between reason and revealed truth.[11]

This picture appears to emerge even more clearly in a letter from Pieter De Bert (Petrus Bertius – 1565–1629, theologian and cartographer) to Georg Richter. Here we learn that the edition of Soner's commentaries on the *Metaphysics* had been entrusted some time prior to 1618 to Richter, who had been a pupil in Leiden of De Bert, a dyed-in-the-wool Arminian.[12] Soner's reputation as a crypto-Socinian must evidently have been public knowledge, and it could not be ruled out that this would cast a shadow even over the philosophical commentaries. After diligently perusing the work and approving Richter's intention of publishing it, De Bert declares himself to be:

> amazed by the inappropriate judgements of certain people, who hold that these texts of metaphysics contain the foundations of the error of the Photinians. In that case one might say the same about logic, rhetoric or poetry. Services of this kind can only distance talented students from honest studies of wisdom, with the result that they flee from the truth while seeking to avoid falsehood. On the contrary, it is clear that the metaphysics of Aristotle no more fosters the unfortunate errors of Sozzini than the follies of the Photinians help to clarify the complexities of metaphysics: they have nothing at all in common![13]

Not much is known about this aborted edition of Soner's commentary, but from what we can deduce it appears that Richter's version was not accompanied by any of the *quaestiones mixtae* (regarding demons, angels and the state of souls after death) which Felwinger instead claimed he had purged it of and which probably represented cause for scandal. Everything seems to point to the value of the commentary Richter was about to publish being exactly what De Bert said it was: namely, a well-argued work representative of the philosophical school of Philipp Scherb, which was moreover not suspected of heterodox sympathies. De Bert and Richter's own heterodox leanings do not seem to me sufficient to conclude that their interest in Soner's commentaries on the *Metaphysics* was conditioned by their confessional inclinations. As regards Ruar, as we saw, nothing suggests that he considered Soner a fomenter of heresy, but as a philosopher only.[14] In my opinion, all this puts into perspective the theory that Soner's commentary on the *Metaphysics* was the expression of a dissimulated confessional commitment, in which he sought and found in Aristotle substantial support for certain specific contents of Socinian theology.

This impressive work instead appears to address other demands, not directly connected either with the construction of a 'natural religion' (a formula currently adopted e.g. by Ogonowski), or with religious heterodoxy, and still less with its theological dogmatic. Which is not to say that theology is absent from the commentary – on the contrary! But it is certainly not a theology commensurable with that of spiritual authorities such as Sozzini, or even of a philosopher-theologian such as Crell, but rather of the incursions *in agro alieno* of an Aristotelian philosopher who wishes to remain such in this work. For this reason, to clarify the features and objectives of the work, I think it necessary to extend the panorama of late Aristotelianism well beyond the figure of Cesalpino or other Aristotelians frequently classified as heterodox. More specifically, I think that Scherb's grand tour in Italy and his mission, once installed in Altdorf, to renew the teaching of philosophy based on Italian inspirations, provide a more relevant context for understanding Soner's work as a commentator on Aristotle. The first question I ask myself is whether it is possible to see, behind Soner's efforts to go beyond the limitations and ambiguities of the contribution of Taurellus, the expression of a school, of an 'Altdorf metaphysics'.

Scherb's master, Tommaso Pellegrini

Various evidence confirms the special interest, and even admiration, displayed by Scherb during his sojourn in Padua in the lectures commenting on the *Metaphysics* held by Tommaso Pellegrini. This can also be deduced from a letter dated March 1603 sent by Michael Piccart, Scherb's other pupil, to the future professor of medicine at Altdorf Caspar Hoffmann (1572–1648). While Hoffman was in Italy Piccart wrote to him regarding the purchase of books, incidentally asking him about Pellegrini, and expressing his regret that he possessed no publications or other writings documenting his ideas. It is easy to imagine that it was Scherb himself who sang the praises of Pellegrini to Piccart. A certain jealousy on the part of Scherb for 'his' Pellegrini transpires from this account, given that he evidently did not allow his pupil and colleague Piccart access to the materials in his possession, presumably consisting of transcriptions of lectures or private conversations.[15] In his most famous philosophical work, the *Isagoge in lectionem Aristotelis*,[16] Piccart recalls approvingly a metaphor used by Pellegrini to illustrate the subject of metaphysics, which again we can assume was related to him by Scherb. Soner too, in his commentary on the *Metaphysics*, recalls how Scherb told him of Pellegrini's explanation of an acoustic phenomenon. Soner's choice of words in this instance is interesting: he speaks of Scherb as his Master (*Praeceptor*), and of Pellegrini as the Master of Scherb.[17]

It seems useful, therefore, to sketch out the profile of a figure of such importance in the establishment of the Altdorf philosophy. On this point, to date, the role of other thinkers has been placed in the proper light, chiefly that of Andrea Cesalpino with whom the Altdorfers had an unsettled score since the time of Taurellus, but the same cannot be said of Pellegrini. The reputation of this professor of metaphysics was certainly undermined by the lack of published works (which Piccart laments and is surprised by) and also possibly by a certain negligence on the part of historians in giving due importance to a phenomenon which has only recently attracted attention. That is, the tradition of the teaching of metaphysics at the University of Padua, from which the students in attendance, both Italians and foreigners, benefited. This teaching was introduced around the mid-fifteenth century to integrate that of natural philosophy in the arts curriculum. It was taught mostly by masters belonging to the Dominican order, within which the so-called Conventuals in particular distinguished themselves in the sixteenth century for their openness towards humanistic currents and a sincere dialogue with secular university Aristotelianism. In practice: a teaching of metaphysics which combined the traditional scholastic *auctoritates* with the results of the reborn study of classical antiquity in terms of philosophical hermeneutics. In this sense, we could speak of a Paduan school of Thomism, or of a Renaissance Thomism,[18] which comprised figures such as Gianfrancesco Beato,[19] Girolamo Vielmi and, of course, Tommaso Pellegrini himself, and developed in close connection with the humanist philology and the lay Aristotelianism of the University of Padua. The sense of this is also to set in perspective certain prevailing trends in historiography (not only Italian): the tendency to overestimate, on the one hand, the conflict between humanist culture and scholastic tradition, and on the other, the critical – in the sense of anti-metaphysical, anti-religious and also anticlerical – scope of Paduan Aristotelianism, turning thinkers such as Cesare Cremonini into *ante litteram* libertines. This teaching of metaphysics, supported by the political authorities and welcomed by the students, was remotely inspired by St Thomas but in actual fact was most attentive to the Greek commentators and the developments of Iberian scholastics. This casts new light on the alleged exclusively naturalistic, anti-metaphysical and anti-scholastic character of philosophy teaching in Padua in the sixteenth century. It also opens up interesting research prospects, considering the importance of this university in European intellectual life at the turn of the century.

This is the tradition surrounding the teaching – albeit with its own peculiar characteristics – of the Dominican Tommaso Pellegrini (or Pellegrino), professor of metaphysics 'according Aquinas' way' (*in via S. Thomae*) in Padua from 1560 to 1583. The esteem in which he was held by colleagues and students has been known for some time,[20] even though it has not been accompanied by an adequate analysis of his contribution as a philosopher and interpreter of Aristotle's *Metaphysics*. As mentioned, the absence of published works has played a decisive role in this oversight and only recently have the manuscripts containing the *reportationes* of his courses in Padua begun to be studied.[21] According to Matthew Gaetano, who was the first to address this material, what is immediately striking about Pellegrini's Aristotelian commentaries is their non-Thomist – and in some cases even anti-Thomist – character. This is illustrated by the fact that Pellegrini bases himself chiefly on the doctrines of Averroes and Alexander of Aphrodisias, the former being the epitomic commentator, whose glosses had accompanied the lessons on Aristotle in Padua for centuries, while the latter was the true great discovery of the humanist era in relation to commentary on the *Metaphysics*. Here two aspects should be recalled. First, Alexander's commentary on the *Metaphysics* began circulating and became an important benchmark from 1527 on, when Juan Ginés de Sepúlveda published his Latin version (which had several later editions). The Spanish humanist was certain of the authenticity of the entire commentary, whereas from Book VI onwards the author is now identified with the Byzantine and Neoplatonizing Michael of Ephesus (twelfth century). Second, fragments of Alexander's authentic commentary were cited by Averroes in his own commentary on the *Metaphysics*, but as far as I know nobody in the Renaissance paid any attention to them, let alone compared them to the corresponding passages of the pseudo-Alexander.

It was, in particular, in defining the subject of metaphysics that, again according to Gaetano, Pellegrini distanced himself from St Thomas. Aquinas excluded God and the other separate substances from the object of metaphysics, since they were the exclusive domain of theology, making them only a 'principle' of the real subject which was 'being in so far as it is being'. Pellegrini instead considers that God comes fully within the subject considered by metaphysics, and to reinforce this idea does not baulk even at violating a methodological dogma (derived from the *Posterior Analytics*) common to the entire Peripatetic tradition comprising Averroes and Alexander, whereby no science can demonstrate the existence of its subject. Indeed, for Pellegrini, metaphysics is engaged precisely in demonstrating its own object, namely the existence of God.

In general, I don't believe it is legitimate to label Pellegrini's positions as non-Thomist or anti-Thomist, but there is a particular point on which I don't agree with Gaetano: namely, the idea that he excluded theology, naturally philosophical theology, from the ambit of metaphysics.[22] Gaetano sees this as being revealed by the fact that Pellegrini objected to Aquinas' ambiguous use of the argument of the eternity of the world to demonstrate the existence of an unmoved substance. Indeed, on the one hand St Thomas, as is obvious for a Christian philosopher, does call this principle into question, but then, not finding anything better – continues Pellegrini – he ends up using it to rationally demonstrate the existence of a divine substance.[23] Well, assuming that Pellegrini's criticism of Aquinas was correct, it seems risky to me to draw from this the general conclusion that philosophical theology is, for Pellegrini, extraneous to first philosophy. In fact, as shown, he considers God and the separate substances to be fully part of first philosophy, part of its object. In short, while we can accept the image of a Pellegrini relatively open-minded in filtering the arguments furnished by all the mediaeval and ancient authorities through philosophical rationality, his strategic objective in constructing a first philosophy through the commentary on Aristotle does not diverge from that of all scholastic thought in general and from St Thomas's standpoint in particular. On the one hand, he adapted to the general standard of the Paduan professors, whose institutional task was to explain the 'mind' of the Philosopher in the best possible way, in line with criteria of philological correctness and rational coherence. On the other hand, however, it seems to me beyond dispute that Pellegrini conceived the metaphysics of the Peripatetic tradition as the science that had the ultimate task of providing a rational basis for theological speculation. Naturally this should not be understood in the sense that philosophy interferes with the specific contents of revealed theology; here we are well this side of apologetic or controversialist scholasticism, especially the hyper-confessional version that was shortly to take over. It should instead be understood in the sense that philosophy of Aristotelian origin guarantees the minimal contents (existence and 'personality' of God, contingency of the world) without which the theological discourse could not even be broached. To this degree, Pellegrini still moves in a Thomist dimension, since he is convinced that the optimum understanding of Aristotle and his metaphysics offers this opening. To clarify this point, and to better understand the meaning of the inclusion of speculation on the separate substances in first philosophy, I think that we have to take some of Pellegrini's texts into consideration. I can start by saying that, for the purpose he had set himself, the acceptance of certain ontological theories present in the authentic part of the commentary of Alexander of Aphrodisias appears of crucial importance.

As Gaetano observes, the subject of Pellegrini's courses was chiefly Books I, VII and XII of the *Metaphysics*.[24] It is easy to show that the choice of these books already implicates a certain systematic idea of the structure and hence of the subject and scope of the Aristotelian sylloge. Based on this idea, the sensible substances–immaterial substances sequence was fundamental for Aristotle. The treatment of the former in fact begins in Book VII (those that precede being general introductions, like Books I and II, or questions of method or 'logics', like Books III and IV) and ends in Book X.[25] Since Pellegrini considered Book XI to be spurious, or in any case useless, this leaves Book XII, which represents the apex of the work, Books XIII and XIV being considered merely a doxographic and dialectical appendix. The manuscript I consulted instead contains the commentary on Books I, II and IV,[26] although I do not think these variations have a particular significance. It is likely, indeed, that in the several three-year courses held at the University of Padua, Pellegrini remained faithful to the guidelines of his interpretation, despite varying the texts of Aristotle on which it was based.

The introduction to this course naturally addresses the subject of the science in question.[27] Following tradition, the argument begins by distinguishing between a principal subject and an adequate one, and then, in the case of the former, between a subject that is foremost in 'attribution' and one foremost in 'perfection'.[28] Essentially, the commentator here is grappling with the classic problem of the apparent duplicity of the subject of metaphysics, as emerging from Aristotle's words at the beginning of Book IV: being in so far as it is being or its ultimate causes? In this passage Pellegrini simply delineates the solution, namely by alluding to two possible subjects but specifying that the principal one – the real one, more peculiar to the science in question, is the first that is identified by the relation of 'attribution'. This appears to be a first allusion to the 'substance' and, indirectly, to the first substance, principle or cause of being in so far as it is being, since it is a subject to which the other categories or determinations inhere or are 'attributed'. The relation of attribution is clarified as a relation of dependency in the being and predication of all beings (the being in so far as it is being) on the substance, respectively expressed by the formulas 'from what' (*ex quo*) and 'because of what' (*propter quod*).[29] In the meantime it is clear that the principal (and not adequate) subject of this science is substances, and prospectively among them the 'abstract unmoved substances' as, moreover, – Pellegrini immediately adds – is clear from Book XII.[30]

At this point Pellegrini opens up a polemic with those who understand the subject in question as a being resulting from an 'undifferentiated' (*per indifferentiam*) abstraction, that is transcendental, common to movable and unmoved substances, with the result that the science in question should deal only with the extremely general properties of the being, such as one, act, potency etc.[31] But this throws open the doors to univocism, which is certainly not the way in which the expression 'being in so far as it is being' is to be understood. The term 'being', Pellegrini explains, is neither equivocal, that is polysemantic, nor univocal, that is signifying a genus, but again is such as to display a relation 'from one and towards one' – *ab uno et ad unum*. This means that it is not the case that it applies *first* to the genus and only *then* to the species (like 'animal' as referred primarily to the genus and secondarily to men, lions etc.), since on the contrary it applies immediately to the species themselves.[32] And so, the unity of the science of being in so far as it is being is given precisely by this relation, which Pellegrini illustrates with the classic example of the attribute of 'health', as attributable in the first place to the animal and by derivation to the other categories.[33]

I feel that these few essential indications offered at the beginning of the course are sufficient to identify the source of Pellegrini's conception of the method and tasks of first philosophy. Without undervaluing the contributions of Averroes or Aquinas, what we have here is a clear retrieval of the interpretation of Alexander of Aphrodisias. Let us now clarify these inspirations and their reciprocal relations.

First, Pellegrini does not appear to move beyond the horizon delineated in Aquinas' commentary on the *Metaphysics*.[34] It is true that Aquinas speaks of *subiectum* only for being in so far as it is being, using instead the expression *finis considerationis* for the cause of the being, whereas Pellegrini uses *subiectum* for both. Beyond this, the intentions of the two Dominicans appear to be to guarantee the unity of metaphysics as a science: this holds together the two aspects, starting from the consideration of the being in general but with its fundamental meaning residing in the discourse on substance (and hence unmoved substance). What strikes me as new in Pellegrini as compared to St Thomas is a different way of explaining this unity. For Aquinas, the consideration of the 'common being and what follows from it' (*ens commune et ea quae consequuntur ipsum*) on one side, and that of God and the immaterial substances on the other, have in common that they result from the 'abstraction' from matter, albeit respectively in different ways. The *ens commune* abstracts 'by reason' (*secundum rationem*) from sensible matter, while God and immaterial substances abstract from it 'in entity' (*secundum esse*), a theory that St Thomas found in Boethius. I think it plausible that Pellegrini had the suspicion that abstraction, of whatever kind, could lead only to mere concepts, hence a theory such as that of Aquinas did not protect metaphysics from the risk of ending up in a sort of general ontology, *within* which philosophical theology could eventually find its place. I suggest that this was why he preferred to seek a justification for the unity of theology and ontology elsewhere, finding it in the theory of the *ab uno et ad unum* relation, which appeared to be better grounded in the Aristotelian texts than the theory of abstraction and, above all, had on its side the support of the most authoritative Greek commentator. We should recall that, for Alexander of Aphrodisias,

> metaphysics is a science the subject of which is being in so far as it is being, that is the totality of the real, which it traces to substance, understood as form, and then to unmoved substance, understood as pure form, without matter, through a relationship which is not only of 'relation to one' (*pros hen*), but also of 'dependence on one' (*aph'henos*). It is therefore a discipline which is at once ontology, that is a science of being, and also, and more importantly, rational theology.[35]

The doctrine of *ad unum et ab uno* naturally emerges from the commentary on the early parts of Book IV of the *Metaphysics* where Aristotle, again in relation to the question of the unity of first philosophy, states that this is not based on a unique object in line with the typical univocal unity of genus (for instance 'animal' as compared to human, lion or insect), but on the unity resulting by the common reference of the 'species' of the being to the substance, the famous reference *pros hen*.[36] St Thomas includes these different types of predication under the category of 'analogy' and 'proportion',[37] using terminology which arguably threw up more questions than it answered. Pellegrini does not use it, resorting to Alexander's straightforward formula. However, the purpose is always the same as that of Aquinas: grounding the unity of metaphysics as, above all, *scientia divina*.

Regarding the formula *ab uno et ad unum*, in line with his approach of explaining Aristotle through Aristotle, Alexander of Aphrodisias illustrates the opening phrases of *Metaphysics*, IV, 2 ('The term being is used in many senses, but with reference to one thing and to one nature' – *pros hen kai mian tina physin*) by resorting to the expressions in the *Nicomachean Ethics*, I, 6 (1096 b 26–8): *aph'henos einai ê pros hen* – 'things that are said to depend on something or in relation to something'.[38] And to explain what the things that are in relation to one or depend on one have in common, Alexander says: 'there is a communality by virtue of the fact that these are things that we say because there is a certain nature of that thing that is in some way visible in all of them; it is because they derive from (*apo*) that thing or have a *logos* in reference to (*pros*) it that they also share its name'.³⁹ The second part of the formula (*pros*) thus appears to allude to a relation or several relations of a conceptual-definitional type, whereas the first part (*apo*) instead refers to a relation of causal derivation or dependence. In short, for Alexander the being of the substance is something in common which is in some way 'visible' in the being of the categories, which is why the being of the substance is what the being of the other categories *derives from*; in this way one can say that the categories can be reduced to substance.⁴⁰

That these considerations are preliminary to the grounding of a discourse on being destined to be theological is fairly clear⁴¹ from passages such as this: 'The genus of philosophy dealing with principles and first causes and substance is at once first and universal; and in fact in what is said by derivation from one and in relation to one (*en tois aph'henos te kai pros hen legomenois*) the first is also universal, since it is itself the cause of being of the other things.'⁴² 'There is then a single science of all being, since being is of the same nature, and it will be above all concerned with the first and principal being, by means of which (*dio*) other beings exist',⁴³ where the *ab uno et ad unum* relation appears to refer to a relation of ontological causality. Or, again, 'first philosophy is a theory about the first substances which also theorizes about all the others the being of which depends (*êrtêtai*) on the first'.⁴⁴ So, although it does not present actual theological contents, Alexander's exegesis supplies a solid background for a theological interpretation of metaphysics, especially if considered in combination with the part of the commentary by the pseudo-Alexander where this interpretation is explicit. A famous passage testifying to this general orientation is the beginning of the commentary to Book XII: 'This book of the *Metaphysics*, usually called book *lambda* by the Peripatetics, speaks of the first and unmoved principle, for which all this matter has been brought to light'.⁴⁵

In conclusion, in Alexander's commentary the quest for the principle that gives unity to the meanings of being, and hence to first philosophy-metaphysics-wisdom, shifts easily towards the discourse on substance, from where it is a short step to the substance that is first in the order of substances (corruptible and incorruptible) which is the cause of being of all the others. Using terminology anachronistic for the second century, one might say that the ontological moment of metaphysics is yoked with the theological; the former cannot be without the latter, since the latter is the apex of the former. It is easy to imagine how this theological extension can be articulated: once the being of categories is traced to the first one, i.e. to substance, and reiterating Aristotle on the principles of substance being the principles of all being, it is therefore a question of finding the *principles of substance*. Then, in *Metaphysics* Book XII we will see how the unmoved mover effectively encompasses them in himself: in Alexander and the pseudo-Alexander, because the first unmoved substance, God, is the supreme final cause (the object of 'love' on the part of the first heaven, which then communicates its motion to the rest of the cosmos);[46] in Averroes and Aquinas[47] because instead the supreme cause is both final and efficient, a variation to which Pellegrini himself explicitly subscribes.[48] In a word, Alexander of Aphrodisias had laid the foundations for interpreting Aristotle in a way that conformed with, or at least did not contradict, the theology characteristic of monotheist religions, with God granting His being to the world, and the world seeing its own 'purpose' in God. This theoretical construction met with the favour of the leading philosophers of Arab and Christian scholasticism.

Soner's commentary on the *Metaphysics*

As I see it, Soner's commentary is in line with this hermeneutic tradition whose leading exponents were Alexander, St Thomas Aquinas and Averroes, and which was taken up again in the sixteenth century by Scherb's master Tommaso Pellegrini, among others. This conception seeks to find the explanation or the 'cause' of being in the characterization of the supreme Being, and is thus a conception far removed from the tendency to explain the supreme Being based on the general, transcendental categories of being. The latter orientation was perhaps already prevalent at the end of the sixteenth century, headed by the Jesuits Pedro Fonseca and Francisco Suarez, and was also significant for the nascent 'ontology' of the *Schulphilosophie*. For Soner, instead – as for the majority of the writers mentioned who preceded him and inspired him – it was a question of building a 'first' philosophy that culminated in the consideration of the first divine substance and then, more specifically, in the relation of the same with its/His 'attributes'. This is why, in the course of the commentary, particular emphasis is given to issues such as the relation Aristotle established between general science and particular sciences, between first and second substances, between substance and accident, between substance and categories, between passions and affections of the being etc. It is as if Soner is probing the potential of philosophical discourse to explain, first and foremost, the concept of the free creation of the world by a personal God. Naturally, all this is prior to and irrespective of any discourse of revealed theology, and through comparison with the entire tradition of Aristotelian commentary. This tradition begins with his 'exegete' Alexander, continuing with the other ancient interpreters (Simplicius, Ammonius), the mediaevals (Albertus Magnus, Thomas Aquinas, Duns Scotus, Jean de Jandun, Averroes) and ending with the 'moderns' (Agostino Nifo, Andrea Cesalpino, Federico Pendasio, Antonio Scaini, Tommaso Pellegrini, the Iberians and the German philosopher Henning Arnisaeus). The method employed is largely that of the scholastic *quaestiones*, by Soner inserted in an *ad capita* commentary on Aristotle's text, which also takes into consideration textual and translation aspects. The terminology used is generally of scholastic origin, seeking not to overdo technical language and always explaining with examples and citations from the original texts. The form adopted for the commentary is also interesting, going against the tide in a time of systematic summaries and synoptic tables. Soner shows that, despite risking a degree of repetition and confusion, this formula can still be doctrinally and educationally effective. The immediate and long-term success of the work proved that it was the right choice. In his preface to Soner's commentary, Felwinger indeed declares that he had decided to publish the book (despite what he saw as its doctrinal danger) precisely because everyone already had their hands on it. In any case, I believe that if Soner chose to follow Aristotle's text from the beginning to the end, it was because he was convinced that it was already arranged to a precise plan, and it was simply a matter of consistently and patiently bringing to light all the consequences and articulations. While fully aware of the wealth of subjects in the work and the difficulty of providing an adequate and exhaustive illustration of them, my intention is to reveal what I see as the structure of this commentary, bearing in mind primarily the context sketched out above, namely that of the late mediaeval and Renaissance commentaries on Aristotle's *Metaphysics*.

The *Prolegomena*

The introductory pages, the *Prolegomena*,[49] provide decisive programmatic clues from which one can reasonably expect general indications about what Soner sees as the scope and structure of Aristotle's treatise. Naturally, it is the canonical discussion about the 'proper and adequate' subject of metaphysics that provides the most important information. Thus we are immediately informed that this subject is 'being in so far as it is being', but given that this is equivalent to 'substance' the proper and adequate subject is ultimately substance, and essentially the first of the series. The clarification that follows is equally important:

we must understand the relation between the first substance and the others as the type of dependence that exists between the substance in general and its attributes, a dependence 'in existence'.[50]

One might say that the complete programme of metaphysics, as Soner sees it, is all here, consisting in 'ascending' to the first substance as that which dispenses being to the things of the world, but this point definitely needs to be further clarified. In addressing the meaning of the 'reduplication' in the formula 'being in so far as it is being', another classic point in such discussions,[51] Soner informs us that the dependence of the accidents on the substance and, above all, of the other substances on the first, is best expressed through the category of the *analogia ab uno*. This is the relation whereby a number of things are held together not because they share a common nature but because the second analogates are obtained from a first analogate by addition, that is by adding various predications. However, 'being in so far as it is being' signifies precisely this first analogate from which the other things descend.[52] In short – not from the start but as its ultimate aim – metaphysics deals with a single substance. Let this be said against those (for instance Timpler, among the *novissimi*) who interpret being in so far as it is being in a purely ontological manner, identifying it univocally with the 'intelligible', or who, more traditionally, consider the ten categories as the 'species' of the being, conceiving it therefore as a univocal genus superior to them.[53] Soner instead insists that the categories are not genera of this kind but 'figures of the predication' that do not inhere to all beings or to the being in general, but *to a specific being*. In conclusion: 'The being in so far as it is being does not signify a common nature of being, because it is not univocal, but the first being on which all the others depend and are called beings as a result of this participation, some in a closer and some in a more remote manner'.[54] Therefore 'being' or 'is' as predicated of things refers to the descent from or dependence on the first being, but does not correspond to any 'real objective common nature' in things.[55] Hence this science is by its essence a 'doctrine of God', since the 'first analogate of the being is God and this science is about Him in the first place', as much or as little as the human intellect manages to grasp solely 'by its own light'.[56]

What appears to me central in the remainder of this part is the negation of the idea of an *ens commune* understood as a real concept existing beyond the individual beings and, in particular, beyond the existence of the first being. This is what is meant by the words of Aristotle which Soner cites on innumerable occasions, whereby ' "human being" and "being a human being" are the same thing'. Consequently, the 'entity' of beings other than the first consists of their relation with the first being, a relation which Soner sees as one of both participation and dependency.⁵⁷ And the analogy between the first being and the others is a concept which does not precede them all, as it would pursuant to the univocal and common concept, but which emerges after this dependency has been established. It is therefore something 'accidental', in other words, added to the first being.

A similar rule is employed in the question of the division of metaphysics into parts and the order of these, as against those who, for various reasons, divide it into a universal part and a special part (presumably the Iberian commentators). They are all wrong, as they start from the assumption that there is 'some common essence of the being in so far as it is being, beyond the first analogate of the being'.⁵⁸ The true division – as, moreover, suggested by Pellegrini who is explicitly cited – is between the general and introductive consideration of the principles and the study of the affections proper to the subject, namely of the being in so far as it is being or the first substance.⁵⁹ The principles are understood as the very existence of the first substance and the first axioms (principle of non-contradiction; principle of the excluded middle). As for the affections of the being in so far as it is being, they can be attributed to the first substance 'by abstraction', eliminating those attributes belonging only to sensible substances. Moreover, the two parts correspond to the plan of Aristotle's *Metaphysics*: preliminary questions and method in the first five books, and then the part addressing the subject scientifically (*epistêmonikôs*) in the last eight or nine (depending on whether or not Book XI is considered authentic), where the inquiry into the common affection of the being (both single, such as *one*, *true*, *good*), and joint (*coniunctae*, such as *cause/effect*, *identical/different*, *principle/what derives from the principle*, *one/many*, *anterior/posterior*, *act/potency* etc.) opens the path to knowledge of the first being.⁶⁰

Thus Soner provides a clear and personal answer to the classic question of whether and in what sense metaphysics is a unitary science. In the course of this, polemicizing with univocist and realist stances and to affirm his own idea of the *analogia entis*, he unabashedly uses expressions of a nominalist flavour.⁶¹ At any rate, this unity – he claims – does not derive from a common nature, but comes instead from the fact of dealing with 'the principles and affections of the being', namely the first being in its relation of analogy with the deriving beings. Finally, given these premises, not only is the splitting of first philosophy avoided, but the division of the work of Aristotle is also defended. As a matter of fact, Soner speaks of Aristotle's *Metaphysics* as the work *in the course of which* metaphysics as a science takes shape. In this sense, Aristotle's book delineates a philosophical path that culminates in the doctrine of Book XII, or rather, the very end of it

(Aristotle's allegory of the general and the army at Ch. X, 1075a 13–15): actually it is only from this point that metaphysics itself as a science begins.[62]

The being and its affections

These *Prolegomena* constitute a sort of summary of the work, comprising the entire programme developed in the course of the commentary. Certain points deserve to be explored further, also to establish similarities and differences with the tradition Soner was inspired by. I see as chief among such points the relation of dependence *ab uno et ad unum*, which is further expounded in the commentary on the first part of Book IV. What is examined here is the central issue of the meaning – neither purely equivocal nor purely univocal – of the term 'being', which instead is used, in the famous words of Aristotle, 'with reference to one thing and to one nature'. So what is the type of conceptual unity identified by the notion of 'being'? Soner replies to the question of whether we can, alternatively, speak of 'analogy' by saying that, in effect, Aristotle introduced two other types of 'genus' in addition to univocity and equivocity. The first is that *ab uno seu ad unum*,[63] exemplified by the relation of dependency of the accidents on the substance; the second is explicitly said to be 'analogous' and the examples of it are the relation between 'fishbone' or 'backbone' as compared to 'bone', or 'ability to fly' and 'ability to swim' compared to 'local motion', or even different types of opposites as compared to the primary opposition one/many.[64] The difference between the two types of genericity is that, in the first case the relation between the terms is not so much of 'proportion' as of inherence, whereas in the second case there is a real proportion, albeit in the Aristotelian sense of 'analogy', namely a similarity between terms belonging to different contexts. Consequently, in the first case the terms are the subject of the same science, while, in the second, analogy places subjects studied by different sciences in relation to each other. So, what are the consequences of these subtle distinctions for the doctrine of being? And, more precisely, which of the two relations describes the being: the first, the analogy of attribution, or the second, the analogy of proportion (as they are called in the schools)?

Soner's reply is that both hold.[65] The first because it sets up a relation of dependency of all heaven and all nature on the first being, from which all things 'have being and live'. And also the second, the analogy of proportion, substantially because the different substances, despite being distinct in genus (incorruptible and corruptible) and consequently being described by different sciences (metaphysics,

physics and astrology), share analogous principles. According to Soner, the fracture between metaphysics as a universal science and as a particular science is avoided, and the two perspectives are conciliated, if the subject of metaphysical consideration is the first being *in so far as it is first analogue*, since it stands for all the other analogates.[66] Having got so far, now the range of investigation of metaphysics has to be restricted to 'the common traits that a certain genus has received from the first being, leaving aside the other [aspects] proper to [only] that genus, for example the physical'. And as these affections 'do not belong to a common nature but belong immediately to the first [being] and through it to the other substances; [hence] all difficulties are resolved if [metaphysics] deals with the first and what is proper to the first'.[67] Again, the universality of metaphysics is not obtained by postulating a universal, common and univocal notion of being, nor does metaphysics renounce universality if it deals only with the first substance, since its affections are common to all substances, irrespective of the genus of belonging. As I see it, all this is a way of showing that metaphysics does not need to waive its classic structure – or what Soner saw as classic, starting from Pellegrini and, behind him, Aquinas and Alexander of Aphrodisias, and also Cesalpino – and evolve towards a form of general ontology to maintain its claim on being in so far as it is being, that is the totality of being. What one might call a theocentric metaphysics perfectly fulfils its role as an 'architectonic' science.[68]

Soner arrives at the same conclusion by denying that there is a real, objective concept of being common to all beings and distinct (*praecisus*) from the concept of the particular beings (that such a 'formal' concept exists in our minds is beyond discussion). He then calls on the authority of Averroes, De Vio and Fonseca to support his theory. In particular he revalues Fonseca's 'third concept' (*conceptum tertium*), introduced for the precise purpose of arguing that the concept of first being is sufficient to explain the being in all its fullness and extension. Although Fonseca was opposed in this by the 'Scotists', Suarez and Arnisaeus,[69] Soner is convinced that it should be reappraised. This concept is:

> in part distinct and in part confused [with the concept of the other beings], as when we conceive the first analogue distinctly while at the same time conceiving the other [analogates] in a confused manner … In this analogous respect, the distinct concept of the first analogue includes the concept of the analogates eminently and virtually: in the same way the concept of father, qua father, includes the concept of son, even if not distinct.[70]

In a word, Soner's strategy is consistently opposed to the idea of a univocally common concept or 'nature' that is either anterior or superior both to the first analogate (or analogue) and to the second analogates. Instead, as Aristotle puts it, where there is a succession *per prius et posterius* there is no need for a 'formally' common nature. 'For me this foundation will continue to stand firm and unmoved until he [Arnisaeus] succeeds in shaking it with stronger reasons or succeeds in reinforcing his own.'[71]

This being established, the other point that I feel is important in this part of the commentary concerns precisely the manner of conceiving the first analogate in relation to its affections.[72] This term, in the first place, includes the classic transcendental formalities (one, true, good), but then much else besides. As we have seen, this subject had already been broached in the *prolegomena* regarding the parts of metaphysics so as to understand (1) the principles and (2) the affections of the first being. Apparently the commentary on Book IV seemed the right place to take it up again, albeit in the light of the ontological clarifications that had emerged so far. I think it legitimate to jump straight to the conclusion, which is reached bearing in mind the parallel considerations of Suarez and Fonseca, which can be summed up by saying that these affections are not 'in reality' (*realiter*) anything distinct from the being, that is, nothing positive,[73] while existing only 'formally' (*formaliter*), namely: 'they do not add anything to the subject except in some respect'.[74]

In view of the way the discourse about being in so far as it is being – which we now know to be synonymous with 'first being', or directly 'God' – is conceived, it comes as no surprise that Soner immediately and explicitly draws theological conclusions from these premises:

> *This is why theologians and philosophers say: everything that is in God is the same essence as God,* since *realiter* nothing is distinct from being in so far as it is being. [If it were] distinct, it would in fact be non-being. But, as demonstrated in the *prolegomena*, being in so far as it is being and the first being are the same thing, and the first being is God.[75]

Therefore, the *affectiones*, such as one, true, good,[76] are not formalities distinct from the first being, but only relations of reason, which appear when considering what is *outside* God. These relations – and this is the crux of the matter – are founded in a *contingent* and not *necessary* way on the indivisible nature of the first being. Thus, before the creation of the other beings, God was not truly 'one' formally, but only really, since strictly speaking formal unity can be attributed to Him only consequent on the existence of a multitude. Soner explains this through one of his favourite metaphors, possibly taken from Cesalpino, that of the geometrical centre, the lines radiating from which are present *realiter*, that is before being sketched out, whereas they exist *formaliter* only after they have actually been traced.[77] And here Soner parts company with Aristotle, accusing him of not being consistent with his own ontological principles: in practice, with the concept of the relation between God and His attributes, presented earlier. Aristotle had indeed deduced from the fact that God is good and hence the object of desire that *there must be* something that desired Him. Moreover, it is likely that, beyond Aristotle, the real target of Soner's criticism was certain of Cesalpino's Aristotelian exegeses which appeared to involve some form of necessitarianism in the *ad extra* action of God.[78] The mistake lies in conceiving the goodness of God, and hence His being an object of desire to the world – the *esse appetibile* – as being present in Him as a formally distinct determination, and hence consequent on Him as of its *foundation* and of necessity. If Aristotle had been consistent with his own principles, Soner continues, he would have seen that it is only *realiter* that the goodness (the oneness, the truth) of the first being is posited as identical to Him, which seems to rule out at the root any necessary derivation of distinct formalities from Him. The first being effectively only becomes the object of desire when he is *formaliter* desirable, namely when what desires Him emerges to being, is 'created'.[79]

However, Soner then extends these considerations to all the attributes of God: wisdom, justice, mercy, power, will etc. *In* Him these are not really distinct but 'all one' and only begin to be distinguished when they are *beyond* Him. Similarly, the centre of the universe, in so far as it is in itself indivisible and identical only to itself, does not face either east or west. But when something 'is propagated eastwards' from that centre, although the centre 'remains immovable and undivided [it] establishes the eastern line'.[80] The criticism of Aristotle comes to a crux when Soner asserts that, in the simplicity that *precedes* the formalities deriving to Him from the various *affectiones*, God is free: 'and just as there is no necessity in the centre to propagate in one direction or another, in the same way [there is no necessity] that God should bring to the outside one faculty rather than another, unless He has previously constrained Himself to one or the other by His own will'.[81]

Whether or not these arguments convince the reader, they illustrate Soner's concern not to justify a necessitarian interpretation of the relation between God and His attributes. I feel that they ought to be completed by others where ontology and theology overlap on almost every page. Here I am thinking in particular of the passages in the commentary in which Soner asks himself whether the 'accidents' of the substance take their being *formaliter* from the substance or from themselves.[82] He replies by means of a distinction: in one sense they are formally distinct and in another one their being depends 'by attribution and denominatively' from the substance.[83] However, he then goes on to explain the ontological relation between the immaterial first substance (namely, being in so far as it is being, that is God) and the second sensible substances. Neither the latter nor the accidents, continues Soner, are formally beings, if considered in relation to the substance to which they owe their being. However, considered in themselves, in so far as they are distinct from each other and from the first substance, both the accidents and the second substances represent different degrees of participation in the being and hence enjoy some type of formal distinction.[84] In these parts of the commentary Soner borrows from Cesalpino (*Quaestiones peripateticae*, II, 1) the explanation of the relationship between the different kinds of substances in terms of 'attribution/addition and subtraction' (*additio/attributio – ablatio*). This is tantamount to saying that one 'arrives' at God as the first being by – so to speak – isolating Him from all possible attributes and relations, while the secondary substances can be defined by explicating their dependence on the first being. Soner's distinction between not-univocal genres of substances (sensible non-eternal, sensible eternal and immaterial[85]), as the basis of the distinction between physics, astrology and metaphysics, is also probably derived from *Quaestiones peripateticae* (I, 4).

In these long and complex distinctions of Soner's, the overlapping of ontological and theological issues is such that it is hard to separate the two. And, here again, the effort is aimed at demonstrating the possibility of thinking, in purely philosophical terms, about two indispensable points of any Theist concept, possibly even in friction with each other. Namely, on the one hand, the creatures' dependence on God in essence and existence and, on the other, their distinction from this dependency, that is, their (relative) entitative autonomy.

Finally, to confirm and specify the theologizing slant of the commentary, I refer to the concluding passage of the exegesis of Chapter 2 of Book VII, glossing Aristotle's famous words about the equivalence of the question of being and that of substance (VII, 1, 1028b 3–5). To grasp this point Soner uses an analogy: 'Just as when someone has to receive a king, although he also has to receive all the king's retinue, it is the king whom he takes particular care of, and he would be called primarily *the king's host* and not host of the king's retainers.'[86] The almost literal coincidence of this formula with that attributed by Piccart to Pellegrini, probably based on Scherb's recollections, regarding the main subject of metaphysics is most singular. 'And Tommaso Pellegrini illustrated this concept using the following comparison: anyone inviting a king or a prince to a banquet also invites his retinue, and hence even the lowest among his retainers; in the same way the philosopher deals first with God, as king among beings, and then with all the other beings in order of importance.'[87] The striking similarity of these two analogies suggests that Soner had the Paduan Dominican in mind when he expressed himself in this way. But if this is true, we should also note the difference between the two stances which, even it is only a difference of emphasis, I think significant. For Pellegrini, metaphysics deals with the king *but must also deal with the other beings*, whereas for Soner the science is to concentrate on the king. The selection of pieces I have proposed to analyse here seems to confirm the centrality of the issue for Soner. Obviously, his commentary on the *Metaphysics* is much more too: suffice it to read his articulated and detailed explanations of Books VII to X dealing with sensible substance and comprising numerous analyses of issues related to natural philosophy, definitional logic and the doctrine of scientific knowledge. The parts examined serve chiefly to demonstrate that for Soner the pivot of the *Metaphysics*, which everything else revolves around, lies in the fusion of the ontological perspective, founded on the *ad unum et ab uno* analogy, and the theological viewpoint. It is thus natural for him to see Book XII as the culmination of the entire work that gives meaning to all the preceding arguments. Effectively, in the commentary on this part Soner takes stock of his entire exposé and reveals his thought in the most characteristic manner.

The commentary on Book XII

Any doubts there might be about the content and structure of Aristotle's *Metaphysics* as the canonical exposition of this *scientia divina* are immediately swept away by the solemn introduction to Soner's commentary on Book XII:

> This book represents the apex of this science and the chief purpose of all the metaphysical work, in which [Aristotle] is now drawing very close to explaining the nature of the abstract and unmoved substances. In fact, what has been discussed so far has been done to lead us gradually from the deep fog of our minds towards the bright light of these substances, to the knowledge of which our minds are, moreover, like the eyes of the nocturnal bird to the light of the sun. And if human genius has ever achieved anything, the sum and summit of it all is shown in this book, in which – all sound minds are agreed – the Philosopher has reached a point beyond which human efforts cannot go.[88]

Immediately after Soner recalls that, in the eighth book of *Physics*, the Philosopher merely demonstrated *that* a First Mover occurs, whereas now he also explains 'how He moves, how He lives, His substantial nature, how many substances of this kind actually exist'.[89] And in another part of the commentary the German philosopher provides a synthetic list of the doctrines which are the 'culmination' of Aristotelian philosophy, namely God's omnipotence, omniscience and perfection, entailing respectively the dependence of all creatures on His being, of intelligent ones on His intelligence, and the universal *appetitus* of beings toward Him.[90]

I don't think these opening words should be undervalued. Echoing the pseudo-Alexander's evaluation of Book XII as the culmination of the work,[91] Soner also immediately introduces the aspect of the weakness of human sight before the truth, recalling the famous passage on the bat (which in the tradition became an 'owl') from Book II of *Metaphysics*. Aristotle has undoubtedly pushed this sight to the limit, but now it is a question of whether and in what way this limit can be pushed further forward, given the urgency of the questions set before the attention of philosophers and theologians by the Christian tradition founded on the Bible. The commentary on Book XII represents a small *summa* of these matters, but before looking at the contents something should be said about the passages in which Aristotle expresses his thoughts about the cognitive possibilities of this science. Particularly useful is a passage from Chapter 7 dealing with how to comprehend *in philosophicis* the existence of a will in God, testified by the Holy Writ, without prejudice to his absolute immobility. Soner says this is the crucial question, which like others of the genre – such as the nature of demons and angels – were not treated by Aristotle precisely because there are no evident reasons for deciding them, but they nevertheless have to be in some way addressed 'on the basis of a philosophical analogy' (*ex analogia Philosophiae*). In such a situation, in the absence of genuine demonstrations, that is, indications of causes and reasons founded on empirical evidence, one proceeds by considering hypotheses consistent with the general principles regulating philosophical discourse. Moreover, the same is true of theology, where the 'analogy is based on Christian faith' (*analogia fidei Christianae*) steps in where there are no demonstrations. Consequently, in such cases it is possible only 'to stutter something' (*aliquid balbutire*), without aspiring to reach conclusions fully justified on a philosophical basis.[92] The metaphor can be clarified by what Soner declares in summing up the conclusion (the merits of which we shall return to): our reason can certainly not positively explain (*assequi ratione*) in what way acts of volition belong to God if we maintain the postulate of His immobility; all we can do is demonstrate the absurdity deriving from admitting acts of volition *within* God, so that we have to settle for arguing *pro parte negativa*! In a word, in certain cases the only card philosophy has left to play is that of non-contradiction; in matters beyond the scientific methodology of the *Analytics*, the only option is to seek what is 'further from contradiction' (*magis remotum a contradictione*). Similarly significant is the parenthesis in which Soner alludes to the relation of these speculations with the awkward biblical accounts: Scripture, he notes, sometimes speaks of God attributing Him a body, mentioning His eyes or His hand. Obviously no one takes literally such expressions in which the biblical writer improperly attributes human characteristics to God (*anthropopatheia*). So why not then adopt the same criterion to judge Scripture every time it attributes acts of volition to God?[93] In short, it seems to me that Soner sees the task of philosophical theology as essentially limited to protecting the discourse about supernatural realities, on the one hand from all the logical absurdities looming over it and, on the other, from the danger of overly enlarging the meshes of anthropomorphic analogy with the risk of succumbing to forms of superstition. That is not to say that we are dealing with a form of religious rationalism; on the contrary, citing Aristotle's *On Divination in Sleep*, Soner admits the possibility of accepting as true realities that reason, due to its intrinsic limitations, cannot explain. It is instead a question of using reason as far as it can go, without expecting to assign it tasks that exceed such limits. But perhaps this is a violation of the way in which the scholasticism of all times has seen the role of philosophy?

Soner's philosophical theology

The fact that Book XII of the *Metaphysics* was the treatise in which Aristotle expounded his theology was almost axiomatic in Soner's time. It was called into question only by stalwart critics of Aristotelianism, such as Patrizi or Gassendi,[94] while being accepted by the majority, including Soner. It is probable, moreover, that neither side was right: the one in denying the treatise any point of contact whatsoever with a theory of the divine, and the other in claiming that everything preceding Book XII was merely an introduction and that the only subject of the entire treatise was the unmoved substances. Contemporary studies have called both postulates into question, demonstrating that for Aristotle 'first philosophy' is in general a quest for the first, namely highest, causes of each genus, i.e. material, formal, final and efficient, and that Book XII furnishes indications only about the ultimate efficient or moving cause, which for Aristotle undoubtedly belongs to the sphere of the divine, in so far as it is without motion, that is, immune from generation and corruption. However, that Aristotle described 'the causes and principles of being in so far as it is being' in only a few passages of Chapter 7 (and possibly 6) of Book XII is simply not plausible.[95] The person who made this theologizing interpretation of the *Metaphysics* practically canonical was definitely Alexander of Aphrodisias between the end of the second and the beginning of the third centuries BC, and it continued at length to exert a direct or indirect influence on the majority of later Greek, Arab and Christian commentators. In the sixteenth century there was a major increase in his direct influence as a result of Sepúlveda's Latin translation of his commentary. As previously explained, the fundamental ontological ideas of Soner's commentary come from Alexander, probably channelled through Scherb and Pellegrini, and in particular that of the *dependentia ad unum et ab uno*, which I see as the hub of the entire commentary. In perfect continuity with this basic approach, the commentary on Book XII is substantially a recovery of Alexander's theological ideas, combined with the attempt to insert them into what Soner saw as mainstream scholastic theology.

It is well known that the most salient trait of the theology of Alexander, or rather of the pseudo-Alexander, as emerging from the commentary on Book XII of the *Metaphysics*, is the idea that God was the object of appetite/desire.[96] This doctrine was one of a pair with that, generally considered typically 'Alexandrist', whereby the famous 'active intellect' of Book III of *De anima* is to be identified with the God of Book XII of the *Metaphysics*. As I see it, Soner simply assumes these elements and attempts to bring them together with the ontological doctrine of *dependentia*. The desired result is a theory of the relation between God and the creatures in which their appetitive dependence on God is equivalent to a dependence of being. All this was probably with a view to a fundamental theoretical result: God is not to be conceived as an 'active' or 'operative' intellect, but as an ever-actual intelligence that understands itself. As such, despite dispensing the *esse*, He remains immovable in Himself, and as a result His simplicity and perfection are preserved.[97]

In the final analysis, this means that Soner feels the pressure of two traditions which he tries to conciliate. On one side, is the mediaeval scholastic tradition that interprets Aristotle's First Mover as an anticipation, an adumbration of God, the creator of being; on the other side, Alexander's exegesis of Aristotle's metaphysics, the most authoritative contribution – along with that of Averroes – and the one more recently restored by humanist philology. This appears most clearly when Soner addresses the classic question of what type of causality the First Mover exercises, namely if it is only an end or if it can also be considered 'efficient'.[98] Indeed, although there are several reasons for choosing the standard, exclusively 'finalist', Alexandrist solution, in the end Soner also admits in God a type of efficient causality. Not in the sense that he directly imparts motion to the heavens in the same way as someone moving a stone – He is, after all, a *speculative* intellect! – but in the sense that He is present in all things as the cause of their being. And this in turn is to be understood in the sense that the first cause generates the being of things precisely by inducing in them the appetite for itself, and this appetite for God, this dependence on God, is for the things 'being'. Soner clarifies that it can be expressed by saying that God is the efficient cause of things in so far as their appetite/being is 'in accordance with' (*secundum*) God, or comes from the 'assistance' of God, in conformity with the extended concept of efficient causality that Soner finds in Alexander's treatise *De anima*.[99]

The topic is taken up again a few pages later, when Soner reconfirms that final causality is not enough and it is inevitable to introduce a form of efficient causality in God. This is not to be understood in the manner of the forces operating in the sublunar world, since Aristotle 'tacitly insinuated a different and more sublime' mode,[100] which is precisely the production of the *esse*. The superiority and perfection of the first cause resides in its primacy in the order of the *esse*, a doctrine that Soner believes he reads in Aristotle although, irrespective of this, he argues that it is grounded in solid reasons.[101] And the first result of this efficiency is the 'creation' – that is, its total dependence on the first cause for being – of matter, whether we believe that the *productio rerum* was in time, or whether like Aristotle we believe it to be eternal. Conclusion:

> This being how things stand, it is clear that not only is God the final cause of things (which everyone agrees about: all things indeed tend towards their principle, from which they come), but also that it is this cause that primarily bestows all being on all things. And therefore it is inappropriate that it be called efficient cause, given that the efficient principle is normally made by something in something else that already exists. God, instead, is at once the author of the thing 'in which' (that is, matter) and also operates without moving and without changing. Therefore He is said to be efficient by emanation not by production.[102]

Similar reasons are then employed to show that God is also formal cause, but in the sense of 'assistant'[103] and not in that of 'immanent', to complete a reconstruction of divine causality that Soner evidently considers generally acceptable to Christian scholasticism. At any rate, the negation of the 'active or productive' character of divine intellect and the confirmation that His only action is instead 'speculative' has all been taken by Soner from Alexander's exegesis.

The real difficulties emerge from this point on. The crux of the Altdorf professor's exegesis of Book XII of the *Metaphysics* is, therefore, the attempt to preserve the immobility of God, while at the same time admitting in Him the insurgence of an act that creates the world. The concept of creation in fact implies the existence in God of acts of volition which threaten the postulate of his inalterability. Soner devotes many long pages full of complex arguments to the question,[104] despite, as we have seen, not expecting a demonstrative and hence definitive and universally convincing solution from them. Much of this discourse is devoted to eliminating possible objections to his proposals, which are thus presented merely as the least contradictory and unreasonable.

And so, how is it possible to comprise the creation of the world in time without attributing an act of will to God, which cannot apparently be made without an alteration in Him in time. Soner's answer to this does not strike me as perfectly univocal: at times it consists of distinguishing a will internal to God (consisting in the simple enjoyment of His own perfection) and in reality identical to his essence, from a will aimed outwards and also external to his essence. Here, once again, what is proposed is the ontological model supplied by the theory of *dependentia*: an analogical relation between the second analogates and the first analogue can exist without anything being changed in the latter. 'Creation' is hence a particular mode of the general divine causality over natural processes, understood as dependence:

> And since this dependency in time did not alter anything of His essence, in the same way also in the principle internal to God, whether it is understood as volition or will, nothing is changed . . . . And, according to his essence, God is not in a certain manner now that the world has been emanated by him, and in another manner before [the creation of] the world. And therefore nor is He according to His will different before and after [the creation]. As now, without any internal change, [He] communicates himself to certain things and distances himself from others (hence their generations and corruptions), just so He allowed the universe to be emanated from Him, whereas before it was not emanated, without any change whatsoever [in Him].[105]

A will conceived in this way not only does not threaten the unity and immobility of God but, according to Soner, also has the advantage of maintaining the freedom of God's creative act, excluding the notion that it occurs in a necessary way, a trap into which, as we have seen, Aristotle himself fell. As Soner explains a little further on, what misled the Stagirite was his conviction that for God, inasmuch He is the greatest good, it is essential and necessary to communicate Himself externally as well as being object of desire. Soner recalls the *dictum* from the *Physics* (see I, 9, 192a 16–19): *existente divino et appetibile, dandum esse etiam, quod illud appetat* ('if there is a divine being which is the object of desire, there should also be something which desires it'), which Cesalpino had adopted while explaining the necessary emergence of the first matter.[106] Elsewhere, however, Soner makes a different distinction, attributing solely to the limitations of human perception the apprehension of God's will as a formality distinct from His essence.[107] As I see it, this confirms that the introductory words to the commentary on Book XII recalling Aristotle's image of the bat were not merely rhetorical.

Whether or not Soner's *rationes* for neutralizing divine will are convincing, there is no doubt that his intention is to preserve God's absolute autonomy from things that derive from Him. And here again is the metaphor of the centre and the line, whereby 'in some way (*quodammodo*) we can understand how something is separable and is, according to its essence, separated from all things and, at the same time the latter are not separable from Him. And how something does not undergo mutation although many mutable things flow from Him'.[108] And, naturally: 'what is said here about the will [of God], holds even more for the other affections, all of which are initiated outside him in such a way as to touch Him without changing Him (*immutabiliter*). Indeed He could not live a most blessed life if He were moved by hatred, anger or mercy like a sea of troubles'.[109]

I feel that the points just discussed are most significant among the issues raised by Soner in his interpretation, especially in the discussion of Chapter 7 of *Metaphysics*. It is true that in the last part of the commentary on Book XII he addresses typical *quaestiones mixtae* of particular epistemological status – angels, demons, resurrection of souls and bodies – that have attracted the attention of scholars.[110] Nevertheless, these seem to me to be rather incidental digressions, extraneous to the central theme of his work as I have sought to define it. The discourse on the angels, for instance, is intended to complete the discussion about the number of celestial intelligences, topical for the commentaries on this chapter of the *Metaphysics*. It seems to me equally rash to dub the solutions proposed by Soner as 'Socinian', whatever that may mean. For example, his polemical lunge against Cesalpino – who to admit the existence of demons in deference to the 'courtiers of the Whore of Babylon'[111] contravened the teachings of Aristotle – takes up an anti-Catholic cliché common among the Lutherans. Similarly, the conclusion of the argument that demonstrates the loss of individuality of the souls of the deceased is typically and tritely Lutheran: since the maintenance of individual identity after death is not demonstrable, the

Antichrist fantasies about prayers to the saints and Purgatory have no sense.[112] That, as has often been upheld, this same concept of the return of the souls of the dead to a common spiritual principle is linked to the Socinian theory of the 'Sleep of the souls' (*psychopannychia*) seems to me somewhat far-fetched,[113] since it can quite simply be considered the application of Averroist or Cesalpino-derived principles to eschatological matters. Or, as I believe more probable, Soner's observations on the state of the souls after death should be seen not so much as a form of acceptance to the Socinian doctrine, but rather as a criticism of Taurellus' assent to this doctrine. This was part of the latter's claim to a Christian philosophy capable of furnishing arguments to confirm the believed truths, finding them beyond the bounds of philosophy, Aristotle's or any other.[114] In this case, in these parts of the commentary Soner is expressing disagreement with his colleague, at the same time justifying the silence of Aristotle on certain subjects that cannot be addressed *ex sensu et ratione*.

Soner and Cesalpino

In my opinion, the digressions related to demons and personal immortality proposed by Soner in the commentary on Book XII, and treated in the manner of *quaestio disputata*, have been overexposed by scholars, who have seen them as the key to understanding his relation with Cesalpino, considered the most important intellectual landmark. However, Cesalpino is evoked only in the passages dealing with these specific topics. He is absent from the part that I see as most characteristic of the commentary on Book XII, in which other Italian Aristotelian philosophers such as Francesco Vimercato and Federico Pendasio are instead mentioned. First, I would say that the heterodox character of the thought of Cesalpino (personal physician to the Pope!) has been exaggerated in deference to a reading conditioned by the interpretations of Brucker, Bayle and Renan, concerned in their different ways with finding precursors of Spinoza's atheism or of enlightened Deism. The hallmark of this interpretation consists in essentially considering the 'heterodox Aristotelians', from Pomponazzi to Cremonini, to be hypocritical when they declare in advance their disapproval of any conclusion that could conflict with the truth revealed by religion. In general, this is seen as a formal, i.e. insincere, submission to authority and a sort of Nicodemite strategy to boot. This reading of Cesalpino aligns him with the heretic Bruno in terms of his philosophic theories.[115] In actual fact, Cesalpino's philosophy does not appear to me to be particularly shocking or novel, but rather to fit within the commonly accepted terms of the debate on the correct interpretation of Aristotle and his natural philosophy. It would also be interesting to assess the link of these 'modernist' interpretations with the very first polemic launched against Cesalpino by Taurellus. In truth, what Taurellus censured in the Pisan (an impious concept of God derived from Aristotle) was exactly what came to be regarded as a merit by later historians, as already mentioned.

However, leaving aside judgements about Cesalpino, my impression is that his role was not so decisive that Soner's commentary on the *Metaphysics* examined here can be seen as merely a continuation or explication of certain theories in the *Quaestiones peripateticae*. Questions in the first two books regarding, for instance, the unity of intelligences, the soul of the world or the necessity of first matter, or those in Book V concerning the immortality and individuality of the human soul, or Cesalpino's theories of demons or spontaneous generation. It's true that Soner uses Cesalpino on various occasions, just as he uses other interpreters of Aristotle, but it's not easy to sustain the notion that his strategic scope was that of coming to terms with the Pisan's alleged heterodox Aristotelianism. To the argument that Cesalpino's Aristotelizing philosophy was characterized by theories such as that of the eternity of the world or of matter, or of God's 'closure' to the world, being sunk in the thought of Himself, one can object that these were the difficulties traditionally posed by Aristotelianism *tout court* for those wishing to relate it to a theology inspired by the Bible. They were difficulties that all the Christian interpreters of Aristotle's philosophy had to address, without for this reason being suspected of collusion or compromises with heretic tendencies. And I repeat, what seems to me a more salient characteristic of Soner's intention is the discourse he opens up in the prolegomenon and goes on to develop at different times in the commentary on the central books, concluding with the final developments in Book XII. As I have sought to show, it is, substantially, a discourse *de Deo et attributis eius*, the entire difficulty of which lies in simultaneously preserving several fundamental principles of the theological discourse which are inevitably in tension with each other: the contingency of creation and the immutability of God; the dependence of the world on God and its 'formal' autonomy. Whether or not his subtle distinctions are convincing, Soner appears most confident in presenting his contribution, which drew on the most valid Aristotelianism of his time. Instead, he shows himself exceedingly prudent, not to say timorous, in addressing the 'mixed' questions, where there is inevitable friction between what is said by Saint Paul and by Aristotle, where clarity is a truly arduous goal and one has to settle merely for a plausible (*verosimilis*) conclusion. However, as I said, these excursions *in agro alieno* are not the nub of his *lectio Aristotelis* and, in any case, not only are there no traces in him of any antinomy between natural reason and the light of faith, but rather his is a quest for a discourse as consistent and non-contradictory as possible on the fundamental chapters of a monotheist theology. Let us note that even Ogonowski, who in the footsteps of Bayle adopts the category of 'antinomy' between faith and reason to evaluate the final outcome of the metaphysics of Soner and of the other Socinians,[116] ultimately acknowledges a certain 'similarity' between Soner and Aquinas.[117] Ogonowski also admits that Soner's Socinian inclination does not emerge in a univocal and distinct way from the commentary and above all that the Altdorf professor 'refrained from taking the decisive step: identifying the anthropomorphized God of the Bible with the abstract God of the philosophers'.[118] To this one could respond that the above-mentioned antinomy is plainly a post-Cartesian anachronism and that it can scarcely be posited as the aim of a thinker such as Soner with his traditionally scholastic philosophical background.

In sum, Soner is simply one of the many ancient, mediaeval, modern and even contemporary readers of Aristotle who interpret the *Metaphysics* as a theology. And, as we have seen, for him this is most satisfactorily achieved by taking Aristotle's ontological considerations as the guiding thread. Moreover, as I have sought to show, it is not true that there are religious – still less confessional – impulses underlying this endeavour, while at the same time it does not seem appropriate to apply here the enlightened concept of 'natural religion' which belongs to different contexts. This is why I agree with Achermann[119] on the futility of hunting out 'deistic' or 'pantheistic' ideas in Soner's language and philosophical theories (and there are certainly plenty to be found!), since the core issue of his philosophy is to avoid the aporias which result from both the absolute transcendence and the absolute immanence of God compared to the world.

What instead seems clear is the desire to be part of the centuries-long tradition of commentators, in continuity with mediaeval scholasticism but with the idea of renewing this through the conspicuous contributions offered by humanism, and especially the rediscovery of the ancient commentators, first and foremost Alexander. In a word, the idea is to furnish the philosophic bases for the fundamental points of a monotheist theology of biblical inspiration, albeit without going in the direction of a 'Christian philosophy' such as that of Taurellus. The *analogia entis* reread in the light of the ontological clarifications provided by interpreters such as Alexander, and interpreters of interpreters such as Pellegrini and Cesalpino, for him represents true progress to be nurtured, albeit without going beyond the frame of reference of mediaeval scholasticism, that of Aquinas and Scotus, who are frequently used and recalled by Soner with esteem and respect, as are their modern followers.[120]

Epilogue: Crell and the critique of Alexandrian finalism

The nucleus of Soner's theology was therefore his attempt to explain the modes of divine causality, remaining within the bounds of philosophical discourse. This, in turn, was substantially understood as analysis of the consequences deriving from assumption of the principles of Aristotle's philosophy. If my reconstruction is correct, the key concept here is the *dependentia ab uno et ad unum*, even prior to providing a response to the traditional question of which of the four types of causality distinguished by Aristotle could be attributed to the first being. Soner does, of course, address the latter issue, but for him the most important point had already been scored, since thanks to the concept of dependency it was possible to explain how the first cause could transmit being to the world while remaining immutable and distinct from it. And the rest too, namely the figure of God as intellect eternally in act and the aspiration of the other substances to resemble Him, were subjects set forth in Book XII of Aristotle's *Metaphysics* and in Alexander's commentary but could, in the end, be integrated with the focal concept of the *dependentia*. These observations serve as an introduction to the last question to be addressed here: the relation between Soner's commentary and the *De Deo et attributis eius* composed by his pupil at Altdorf and leading Socinian theologian, Johann Crell (1590–1633), which aspired to present an official version of the philosophical theology of the Antitrinitarian movement.[121] Considering that the critical edition of this work is shortly to be published, perhaps one ought not to speak too soon; therefore I shall restrict myself to simply offering some hypotheses which may be confirmed or contradicted when the philosophical design underlying Crell's treatise is more clearly focused.[122] The connection between this work and Soner's commentary to *Metaphysics* was sustained by Ogonowski, who interpreted Crell's attacks on 'heterodox' Aristotelianism as directed jointly at Soner and Cesalpino. Crell was thus voicing the attitude of the theologians of Raków, aware of the incompatibility of this version of Aristotelianism originating from Padua and the 'humanist' version of biblical theology current in Socinianism.[123]

Without calling into question the pivotal point of Ogonowski's reconstruction – namely, Crell's hostility towards Cesalpino's Aristotelianism – there may be doubts about whether Soner too was included in this criticism. In fact, he is never mentioned by name by his former pupil who in polemizing always refers to a collective subject. It can be assumed that Crell's silence about his Altdorf professor was due to the fact that, all things considered, he did not see significant progress in his doctrine compared with Cesalpino's; more specifically, he deemed ineffective the efforts of his former teacher to escape the aporias (theological 'necessitarianism') implicit in Cesalpino's concept of God. Crell has no need to distinguish Soner from Cesalpino, and hence refer to him directly, for the simple reason that he traces both back to the common Alexandrist root, namely the theory that God, as pure *speculative* intellect, an act of intelligence always turned to Himself, through the sole presence of this act can rouse matter into being. Consequently Crell saw no point in Soner's – effectively rather tortuous – clarifications regarding the 'efficient' causality of God or the contingency of the world as regards divine essence, once the first cause has become that very type of intellect.[124]

Bypassing all the exegetic and theoretical work of Soner in this manner, all Crell does is take up the criticism levelled at Cesalpino (and Piccolomini) at the time by Taurellus in the works of 1597 and 1603, respectively, the well-known *Alpes Caesae* and the less known, though not less voluminous, *Kosmologia* and *Ouranologia* pursuing the same path in the construction of a peculiar 'Christian philosophy'. I believe that the possible relation between Crell and Taurellus is hence a topic which should be investigated.[125]

Regarding the *pars construens* of Crell's theology, as known, the solution proposed by him, in complete severance from Aristotelianism (and Aristotle), was to declare that God is an active intellect operating through 'judgement' (*consilium*), that is deliberation on the means in view of the ends, in other words on the model of the human agent pursuant to the description in the *Nicomachean Ethics*.[126] At this point, however, the discourse on the attributes of God comes to the surface, which is undoubtedly the central topic of Crell's treatise. This discourse, which occupies the second half of the work, appears inter alia to make some further concessions to *anthropopatheia*, the metaphorical language about God, than Soner was willing to do.[127] Indeed, Crell has no qualms about stating that free will is *in* God.[128] He was very probably aware of the philosophical and theological aporias implied in this, but seems to think it a price worth paying for retrieving the notion of a provident God. It would, moreover, be interesting to know from whom Crell took inspiration in elaborating his concept of *libertas indifferentiae* in God, namely a surplus of autonomy apropos the causes preceding the act of volition, present to a degree in human will and absolute in the divine.

Here Crell uses the term *autexousion* as synonymous with *liberum arbitrium*.[129] While Alexander of Aphrodisias himself is not to be ruled out as a source, since in *De fato* he uses this term with reference to the concept of liberty,[130] or even the patristic sources, I would assume that Crell's relations with coeval scholastic theology, especially the Hispanic variety, ought first to be clarified.[131] However, apart from all this, there are many elements for identifying the 'Socinian' natural theology of *De Deo* as a continuation of Taurellus' polemic with Italian Aristotelianism and a renewal of the project of Christian philosophy.

Naturally Crell and Soner operated in different contexts and with different aims. Crell was essentially a theologian for whom the biblical concept of a provident God was more important than the consistency of the discourse on God with the principles of Aristotelian philosophy (or what were passed off as such through adroit exegetic operations).[132] For him, Aristotelianism was more than anything an obstacle on the path to the formation of a natural theology fitting to the biblical postulates. Soner, on the other hand, saw himself as last in the line of a tradition of exegetes of the *Metaphysics* for whom the science of being is *in itself*, without conforming to non-philosophical requirements, destined to be converted into theology. The synthesis of humanism with old and neo-scholastic exegesis of Aristotle proposed by Soner has certain important advantages. On the one hand, Aristotle's philosophy, intelligently interpreted, contains reasons for denying the pointless opposition between reason and revelation; on the other, it provides a debating platform for the more complex matters without yielding to the temptation to 'confessionalize' them, as proved by the fact that thinkers belonging to very different religious traditions had reasoned on this basis for centuries. And perhaps there is also a third advantage: avoiding the watering-down of metaphysics into a 'transcendental science' effectively of use solely for the compilation of lists of beings and philosophical lexicons, which would indeed have been a scholastic outcome, in the pejorative sense of the term. A few decades later Jakob Thomasius came to the rescue of this perspective of a theologizing metaphysics, and it is probable that his pupil Leibniz judged it appreciatively.[133]

Part Three

Praxis

4

The Aristotelians and the New Science of Politics

We have observed in the previous chapters the continued vitality of a long and illustrious exegetical tradition of metaphysics of a more or less remote Aristotelian inspiration, even at the end of the seventeenth century. Conversely, regarding the part of practical philosophy that became known as 'politics', according to the reconstruction prevailing among historians, the modern age seemed to have marked a caesura with the past, rendering futile all efforts to retrieve the ancient models, especially that of Aristotle. This in turn dealt a mortal blow to the concept of politics and its aims set forth in the eight books of Aristotle's *Politics*, adopted by mediaeval scholasticism and also taken over by early modern humanists. The rejection of the ancient models then gave rise to a 'political science' focused on the principle of sovereignty and the question of management of political power, in parallel with the renewal of natural science that led, some decades later, to the scientific revolution and the definitive eclipse of Aristotelianism. All this was brought about, inter alia, by the great philosophical syntheses of Hobbes and Spinoza and the school of natural law, which definitively undermined the preceding concept, resetting the political discourse on completely new foundations.

However, if we look at the elaboration of this discipline carried out in schools, the story appears a little more complex. The pattern of a simple succession or substitution of one 'paradigm' with another does not seem entirely appropriate to describe the dynamics of political philosophy taught in upper schools and universities. Professors of politics of the late sixteenth and early seventeenth centuries, who trained on the texts of Aristotle, did not apparently interpret the lesson of Machiavelli's *The Prince*, Bodin's *Republic* and Lipsius' *Politica* as a mere break with tradition that ushered in a new discourse on the 'reason of state' or on the 'mysteries (*arcana*) of politics'. Indeed, the Aristotelians appeared to think it possible to assimilate the theoretical novelties of the time within the framework of philosophy inspired by the Stagirite's *Politics* and his practical philosophy in general. Historians should not underestimate this effort to provide students with an updated political discipline, even solely on account of the objective difficulty of the enterprise; in fact, as we shall see, with Hermann Conring it reached an impasse. Meanwhile, however, in the early-seventeenth-century writers inspired by Aristotle, the clash with modern politics stimulated profound reflection on the central category of his practical philosophy, the *prudentia*, and on its capacity to assume functions appropriate to the practical and theoretical demands of the time. Therefore, in the first part of this chapter, I take a closer look at how some prominent professors of the early seventeenth century dealt with the topic of political counsel, the primary arena for the practice of prudence. In the second part I discuss the theoretical consideration and didactic practice of Hermann Conring and his school in the area of *prudentia civilis* and his ambiguous relationship with Aristotle's *Politics*. My ultimate hope is that the sample examined will adequately illustrate how, as far as political theory and teaching is concerned, the encounter between modern thought and academic Aristotelianism gave rise to different results, ranging from a synthesis of Peripatetic political thought to works that dramatically posed the question of the effective compatibility of Aristotle's conception with modern political thought.

The *prudentia civilis* of the political adviser in the early *Schulphilosophie*

Chapters 22 and 23 of Machiavelli's *The Prince* are conventionally taken as the beginning of modern thought on the subject of the adviser, all the more so because they contain certain motifs that are constants in subsequent political literature – first, the link of this topic with that of prudence and, second, aspects such as the relations between the counsellor and the person of power, the latter's selection and assessment of the advisers and making decisions on the basis of the advice received. However, another source of the modern concept of prudence in advising is undoubtedly the large, and frequently anonymous, sixteenth-century production of books of counsel, maxims and precepts that were widely available to the great political writers of the century and inspired many of their ideas.[1] This literature encapsulated a wealth of individual experiences and historic reflections expressed in aphorisms to provide rules of conduct for those engaged in public life. In the second half of the sixteenth century the eminent Dutch humanist Justus Lipsius – who revisited Stoicism and, in his own manner, disseminated and supported the theories on the reason of state[2] – revived a concept of civil prudence which was essentially a synthesis of these two traditions. In Book III of his *Politica* Lipsius confirmed that the question of the counsellor belonged to the sphere of *prudentia*, understanding this as the capacity to act in a real situation and on the basis of experience as well as the historic knowledge acquired from books. It was Lipsius too who, in the same text, presented the sequence of the *loci* making up the subject of the counsel and the counsellor, which substantially continued to be the model in subsequent treatises.[3] Lipsius' exposé was in fact readily consulted also by the numerous authors of political *disciplinae* active in the Protestant academic world, if only for the fact that he had provided a systematic arrangement of a largely new subject.

This dependence on the author of the *Libri politicorum* of certain exponents of the young *Schulphilosophie* – the academic system of philosophy teaching in German-speaking territories at the time of the Reformation – was already indicated in 1633 by the famous scholar Gabriel Naudé in his *Bibliographia politica*, where they were in effect lumped together. In the context of an overview of writers on *civilis prudentia* – and following a lengthy excursus on ancient, mediaeval and Renaissance literature on the question of the state, which for Naudé culminated in Jean Bodin's *Six Books of the Commonwealth* – the only role left to them was that of exhausted followers: 'everything that was then added by Justus Lipsius or by Timpler or by Keckermann can be positively appraised mostly for the style or the easier method, but not because there is some new content in it'.[4]

Leaving aside the overall judgement about the originality of these authors, the association between them proposed by Naudé is not surprising. The works of political philosophy produced in Protestant circles at the beginning of the seventeenth century were not restricted to dry scholastic exposés where neoclassical (neo-Aristotelian and neo-Ciceronian) inspirations are somehow filtered through the theological thought of Luther or Melanchthon. They also illustrate the massive presence of the typically sixteenth-century political issues connected with the birth of the modern state. Additionally, they bring to the fore how the concept of *prudentia civilis*, despite being presented as a continuation of the classical political ideal, has no few points of contact with the evolving idea of new political science, and hence with the qualities that are crucial for the modern political agent, the sovereign and the magistracies emanating from the same.

Therefore it seems useful to take into consideration some works of this type, more or less in the nature of textbooks, to see in what way the topic of the *consiliarius* and the virtue of *prudentia* proper to him, and characteristic of political science in the early modern age, is addressed in the context of the

Aristotelizing and neoclassical language of certain Protestant scholastics. This will show how the categories of Aristotelian matrix were adapted to tasks that were extremely new in historical terms. It will also show how the impression of uniformity and repetition that this literature provokes at first sight begins to dwindle with the realization that each writer has processed the material in line with objectives linked to his own institutional context and his own intellectual exigencies.

Here I restrict myself to a small sample of three well-known authors: Clemens Timpler (1563–1624), representing the *Gymnasium Academicum* of Steinfurt, and Bartholomäus Keckermann (1572–1609), professor at the *Gymnasium Academicum* in Gdansk. With them we will consider also the professor at Herborn, Siegen (Germany) and Emden (Netherlands), Johannes Althusius (1557–1638). The works considered here were published in the space of a few years, between 1608 and 1611. More precisely, Keckermann's *Systema disciplinae politicae* and *Apparatus practicus* were published in 1608–9; the second edition of the *Politica metodice digesta atque exemplis sacris et profanis illustrata* by Althusius was published in 1610; the third part of Timpler's *Philosophiae practicae systema methodicum in tres partes digestum*, the part dealing with politics, dates to 1611. In addition to their chronological closeness, these works also share a family resemblance, primarily more or less close links with so-called political Calvinism. The three writers also knew each other well: Keckermann makes several references to the first (1603) edition of Althusius' treatise, and Althusius in turn cites Keckermann in the second and third edition of his work (1610 and 1614 respectively),[5] while Timpler mentions both the others.[6] Nevertheless, several substantial differences between the treatises should not be overlooked. Timpler's is the least original of the three, the one closest to a dry student textbook. Keckermann's *Systema*, on the other hand, is an impressive synthesis of the political problems of the time, with interesting references to the contemporary history of the Polish Republic in the international context. Finally, Althusius' *Politica* displays a theoretical originality that was immediately recognized, and which even recently has attracted the attention of historians of political and legal thought and other scholars.[7] Another difference to be noted among the writers themselves is that Timpler and Keckermann came from an essentially philosophical or theological background, while Althusius had trained as a jurist. Similarly important is the fact that the first two spent their entire lives teaching in their respective gymnasia, whereas the academic work of Althusius went hand in hand with political activity. In addition to the various minor offices he held, he was the mayor of Emden in Eastern Frisia in the years of the war between the Dutch Provinces and the Habsburg Empire. However, from a certain point of view it can also be said that Keckermann's perspective was not so distant from that of Althusius since, like Emden, Gdansk was an important centre of international marine trade dominated by a (Reformed) Calvinist civic elite, and in both cities the crucial issue was the coexistence of different confessional trends.

Timpler

Considering the way these writers address the subject of the political counsellor, one has the distinct impression that, by the early years of the seventeenth century, a standard, topical arrangement of the subject had crystallized: a succession of thematic units and subunits repeated almost without variation in all the texts. This holds both for the positioning of the subject of the *consiliarius* within the context of the entire chapter *de gubernatione*, and also for the internal development of the subject itself. Looking at the index of contents in Timpler's treatise (Book III)[8] immediately reveals the way the writer has organized his treatment around these two aspects. The chapter on the adviser follows the discussion of the principal figure in the exercise of power (the *magistratus*) and is developed in the course of the explanation of the function of government in its numerous and varied aspects. The role of the counsellor is addressed together with that of other ministers (*administri/satellites*) and that of the legates-ambassadors, and this same order is also followed by Keckermann and Althusius. Moreover, the presentation of the figure and function of the adviser is also highly standardized, with all three writers repeating more or less the same aspects. For instance: whether the magistrate needs the counsellor, how many counsellors are necessary, the preferable age, social background and country of origin (national or foreign), the requisite moral characteristics and in what way the magistrate should take their advice into consideration, and so on. The only point that Keckermann and Althusius include but Timpler leaves out is that regarding the senate or similar institutional bodies with consultative functions.

As mentioned, this structuring of the topic is not an original feature of the scholastic textbooks, since it was already to be found, with slight variations, in a famous work such as the *Politica* of Lipsius (in Book III) which I believe can to all intents and purposes be considered the source of inspiration for these authors. While the Flemish humanist constructed his argument – as was his habit – through an appropriate composition of passages and precepts taken from ancient writers, these professors were more attentive to the methodical aspect of their treatment. In practice, this resulted in the adoption of an order of exposition of the kind used in the period following the reforms of Ramus, which then became definitively established with the circulation of Keckermann's treatise. In general, the *praecepta*, containing the essential elements of the subject, were followed by *quaestiones* that developed the main points, also by comparing different opinions. *Tabulae*, placed before or after the body of the treatise, offered a synoptic overview of the subject as a whole and its ramifications, with a preference for dichotomies and designed to facilitate mental assimilation and recollection. Timpler himself acknowledged that the purpose of his work was primarily to provide a guide for organizing the numerous and complicated political questions. He also admitted that his personal knowledge of the subject was merely a scholarly one, since he had never held political office and had no practical experience of politics.[9] This professor of the *Gymnasium Illustre* in Steinfurt can be grouped with the other eminent academic exponents of the Reformed movement such as Rudolf Goclenius senior, Otho Casmann and Keckermann himself. He is a perfect example of how academic Aristotelianism substantially took up the task of assimilating early modern political theory as it had developed in the course of the sixteenth century. I shall now try to summarize how he did this, starting from several texts of a programmatic nature and moving on to the specific subject being dealt with here.[10]

In the *Epistola* placed at the beginning of the political part of the trilogy, Timpler explains the ideas that guided his work. He places emphasis on the concept of *prudentia civilis*, insisting that this is equivalent to the *dýnamis politikê* alluded to at the beginning of the *Nicomachean Ethics* (I, 1, 1094a 10-15): the capacity of governing the city. In the same way as Aristotle, Timpler defines this as 'the main one and the more architectonic' (*kyriôtatê kai málista architektonikê*) in relation to the other capacities, for instance that of governing one's own family or one's life. However, to acquire the corresponding specific prudence it is necessary both to gain specific knowledge – especially from history – and to acquire specific experience. Necessary, but not sufficient, as the aspiring statesman has to make a further step beyond the purely empirical level to reach a more 'scientific' one. This means that the governor has to acquire the capacity to personally elaborate the universal *principia et praecepta* that are the real fundamental components of the *ars politica*. Although here Timpler is referring to the passages at the beginning of the *Metaphysics* and Book VI of the *Nicomachean Ethics* that everyone had in mind,[11] these definitions at the very beginning of the work have a decidedly modern tone. This is due to the fact that he replaces Aristotelian practical philosophy (of which politics is an element) with a discourse aimed at the application of rules and precepts to concrete action. Indeed, the very first phrase of the actual treatise states quite simply: 'Politics is an art that demonstrates how to build and how to govern the republic in the best possible way'.[12] Another definition found in these early pages states that politics is a discipline serving 'the political magistrate who wishes to exercise his power properly'.[13] Substantially, therefore, Timpler sees politics as a technique for statesmen, and his treatise is simply a guide for those exercising the power of government who require a minimum of theoretical foundations, which must necessarily be conceived as guidance for practice. Considering this qualification of the *ars politica* as a practical instrument, it comes as no surprise that most of the work is devoted to the question of *gubernum*, in both its secular and its ecclesiastic-religious dimension.

The work focuses on the function of the magistrate (Books II–IV) and this is the context in which the specific role of the *consiliarius* is addressed (Book III, Ch. 3). According to Timpler's definition – couched in the characteristic post-Ramist terminology – the latter is the 'instrumental efficient cause' in the exercise of the *imperium*, while the magistrate of whom the adviser is an official is the 'principal efficient cause'.[14] Timpler's exposition takes the form of *quaestiones* that call for a choice between two alternative options (*An* ...?), going on to provide arguments for and against, supported in turn by references to classical literature, biblical texts and contemporary literature (with Tolosanus – alias the French jurist and polymath Pierre Gregoire [1540–97], very popular among Reformed scholars – possibly the writer most frequently cited). What I see as particularly noteworthy in the treatment of the magistrate and the counsellor is the insistent criticism of ideas grown out of Machiavellian political thought. According to Timpler, the link between politics and morality must be preserved, in relation to the activity of both the chief magistrate and of his 'instrument', the adviser.[15] This actually refers back to Timpler's original elaboration of a general theory of action that he calls 'praxeology',[16] which holds that it is important to know the moral quality of the action itself pursuant to socially accepted criteria. It is therefore important that the activity of the magistrate too, and of those that help him in the imperium – counsellors, ministers, legates – are subject to the same criteria. This is exactly what I see as Timpler's characteristic trait, which is also in effect the leitmotif of the chapter on the counsellor: the evident evolution of the category of *prudentia-phrónêsis* derived from the Aristotelian tradition in the direction of the theory sketched out in his praxeology, which pivots on the essential approval or non-approval of the actions of the politicians on the basis of their moral quality. Obviously this leaves other aspects of the Aristotelian conception on the sidelines, such as how fitting the means subject to deliberation (*boúleusis*) are to the desired ends, or the practical efficacy of the action itself for the achievement of a righteous end.

Althusius

Unlike Timpler's work, the *Politica metodice digesta atque exemplis sacris et profanis illustrata* by Johann Althusius (or Althaus)[17] is considered to go beyond the pragmatic horizon of the scholastic political treatises of the early seventeenth century, providing original notions of political theory. This is not to say that the treatise lacks certain characteristic features of this genre of works; for instance: the principle that politics, understood as public activity, is a distinct *ars*-technique and the idea that a new *scientia* is required to teach this art, a discipline which – conforming to the rules of the Ramist method – includes only 'essential or homogeneous' elements.[18] The graphic layout is also scholastic, with lengthy passages in italics commenting and developing the text in apodictic form in normal type.

Althusius' thought was salvaged from oblivion in the second half of the nineteenth century by the legal theorist and historian Otto von Gierke, in search of modern precursors of a federal notion of state.[19] Since then, even up to recent decades, his *Politics* too has attracted an attention not enjoyed by the other scholastic political manuals of the time.[20] Of particular interest was Althusius' theory of the *consociationes* – with features redolent of Montesquieu's 'intermediate bodies' – namely the political and social bodies operating between the sovereign and the people. This theory, which has its roots in political Calvinism and also in the tradition of mediaeval secular and canonical *ius*, was openly opposed to Bodin's theory of absolute sovereignty. Althusius in fact identified two principles underpinning the political body. On the one hand, the rules of the Ten Commandments that are the basis of 'symbiotic' life, that is, of the bond that holds together each of the aforesaid intermediate bodies. On the other hand, the rights of supreme power (*iura maiestatis*), as a result of which the body politic as a whole forms a totality.[21] Another characteristic point, possibly in polemic with Bodin, is the statement that the *proprium* of political science is the 'fact' of the existence of the *maiestas*, whereas *iurisprudentia* deals with the merits and rights deriving from this fact, from which a certain primacy of political theory over law can be deduced.[22]

Starting from Bodin's *Six Books of the Commonwealth* (1576) the close relation between the new science of politics and the concept of *maiestas*, as well as the emphasis on the juridical and institutional expressions of the latter, were the distinctive traits of modern political thought. Althusius basically adheres to this approach, but interprets it in a democratic sense. Indeed he objects to contemporary 'jurists and political writers' (essentially to Bodin), who assign *maiestas* exclusively to 'the Prince and to the highest magistrate', proudly declaring that: 'I, with a few others, affirm the opposite, namely that majesty belongs to the symbiotic body of the society as a whole'.[23] On the other hand, the ideas that the *politica Iudeorum* represented a paradigmatic regime, or that a definite political doctrine could be derived from the Ten Commandments,[24] are probably concepts connected with Calvinist political thought, namely with that of the theorists of the so-called 'right of resistance' such as Lambert Daneau, Theodore Beza, François Hotman or the author of the *Vindiciae contra Tyrannos*. Finally, Althusius' crucial concept of symbiosis and the insistence on the fact that the citizens participate in a community of reciprocal rights and services (*communicatio iuris et operum*) harks back to an essentially classical model. In the light of this model, politics is focused on the concept of life in communities legitimately established for the purpose of pursuing the search for the good life and not the acquisition and maintenance of power. This is not the place to go into detail about Althusius' ideas about how the body politic is organized, so I shall simply cite some passages regarding concepts such as *symbiosis* or *communication* as a way of introducing his thoughts apropos the political adviser.

Discussing the characteristics of the kingdom, the major political community (*universalis publica maior consociatio*; Ch. 9), Althusius sees the 'communication' mentioned earlier as something of a bond 'binding this body and this association is the consent and the trust *reciprocally* given and accepted between the members of the Republic; it is, therefore, a tacit and explicit promise to reciprocally provide substances and actions, help, advice and common rights, as required by the utility and necessity of the universal social life of the kingdom'[25] (italics mine). I should point out that the formula *ultro citroque*, deriving from the definition of contracts in civil law, has been translated here by 'reciprocally'. The promise underlying civil life is hence an obligation to exchange, including the exchange of 'advice'. A similar point is made in another of Althusius' works, the *Dicaelogica*, a treatise on universal law: the very core of political symbiosis consists at all levels of the exchange of various benefits, again including advice: 'those who, on the basis of a communion of utility, of certain advantages and disadvantages, help and advice, form a common body are considered united voluntarily and by consent'.[26]

This conviction that a certain *consensus/placitus* is the basis of the political community is a characteristic trait of Althusius' thought. Even if people naturally seek life in a community, they become members of political bodies as the result of a conscious act of will and, in formal terms, of a contract. Incidentally, the formula *auxilio et consilio* is also worth noting, since it recalls the obligations of the vassal towards his or her lord in the feudal system, which on the other hand strengthens the impression that some aspects of Althusius' thought are rooted in the Middle Ages. In any case, both the *Politica methodice digesta* and the *Dicaeologica* mention counsel as one of the fundamental goods, the exchange of which establishes the political dimension of the community.

The practical application and a more complete exposition of this theoretical principle of a universal nature – advice as the subject of *communicatio* between the components of the body politic – is found only in the subsequent sections of the *Politica*, more precisely in Chapter 27 where Althusius discusses the counsellor of the chief magistrate of the Republic.[27] This chapter comes after a series dealing with the function of the magistrate himself, who exercises his power in the name of the people that he represents, safeguarding the principle whereby he is 'greater than singles, but smaller than the whole community' (*maior singulis, sed minor universis*). It is important to note that in this formula 'single' does not refer so much to individual persons as to the single *collegia* or *consociationes*.[28] This therefore means that only the *universitas*, the Republic as a whole, is legitimized to possess the *maiestas* which no particular person (individual or association) is entitled to. The magistrate is an official subject to the will (*placitum*) of the community, or eventually of its components. At the same time, apropos the topic *the adviser of the magistrate*, its development in Althusius' version is seemingly similar to that of Timpler. In both cases this question is part of the more general topic of *prudentia civilis*, understood here as a stable intellectual disposition which is the distinctive trait of the righteous, competent and efficacious magistrate. However, Althusius' presentation is quite different from that of Timpler. First, on account of the strong prescriptive emphasis, which effectively transforms it into a collection of advice and instructions addressed to magistrates performing their functions. Second, as a result of his marked Biblicism, since the overwhelming majority of his literary references are derived from the Scriptures, mostly the Old Testament. Finally, in his more explicit use of Renaissance literature about the art of government, the reason of state, the *arcana imperii* etc., with frequent citations from or references to writers such as Scipione Ammirato, Arnold Clapmar, Innocent Gentillet and Giovanni Botero. The classic questions of political theory in the post-Machiavelli period are exhaustively discussed. For example: the populace is a many-headed monster and the Prince must be well versed in the techniques for manipulating its emotions;[29] the mutability of the populace is the principal cause of instability in the state so that the Prince must know how to deceive it through dissimulation;[30] the Prince ought to be suspicious, even of his closest counsellors and ministers; the *aula* and the *aulici*, the court and its members – the circle closest to the magistrate – are of crucial importance in government, as they represent a sort of microcosm governed by its own laws and specific conventions.[31] The first concern of the potentate should be to protect the stability of the state, continually threatened from without and within. In this context, the counsellor is essentially a professional whom the magistrate consults for advice about stabilizing his power. In Chapter 27 this figure of the counsellor finally appears, sketched in a few, effective phrases. The advisers are 'trusted men, experts in human nature, who provide salutary suggestions and, like experts on storms at sea, help to keep hold of the helm, even though they have no authority, power or jurisdiction'.[32]

Although it is not the most original aspect – having already been discussed by the Spanish humanist Fadrique Furió Ceriol[33] and others – perhaps one of the most characteristic elements of Althusius' presentation of the political adviser of the Prince / Supreme Magistrate / Sovereign is the extension of the subject to include the more institutional forms of counsel. In other words, the local assemblies (regional, provincial, civic), the senates of the kingdoms and, at a higher level, the groups of the so-called 'ephors', the most important figures in the state who enjoyed a special legal status and a particular prestige (Chapter 18). It is in fact important to remember that in political Calvinism the role of the latter was not restricted to consultancy offered to the chief magistrate,[34] since they also possessed a much more substantial 'right of resistance' in the face of potential abuse of power by the magistrate. As a result, it appears that in Althusius' description the sphere of the activities and prerogatives of the counsellor is very broad and ramified. It extends from the traditional role of the court official – who whispers shrewd suggestions into the ear of the Prince – to the effective function of a check-and-balance type proper to the Greats of the realm. Indeed, the advisers are legally and morally legitimized to refuse to obey the *summus magistratus* (as examples of this position Althusius generally mentions kings, such as those of France, Belgium or Poland, or emperors, such as the German Emperor) when he becomes tyrannical, up to the point of even heading the revolt of the populace in case of necessity.[35] Thus they collegially represent the universality of the associated populace, and as a result their *maiestas* is superior to that of the supreme magistrate.[36] In the light of all this it seems clear that the counsellor, in a broad sense, is not just an expert, an instrument of the sovereign, but also possesses a constitutional rank, which becomes particularly important in the case of – so to speak – states of exception, such as wars, revolutions or major civil and religious reforms. At such times, Althusius clarifies, decisions must be taken by the magistrate with the consensus of the *universitas*, the body politic of the Republic in its entirety. In fact, the person holding the power to govern is nothing more than a delegate, an agent, who is not entitled to take complex or extraordinary initiatives without an explicit mandate.[37]

Therefore, the reflections of Althusius on the subject of the political counsellor faithfully reflect the main lines of his political-constitutional thought, comprising classical (Aristotle, Cicero), mediaeval and early modern inspirations of a religious, juridical and philosophical nature. The *consilium* is also a particular aspect of the more general category of *prudentia politica*, which Althusius describes using the examples of the wise king of Israel alongside the ancient (Seneca, Cicero) and modern (Lipsius) definitions of this virtue. However, beyond all this, it does not appear to differ substantially from the practical rationality founded on experience and aimed at the right decision and action described by Aristotle in the *Nicomachean Ethics*, *phronesis*: the virtue proper to the statesman.[38] Nevertheless, perhaps the reference to theoretical models and literary inspirations is less important for understanding Althusius' reflections on the counsellor and the magistrate than reference to the context of the Dutch Revolt (*bellum Belgicum*), and Spain's attack on the autonomy of the United Provinces, to the leader of which Althusius dedicated his work.[39] He was defending with his pen the value of a model of *consociatio*, of 'federal' political organization: the materialization of the political prudence envisaged by the politicians and philosophers of every era.

Keckermann

Keckermann wrote a massive treatise with the characteristic title *Systema disciplinae politicae*,[40] a *summa* of issues connected with politics. This work was essentially conceived for the students of the *Gymnasium Academicum* in Danzig and the material was arranged according to methodical rules of Ramist origin. It was officially inspired by the political philosophy of Aristotle, but actually comprised contemporary political issues as emerging in the works of famous writers of the time, such as Jean Bodin, Tolosanus, Lambert Daneau, John Case, Johannes Althusius, Otho Casmann, Justus Lipsius etc. The topics focused on the concepts of sovereignty and the legitimation of state power, the relation between political power and religious authority, that of the coexistence of different confessions within the same territory and, finally, on the development of the bureaucratic structure of the early modern state. As regards the elements of political philosophy present in this work of remarkable dimensions, it should be said that in tracing the process of formation of the political society described by Aristotle in Book I of the *Politics*, Keckermann explicitly distances himself from this when he states that the cities also emerged 'from fear' (*ex metu*),[41] taking his cue more from a species of anthropological pessimism of biblical origin, possibly filtered through Saint Augustine, than from the classical tradition.[42]

Like the works of Timpler and Althusius, Keckermann's *Systema* too responds to practical and didactic requirements. Consequently it cannot afford to leave out anything that might be relevant or useful for his students – mostly from the city of Gdansk itself and from Pomerania – approaching public life at the beginning of the seventeenth century. Naturally the figure of the political adviser has to be addressed here too, but to find it we have to wait until Chapter 5 of Book V.[43] But these pages, where the topic is presented in the same by now crystallized form as in the work of the other two writers, grasp our attention much less than other more interesting works in Keckermann's vast corpus. I am thinking in particular of a text written during the last years of his career when he devoted his remaining energy to practical philosophy.[44] This work, the *Apparatus practicus*,[45] is a long list of *loci communes*: the key themes dealt with in the canonical triad of practical disciplines (economics, ethics and politics). This type of thematic repository supplies the basic material which then has to be processed through the functions of the logical faculty. It is to logic that Keckermann attributes the art or ability of expounding a topic, discussing it 'dialectically'.[46] In the section on prudence, a large part of the *loci* concern its *pars consultrix*- providing counsels (as distinct from the *diiudicatrix*-assessing), understood as an 'intellectual' habit and divided in turn into the ability to give advice to others and to personally evaluate the advice received. Behind these distinctions stand the figures of the prince-magistrate and his adviser, both hopefully well trained in the art of logic taught at the gymnasium of Gdansk.[47]

Apart from these processes of classification, triggered by the dichotomies favoured in Ramist logic, to understand Keckermann's thinking about the counsellor I believe that one needs to look at a particular element of the definition: the adjective 'intellectual'. I also think that Keckermann had in mind that Aristotle had included *phrónêsis-prudentia* among the 'dianoetic dispositions',[48] that he had, so to speak, attempted to intellectualize *prudentia*, and he himself took up the same path continuing the operation in his own way. We shall not be straying far from the truth if we admit that here Keckermann uses the term 'intellectual' in the fairly narrow sense of 'logical', and if we understand this logic not so much as a technique of inferential procedures (syllogisms) as the art of invention and ordering: respectively, the capacity for the topological analysis of a given topic, and that of arranging what is found in an ordered manner. In a word, what was meant by 'logic' (or 'dialectic') in the late Renaissance, especially in the circles influenced by Ramus and his followers. This also means that in Keckermann the issue of the *consilium politicum* can be traced to the question: how does one teach the Prince or his counsellors the rules for forming sound opinions, where 'sound' primarily means irreprehensible in terms of their logical (in the sense just mentioned) construction? And, more precisely and in practice: when a problem emerges in the government of the Republic, how can one train the Prince and his men to clearly define the terms and elements of this problem, arrange them in an ordered sequence and then grasp the entire sequence at one glance?

To take a closer look at this point we now turn to several texts derived from Keckermann's academic entourage (colleagues and pupils) and published together with his own other works. More specifically, these are found in a posthumous volume containing academic disputes and similar materials,[49] also dealing with practical philosophy. The importance of the practice of public debate in the schools of the modern age goes without saying. It was institutionally important as a requirement for obtaining academic qualifications, but also in terms of intellectual history, since the formation of a *habitus disputandi* was considered possibly the chief result to be expected of academic education. In any case, even if they were frequently printed with the name of the candidate or student (known as *respondens*), these *theses disputatae* (*assertiones* or *sententiae* and also other names) generally represented the theoretical approaches of the professor-promoter, who could play the role of *praeses* in the public debate. This is certainly the case here and so we can consider these texts as expressing the point of view of Keckermann's school or of Keckermann himself.[50]

The topic we are dealing with appears in the specifically political section in the thirty-first dispute. This is followed by three 'discourses on counsel, the counsellor and consultation', written by Andrzej Rej (1584–1641, the grandson of the great Polish Reformed writer Mikołaj, as he himself notes),[51] preceded by a letter from Keckermann himself in which he solemnly states that 'in politics this topic [counsel and counsellor] has the status of a principle on which not only the entire discipline of politics depends, but also the reason [why it is taught and learnt], namely: to guarantee public safety'.[52] In his own introduction Rej in turn strives to justify the originality of his contribution to the literature on the argument. He claims it as a fact that, in terms of political literature, our period is superior to any that went before, even the ancient era, 'in both military and civilian sectors'.[53] Nevertheless, in all this immense production, and in general in the minds of his contemporaries 'there is more science than conscience'. Indeed, there is a failure to respect the principle endorsed in the *Nicomachean Ethics*, whereby for the *consilium* to be *bonum* (Aristotle's *euboulia*), it is not enough for it to have a good effect, that effect must also be brought about in the right manner and with the right means.[54] This is, evidently, a criticism of the presumed amorality of the contemporary literature on the reason of state, but it certainly does not reflect the originality of Keckermann's school. As I see it, this originality is to be sought in other passages, especially in the chapter on the *consilium* that precedes discussion *de consiliario et consultatione*, where the usual material, commented with abundant references to sixteenth-century literature, is in some way comprised within an Aristotelian framework.

Thus, *consilium* is defined as the deliberative aspect of *prudentia*, what Aristotle embraces with the verb *bouleuesthai*: the capacity to take decisions and carry them through.[55] Here what is truly essential is the formation of judgement (*iudicium*) in the phase preceding decision and action, and this is exactly where Rej believes he has made an original contribution, while obviously continuing and clarifying the teaching of his master Keckermann.[56] It is important – Rej continues – that someone has finally described these mental-logical processes that precede action, especially since the argument had hardly ever been addressed. The only other person to have written something about it was the Byzantine Emperor Leo VI (ninth to tenth centuries) in his treatise on military tactics, the book *De bellico apparatu*, published in a Latin version by the Cambridge professor of Greek John Cheke in 1554.[57] Rej explains that the *consilium* is fundamentally a conjecture, a wager on what should be done so that the action will be effective. This is why special logical instruments are required, such as can be specifically applied to future and singular events.[58] Nor is it a coincidence that Keckermann himself, in the second edition (1608) of his main work on logic, the *Gymnasium logicum*, added *praecepta* dealing precisely with how *consilia* should be constructed in adherence to the rules of logic.[59]

Therefore, according to Rej, it is patently clear that the politicians and their advisers are expected to have specific competence in specific sectors (military, legal, economic etc.) as well as a general knowledge of the problems of the state. Nevertheless, the universal processes and methods for issuing 'judgements' (that is, conjectures) are the domain of logic, i.e. the *artificium* that brings the natural gift of formulating conjectures to perfection.[60] It can hence be argued that Keckermann and his school concentrated on the universal rules of the silent mental discourse that precedes decision and action. The point is that this 'intellectual act' is directed at *futura contingentia*, hence something that is by its very nature undefined and ambivalent (*ambiguum*).[61] Individual and future events are unique and unrepeatable and cannot be treated as the particular cases of a universal rule known in advance. In order to eliminate, or at least minimalize, the unpredictability of such future events, Keckermann and his school envisage a logic focused on conjecture, substantially modelled on the topological analysis typical of Renaissance and neo-Ramist dialectics, of the kind already familiar from other of Keckermann's works. In formulating his counsel the adviser must take into consideration 'what precedes, what is connected with and what follows the particular circumstances of place and time'. In addition, 'the arguments derived from the causes, effects, properties and parts' must also be taken into account.[62] In other words, all the information about the consequences of a given decision that appears useful in order to avoid uncertainty (*ad tollendam ambiguitatem*).

In conclusion, an appraisal of these theories, setting them against the background of their time and the milieu in which they emerged and for which they were conceived, can start from an observation found later on in these *Discursi*, when Rej reflects on the requisite training of the counsellor and more specifically whether he ought to be familiar with eloquence and rhetoric.[63] Rej replies in the affirmative, while specifying that this is only useful when the counsellor is acting externally, for instance as an ambassador, whereas in general 'counsel is a purely mental construct, unrelated to emotions or language, proper to logic rather than rhetoric. Indeed, the best advice is formulated in a few, bare words, and is best constructed and expressed when devoid of verbal ornament and rhetorical figures.'[64]

Obviously these texts of the Keckermann school repeat the rich literature on the topic of *de consilio et consiliario*, while at the same time seeking to position it within an Aristotelian framework, developing in their own way the customary category of *prudentia* as a dianoetic virtue. The logical aspect is underscored, but without overlooking the moral content, the fact that it is directed towards the right end (otherwise it would be *calliditas*, cunning or even the art of deception). However, when – in the midst of all these noble elements of Aristotelian derivation – one attempts to define the functional meaning of these theoretical contributions of Keckermann and his school, and hence their historical specificity, what in the end appears decisive is the focus on logic. It seems to me that what we are looking at here is nothing more than the theoretical systemization of a technique for elaborating political advice that is easy to learn and apply because it is based on simple topical schema. If one were then to ask whom it was aimed at, the first figure that comes to mind is an official working in the *aulae* of the centres of state power in the early modern age: a specialist in administration, a civil servant in the service of the kings and local territorial princes of Central Europe in the early seventeenth century. An *artificium* of this type for the drafting of clear, well-ordered opinions, tending to the brief and probably better in writing, could undoubtedly be useful to a professional figure of such a kind. It is certainly a figure engaged in territorial bureaucracy, dealing more with management of the current affairs of the administration than with the collaborative devising of political strategies; a public official, not lacking a degree of classical culture and abreast of the literature of the time, all, however, apprehended in a few years of intense scholastic training that is very far removed from high-level humanist and philological education; a figure unquestionably lacking the Promethean aura of the political counsellor rendered familiar by the post-Machiavellian literature on the reason of state, with all his intellectual sophistication and moral ambiguity.

Reason of state and political Aristotelianism: Hermann Conring and the troublesome legacy of the *Politics*

The term 'political Aristotelianism' has been used primarily by Italian and German scholars to indicate a renewed interest in Aristotle's political thought. This revival took place not so much – or not only – within the general movement for the retrieval of the ancient tradition characteristic of the Renaissance, but more particularly in Germany between the end of the sixteenth century and the first half of the seventeenth.[65] More precisely, it occurred within the context of a new type of reflection on politics essentially connected with the appearance of premodern forms of state and the contemporary decline of the universalistic forms that characterized previous periods.

In general, the category of 'Aristotelianism' referring to political thought at the time of the literature on the reason of state needs to be disambiguated. It has in fact been used as a sort of umbrella term for the most diverse phenomena, including for instance Iberian neo-scholasticism, the mature fruit of which was the doctrine of international law of the School of Salamanca, and the vast and sophisticated work of philologists (largely Italian and Flemish) on the text of the *Politics*, only apparently unyoked from the current debate on political theory. Different again, within the context of Central Europe in the period of confessionalization, was the flourishing of a particular type of 'Aristotelianism' in political theory, linked to the specific question of the legitimacy of the nascent local territorial powers. Therefore we have to steer clear of the notion that the Aristotelianism of the time was an ideological-doctrinal whole of closed and stable confines that could be seen as a school or a clearly defined philosophical stance opposed to others. This notion – if indeed it ever was formulated and approved – has been justly belied by the research of the last decades. The politics and the practical philosophy harking back to Aristotle has instead been assigned the status of a paradigm (Manfred Riedel) or a language (Quentin Skinner, John Pocock), or a code or a community of discourse (Merio Scattola). In other words, in even more abstract terms, it is an open structure, a space that does not strictly determine contents and conclusions, but accommodates them and even makes them possible. Possibly even better, in my opinion, is a characterization not only aimed at the linguistic-methodical aspects, but one that sees these in connection with precise fundamental philosophical stances, pretty much shared by different thinkers and different generations of thinkers. Political Aristotelianism would therefore be 'a set of specific *loci* and thematic, conceptual and "linguistic" habits, defined on the one hand by a series of principles, implicit and explicit premises of a more general theoretical order, and on the other by a large quantity of doctrinal contents or particular argumentative *loci*'.[66] As a topical repertory it comprises, for instance, reflections on issues such as: the subjects of politics; the function of different genres of cognition (*techne, episteme, theoria, prudentia*) in politics; the particular role of 'phronetic' understanding in public action; man's political nature; slavery and barbarism; economy and chrematistics; citizenship and education; the typology of constitutions, their conservation and subversion-revolution; civic functions within the *polis* and many others. As a theoretical mindset it is 'ultimately governed by its own profound internal logic – and naturally by the use of particular forms of rational exposition – bound by an intimate solidarity albeit without excluding contradictions and aporias', and 'responding to specific problems primarily on the basis of premises or values'.[67] And these are simply the theoretical principles derived from anthropology (the political nature of the human being, the correspondence between reason and virtue in the 'good life'); from ethics (the hierarchical and harmonious order of ends, the value of the mean); from ontology-metaphysics (the repose attained at the end of the process, understood as perfection); from epistemology (correspondence between ontological ambits and knowledge) and so on.[68] In sum, as authoritatively argued, if there is a system in Aristotle it is only a system of 'problems' held together by a conceptual structure largely transversal to the individual ambits of research. Such a system is always susceptible to new uses, or partial uses; in other words, it can be subject to a degree of tension without this causing it to lose its identity.[69]

Applying these concepts specifically to the political Aristotelianism of the late Renaissance, we could say that this shouldn't be identified with particular solutions of political theory or defined forms of constitution, although obviously attempts are made to turn Aristotle into a champion of one or other regime. Understood in these terms, the vitality of the notion of 'political Aristotelianism' for modern political philosophy is possibly confirmed by an overview of the seventeenth-century *Schulphilosophie*. From this perspective we now attempt to analyse the case of one of its most eminent exponents, Hermann Conring (1602–81), a professor and a scientist renowned for his broad scientific interests in medicine, and to an even greater degree in the fields of law, history and politics.

Prudentia civilis as a cognitive habitus for the reason of state

In a 1986 article Horst Dreitzel addressed the question of continuity and discontinuity between Hermann Conring's political philosophy and Renaissance political Aristotelianism – and through this, classical political Aristotelianism – illustrating the complexity of a dynamic that cannot be reduced to overly simple formulas.[70] Nevertheless, if one wished to identify a central theme in this complexity, I would say that, especially after Conring's definitive return to Helmstedt in 1632 following his studies in Leiden, the objective of elaborating a political science, understood as the discourse that derives rules of conduct and operational guidelines for governors from universal theoretical principles, emerges ever more clearly. The context and benchmarks of this endeavour were the literature on the *arcana imperii* or on the reason of state,[71] the neo-Stoicism of Lipsius, Bodin's theories on sovereignty, the proto-constitutionalism deriving from monarchomach literature, and the reflections of Althusius and Arnisaeus on the constitution of 'civil society'. Last but not least, the political situation of the *Reich* during the Thirty Years' War led numerous political thinkers to seek the foundations of legitimacy of the state in the particular history of German law. All this could be summed up by saying that Conring was interested in a theory of sovereignty that legitimized the early modern form of political power, seeking to elaborate within this context collections of precepts for statesmen that taught the techniques for the formation and conservation of the state. At the same time, equally clear is Conring's effort to remain true to Aristotelian practical philosophy, which attributed to political theory the task of guiding those in power to pursue the happiness of civil society, as can be inferred from several of Conring's pronouncements, such as that expressed in a letter he wrote to Caspar Schoppe, one of the theorists of the reason of state: 'The conservation of the state is not the sole end at which a politician aims, but also the happiness of civil society, which is to be attained through the practice of virtue and a sufficient availability of other goods.'[72] Consequently, the concept of *prudentia* became central, since it could apparently anchor two aspects of political science that Conring was particularly keen on. The pragmatic and public/civil aspect, since – in an academy bound up with a territorial principality that was part of the Germanic Empire – the objectives of political education included preparing the future managers of the civil, military and religious administration, who required a solid education in how to conduct the *respublica* in war and in peace. The concept of *prudentia civilis* understood in this manner is well represented by the title of one of Conring's most theoretically detailed works as a politician: the *De civili prudentia liber unus quo prudentiae politicae, cum universalis philosophicae, tum singularis pragmaticae, omnis propaedia acroamatice traditur*.[73] Here it is made clear that such prudence comes from the combination of a theoretical (philosophical) part with a pragmatic part that substantially consists of the illustration of the various administrative organs and the different phases in the life of the state. The methodological slant of the treatise is indicated by the terms *propaedia* and *acroamatice*. We shall return later to the second of these, while the first indicates that the proposed exposé is not about political science as such – namely, directed at praxis – but rather about its underlying methodological (philosophical) principles: the limitations and possibilities of a knowledge of political subjects that responds to scientific criteria. In this way Conring believed he could compare himself to Socrates, Plato and Aristotle, in so far as they managed to redeem civil prudence from the degeneration wrought by the Sophists.[74] And these very characteristics refer back to the second aspect of *prudentia*, as understood by Conring: the fact that it represented a universal knowledge not limited by space and time. This distinguishes it from the particular legislative systems that are the subject of law, which is merely a snapshot of historical situations and particular traditions.[75]

That said, perhaps we can amend the opinion of Gerhard Oestreich who, in his influential contribution to the history of the formation of modern political theory, maintains that the category of *prudentia civilis* in its early-seventeenth-century sense, that is in the incubation period of the absolutisms, is a concept propagandized above all by Lipsius' *Politica*.[76] It seems to me, instead, that it is not necessary to indicate neo-Stoicism exclusively as its origin or as the context in which it spread, since it is an ideologically or philosophically transversal term[77] and a Peripatetic provenance could equally well be argued. Suffice it to think of the tendency to reduce Aristotelian practical philosophy to prudence so deeply rooted in the history of Aristotelianism, especially scholastic, late mediaeval, Renaissance and, above all, Reformed. Indeed, it was commonly accepted that practical philosophy was nothing more than the teaching of the three 'prudences' – individual, familial and civil – mirrored respectively in the *Nicomachean Ethics*, the *Economics* and the *Politics*.

In any case, the Aristotelian derivation of this notion, the transformation of the Aristotelian *phrónêsis* into *prudentia* and the promotion of the latter to the principal figure of ethical-political investigations were all points proposed by Conring in a *Disputatio de civili prudentia* of 1639, in the early years after his return to Helmstedt from Holland.[78] Here we read that, as Aristotle taught in Book VI of the 'ethical books', prudence is the habit of mind that concerns what is good and bad for humankind, while civil prudence is what teaches what is beneficial or detrimental to civil society in particular. Consequently, the experts in civil prudence (*civilis prudentiae periti*) are not only those who know what is useful to civil society, but also those operating for its good, either directly within it or by telling others what they ought to do; this is the *architectonic* function of those who know not one but all types of political society, and hence are potentially *capable of governing* all of them.[79] The remaining forty-four theses of this dissertation contain all the principal motifs also found in the text that will be dealt with in greater detail – Conring's introduction to the *Politics* – so that it is not necessary to go into them here.

However I would like to focus attention on one point: the clarification of the acroamatic character of Aristotle's books of *Politics* in the context of the definition of the method proper to *prudentia civilis* as political science.[80] The continuous recurrence of this theory in the academic writings connected with Conring's political teaching in the decades around the middle of the seventeenth century is significant. To illustrate this fact one can take another *disputatio*, again 'on the best writers on civil prudence', defended twenty years after the first by one of his pupils, Georg Johann Völger, who accurately expounds the key points and the scope of the issue. The discussion and publication date to 1659, in other words a considerable time after most of Conring's work on the *Politics*.[81] This pupil appeared to be particularly interested in the type and quality of the knowledge that can be supplied by civil prudence, not simply as a scholastic discipline, but as a *habitus* rooted in the statesman by effect of the discipline itself. This habitus can be broken down into the science of universals and the experience of details, and hence into the ability to apply universal laws to the detail, which in this case consists of a decision to be taken or an action to be performed. The specific characterization of civil prudence is thus derived from the general characterization of the *phrónêsis* of the *Nicomachean Ethics*, VI, 7, which in substance means that before acting the politician must elaborate a 'practical syllogism'.[82] The clarification of the meaning of the term 'pragmatic', which was also used by Conring, is of great interest. It is in fact opposed to a merely logical type of knowledge, related to opinions about things rather than the things themselves (the *prágmata*). The pragmatic statesman must therefore possess a 'scientific' (*epistêmonikê*) and not just 'opinionative' (*doxastikê*) knowledge, which means proceeding in accordance with a cognitive method of an analytic type, capable of ascending to firm principles by induction and subsequently of generating fully demonstrative syllogisms from these principles. The intellectual *habitus* typical of the politician – which has numerous analogies with that of the physician – therefore consists of equipping oneself with a solid inductive base through the study of history, of checking the correctness of the general conclusions derived from this induction and of the correctness of the syllogisms which, as we have seen elsewhere, have a practical outcome: namely, an action.[83] It would be interesting to compare this procedure with the famous *regressus* conceived and taught by the Padua school, even though here the explicit reference is – as well as to Aristotle in person ('just as Nature has experimented the strength of human genius in Aristotle alone, so Aristotle has done in his analytical work alone'[84]) – to one of the less-known sixteenth-century theorists of scientific demonstration. This was the Turin physician Bartolomeo Viotti, possibly selected by Völger both for his familiarity with the question of demonstration in medicine and for his polemic with the 'dialecticians' such as Ramus.[85] These observations serve primarily as an introduction to a species of annotated bibliography of the political writers of all times, furnishing a criterion of reading and appraisal of the same. This is indeed sufficient for the author to distinguish the 'acroamatic' writers and texts (analytic, scientific, serious etc.) from the 'exoteric' (dialectic, educational, popular etc.)[86] and, for example, to disqualify the writings of Plato as merely 'dialogistic': in other words, only dialectical and not strictly methodical. It also allows him to claim the utility of reading the works of Cicero, but only on account of his enormous political experience and vast culture, while they leave a great deal to be desired in terms of method. Indeed, his works rarely reach the level required of political science/prudence since they stop at a 'dialectical-rhetorical' stage, corresponding to the Aristotelian doctrine of the *Topics*.[87]

In this way, in Conring's school the postulate of the suitability of politics – understood both as a scholastic discipline and as an intellectual-practical habitus – for a recognized scientific canon was resolved by taking up several qualifying aspects of the epistemology of Renaissance Aristotelianism. What is more specifically important here is, on one side, the exposition of an analytical method, in actual fact equivalent to a demonstrative method of an empirical deductive type that harked back to the Italian sixteenth-century tradition of reflection on the methodological thought of Aristotle and Galen. On the other side we come up against the reinterpretation of a theme that cropped up at the time of the new reappropriation of Aristotle's texts in the Renaissance: that of the distinction between scientific moment and – as it were – 'popular' moment in the Stagirite's own teaching. From a formal point of view, therefore, in the middle of the seventeenth century a neo-Aristotelian scientific method applied to politics seemed entirely plausible; in other words, the possibility of creating a new science of politics with civil prudence as its nucleus. The relation of this late-Renaissance canon with the principle of the practical science theorized by Aristotle himself in the first chapters of the *Nicomachean Ethics* is obviously debatable. Here, in fact, the reflection on praxis is assigned a 'typological' method,[88] leaving the stricter demonstration outlined in the *Posterior Analytics* to mathematics. It should also be recalled that, for Aristotle, practical philosophy is always a form of 'theory' of scientific knowledge, and is therefore in a certain sense incommensurable with Conring's pragmatics, essentially conceived to serve action. In any case, these texts from the school of Conring appear to illustrate the need to extend logical instruments originally conceived for the natural sciences to the practical sciences too, and hence to politics, even in its operational dimension.

The limits of Aristotle's *Politics*

Aristotelianism therefore sought to update its method to meet a need for scientific rigour in step with the times. It apparently managed to do so with a certain success and without complexes vis-à-vis the doctrines of natural law and absolutism, which claimed the need for a break with the theoretical and epistemological foundations of political doctrine. The difficulty of pursuing a neo-Aristotelian approach emerged instead when the attempt was made to fill a new subject such as civil prudence with the contents offered by Aristotle in the surviving texts. This subject proved to be exorbitant for a writer whose horizon certainly did not take in the modern state and its problems. The classicism of Conring and his circle was therefore sorely tested, with the results described here.

Conring's university career took place almost exclusively at the University of Helmstedt, which had experienced all the same challenges as similar universities in Central Europe at the time, under strong pressure to adopt the reforms in teaching proposed initially by Petrus Ramus and later by ranks of his followers. As regards Helmstedt, it should be remembered that the academic authorities had tolerated teaching in the Ramist manner only in private form, and that in 1624 the ban became total, so that it is legitimate to number it among the Aristotelian universities. As we have seen in a previous chapter, the action of figures such as Cornelius Martini (1568–1621) and Johannes Caselius (1533–1613) was decisive in the imposition of this approach. One might add that the opposition to Ramus seems more pronounced in Martini, whereas Caselius was one of the leading exponents of the European *Respublica litteraria* around the turn of the century. He had an important friendship with the leading Florentine humanist and philologist Pietro Vettori (a writer Conring held in the highest esteem), from whom he derived the philological method of reading Aristotle.

Following Hotson, I would say that, in general, the conflict – between Aristotelians and Ramists, between Ramists and anti-Ramists – can be brought back to the opposition between two methods of teaching. One was based on the philological reading of the classical texts, by its nature elitist in view of the amount of time and elevated skills required. The other was based on the systematization of the disciplines, on textbook summaries that could furnish a ready-to-use product for the extended audience of students and professors that had emerged in the numerous schools and academies of Central Europe following the historic processes set in motion by the Reformation.[89] Obviously, this perspective focused on academic training and on philology does not exclude taking other, more ideological, aspects of the conflict into account. In effect, the strong resistance to Ramism in Reformed academic centres of the late sixteenth century was due to the fact that it was perceived as a serious threat to the dominant Melanchthonian-Aristotelian synthesis or, more precisely, as a risky attempt to replace Melanchthon as the Pole Star in the field of education. However this may be, it can never be sufficiently stressed that, after Ramus, things would never be the same again. Even those who were not willing to renounce Aristotle – and they were many, especially in the more important centres such as Heidelberg, Wittenberg, Leipzig and Gdansk – nevertheless found themselves addressing the issue of rendering study of his works more rapid and systematic, calling into question the principle of direct reading. This was the path taken up by staunch Aristotelians such as Keckermann in Gdansk, a model that was followed by many and appeared to provide a good example of equilibrium in the essential tension between innovation and conservation. But it was far from being the only path followed. Aristotle's texts, which had been made more readily available by humanist philology, still exerted a charm that no conversion into systematic form could suppress or elude. This general problem encountered specific complications in relation to politics and political theory.

The young Conring already had to address these complications, as indeed did all the university teachers in Central Europe where, as it turned out, an Aristotelianism reworked by factoring in Ramist principles became the most frequently adopted solution. The most recent reconstructions of Conring's life and academic career – which substantially coincide – emphasize the fact that, at least at the outset, the pro-Aristotle option was due more to the pressure exerted by the dominant ideologies of the Academia Julia than to a stout personal conviction. The experience of the *libertas philosophandi* during his time at the University of Leiden in the second half of the 1620s had been marked by the cosmopolitanism of the environment and contacts with intellectuals of the calibre of Hugo Grotius and Gerardus Vossius. This contrasted with the provincialism of Lower Saxony under the Dukes of Brunswick and with the Melanchthon-Peripatetic orthodoxy observed at the University of Helmstedt.[90] Nevertheless, it is significant that from the very first programmatic documents of his activity, the two *orationes* 'in praise of Aristotle', Conring specifies the meaning and the limits of his adherence to the Stagirite's philosophy. These speeches were published in 1633, but had been declaimed, one on 20 September 1632 and the other the following year.[91] Apparently, the printed text differs from the delivered speech and is the result of negotiations between Conring and his mentors at Helmstedt, the theologians Georg Calixtus (1586–1656) and Konrad Horneius (1590–1649), who urged him to tone it down.[92] In effect, the published work expresses a balanced position in which the principle of authority is harmonized with that of the necessary freedom and autonomy in the quest for the truth. Conring indeed states that 'it is not appropriate for those seeking knowledge to swear by the words of Aristotle, or that in demonstrating their own scientific competence they restrict themselves to showing that they understand his thought'. This is nothing more than a superstition, which Aristotle himself would stigmatize, since the 'adept (*mystes*) of the Lyceum is not he who repeats the precepts of the master by heart, but he who makes them his own, honing his own judgement: and we all know how much we can gather using our own judgement!' Consequently Aristotle should be considered not as a 'dictator', but as a 'prince', he who, in expounding a problem, offers the starting point. Instead, what happens is that people pay lip service to him but then actually turn to other masters, or he is placed on a par with other thinkers without due consideration for his authority.[93]

In this statement Conring conciliates pre-enlightenment accents ('using one's own head') with a partially positive evaluation of the principle of authority in so far as its function is, so to speak, more regulative than constitutive. Aristotle defines the issue and the point from which its discussion should start, allowing total freedom in its ulterior development and results. Given these limits or conditions, there is no reason to reject Aristotle's authority, after which the *oratio altera* lines up the arguments that could still justify the adoption of Aristotle in the universities in the third decade of the seventeenth century.

Among these, the emphasis on the modesty of Aristotelian 'theology' seems to me particularly important. This should not be ascribed – Conring insists – to a speculative weakness on the part of Aristotle, but rather to his wisdom in having recognized the limits of philosophical reason and refusing to venture into treacherous mystical-religious speculations. Here Platonists and Neoplatonists, both ancient and modern, are attacked not only for having failed to adhere to these criteria of wisdom but for having tended openly and dangerously towards superstition. What is even more important, however, is that Aristotle has made a decisive input to the other part of metaphysics, what we might call 'ontological', concerning the concepts of substance, act, form etc., while all the mediaeval scholastics have done is to complicate his clear and simple doctrine. What seems to be evident here is Conring's intention to limit rational theology to those aspects that can be based on a purely ontological doctrine of being, in line with an approach that had already been consolidated at Helmstedt at the time of Cornelius Martini.[94] According to Conring, this *deminutio* of metaphysics in general paves the way to acknowledgement of a certain primacy of practical philosophy. This is indeed Aristotle's greatest glory, since in this field he outclassed everything produced by the other ancients, especially Plato, in terms of order and completeness of exposition. However, Conring's most salient characteristic is perhaps his opinion of the moderns, and here he addresses the 'jurists' first and foremost. In the *oratio altera*, Conring argues with them again on the very subject of *prudentia civilis*, an expression which they have usurped for their discipline. Their Coryphaeus is Bodin, who would like to relegate Aristotle *ad umbram et otium* ('to the shade of retirement'), would like to reduce practical philosophy to an erudite – ergo useless – pastime, at the same time making politics into a province of law. Conring's rejoinder rests on two arguments: (1) law is limited by the fact that it deals with the contingent and the local, while civil prudence is a universal discourse and hence more rigorous. Moreover, unlike law, which offers only a description of actual situations, prudence is a guide for maintaining or restoring the health of the republic, obviously on the medical model: just as the physician does not restrict himself to diagnosis but must indicate the remedies that lead to health, in the same way, mere knowledge of the laws in force says nothing about how just or opportune they are.[95] (2) Philip of Macedonia, his son Alexander and the latter's generals, and even his mother – all people whose exercise of power was their life, and hence not philosophers or intellectuals – withdrew 'to the shade' to study this prudence. The most notorious case is naturally that of Alexander the Great, who was hungrier for power than for food, but who did not disdain listening to his master philosopher. In short, while Machiavelli (*Hetruscus ille*) had substantially simply copied Aristotle while pretending not to (*clanculum describere*), but at the same time without denigrating him, Bodin's stance was due purely to envy (*aerugo*) of the Stagirite.[96]

Already this praise of Aristotle's *civilis prudentia* or *doctrine* includes a mention of the unfortunate loss, not only of the Stagirite's books *de regno, de coloniis, de legibus* which he had written for Alexander, but above all of part of the *Politics* itself: in effect, the main treatise (... *if only were undamaged those political books which survived! ... integra essent illa quae supersunt Politica volumina!*). And the conclusion too touches on a topic found in the Introduction to the *Politics*: the lack of interest of generations of writers and philosophers that came after Aristotle in the most 'architectonic' of practical sciences. As we shall see, the texts themselves, the eight books of the *Politics*, paid the price of this oversight. In sum, considering the rarity of expositions or comments on this treatise, and considering its superiority to everything written by the generations that came after Aristotle, the implicit conclusion is that the reading of the *Politics* must be undertaken again, since it is still crucial in the seventeenth-century academies.

Finally, a last point in this *oratio* needs to be remembered. A long explanation is devoted to the customary question of the difference between Aristotle's acroamatic and exoteric teaching. However, here the epistemological aspect is less important since the discourse tends instead to come up against the 'Machiavellian' problems of the secrecy or publicity of political knowledge and of the relation between politics and religion. Here Conring begins by praising Aristotle, who has wisely selected the targets of his teaching, aligning the teaching with the ability of the learners. He then comes to the point when he asks himself about Aristotle's parsimony in matters of theology. In actual fact, Aristotle was well aware both of the need for a religious sanction of the rules of civil coexistence, and that an overly impertinent investigation of the divine mysteries by the philosophers could erode trust in religion itself. The wisdom of Aristotle and the Peripatetics therefore consisted of not rendering their opinions regarding the gods accessible to the entire public, unlike the atheists and Epicureans who failed to show such responsibility, making their misbelief public and thus undermining the bases of civil coexistence.[97] Here we are dealing with an Aristotle who was, in his own way, Machiavellian, which is not so surprising after all. At the end of the sixteenth century the fact that the Stagirite and the Florentine secretary had a lot in common, or rather that the latter had taken a great deal from the former, was almost a truism, and was an opinion that Conring read primarily in Daniel Heinsius. The difference between Aristotle and the 'Etruscan' was rather that the latter did not hesitate to expound in public what ought instead to have been confined to a circle of competent listeners. In short, Conring rejects the so-called *interpretatio obliqua* of Machiavelli, the theory that the purpose of *The Prince* was to neutralize tyrannical governments by making known their mechanisms of action, while in a certain sense he reproposes it for Aristotle, conferring a particular meaning on it. Aristotle indeed revealed the occult and unjust mechanisms of tyrannical power, but did so for the benefit of a tiny intellectual and moral oligarchy which alone was capable of making good use of such knowledge. Conring addressed this question in greater depth in the later treatises on civil prudence of the 1660s, enriching it with observations on the relation between the conquest and management of power and moral virtue, but – in my opinion – without venturing beyond the path mapped out here. In a word, for him *civilis prudentia* is the same as the acroamatic political science of Aristotle, but in the wrong hands it can become mere shrewdness (*calliditas*), serving rulers without moral scruples or simply not being understood at all. Most importantly, he who merely exerts power *veluti si Deus non daretur* cannot be defined as a politician, as certain hasty interpreters of Machiavelli would have it.

In sum, the *oratio altera* sets forth some of the arguments that could be produced in the third decade of the seventeenth century to justify the presence – and even a certain dominance, albeit no longer absolute – of Aristotle in academic teaching. It does so by taking up topics characteristic of the Renaissance tradition, but also of the scholastic, derived from Melanchthon and opposed to Ramus. However, as we shall soon see, there was a weak point in this programme.

Conring's edition and interpretation

Now, finally, we come to Conring's edition of Aristotle's *Politics*.[98] This was published in 1656, although an initial version had already been prepared about twenty years earlier, not long after the *orationes*. Unlike the first edition, that of 1656 also included the Greek text, substantially a reproduction of that of Heinsius (based on that of Sylburgius, in turn based on that of Vettori). Another novelty was the introduction of paragraphs for the visual identification of the sentences containing a logically complete thought, *ad maiorem facilitatem lectoris*. The Latin translation alongside the Greek was that of Vettori, replacing Giffen's translation in the first edition, while the new introduction was about twice as long as the previous one, substantially acting as a commentary. Other additions included a list of *emendationes* of the Greek text, a list of chapter titles and rows of asterisks (161 according to Völger) where Conring felt there were lacunae in the Greek text (so that the reader would not waste time racking his brains, but simply move on).[99]

Certain programmatic clues emerge right from the dedication to Johann Philipp von Schönborn, Archbishop-Elector of Mainz. First, Conring asks himself, why Aristotle's political books again? The fact is that antiquity has produced nothing comparable to this work, and neither the mediaevals nor the moderns have penned any work of similar standing. As Conring sees it, Aristotle's superiority is due (1) to the 'ability to teach and provide demonstrations' (*docendi et demonstrandi peritia*), namely, the order of the exposition and the rigour of the conclusions; and (2) to the vast empirical basis (*notitia historica*) on which Aristotle conducted his reflections (158 constitutions of cities, according to Laertius, others attribute to him up to 255), as a result of the extreme variety of political regimes in Greece at the time, greater than the present, dominated largely by mixed regimes.[100] On the grounds of the epistemological principles outlined earlier, this empirical base is essential for the generalizations obtained *via demonstrationis* to be epistemically interesting.[101]

Conring states that the *Politics* was conceived on a tripartite model, which at the same time constitutes the whole body of the doctrine of civic matters (*corpus integrum* of *doctrina civilium rerum*), i.e. of civil prudence as science. This model consists of the following points in this order: (1) 'some common elements' (*communia quaedam*); (2) 'all the institutions and laws of the best Republic' (*omnia instituta ac leges optimae reipublicae*); and (3) 'anything that could corrupt or preserve any of the other Republics' (*quaecumque idonea sunt corrumpere sive conservare quamvis ceterarum rerumpublicarum*).[102] This – Conring continues – is the programme Aristotle effectively implemented in the *Politics* but, unfortunately, the text that we have today is seriously mutilated and corrupted by the ravages of time, which have deprived us of four books of the *de optima republica* section, not to speak of other gaps and movements of passages within the original text.[103] Nevertheless, despite these deficiencies, Conring insists that, even today, the learning of civil prudence has to be based on an understanding of Aristotle's treatise.

In the preface addressed to the 'benevolent reader', Conring expresses his appreciation of those who, for over a century, have devoted themselves to editing, translating, paraphrasing, glossing and commenting on the text of the *Politics* (starting with Sepúlveda, then Giffen, Vettori, Montecatini, Heinsius, Zwinger, Gesner etc.). The point is that the damage suffered by the text has been generally undervalued. The 1656 edition is the culmination of a more than twenty-year-long attempt to establish the entity of this damage and to repair it. Conring furnishes it with a long Introduction, put after the text of *Politics* and compiled in the manner of the Neoplatonic commentaries on Aristotle of the Imperial Age, initially addressing various canonical questions about the authenticity of the work, its place within the system, purpose etc.[104] Here I will not follow Conring in detail as he offers an interesting overview of the history of the *Politics*, especially over the last 150 years when, with the rebirth of *litterae*, the lacunae inherited from the Arab and Christian Middle Ages were resolved, producing Latin versions, commentaries and other forms of reading and interpretation of Aristotle's *Politics*, not to mention the availability of the Greek text.[105]

The fundamental issues are the same as those addressed by Conring in the writings discussed earlier, dealt with in greater detail here. The first is that of the serious mutilation suffered by Aristotle's text, of which only eight books out of twelve have survived, no less than four of the six devoted to *de optima republica* having been lost. Conring makes comparison with the famous list of Aristotle's works contained in the *Vitae philosophorum* by Diogenes Laertius. Here we read of a *politikê akróasis* (course of political lessons) in eight books, which obviously clashes with Conring's theory. The proposed solution is to read *physikê* in place of *politikê*, all the more so since a *Physics* in eight books has in effect come down to us. However, the list also contains *Politika* (political matters) followed by α β, which in Greek indicates the number 2. But since the tradition contains no trace of a *Politics* in just two books, for Conring it is quite simple and straightforward to adopt the theory of Heinsius, who had suggested placing an *iota* before the *beta*, giving ιβ and hence twelve, *quod erat demonstrandum!*[106] Whether such conjectures have grounds or not, what is more important is that Conring rejects Heinsius' other conclusion: that these twelve books on 'political matters' are of a non-acroamatic and hence exoteric character.[107]

Retracing the lengthy debate of the last century about the meaning of Aulus Gellius' report on Aristotle's teaching in the Lyceum, and having correctly divided it into two phases, the Italian discussion (Sepúlveda, Ferrari, Vettori and Sigonio) and its resumption in Altdorf (Scherb, Piccart and Goldast),[108] Conring in the end brings it down to the question of the character of the *Politics*. Furthermore, considering what has been said in the previous pages, I feel it is essential to clarify the reasons for the explanation of Heinsius that Conring rejected. The Dutch humanist considers the *Politics* an exoteric text so that he can then hypothesize the existence of another secret work on the *arcana imperii* – in practice on the iniquity required by the statesman to conquer and conserve power – that Aristotle transmitted in private to Alexander and Philip. According to this hypothesis, these same contents were then included by Aristotle in his *Politics* but in an ambiguous and concealed manner, precisely because, as this book was a publication, it would not otherwise have been possible to spread such disquieting teaching in any other way. In short, Heinsius' interpretation produces a Machiavellian Aristotle, triggering the reaction of Conring who argues that, although it is true that in Books IV to VI of the *Politics* Aristotle in practice anticipates the entire Machiavellian doctrine on the conquest and maintenance of power, this does not mean that their intentions were the same. On the contrary: 'This most wily master of perversity may well have copied all his teachings from Aristotle, artfully concealing the plagiarism, but with one difference: Machiavelli unscrupulously and absolutely unwisely recommends them to all statesmen, whereas Aristotle, much more correctly and sagely, wrote that they are suited only to dictators and tyrants.'[109] This is something like the *interpretatio obliqua* again, the benefit being attributed to the Stagirite and denied to the Florentine. Indeed, Aristotle described the arcane mechanisms of tyrannical power, clearly not to approve them but to unveil them, whereas Machiavelli intended them to be applied, as normal, to all types of regime, losing the distinction between good and degenerate forms of constitution.

Once the acroamatic character of the *Politics* has been claimed, it leads to precise methodological consequences: the application to practical matters of the principles expounded by Aristotle in the *Analytics*. Politics adopts a form of demonstration that starts from 'proper' (not common, as in the case of dialectical reasoning) and 'necessary' principles, such as human nature (an allusion to the definition of the human being as a political animal) and the existence of civil society. Conring is convinced that he can in some way get round Aristotle's advice in the first book of the *Nicomachean Ethics* not to expect the precision of mathematics in practical matters. To do so he resorts to these postulates – spread in Germany by Altdorf Aristotelianism – although here he prefers to recall the Neoplatonic commentators Simplicius and Philoponus as forerunners.[110] In these passages Conring actually appears to focus more on the question of the 'best listener or reader' (*optimus auditor* or *lector*) of the *Politics* than on the demonstrative character of political discourse. By revisiting a question topically addressed by Renaissance commentators, he wonders how to get round Aristotle's advice in the first book of *Nichomachean Ethics*, where he does not recommend the study of practical philosophy to anyone who has little life experience. Indeed he concludes that, *Politics* being an acroamatic matter, it is directed at a selected audience of students in possession of a broad base of empirical knowledge acquired, if not by direct experience, at least through the study of history.[111]

What has been noted about Conring so far places him substantially in continuity with the Renaissance and late Renaissance tradition of political Aristotelianism. Naturally, on condition that such Aristotelianism is seen as a political doctrine inserted within the framework of practical philosophy and, hence, related more to the principles of a teleological (eudaimonistic) ethics than to the science of law, either natural or positive. The obvious model for such discourse was Aristotle's *Politics*, to be read along with the *Nicomachean Ethics*. But in what follows some cracks appear to emerge. As mentioned earlier, the first element of the tripartite breakdown of the *Politics* in expounding the discipline of *prudentia civilis* referred vaguely to *communia quaedam*. Returning to this issue, Conring now directly addresses the significance of the first book of the *Politics* – where presumably these *communia* are presented – in relation to the rest: 'Moreover, what does this discourse have to do with the politician if there is nothing in it concerning the res publica?'[112] Clearly such a question is based on the assumption that Aristotle saw the key theme of his treatise as the *respublica*, or more specifically its various forms: essentially, the constitutional structures and political regimes. But if this is the real subject of the *Politics*, then the first book is no more than a kind of prelude relating to the *materia civitatis*, the forms of organization preceding the political form, the *societas civilis*. This *materia* is provided by the families and villages, that are *subsequently* 'well established' through a 'constitution' (*politeia*).

Here, some interesting linguistic clues in Conring's text call for reflection. He states, for instance, that 'just as every craftsman must possess some knowledge of the subject he is dealing with, so the statesman too must be familiar with *materia civitatis*, the lower societies or "parts"'.[113] Apparently, then, politics as a discipline is considered here less as a form of philosophy than as a *techne*, or rather an applied theory on how to establish and preserve states (*de republicis instituendis et conservandis*) according the various regimes (aristocratic, democratic, tyrannical …). Moreover, the way Conring talks about it brings out even more clearly its characterization as a 'science' in the specific sense of Aristotle's *Analytics*, in vogue again in the late Renaissance. The contents of the first book (*de servi, domini, possessionum, mariti, uxoris, liberorumque natura*: what one might call the pre-political relations between private individuals) are indeed treated like an exposition of the 'essence of the subject' (*subiecti natura*). In other words, like the enunciation of those principles which, on the basis of Conring's preferred interpretation of the *Posterior Analytics*, are beyond the competence of science.[114] Ergo: the doctrine of Book I is, strictly speaking, merely a preliminary, upstream of civil prudence, the treatment of which effectively begins in Book II and even more clearly in Book III.[115] It begins but is then, unfortunately, brusquely interrupted at the end of this book.[116] And here we come to the heart of Conring's argument, since he sees as the key point the condition in which Aristotle's *Politics* has come down to us: the material state of the text.

Without pursuing the detailed, almost chapter by chapter analysis of the text of the *Politics* offered by Conring, which takes into consideration around a century of related discussions, we jump straight to the conclusions. These are shown in Table 1 which illustrates the difference between the original form of the text, as assumed by Conring, and its current state after over twenty centuries of tormented transmission:

Table 1 Conring: the original structure of the *Politics*

	Original order of the *Politics* according to Conring	**Now corresponding to**
1	Materia civitatis	Book I
2	*Constitutio sive Ordinatio civitatis ex aliena sententia*	Book II
3	*Constitutio sive Ordinatio ex propria sententia in genere*	Book III
4	*CsO in specie: De Optima Republica (de aristocratia)*	Book VII
5	*CsO in specie: DOR (de aristocratia)*	Book VIII

(continued)

Table 1 Continued

	Original order of the *Politics* according to Conring	Now corresponding to
6	*CsO in specie: DOR (de aliis rectis rebuspublicis)*	Missing
7	*CsO in specie: DOR (de aliis rectis rebuspublicis)*	Missing
8	*CsO in specie: DOR (de aliis rectis rebuspublicis)*	Missing
9	*CsO in specie: DOR (de aliis rectis rebuspublicis)*	Missing
10	*De declinantibus ab obtima forma*	Book IV
11	*De declinantibus ab obtima forma*	Book V
12	*De declinantibus ab obtima forma*	Book VI

There was no shortage of speculations and hypotheses about the original structure of the Aristotelian text among the Renaissance writers cited by Conring, as all were agreed that the one available featured lacunae and inconsistencies.[117] Conring's reconstruction essentially assumes that Book III was directly followed by those now numbered VII and VIII, followed in turn by the four books now missing. The significance of this solution can be summarized in the following points:

1. Book I is simply a philosophical introduction relating to the *subiectum* or to the lower parts of political society.
2. Aristotle constructed the *Politics* around the doctrine of the optimum republic, the best form of constitution, in practice the aristocratic or royal form.[118] It can be added that:
3. The most useful part of this treatise was that comprised in Books VI to IX of the original numbering. Unfortunately it has been lost[119] and can only be intuited by hints and allusions scattered in other books. Presumably, Aristotle had addressed these issues in detail, seeing that Plato had already done so in the *Laws*.

At this point it is obvious that, considering the movement of passages from one place to another, the loss of books and other minor lacunae, the condition of the text is precarious if not actually hopeless. All the more so as, after so many centuries, it is unreasonable to expect a codex in such a condition as to transmit the *Politics* exactly as it came from Aristotle's hand.[120] Conring is very scrupulous about bringing textual arguments to support his theory, discussing and, where necessary, dismissing the various hypotheses of Heinsius, Giffen and Muret. Nevertheless, there remains the suspicion that all these efforts, and what is at bottom Conring's disappointment with Aristotle's *Politics*, are simply the consequence of an elementary misunderstanding: having overestimated the scope of Aristotle's text. In effect, the Stagirite takes as his subject the constitutions, and the best of them, albeit not conceiving them as abstract formal-legislative systems but always in relation to the social and economic relations existing in the particular *poleis*. Can we be sure – as Conring, along with the Aristotelians of his time, appears to have been – that Aristotle's attention was indeed focused on the mechanisms of government, the institutions, the offices, in short the administration? And can we be sure that Aristotle's investigation of the *aristê politeia* (*Nich. Eth.*, 10, 1181b 22), the 'optimal constitution', did indeed signify the quest for an ideal constitutional model, irrespective of the historic, social, political and economic particularities of each state? And what about the overlapping of this kind of discourse with *prudentia civilis*? Actually, for Aristotle the *phrónêsis* is a particular virtue, the prerogative of prudent statesmen such as Pericles, hence something essentially different from the part of practical philosophy dealing with the *polis*. Lastly, can we be sure that what philosophy – little or much – there is in the work is confined to the first book, the rest being essentially a reflection on constitutional forms and their stability or lability? In short, it seems to me that Conring – and possibly many of the sixteenth- and seventeenth-century writers that he discusses – wanted the *Politics* to be a treatise on political science in the modern sense. Failing to find in it what they were primarily looking for – a theory about the optimal form of state (naturally, a monarchy or a quasi-monarchical form) and constitutional-legislative regime – they preferred to assume that the surviving text was seriously mutilated and corrupt.

If this reconstruction is correct, it is hard to avoid the impression that Conring, and with him the entire Renaissance tradition including Sepúlveda, Vettori, Giffen and Heinsius etc., ended up in a blind alley. In the middle of the seventeenth century what is the point of continuing to speculate on the form and contents of an Aristotelian text so cruelly treated by time? One might as well write one's own treatise on *prudentia civilis*, bearing in mind the guidelines of Aristotle's practical philosophy and, more importantly, the needs of teachers and students who are looking for a methodical, complete and above all useful treatment of the subject. Which is exactly what Conring did in the years immediately following, writing both acroamatic (*De civili prudentia*, 1562) and exoteric (*Propolitica, sive brevis introductio ad civilem philosophiam*, 1563) treatises on civil prudence.[121] The biographies describe him as increasingly less interested in Aristotle and totally absorbed by political questions of a modern type.¹²² He was convinced that politics was a specific sector with its own laws, and was intent on exploring the concept of the state as a sovereign territorial entity, laying the foundations of the typically modern science which within the space of a few decades came to be called statistics. In a sense, these theoretical works were continued and developed in Conring's activity as a counsellor to various European political players – including the King of France – on questions of territorial sovereignty rights. In this context, his commitment to a conceptual definition of the nature of the Roman-Germanic Empire, based on the premise that the Roman Empire too ought to be seen as a territorial state like any other, is very significant.¹²³ Even in his teaching of political theory there came a time when Conring decided to do without Aristotle and teach using the *Tabulae* of his Helmstedt colleague Balthasar Cellarius.¹²⁴ This work was a synthesis of theoretical statecraft and practical governance with a clear and manageable structure, where references to Aristotle were largely rhetorical and ornamental. Considering the accumulated authority, and also the fact that the Ramist polemics had by then lost their sting, it must have seemed quite straightforward to Conring to simply waive Aristotle's *Politics* in favour of a more methodical and pragmatic way of teaching.

Now we are in possession of various elements to appraise this stylish revival of Renaissance Aristotelian philology at the time of the seventeenth-century maturing of the *Schulphilosophie*. As we have seen, Conring's *Introductio* is peppered with moments of severe perplexity, even despair, caused by the entity and gravity of the damage suffered by Aristotle's text. On the one hand, Conring stresses that Western political theory has not given due merit to its fundamental text. Yet, on the other hand, this same text appears to be unusable – especially in a university curriculum – since it is lacking the most salient part, addressing the form of political regime to be considered as a model for the state. This deficiency is important precisely in the light of the fundamental theoretical premises Conring starts from. Jurisprudence had been charged with the defect of particularism and of being confined to the description of factual states, whereas the task of political science was to elaborate universal models of normative value, pointing a way towards recovering or invigorating the health of the *respublicae*. But if Aristotle's *Politics* is lacking the very part which was to serve this purpose par excellence, what use is left for it? Although it is not actually spelt out, everything points to the fact that, for Conring, Aristotle's treatise, baptized by the authority of the Philosopher, was as cumbrous as it was – at the end of the day – useless.

One may then ask the more general question (not restricted to the use of the *Politics* for teaching purposes): is it legitimate to consider Conring's political science as a metamorphosis of political Aristotelianism? A profound metamorphosis, even, but always located within the confines of that specific tradition (or paradigm or lexicon). The answer must perforce refer to the way that we understand this same tradition. This brings us back to the initial considerations, and the revival of the idea that political Aristotelianism was a thematic repertory. At the lower level, that of political-constitutional issues, this repertory was open to additions (and omissions) linked to historic contingencies. At the upper level it was, however, consistent with general principles that went beyond the horizon of politics, drawing on epistemology, anthropology and even what we would now call ontology. That said, I think the answer to the question can be put as follows. First, it is certainly not the abandoning of commentary on the *Politics* that should lead us to see Conring as a deserter of Aristotelianism, as much perhaps as his formulation of a 'political science' fitted to the historical context, understood as a doctrine of the state and an academic discipline on how to govern it. On the other hand, it is also true that Conring makes the utmost effort to maintain this new doctrine in the furrow of Aristotelian epistemology, obviously as he knew it from late-Renaissance reflection. I think that this intention emerges clearly in the 'acroamatic' treatise *De civili prudentia*, the central section of which is aimed at demonstrating the epistemological specificity of the practical sciences. These deal with the world of social and historical experience and hence cannot have the absolute precision of mathematics or geometry, without this meaning that they are not scientific. The laws formulated by the practical sciences are still of a universal character, but it is a universality that is not absolutely valid or without exceptions, but 'mostly' (*ut in pluribus*), and this is precisely because the reality that is subject of these sciences has an irreducible margin of variability, contingency and unpredictability. Conring insists on one concept: the category of necessity also applies in the explanations of practical sciences, but this is a specific usage adapted to the type of reality it is applied to: the sphere of 'things to do' (*ta prakta*) not yet present and given. Hence necessity is spoken of in the practical sciences too, but it is of the type Aristotle defines as 'hypothetical', what we would now call 'conditional': if you wish to obtain *this*, you have to do *this* and *this*. Obviously, all this in turn assumes the general determinations of Aristotelian ontology and theory of causes. In this way modern civil prudence conforms with the traditional breakdowns of classical or premodern rationality defended by Conring in the face of temptations to undue extension of the *ordo geometricus*. This is indeed the focus of the central books (VII–X) of the work. It seems to me that the inapplicability of mathematical 'analysis' to practical knowledge – i.e. the idea that the principles at which one arrives starting from empirical observation are *necessarily true* (an anti-Hobbes notion?) – is clearly formulated by Conring in *De civili prudentia*,[125] where the definition of analysis produced by Pappus of Alexandria is cited as a model that does not apply to politics.

In such a context, Conring's insistence on the value of history, that is, on empiricism as the foundation of the generalizations of phronetic knowledge, is understandable. Knowledge based on historical induction can do its utmost to reduce the margin of imprecision in our universal conclusions but can never eliminate it completely. The epistemological alterity of politics compared to the precise sciences is thus safe, and other architectonic principles typical of political Aristotelianism also appear to hold firm, starting from prudence being constitutionally linked to the pursuit of the righteous end, that is, consistent with the good of both the individual and society. This in turn implies reiterating the consistency between ethics, anthropology and politics, releasing the latter from the solitude to which it had been relegated by certain literature on the *arcana imperii*, based on a unilateral reading of Machiavelli. It seems to me that Conring's interpretation of the latter – his condemnation of the Florentine for having unduly extended the rules of tyrannical conduct to every regime – confirms this judgement.

Therefore, with a view to defining the political Aristotelianism of Hermann Conring, the abandonment of the direct reading of Aristotle's *Politics* in the 1650s is only one aspect, and not even the most important, being related simply to the need to find new modes of teaching better suited to the times. It is more significant that Conring assumed positions in substantial continuity with the general epistemological assumptions of Renaissance Aristotelianism. In fact, he considers his own overexposure of the theoretical and practical habitus of civil prudence to be consistent with the classic paradigm of knowledge, and alternative to modern political science founded on natural law and developed taking mathematical or geometrical demonstration as a model.

Further research would be desirable to more clearly define the confines of Conring's strictly philosophical thought. Such study is still lacking and would need to take in not only his political work but also the inspiring principles of his work in the medical field. From the perspective sketched out here, interpreting political Aristotelianism as loyalty to certain principles capable of inspiring solutions, which inevitably have to be adapted to the particular historic moment,

I feel that Conring can be firmly placed in that intellectual ambit. Obviously, even from this perspective not everything comes out right, because Conring also to a degree calls into question – this time in harmony with modern political and anthropological thought – the Holy of Holies of Aristotelianism: the principle of the political nature of the human being. Again in the *De civili prudentia* we read that the reasons brought by Aristotle, followed by many others, to prove this assumption and its corollary – that only in the *civitas* is humanity happy – have insufficient demonstrative (apodictic) proof. The exercise of virtues is indeed possible even at a distance from civil society, since apparently communities of a lower level such as families or villages are sufficient. Further, the 'civil society' (*coetus civilis*) is necessary only to satisfy an eventual cupidity for luxury goods, whereas it is a useless superstructure if people can restrict themselves to that 'rough and simple', 'holy and natural' life which they were content with in the golden age. In short, at most Aristotle demonstrates that humans have an innate, generic propensity to a form of social life, but it is not that specific to the *civitas*.[126] Hence, if humans create *civitates* they do so not so much to be happy as 'for the power of doing violence to others or to protect themselves from the violence of others'.[127] Clearly it is not necessary to delve any deeper to see that, in the mind of the author of these reflections, a sort of chasm is opening up with the classical political conception and that of Aristotle in particular. This emerges primarily through the surreptitious identification of the *civitas* with the modern state and its power, not to speak of the appeal to a natural, pre-political state as being essentially sufficient for the achievement of human well-being.

Aftermaths

Judgement of Conring's Aristotelianism is therefore necessarily complex, even only considering the philosophy immanent in his writings. Things appear possibly even more ambivalent if we consider his work as a 'deconstructor' of the *Politics* in the context of his university teaching and set this in historical perspective. Perhaps the most interesting opinion here is that to be found in a text published in Helmstedt in 1715: a preface to the list of arguments in Aristotle's *Politics* drafted more than a century before by the famous Altdorf professor Michael Piccart.[128] The anonymous author (definitely a professor at the *Academia Julia*) complains that the *Politics* has not been published for over fifty years – effectively since Conring's edition – so that to illustrate the contents of Aristotle's book to the students he ended up resorting to these *argumenta* by

Piccart which are over a century old. And Conring himself has no small share in the responsibility for this state of abandon, since 'he impaired rather than fostered the authority of the work',[129] bringing to light all its shortcomings, both regarding the state in which it has reached us and by demonstrating that the Aristotelian text is *originally* obscure, ambiguous and repetitive. This undermined the readers' trust in Aristotle's text as a repository of coherent and profound thought; in other words, Aristotle was no longer perceived as an authority.

In actual fact, the author of the preface reflects on the historic crisis of Aristotle's philosophy and of political Aristotelianism, and observes that there are more profound reasons explaining the obsolescence of the *Politics*. First, nowadays it is considered not very useful for learning since it is too theoretical.[130] But above all, as notably pointed out by the famous Samuel von Pufendorf, Aristotle has in mind only and exclusively the Greek cities and their institutions, demonstrating that he 'appreciates above all their liberty, which is a serious defect for a universal discipline serving the whole of humankind'.[131] Another thinker contemporary with Conring, Johann Heinrich Boeckler, goes even further, saying that for this reason we can say that Aristotle has offered only:

> a particular case (*specimen*) rather than a complete body of civil doctrine [given that] he illustrated little or nothing of the monarchic regime, and, good Greek that he was, engaged eagerly in favour of democracy, measuring everything on the model of the republic, and subtly representing an idea of the monarch and the monarchy as impossible to carry through, or instilling horror of the same with a serpent-like cunning and mysterious reasonings, while at the same time not hesitating openly and abundantly to expound the wrongdoings and the methods of tyrannical power.[132]

These and other of Aristotle's defects essentially derive from an original mistake, having considered the human being as a political animal, whereas it is known that 'a human being is by his nature ever ready to bring about [political] revolts and that this principle is denied by many reasons adduced by Hobbes, Pufendorf, Thomasius, Gundling etc.'.[133] In other words, the author upholds the notion that love of freedom and trust in the social nature of the human being and their political translation into republican and democratic regimes – components of an ideology of which Aristotle was standard-bearer – are Greek idiosyncrasies. Modern *scientia civilis* ought instead to aim at universality, which its supporters maintain is achieved by resorting to concepts such as natural law, sovereignty (absolute), state of nature and contract. This is the main reason why political Aristotelianism is at variance with the spirit of the seventeenth century, with the thought of Hobbes, Spinoza, Pufendorf and the like and its implicit anthropology.

If this stocktaking of the Renaissance attempt to relaunch Aristotle's political philosophy – an attempt that substantially failed in the face of the *novitas temporum* – is correct, then Conring's position emerges as ambivalent. On the one hand, this philosophy continued to be his benchmark, little inclined as he was to yield to the modern sirens of Bodin, Hobbes or Grotius. On the other hand, this same practical-political philosophy, with all its premises and corollaries, tended to remain in the background of Conring's teaching and literary activity. It was almost relegated to the rank of a speculative exercise of little use in the educational requirements of the governors of the state or even in the resolution of the political and diplomatic controversies of the time. Adding insult to injury was the blow dealt to the work that continued to be the hub of that philosophy, Aristotle's *Politics*, which through Conring underwent a sort of deconsecration that removed its special status as an authoritative text. Finally came the corrosion of several of the theoretical bases of political Aristotelianism, a corrosion from within since, as I have sought to show, Conring made his own contribution.

5

Franz Tidike's *Disputatio de fato* and the Teaching of Moral Philosophy at the Toruń Gymnasium at the Turn of the Seventeenth Century

The Toruń Gymnasium, a Reformed *Hochschule* of the Polish Commonwealth

From 1569 the city of Toruń and so-called Royal Prussia was part of the political body of the Polish Commonwealth while, from the confessional and cultural point of view, obviously remaining in the area of the German Protestant Reformation. In the wake of the general relaunch of the Reformed educational institutions in the last decades of the sixteenth century, which in Poland also involved the centres of Gdansk and Elbląg, after 1594 the authorities of Toruń revitalized the existing six-year school, turning it into a *Gymnasium Illustre* with a ten-year course of studies, following the famous model elaborated by Sturm and adopted in Strasbourg. The strategic goal of the city authorities (in particular Heinrich Stroband, mayor of the city from 1587 up to his death in 1609) was to create an academic centre of interregional, even international, rank, also taking advantage of the *pax religiosa* established in the Polish *Respublica*. The underlying idea was to attract students of Reformed confession from the Kingdom and from the countries gravitating around it, such as Pomerania, Transylvania and Lithuania. Historians agree that this plan was felicitously accomplished during the first decades of the seventeenth century, one of the finest periods in the history of the school, as witnessed by the number of enrolments and their geographical range. It should also be remembered that the success of this plan was due to the ability of the city authorities to keep the gymnasium free from religious conflict, entrusting its management to lay people and adopting a humanistic teaching programme based primarily on Melanchthon's textbooks, albeit not unrelated even to an Erasmian inspiration. This characteristic mission of the school must certainly be linked to the historic role of the city of Toruń itself, in 1595 seat of an important synod of the various Protestant factions (Lutherans, Calvinists and Bohemian Brethren, with the exclusion of 'radicals', i.e. Anabaptists and Antitrinitarians). The synod ended in a compromise and in a spirit of peace, although it had not been possible to come to an agreement on the main theological and ecclesiastical points at issue.[1]

The teaching of ethics in Toruń seems to me to be a good illustration of how, in the world of German-language upper schools and universities in the Reformed area, the didactic orientations of the individual institutions were often conditioned by local political, social and cultural factors, making it difficult to reconstruct a picture that is both detailed and general. In the case of Toruń, the professors of the gymnasium were invited to collaborate in the revitalization project already mentioned, which gave rise, among other things, to an intense production of school textbooks. It is noteworthy, however, that the latter rarely took the form of systematic, 'disciplinary' treatises, as in Keckermann's Gdansk. To put it succinctly, it is as if the school, without yielding to Ramism, but also without adopting the most modern forms of Aristotelianism, thought it safer to refer to the early-sixteenth-century culture of humanism, with Melanchthon – the undisputed authority of all Protestant confessions – as a point of reference among the moderns, and Cicero among the ancients. In this situation, aside from ritual tributes to the authority of the Stagirite, the legacy of Aristotle and Aristotelianism does not appear as the focus around which the teaching of philosophy was organized. The *Nicomachean Ethics* was neither the only nor the most important reference text for the teaching of ethics, which was given a decidedly practical and moralistic imprint. Philosophical ethics itself was seen less as an autonomous discipline and more as an interweaving of anthropological, moralistic, cosmological and theological concepts.

Tidike's ethical thought

I believe that a good illustration of these trends is provided by a typical school text, a *disputatio de fato*, published in the early seventeenth century by Franz Tidike (b. Gdansk, 1554, d. Toruń, 1617), an interesting figure of professor teaching at the academic gymnasium of Toruń in the decades around the turn of the seventeenth century. He was a philosopher, a theorist of medicine, a physician and a pharmacologist, as well as being engaged in the reform of the gymnasium where he taught several disciplines. In view of this multifaceted activity, it is not easy to trace all its developments or to identify an overall interpretative key. In a previous study I examined Tidike's philosophical ideas, referring in particular to two texts – *Disceptationes philosophicae* (1590), focused on Aristotle's doctrine of categories and predicables, and the vast synthetic *Microcosmus* (1615) – attempting to find a thematic link between them.[2] The conclusion I came to was that, over the years, Tidike fairly consistently elaborated a philosophical approach, including a philosophy of nature, focusing primarily on concepts – such as the soul of the world or analogy/sympathy – linked to Renaissance Neoplatonism, or at least to concordist models typical of the early sixteenth century. The *Disceptationes* was a work that emerged in the scholastic environment of Leipzig, in which Tidike defended his Peripatetic and Melanchthonian orthodoxy, whereas the *Microcosmus* aspired to go beyond the academic world. In the passage from one to the other Tidike had shed the need to present himself as an Aristotelian. The Stagirite thus became one of four authorities, the others being Hippocrates, Plato and Galen, on which he could construct his Neoplatonizing and, in effect, eclectic synthesis.

Here, on the other hand, I wish to return to an appraisal of the more scholastic Tidike, with particular reference to a publication of 1609 in which he brought together his writings on moral philosophy.[3] He included among these a short *Disputatio de fato*, one of the classic topics of Renaissance Aristotelianism. The discussion of fate had persisted throughout the sixteenth century, starting with the publication of the Latin translation of the *On fate* (*Peri heimarmênês*) by Alexander of Aphrodisias (1516), through to Pomponazzi's major treatise *De fato, providentia et praedestinatione* and the writings of Juan Ginés de Sepúlveda, Simone Porzio,[4] Giulio Sirenio etc., not to mention the innumerable contributions commenting on various key Aristotelian passages in the *Nicomachean Ethics*, *On Interpretation* and the *Metaphysics* in particular.[5] However, as we shall see, neither in the strictly ethical works nor in this *disputatio*, straddling ethics and natural philosophy, is the reference to Aristotle essential for Tidike. It seems to me, indeed, that we can note a progressive marginalization of the Stagirite, or a use that is, all things considered, purely instrumental. This is what I intend to explore here, along with the intellectual interests at work in Tidike's thought.

First, a few observations on the 1609 publication as a whole are called for. We can dispense with the detailed account of the contents of its two principal parts – the translation and commentary on the Pseudo-Aristotelian *De virtutibus et vitiis* and an *Isagoge Ethica* – since this work has already been done.[6] What follows is intended as a contribution to the interpretation of these writings in the context of the history of philosophy around the end of the sixteenth century and beginning of the seventeenth. They will be considered in parallel, since they express the same thought but with different modes of exposition.

The first aspect to note is that the translation and commentary on *De virtutibus* and the *Isagoge* are accompanied, as a sort of appendix, by certain texts in the typical form of *theses disputatae*. The first of these is the *Disputatio de fato*, followed by a *Disputatio de summo bono*, a *Quaestio utrum honestum constet natura an opinione* and finally by the *Themata disputationis de voluptate et dolore*. In the letter dedicatory that introduces the entire collection, Tidike recalls how he had begun to reread the pages containing his past philosophical meditations and how the revision and reworking of these neglected texts with a view to publication had brought him solace and relief from the 'melancholy' caused by his work as a city physician. Most of this material must have dated to his time in Leipzig and been connected with his teaching activities there. This is especially true of the four texts in the appendix, which clearly originated from the scholastic exercises in disputation.[7] Reconsidered and rewritten 'to conform to a more resolute and mature judgement', this material is now ready, as it were, to emerge from the classroom for the more general benefit of a public not restricted to students of the gymnasium.[8] This appears to be the sense of the observation that opens the commentary on *De virtutibus* and can be extended to the entire collection: comparing *De virtutibus* to another famous apocryphal text, the *De mundo ad Alexandrum*, Tidike explains that in both cases we are dealing with works that were not penned directly by Aristotle, but by a writer totally faithful to his thought (*doctrinam Aristotelis penitus referens*) who wished to expound the ethical doctrine of the Master for the benefit of a patron or a dear friend (*in gratiam alicuius magnatis vel amici, cui bene voluit*).[9] Not without reason, adds Tidike, from a certain point on the *De virtutibus* was included in the editions of the authentic works of Aristotle,[10] almost as if to integrate a treatment that had not been sufficiently developed in the two major *Ethics*, the *Eudemian* and the *Nicomachean*. In short, even though it is not comparable to Cicero's *De officiis* as maintained by one of its Renaissance translators, Alexandre Chamaillard,[11] this work is at least very useful for a compendious knowledge of Aristotle's doctrine, partly as a result of its perfect topical articulation: 'On virtues and vices and on those things linked to both of them, their properties, connections and consequences' (*de virtutibus et vitiis, ac de utrorumque adiunctis, proprietatibus, cognatis et consequentibus*). Nevertheless, it will still always be a 'popular' and 'exoteric' treatise which hence, programmatically, does not aspire to the 'acroamatic' level.[12]

Virtue as self-control

It should be clarified at the outset that the indications to be derived from Tidike's work on *De virtutibus* already reveal a great deal about how he sees the task of philosophical ethics and the reasons for teaching it. In short, there appear to be two lead concepts: (1) the core of Aristotle's teaching is a doctrine that pivots on the topic of the virtues, more precisely those traditionally known as 'cardinal'. The list of these is effectively the one rendered canonical by Cicero in *De officiis*: *prudentia, fortitudo, temperantia* and *iustitia* with the addition of *liberalitas*;[13] and (2) if there is a theoretical aspect in philosophical ethics too, it is fairly negligible because what is actually important is to delineate a practical ethic. The at once prescriptive and paraenetic value of moral teaching is pre-eminent, in other words: the efficacy of the ethical discourse in moulding character and personality.

Therefore, Tidike retrieves a text which – whatever its origin[14] – is the expression of a post-Aristotelian, Hellenistic and probably Stoicizing ethic, because he perceives it as being in harmony with his own way of conceiving the *ethica disciplina*. Indeed, he illustrates the arguments of *De virtutibus* above all on the basis of the writings of Cicero and Plutarch and other ancients even more than those of Aristotle. Not to mention the fact that, starting from *fortitudo* (33), Tidike also draws numerous teachings and moral exhortations from the Holy Scriptures. So now we come to his reflections on the central concept of virtue. By his own account this is the same as *honestum*, and also as *decorum* (gr.: *to trepon*),[15] the only thing that is good in itself and the only thing truly worthy of praise (*encomium*), while goods of other kinds, such as wealth or health, are such equivocally or popularly (*vulgo*), while in actual fact they are at most the object of mere 'appreciation' (*commendatio*). In effect, praise and blame are by Tidike considered as the natural outcome of virtue and vice respectively and not as subjective judgements depending on opinion.[16]

As regards the definition of virtue, Tidike alludes preliminarily to an *arete* understood as an accomplished or excellent state of anything ('an eye', 'a horse'), while making clear that this is merely a generic (*latus*) sense of the word, not fitting the specific, i.e. ethical, matter he is dealing with. Another broader, *popular* definition of virtue is the one found in the *Rhetoric*, where it is said to be a *dýnamis*, i.e. a capacity to achieve public benefits, which is why it results in virtues such as justice and liberality.[17] However, when we come to the strictest (acroamatic) definition of virtue, it is undoubtedly that supplied by Aristotle in Book II of the *Nicomachean Ethics*, namely virtue as a mean (*estin ara hê aretê hexis proairetikê en mesótêti ousa têi pros hêmas, ôrismenêi logôi kai hôs an ho phrónimos oríseie*: 'Virtue is a habit with the capacity of deliberating and consisting in the mean relating to us; [this mean] is defined by reason and as a prudent man would define it'[18]). Tidike first translates this passage literally into Latin and then provides a paraphrase of it which strikes me as interesting:

> Virtue understood in the strictest sense, that is when speaking of human virtue, is nothing more than solid intention and constant will, which is learnt and reinforced by continual exercise and which is bred from the depths, to live in an upright and praiseworthy manner according to the dictates of the right reason that is innate in us and which we therefore call the Law of Nature; and then to do nothing other than what conforms to the right reason, in which all of us participate.[19]

The first part of this passage refers to the theory of the acquisition of the habit of virtue through exercise and discipline, which was one of Tidike's favourite topics even in his other ethical writings. The second part introduces concepts that are less evident, or even absent, in Aristotle's text, namely the 'right reason' and 'Law of Nature', objective criteria of moral judgements, here set in relation to each other. In a *quaestio* included in the anthology, Tidike associates these same concepts with that of the well-formed conscience, capable of distinguishing between good and evil.[20] The contents of the *Isagoge* can help to clarify this. It introduces the concept of a state of moral integrity – of harmony between *mens* and *appetitus* – preceding original sin and unknown to the pagan sages,[21] arguing that education through philosophy and other sciences can and must tend to the recovery of this state.[22] I see these topics as substantially comprised in the perspective introduced by Melanchthon, which holds that philosophical-pagan ethics and ethics inspired by the Holy Scriptures are different. But they are not contradictory, since the former is none the less based on the remnants of a moral law which, despite the decadence of humanity following original sin, is still present within the conscience and can guide human action towards good. In this sense, pagan ethics are preparatory to Christian ethics.[23] In Tidike's version this concept – which is explored further in the *Isagoge* – is expressed by arguing that the ancient philosophers and moralists in actual fact described only the secondary causes of corruption and vice – celestial influences, elementary temperaments and bodily structures, parents, forms of education – concealing the true cause, which was the fall of our first parents tempted by the devil, that can be apprised only if the reason 'is further instructed and perfected by the Word, the sentence and the judgement of God'.[24]

Within the discourse on virtuous dispositions Tidike places particular emphasis on the virtue of *prudentia*. The acquisition and consolidation of this is based on two foundations, the right reason or right rule, which is its remote cause, and education as its proximate cause. Described in Aristotelian terms as a 'dianoetic' virtue, the description of *prudentia* furnished by Tidike is mostly inspired by Cicero: prudence is the knowledge of what should be pursued and what avoided (*De off.*, I, 153), the organ of discernment between good and evil,[25] as a result of which it can rightly be declared the 'mother of all virtues'.[26] In actual fact, Tidike assigns it a prevalently paraenetic function in the economy of moral life (*dictare, monere, suadere*).[27] This slightly overshadows its function of appraising and choosing the means with a view to the right end present in the classical, Aristotelian concept of *phronesis*, which was fully expressed in the form of rationality habitually referred to as 'practical syllogism'.[28] This understanding of the fundamental concepts of ethics seems to me functional to Tidike's general idea of the virtuous life, the life guided by prudence. The task of this virtue is substantially that of imposing a modus on the sphere of the impulses and the passions (*to orektikon*).[29] This is, moreover, an evident theoretical amendment made by Tidike to the doctrine of the Pseudo-Aristotelian *De virtutibus et vitiis*. The latter adopts the Platonic tripartite division of the soul, whereas Tidike prefers the breakdown taken from the beginning of the *Nicomachean Ethics* which, as he emphasizes, is also consonant with the Holy Scriptures: the simple opposition of two parts, right rule / prudence and appetite. 'The reason is like a lord who commands, the appetite like a subject and servant, who is bound to accept and admit the government of the reason and to be virtuous.'[30] It should be added that the bipartite division taken from classical psychological doctrine then has to deal with the introduction of a third element, the conscience – of scriptural-religious derivation – but without Tidike clarifying exactly how all these factors of moral life are related to each other.[31] In any case, all this can be summed up by saying that what is proposed here is an ethics pivoting on the notion of moral virtue, which in turn is understood substantially as self-control. In effect, if different virtues are only different forms of self-control, the question arises of how virtue in general is to be distinguished from that particular virtue which is continence (gr.: *enkráteia*). In effect, Tidike sees both in a relation of continuity, by explaining that continence is the situation when the governance of passions by the right reason is still painful and uncertain, whereas full virtue is attained when reason pacifically and 'pleasantly' controls irrational impulses, since a firm 'habit' has been established within the soul. Obviously, simple continence is more common, whereas perfect virtue is statistically very rare, since it known solely in the few examples of 'very holy men' recorded in Scripture and in hagiographies.[32]

The moral task of ethics

Essentially, then, Tidike's is an 'areto-centric' ethics, in the strict sense of *arete*-virtue chosen by him: the capacity of the individual to mould character by dominating the appetites. As already said, this approach is in harmony with the tradition of post-Melanchthon scholastic teaching, which in any case required no small shift from the focus on *eudaimonia*-happiness-flourishing life that emerges from Aristotle's ethical treatises as a whole. The – so to say – neo-Stoic tendency becomes explicit in a passage such as this, dealing with happiness:

> Even though for Aristotle happiness is something made up of all the types of goods ... both of the soul, such as the intellectual and moral virtues, and of the body, such as health, beauty and strength, and the exterior goods, such as wealth, friends and glory, nevertheless and fundamentally it lies in virtuous deeds ... so much so that the Stoics established that this alone was sufficient for a good and blessed life.[33]

As said, Tidike is not particularly inclined to develop the theoretical aspect any more than is strictly necessary. The few metaethical elements, such as the bipartition of the soul and the definition of virtue or prudence, are certainly not the focus of his discourse. In this doctrine the theoretical aspect (*doctrina ... qua erudimur ... quaeque explicat*) is at the service of the practical ([*doctrina quae*] *viam virtutis nobis aperit atque ostendit*), as we read in the opening page of the *Isagoge*. While the science/art of living dilemma is characteristic of philosophical ethics,[34] Tidike's slant is indubitably towards the second alternative. In fact, as he says, the purpose of ethics is to 'produce', 'bring to birth' or 'fabricate' virtue in the individual, its seeds having been induced in (general human) nature by the 'supreme author of every good thing' (*summus autor omnis boni*). Ethics is substantially an art, a technique of living, and like all the other arts or techniques, all it does is introduce a specific form (virtue) into a specific subject (the irrational part of the soul). This signifies simply that 'the unbridled and recalcitrant appetites' are tamed,[35] and thus transfigured into love for God and men. Consequently, *philautia* or *amor sui* is the most basic vice as Tidike maintains, mindful of St Augustine.[36]

In clarifying his thought,[37] and taking inspiration from the analogy between medicine and philosophy, Tidike divides the latter into speculative and active parts. Speculative philosophy is pure knowledge, which comprises both the *scientia rerum* and the *cognitio boni et mali, turpis et honesti*, that is, the set of dianoetic habitus mentioned by Aristotle in Book VI of the *Nicomachean Ethics*. In this way 'active philosophy' is isolated from the cognitive habitus and, consistently, its only task consists in 'prescribing its virtues to the appetite, those that we call moral virtues, which are: generosity, temperance, etc.'.[38] Active philosophy is no longer science but education, in the sense of correcting the faults of the soul and the body until virtuous habits are established.[39]

As a result, it is the prescriptive aspect of ethics that Tidike favours.[40] And the first precept – derived from Galen – is that of recognizing one's own vices by trusting oneself to other people capable of seeing us from outside and telling us honestly what is wrong with us.[41] This is followed by others taken from the *Nicomachean Ethics*, again connected with the notion of moderating irrational impulses.[42] Once again, it is not sufficient that the precepts are known without being put into practice, as taught both by Jesus, in his attacks on the Pharisees, and by Aristotle, associated here with Pacuvius and Gellius. Here too the key idea of these reflections of Tidike's emerges: that of the conscience as an 'incessant stimulus, embedded deep in our soul, like eyes continually watching us, which like a spur never ceases to warn us of our duty, and energetically and effectively urges us to put into practice what we have learnt from the doctrines of the wise men and from their precepts, and that we have accepted and made our own'.[43] Hence the importance of reading and meditation on authors 'whose books are overflowing with salutary precepts for conducting life'.[44] The canon comprises writers of the Old Testament (Psalms, Sirach and the Prophets), the New Testament and then the *ethnici* Theognis, Phocylides, Pythagoras, Solon, the fables of Aesop and so on. Then, among the moderns, Vives,[45] the *Apophthegms* of Erasmus,[46] the *Gnomology* of Stobaeus,[47] the *Regulae vitae* by David Chytraeus,[48] and finally the lives of classical heroes and Christian saints. In short, a literature made up of *gnomai*, maxims, aphorisms and examples.[49] Tidike also adds that even more effective than mere readings are certain spiritual practices such as the meditation on the judgement of God,[50] rumination (*recordatio*) on past sins under the stimulus of the 'torture of conscience' that never leaves us in peace day or night.[51] Rather, this last exercise is the 'greatest teacher' of moral improvement.[52] Alternatively, Tidike suggests a day-by-day rebuke (*quotidiana reprehensio*) of the judgements made of us by others, both those that are just and severe, which we accept in good grace, and also the calumnies, which help us to practice patience and trust in God, the only just judge.[53] Towards the end of the *Isagoge* is an extensive crypto-citation (*quidam pie sane scripsit*) from *The*

Imitation of Christ in Castellion's popular revision, which is very significant for the interpretation of the entire text.[54] It would indeed be quite plausible to argue that this classic of modern Christian spirituality, with its marked moral practicism, the appeal to perfection of the self, the importance of good conscience and trust in God alone, is the source of inspiration for Tidike in these pages, and in general for his ideas about what the role and articulation of the scholastic philosophical ethic should be. To assess this doctrine in a historical perspective, one could argue that this overexposure of virtue as the pivotal theme of a neo-Aristotelian ethics is more than likely to be widespread in the context of the main trends in the Reformed scholasticism of the time. It can be traced in other authors, such as Tidike's fellow citizen Keckermann, and other Reformed commentators on the *Nicomachean Ethics* (for instance, Andreas Hyperius, Pietro Martire Vermigli, Viktorin Strigel, Rudolph Goclenius et al.[55]). What seems to distinguish Tidike's arrangement is its pronounced practical character directly aimed at the moral education of its recipients, so much so that at times he appears more at ease in the role of spiritual director than that of philosophy teacher. On the other hand, precisely the need for training in moral discipline, and hence recourse to the categories of sin and conscience – as well as a certain propensity (particularly evident in the *Isagoge*) to mixing philosophical ethics of classic origin with ideas of a religious and scriptural origin (an allegedly Christian ethic) – suggest that Tidike felt somewhat hemmed in by a strictly philosophical ethic. The idea of a theological ethic, or a practical theology, with a crucial emphasis on 'what has to be done' (*facienda*), moral discipline, and a 'practice of piety' guided by conscience illuminated in turn by faith,[56] began to make headway starting from Lambert Daneau (*Ethice Christiana*, 1577). It continued with Ramus and Amandus Polanus, through to the authors of Reformed casuistry, including the puritans William Ames and William Perkins, and Johann H. Alsted on the Continent. I do not wish to say that Tidike went so far as to see his ethical teaching as part of an exclusively theological agenda, but simply to underline his evident interest in numerous important topics of non-Aristotelian and non-philosophical origin that were closer to this second tradition.

In any case, at the end of the work Tidike brings up a passage from the *Problems* of Alexander of Aphrodisias in the translation by Theodorus Gaza, in which moral questions and naturalistic categories are admirably combined. It is hard to imagine a better gloss for this synthesis of Aristotelian natural philosophy, Stoicizing moralism and modern Protestant spirituality, not without echoes of Erasmus:

If, beyond the agent, there is an aptitude in the patient subject to influence the causes of the passion, then perhaps, even we, if we arm our souls with piety, if we maintain the body through a sober life, if we content ourselves with little, despising the superfluous, then perhaps, in the end, we may succeed in remaining immune from the defects of human nature, as far as this is possible through human efforts. In other words, we may not provide any opportunity to the agent to do anything to the patient subject, whether that agent be a dangerous demon, or a heavenly body or any other agent that, from without, contributes to our error or our vice.[57]

And with its mention of such external conditionings of our conduct and of the importance of resisting them, this passage provides an excellent introduction to Tidike's work on fate.

The *Disputatio de fato*

In the same ethical anthology,[58] but with separate numbering (A2r–a3v and 1–48), are four other texts: three *disputationes* – *De fato et rebus fatalibus*, *De summo bono seu felicitate humana* and *De voluptate et dolore* – and the *Quaestio utrum honestum natura constet an opinione*. These largely date to the Leipzig period,[59] and they were probably selected by Tidike and then revised for this new edition. They display the typical subdivision into points of the length of one paragraph – each supporting a particular argument and all together providing a coherent doctrine on the proposed topic – that confirms their origin in the public academic debates. These were a characteristic of the German universities, although in Leipzig they were given even greater stimulus with the arrival of the famous Aristotelian professor of philosophy Simone Simoni (1532–1602), to whom Tidike elsewhere expresses his admiration and gratitude.[60] Among other things, Simoni had also established an informal structure, the Academia acutorum, which brought together the more gifted students and was based on the practice of frequent dialectic debates.[61]

The longest of these texts (half of the total: 1–23, divided into fifty-four *assertiones*), and the only one with a preface, is the first, which reveals several interesting corollaries of Tidike's ethical reflection. I shall therefore analyse in greater detail the *Disputatio philosophica de fato et de rebus fatalibus*, providing a full translation in the appendix to this chapter, while at the same time seeking to offer an interpretation from a historical-philosophical angle.

Tidike's preface delineates the objectives that led him to address the topic, as well as indications about how the discourse, which goes beyond the limits of mere theology, is to be understood. He begins by recalling how the very word 'fate' has become suspicious to philosophers and theologians on account of the various depraved and absurd doctrines with which it has frequently been associated. More specifically, both in philosophy and in religion, the theory that God is the efficient cause of anything that human beings do and the idea that it is impossible to resist such action, ought to be considered dangerous. In short, the aim is to halt the spread of a fatalistic sentiment with clearly negative moral consequences, demonstrating the untenability of theories on which it is implicitly founded. In this respect, Tidike claims that all he is doing is repeating the 'sound doctrine' received from his teachers and, in any case, that he is acting as a philosopher making only a momentary *excursus* into theology. Indeed, in this matter philosophy can help us to understand many truths immune from impiety and blasphemy, but only on condition that we do not take the words at their face value. It is true that there are philosophical theories that *appear* unacceptable and scandalous in religion, but this happens only because often men are not capable of grasping – beyond the 'overly profane' meaning of the expressions used or the sometimes ambiguous, and sometimes incautious and provocative, manner in which they are presented – the way in which they conspire with 'the sole truth of things'.

As regards the *Disputatio* proper, I think it can be broken down as follows into three main parts, within which other thematic sections can be identified:

1–7:   On fate as a causal chain ('Stoic' fate)
8–19: On 'astrological' fate as the order of nature – *dubia* and *solutiones*
20–53: On fate as God's providence

    28–9:   marriages
    30–2:   upheavals of the empires
    33:     punishment of crimes
    34–8:   success and failure
    39–49: the terms of life and death (digression on medicine: 43–48)
    49–53: On the prescience of God

54:    Conclusion

I shall now try to summarize the contents of the *Disputatio*, followed by some observations on what I see as the most remarkable points.

Tidike begins by observing that it has become common to attribute to the notion of 'fate' the meaning attributed to it by the Stoics: that of an uninterrupted series of causes proceeding from God to all the parts of the universe, a concatenation that holds together past, present and future events, making them derive from God's decision to impose this order on nature. However, once this order is determined not even its Author can suspend it, leading to the paradox that God depends on what He himself has created (5). However, since this theory nullifies both God's freedom and ours, it is 'all a fable' (6). It is much more plausible to see fate as a 'certain and stable' force that acts on nature, and this is 'astronomical and physical' fate (8): the *vis* exerted by heavenly bodies through which they govern the world, as everyone admits (9). The answer to the question of whether this government implies that the heavenly bodies have a compelling influence on the human soul (11) is that, given the radical ontological alterity between heavenly bodies and spiritual substance, it is impossible that one acts upon the other (12). Nevertheless, since the soul operates through bodily means such as innate warmth and pneuma and it is plausible that the heavens can influence such 'instruments', then the immaterial soul and its functions are also to a certain extent influenced by heavenly bodies (13–15). Such influence is naturally stronger for the 'part' of the soul presiding over the vegetative and sensorial functions, and much less so for the 'mental and rational' part, on which innate qualities and morals depend (16). As regards the latter, education and exercise have much more influence than the heavens, since the bodily dimension directly influenced by the heavens is at most responsible for generic inclinations which can be resisted (17). Regarding the second question about the causative force of the heavenly bodies on individual events, 'chance' cases in the life of the individuals (10), all that can be said is that the action exerted by those bodies is only indirect, since they act directly on the corporeal qualities and through these, indirectly on individual character and nature. Even if this has a remote effect on, for instance, marriage, success and failure, birth and – above all – death, in actual fact the direct cause of these is – for those who believe – divine providence (18). Therefore, as Cicero rightly admonishes, the astral fate is not the cause of everything that happens (19).

Having spoken of fate in the 'Stoic' and 'astrological' sense, the discussion moves on to a sense 'more adequate from our point of view': that of divine providence understood as both government and as 'precognition' of individual events (20). Apropos this, first it should be noted that, while it is true that God knows each event in its singularity – as will be clarified in the final part – that is not the same as saying that He wishes each event and is the Author of it (21). Here Tidike makes certain clarifications: God is the cause of both the existence and essence of all things, and can hence know the thing in its essence at all times

(22). As regards its coming-to-be and passing away ('becoming'), on the other hand, a distinction has to be made between what He knows and makes to be and what He knows only (23). Consequently, to state that nothing can happen without being imposed by God is a patent exaggeration (24). The truth is that God is not at all the Author of certain things, but despite this they are placed under His providence, in the sense that He knows them and 'allows' them to happen. This, for instance, is the case of criminal deeds (25). In the case of providence too, popular parlance makes frequent recourse to discourses and concepts of a Stoic flavour: 'fatal' marriages, major political upheavals, success and failure in everyday life and in society, criminal punishments, births and deaths are all directly attributed to divine causality (26). This, however, is nothing more than a manner of speaking that men exploit to avoid taking responsibility for their own actions (27). These categories of human events are then scrutinized so as to understand how human free will and providence apply within them. The first case addressed is that of the 'fatal' marriages: did Laius, Aegisthus and David fatally wed Jocasta, Clytemnestra and Bathsheba respectively because God so wished it? Certainly not; the will of each of these heroes was free of all theological necessity (28)! Obviously, if the marriage is legitimate and honest, God may approve and favour it and in this sense it is 'fatal'. Nevertheless, there are many marriages that He would not wish for and yet He allows them to happen (29). The case of major political upheavals is more complex. The fall of empires cannot be attributed to mere ageing or natural cyclicity but directly to divine will and causality, since God decides when they begin and end (30). While it is true that in Book V of the *Politics* Aristotle explains the ethical, social and economic – i.e. human – factors in revolutions (31), it is none the less eminently a matter of divine providence, which uses the actions (and crimes) of individuals as the means and opportunities for achieving its ends. So we cannot say that God required Paris to abduct and marry Helen to finish Troy off, but He took advantage of the opportunity offered by Paris, as a free perpetrator of his crime, to destroy Priam's empire (32). In the same way, the punishment for crimes committed is to be seen as an opportunity to make amends offered to the criminal by God (33). The case of good and bad luck in everyday life and social success and failure is similarly articulated: fate and providence can be called into play here, but always with caution so as not to succumb to Stoic fatalism (34). The required precept is indeed to entrust the successful outcome of our efforts into the hands of God, as the sole cause and Author of human fortune (35). At the same time, however, one must not waive the principle – confirmed both by the wisdom of proverbs and by Cicero – that frequently it is in the power of men, as a result of their virtuous habits, to help their neighbours (36) and also, as a result of vicious habits, to do them harm (37). All things considered, in this sphere of events God allows human beings to act in one way or another and 'concedes' the realization of their plans. He is a moderator who intervenes in human reality in different ways, introducing obstacles and offering opportunities. He exerts a dominion over our will, but it is of a 'political and milder' kind rather than of a 'master–slave' nature, establishing ends for human efforts that are not necessitating in themselves but allow free agency and deliberation in the agents. This is enough to be able to say that each human being is the forger of his or her own destiny, and that freedom of decision and providence are compatible; here Tidike remembers to speak 'according to philosophy' (38). Finally, this same popular mentality, spontaneously inclined towards 'Stoicism', speaks of the time and manner of everyone's death as a destiny dictated by God that man can do nothing about, but this manner of thinking and talking is 'unworthy of a Christian' (39). Furthermore, this fatalism leads people to the conviction that all action is pointless (the famous 'lazy argument'), and the futility in particular of resorting to medical treatment (40), thus implicitly denying that God's action in the specific case avails – as indeed it does – of the mediation of nature as a second cause (41). Death is no more than the lapse of the connection between body and soul, when the innate warmth channelled by the pneuma comes to an end. The causes of this ending are already in nature, in elementary and humoral dysfunction (42), but to address them we have been given medicine. And so, life and death depend on the skill or lack of skill of the physicians, not on fate (43). However, even medicine cannot always win over disease (44), which again demonstrates the efficacy of providence. If God wants to call someone to Him, He can do so through the second causes, reinforcing the strength of the disease or preventing the efficacy of the treatment. In this case the death may indeed be called fatal, and medicine can do nothing to stop it, but here too it is not unalterable necessity, since one can resort to prayer and plead with God to change His decision (45). And necessity does not come into another two cases either: suicides are fully responsible for their own deaths, while those who have lived 'with prudence' and have accepted the physicians' advice are themselves the reason for the prolongation of their life (46). The reasoning of the fatalists – it is pointless to resort to medicine since being cured or not is in the hands of destiny – does not hold up. More precisely, their assumption is false if taken in absolute terms, while it could be true in a conditional sense: one is fatally cured *if one takes medicine*, if the human action cooperates with the success of the fatal action: fate (here divine providence) and human will do not rule each other out (47). Dying is inevitable, but not dying in a certain way and at a certain time. In reality, everything is subject to fate, but not to the same degree: there are events that are absolutely necessary, others that are statistically more probable and others where the probability of their occurring or not is the same. Most events conform to the course of nature, but there are certain, very particular, events that derive from the direct intervention of God: namely, miracles (48). In general, then, there is no necessity in human events; this is founded on the real existence of the category of the possible that the Megarians wished to deny. And nor does the attribution to God of the prescience of future events exclude their possibility (49), because the certainty of divine cognition does not confer necessity on events. Then there is a brief mention of the solution to the problem of future contingents given divine prescience: God's knowledge of the future and contingent event depends on the event itself, hence God knows it as contingent. Nevertheless, He still has a certain knowledge (50) since He sees it not as future but as eternally present, existing as He does in a non-temporal dimension (51). Therefore one cannot, strictly speaking, say that God foresees, because He sees all things in an ever-present and not prior actuality (52). Our condition is different: we see the future as indeterminate, for us its truth is indeterminate, in the sense that it is 'really' indeterminate (and not only that we cannot subjectively perceive its determined truth, as in the question of whether the number of stars is even or odd) (53). The conclusion, which summarizes these philosophical considerations, is that everything is subject to fate, but in different ways, and in any case the 'potentiality–possibility–contingency' [= *dýnamis*] must be admitted in what comes to pass.

Let's begin with some observations about the preface to the *Disputatio*. First, Tidike presents his text like a theodicy with a polemic objective. The target is not so much other theological or philosophical theories as a widespread *communis opinio*. There are references throughout the work to the *vulgus* and its ill-considered way of thinking and talking. Later I will propose an explanation for this attitude on the part of Tidike. Second, Tidike's comments regarding the limitations and potential of philosophy in explaining a – so to speak – interdisciplinary subject such as fate need to be stressed. It is plausible to posit the general context as that of Melanchthon's ideas on the positivity of natural reason, as a residue of the *imago Dei* (and in any case subordinate to the revealed truth in the Scriptures). Since Tidike makes reference to the tradition of the *sanior doctrina* of his tutors, it seems logical to take as a direct point of reference Joachim Camerarius the Elder, assistant to Melanchthon and an intellectual and moral authority at the University of Leipzig up to his death in

1574. The stance of Camerarius is illustrated in the pages of his commentary on the *Nicomachean Ethics* dedicated to the moral dimension of the question of fate, where it is not hard to find similarities with Tidike's arguments in the *Disputatio*, for example on the risk of merging philosophy into theology, despite the superiority of the latter and on the utility of a philosophical analysis of the question of fate.[62]

Connections with the ideas of Tidike's other teacher, Simone Simoni, are harder to find. I believe that the reason for this is twofold. First, an exhaustive synthesis of Simoni's philosophical thought has not yet been produced. Second, although Tidike praises him as a teacher of both Aristotelian philosophy and medicine, his influence on Tidike was probably restricted to the latter, conceived as a sectorial science. It is well to recall that from 1573, the year of Tidike's arrival in Leipzig, Simoni – nettled by previous experiences such as the troublesome relation with Theodore Beza in Geneva or the long philosophical-theological polemics with Schegk – evidently decided to concentrate on medicine, as confirmed by his publications in this period.[63] Nevertheless, Tidike's conviction of the legitimacy of the philosophical investigation of a subject that brings the question of providence into play, and hence implies excursions into the theological field, does not contradict the attitude expressed by Simoni in his published works; rather the contrary. Simoni is generically classified as an Averroist, especially for his adhesion to the theory of the unity of the human mind. He derived this doctrine from the study and frequentation of the principal exponents of sixteenth-century Italian Aristotelianism, Francesco Vimercato (their 'prince'), Marcantonio Zimara, Francesco Piccolomini and Genua (Marco Antonio Passeri).[64] Yet, his statements on the relation of this purely 'physiological' theory with the revealed truths do not make him a mere supporter of the Averroist theory of the double truth: the coexistence and reciprocal impermeability of two systems of thought. As shown by his polemic about the sacraments with the Lutheran theologian Jakob Schegk, Simoni justified the use of Aristotelian philosophy in certain matters – sometimes burning issues – that were not strictly the pertinence of the philosopher. Nor is it hard to find scattered through his writings statements that – with reference to Thomas Aquinas, generally considered by Simoni as the maximum scholastic authority – reveal trust in the capacity of natural reason to grasp certain fundamental truths about God, leaving to religion the revelation of the more specific contents of Christianity.[65] Or the fact that not even Aristotle always remains within the boundaries set by physiological principles and indeed, on the contrary, attempts excursions *in agro alieno*.[66]

Moving on to the *Disputatio* itself, it seems that the structure is quite clear, as indeed is the guiding thread (explained in the preface): coming to terms with the idea that admitting fate entails 'Stoic' fatalism. What is less clear is the distinction between 'physical and astrological' fate and 'providence'. Beyond the fairly obvious observation that the former comprises the impersonal and automatic forces that condition our action, whereas the latter refers back to a free and personal agent, at times it seems that these are different names that we give to the same things (see the beginning of *assertion* 20). Probably the point is this: whether or not they are different (and only conceptually or also really?),[67] what Tidike is concerned with is demonstrating that under no circumstances are we dealing with a *vis* that makes necessary the things that depend on it. In short, without putting too fine a point on it, any theoretical framework for the sentiment of unwitting resignation so widespread in the words and feelings of the populace has to be done away with. In practice, more than half of the text is devoted to fate understood as providence, to demonstrate that there is nothing Stoic in this notion. Divine omnipotence and omniscience neither make the course of events always inevitable, nor render human initiative vain or illusory. What thus emerges is the image of a personal God who guides the world but without tyrannizing it, waiting for the latter to autonomously offer Him opportunities to intervene with His providence. And this holds even for those cases, such as major political upheavals, in which there is a tendency to see the direct hand of the Creator. Or alternatively that He 'leaves be', consenting to human actions that are not pleasing to Him, almost as if deliberately bridling His own power. Conversely, there emerges the image of a human agent who is truly responsible, despite operating under the assiduous and infallible (but also loving) supervision of his Creator.

The *Disputatio* is an occasional scholastic exercise probably fished out of the bottom of some drawer. As a result it naturally does not have the ambitions and the speculative force of the benchmark Renaissance work on the subject: Pomponazzi's *De fato, libero arbitrio et praedestinatione*, especially with its fifth book on predestination.[68] Nor does it exhibit the diligence and didactic completeness of another fairly famous work, chronologically and culturally closer to Tidike: the *De fato* in nine books by Giulio Sirenio (Serino or Serina, 1553–93), a hefty neo-scholastic synthesis of the subject in the Tridentine spirit.[69] In general, there are no evident or explicit references in the *Disputatio* to this or other works relevant to the contemporary debate on fate. If I am not mistaken, the only sixteenth-century authors cited are Melanchthon and

Scaliger (see notes on the text). Even the references to ancient philosophical literature are restricted to certain classic passages from Aristotle, Cicero's *De fato* and little else. Rather more surprising is the absence of any reference to the *On fate* by Alexander of Aphrodisias, who shared with Tidike the polemic against the Stoic mentality and philosophy widespread in the Imperial era. However, in its fundamental inspiration, the work can be linked to Melanchthon's *Initia doctrinae physicae* and its concept of the relationship between natural philosophy and Christian doctrine. In fact, without aspiring to open up an authentic philosophical discussion, the *Disputatio* settles for establishing the general boundaries that ensure the plausibility of the discourse on providence, *quos ultra citraque* there is the risk of sliding into absurd and possibly even heretical conclusions. A minimal basis of theologically correct principles, which demonstrate the harmony of free will and providence, Nature and Grace, in the selfsame spirit of the *praeceptor Germaniae*. Within this context, Tidike's personal emphasis can be discerned in several characteristic themes. One of these is the radical inhomogeneity between the rational soul on one side and elementary corporality on the other. This idea, which I feel steers his philosophy towards a sort of Neoplatonizing spiritualism, emerges throughout Tidike's work. It is present in the *Phytologia*[70] and returns in the *Disceptationes* to the *Microcosmus*;[71] it is also implicit in the dichotomy of the parts of the soul in the ethical texts already discussed. The question of the heavenly bodies as one of the factors influencing the moral character of individuals (along with temperament, physical structure, parents, education, diet, etc.) had already appeared in the *Isagoge ethica*.[72] In order to clarify the way this influence acts, Tidike had there made a distinction between moral *dynameis*, *affectus* and *habitus*: habits are either virtuous or wicked, derive from the action (effective or not) of the *mens* on the affects and are liable to moral judgement. Affects are natural predispositions and are irrelevant from a moral point of view. Both habits and affects are to be differentiated from 'potential' dispositions, which are oriented towards a specific affect or habit, even less liable to ethical evaluation since even less 'dependent on us'. The *animi mores*, inasmuch as they result from the body's temperaments, according to Galen's famous formula, should be understood exactly as the latter, i.e. as natural predispositions, not as affects or, still less, as well-formed habits. Incidentally, Tidike's conclusion is that preceding natural factors, which are exempted from our control, do not determine moral habits (*non inferunt necessitatem moribus animi*). The latter fully depend on us in the sense that we can mould them through 'discipline and doctrine'. In conclusion, Tidike admitted that astral influence is possible but only indirectly, through an influx on the mere predispositions or inclinations of the individual and certainly not on vicious and virtuous habits already acquired. This complies with the principle that the soul is ultimately responsible for these and that the soul is essentially of a spiritual nature, even if it can effectively make use of material instruments that facilitate or obstruct its activity. The argument in fact ends with the old saw *sapiens dominabitur astris!*[73]

Then there is an even more characteristic point. In the *Isagoge* Tidike argued in favour of freedom and of the efficacy of human initiative, especially if this is exercised in the form of scholastic education and moral self-improvement (through the particular ascesis of the conscience that Tidike calls 'philosophy'); in the last part of the *Disputatio de fato*, also, theory and practice of medicine are represented as factors in this process. Here, indeed, the subject of medicine is addressed as the typical arena in which the contest between divine providence and free human initiative is played out. If truth be told, it almost seems as if Tidike wrote – or rewrote – the *Disputatio* with precisely this intention: to clear the decks of various pseudo-theological objections regarding the operation of the physician, clarifying that such intervention is necessary precisely because it allows God to help us. The 'sloth' of those who refuse to turn to a physician because they are convinced that what is going to happen will happen anyway or that, in any case, we are in God's hands, is a theoretical misunderstanding – naturally Tidike takes up Chrysippus' theory of co-fatality[74] – and probably also a sin against providence. And I would not rule out that these parts *pro arte medica* were added by Tidike only at a later date, at the time of the re-editing of the *Disputatio*, probably giving a specific purpose to a discourse that was more generic in its original version. Tidike had already been engaged in his noble but perhaps not universally esteemed profession in Toruń for many years now and, to defend it from the discredit cast upon it by *mulierculae et alii plebeii*, had thought it expedient to pull from under the feet of this insipient multitude the rug of the Stoic theory of fate or theological necessitarianism. It was a battle close to his heart and one in which he had already engaged, as he devoted an entire treatise, taking the form of an humanistic dialogue, to the defence of medicine and of the good repute of physicians 'against those, who whip the art of physicians'.[75]

In any case, the *Disputatio de fato* emerged from this tangle of reasons connected with Tidike's personal interests and others deriving from the age-old problem of finding a place for cumbersome Reformed theology in the late humanist curriculum. The work is not without its interesting aspects: for example, sections 39–49 anticipate the debate *de vitae termino* that was launched in the 1630s by the Dordrecht physician Johan van Beverwijck's (Beverovicius) *Epistolica quaestio*,[76] despite which it went unnoticed and there is no trace of it in the famous annotated bibliography of Arpe. In general, Tidike had little success with posterity as a writer, despite a non-negligible production that culminated in the major synthesis of the *Microcosmus*. In the light of the ethical works considered here, and in particular the *Disputatio de fato*, the reasons for this neglect can perhaps be explained as follows. A discussion on fate and providence from the perspective of natural philosophy, associated with ethical topics and set against the background of the characteristic themes of Reformed theology, made Tidike a direct heir of the intellectual tradition initiated by Melanchthon, probably assimilated into Lutheran Leipzig through Camerarius or his pupils. As we have seen, in perfect Pauline spirit, study of the providential order disposed in nature by God is a premise for bringing the mind closer to the order of Grace, and the physiology that explains the cosmic machine extending from the heavenly bodies to the human soul needs to be substantially understood in order to be prepared to listen to the revealed Word.[77] However, in the second half of the century, in the Reformed universities this intellectual system typical of the early Reformation was destined to a substantial revision. When the confessional debate began to open up within the Reform movement, and rapidly assumed the character of a bitter conflict, the contenders began to feel the need to resort to more refined and efficacious intellectual instruments than those of the humanist-based and philosophically concordist natural philosophy of Melanchthonian inspiration. The time had come for a theory of demonstration and dialectical confutation of Aristotelian matrix and, above all, for metaphysics. It was at this point that, in Wittenberg, Leipzig, Heidelberg, Tübingen and elsewhere, through the stimulus of theologians trained in mediaeval scholastics such as Pietro Martire Vermigli and Girolamo Zanchi, theology began to look less towards natural philosophy and more towards the science of being, which in this way became a crucial element in the scholastic curricula. It was inconceivable to argue with Papists and Arians about the core issues of sacramental theology and Christology without having mastered concepts such as 'species', 'substance', 'nature' and 'quality', in other words without the ammunition furnished by the *regina scientiarum*. Tidike's *Disputatio de fato* instead appears to belong to an intellectual season and climate preceding this development, when *physica* or physiology was the architectonic science on which both medicine and ethics depended and the first rung on the ladder leading to theology.[78] The same can be said of his other works. Even the most important one, the *Microcosmus* – despite appearing when the seventeenth century was well under way – seems with its concordist tendencies outdated in the face of the rampant spread of confessionalism. This may have been partly due to the fact that Tidike worked in the irenically oriented Toruń and not at a university like those of the Reformation capitals, Heidelberg and Wittenberg, which were constrained to enter the fray of the religious controversy. In fact, the curriculum of the Toruń gymnasium does not appear to have been affected by these tensions, and for long decades continued to be substantially tied to ethical Melanchthonism and the humanist culture of the early sixteenth century.[79] The text of the *diputatio* follows.

Appendix

Disputation on fate[80] and fatal things, once publicly held in Leipzig and submitted to public approval, after being subjected to quite severe censorship and examination by the Philosophical and Theological College.

Published in print in the very same place, now reviewed and newly assessed for the advantage of students.

By the authorship of Franz Tidike, philosopher and physician.

To the sincere reader, a preface.

The term Fate has been disapproved and mistrusted for a long time by wise men, and by theologians no less than by philosophers. To the point that, for many centuries, over and over again and everywhere in the schools, many have propagated numerous theories. And not of one type only, but divers, and sometimes (as in the case of the Stoics' delirium) so despicable and absurd, so rude and horrible to be heard or to be uttered, that they could not be accepted in any way, if one wished to save religion and its efforts to be righteous. There is no doubt that this question is one of the most serious and momentous among those ever addressed in religion and in philosophy, wherein it is extremely easy to fall in error, nor are they without risk. None the less, we must not estimate [those questions] so hard that we simply end up abandoning the discussion of this topic in the common assemblies of teachers and students. Indeed, what a vast quantity of errors in human souls has been caused by the fact that this question has been treated without due care. Oddly enough, this is more than sufficiently shown by the ordinary speeches of insufficiently learned men discoursing on fate and fatal things and claiming that God is the efficient cause of all their actions, even of the most insensate ones. This opinion infects many with its evilness, since they deem – as though they were at the school of some Zeno or Chrysippus – that everything is subject to fate in such a way that whatever they plough (as they say), wherever they sail, whatever they attempt, undertake, determine, act, either well or not, either wisely or not, all this happens because God wants, accepts, incites, acts and, in general, in such a way that everything which happens, must happen, as they say, according to God's command, against which everyone is powerless. In this way they can justify everything. In order to uproot this major error from human souls, where it has already deeply penetrated, it would be profitable in what follows to reaffirm the teachings on fate and the things subject to it that we have learnt from our illustrious preceptors, who followed the safer doctrine. Thus, hopefully, no one ought to regard it as merely meticulous, but rather as fruitful and indispensable. As to myself, I resolved to set down this disputation in order to expound the matter – which is extremely risky in this kind of speculation – under more clear-cut headings, and put forward some of them more openly. Also in order to offer something more than mere slavish adherence to the definition of the topic (since I am well aware that this kind of proposition should not be lacking supplementary arguments and strictly closed in its proper terms), with the aim of not adding further darkness to a dark and difficult question by an inopportune brachylogia (which is in any case inevitable, considering the magnitude of the matter at issue). The present argumentation is in part common to the theologian and to the philosopher. Therefore, for a better assessment of the question, while mainly acting as a philosopher, I could not refrain from sometimes intruding myself into the fields of Sacred Theology, though neither overly nor – as far as I can see – exceeding the manner of a philosophical disputation, but [discussing] everything in a philosophical style. Meanwhile, I would be glad if all readers did, at my request, what the sincere ones do spontaneously (nothing indeed is so rightly expressed that could not be distorted or deflected in a strange sense by those who do not understand or who wish to interpret it quibblingly). Furthermore, that all may refrain from pedantically examining every single little word (if any might appear to be uttered unadvisedly) adopting too severe a yardstick, but will rather consider and evaluate what in it is right or wrong from the entire disputation (indeed, not everything can be said in just one place). Meanwhile, sincere reader, remember what Cicero said,[81] namely that true philosophers can be recognized not by isolated words, but by continuity and perseverance. And also ponder that many different things are said correctly and safely by philosophers, who cannot be accused of being blasphemous since they are in fact concerned with the sole truth of things, whatever the words [used to express it]. Those things, though true, sometimes appear unacceptable in religion, either due to a somehow overly profane meaning in the expressions used (even Plato warns that one should speak of God only cautiously and as if He gives birth to those words) or because of their ambiguity or irreverence, which in different ways have succeeded in scandalizing many, as repeatedly happens.

Philosophical disputation on fate and on fatal things

Assertion I.

So far the term fate has been used in many contexts. In general, it designates a force which is dispersed far and wide in nature and bestows all things. Since this force is diverse in different things, it is considered as exerting its power diversely in different things.

II. Everyone is familiar with the famous opinion of the Stoics,[82] who constantly maintained that all human events are bound by an inextricable necessity in their happening. All their causes can be traced back to the supreme God, who from eternity has established a species of certainty about things, universally and singularly, the greatest and the least, both those which have already occurred and those which are to follow in the future. All things are subject to that [determination], without exception and singularly, as to a sentence which from time immemorial has been divinely set forth. For all singular things [He] has prescribed that they can never deflect by the width of a nail, as they say.

III. Whence derive these words, *moira, peprômene, heimarmenê, fatum* etc., as if to all things their own lots had been allocated, and to each single thing its destiny, which have been established since time immemorial and prepared by virtue of an irremovable decree. This is, they say, *the allocation of a part and the being destined* and what is sanctioned by presaging or by a word, as a future which is determined.

IV. And further: they connect the efficient causes of all the effects, both the lesser and the greater and the most distant, by means of a continuous and infinitely uninterrupted sequence starting from God Himself, and deriving from Him a law and an order diffused through all the parts of this universe, from the highest to the lowest, a fixed and stable order, against which nothing can ever be done. Even its author, God Himself, can do naught against it, even though He should greatly wish to.

V. [By means of this reasoning] they argue that all that has previously occurred since time immemorial are the causes – indubitably immutable – of all that has come after in all the following times. Furthermore, universally what comes after is intertwined and connected with what precedes by an indissoluble bond, by way of a chain, so that as the second things are tied to what is first and similarly the first depend on the second things. Consequently, they claimed that even God, after this order has been set, is wholly dependent upon created things.

VI. This *natural order of the whole*, whereby *from eternity some things follow others* so that *such an interdependence is unalterable*, to quote the sixth book of the *Attic Nights* of Gellius,[83] is called *Fate* by the Stoics. However, since in this way no freedom remains to God's will, which is supremely free, nor to human will, which is simply free, such fate according to us is an invented fable.

VII. It is right to say that there occurs in nature a conjunction of causes and effects, universal and particular, which is restrained within a certain order, so that universal causes govern particular ones to a single, certain effect. However, neither is this sequence of causes so [powerful] as to control something almost infinite, nor do all things without distinction follow an immutable law of consequence, capable of nullifying their proper freedom, nor, still less is [that order] capable of hindering God's will, as an obstacle tied to His feet, impeding Him from attempting anything against it.

VIII. Far better are those who admit that there is in heavenly bodies a certain and stable virtue affecting all these inferior things, both living and not, according to its proper mode and order; they confirm that this very power is what is commonly named astronomical or physical fate.[84]

IX. No sound mind will deny this heavenly force, which with a certain continuity openly turns to human affairs and insinuates into them. In fact all also admit to the belief that the superior parts of the world govern inferior nature almost in its entirety, namely in relation to the primary qualities and also to the secondary, not less than to the ones which are called third or occult and to all the things that emanate from these qualities or follow upon them.

X. There is at least one point that in this section poses a very hard question: namely whether the heavens with their proper and innate power over human kind are or are not able to forge the destiny of every human being. Or, further, to be the cause of various events affecting the mortals such as, e.g., a lucky or unlucky marriage, the fortune or the misfortune of the family patrimony, giving birth to a numerous and healthy progeny, an honest or dishonest manner of life, success in affairs and business and, finally, a peaceful or not peaceful departure from this life and so on.

XI. Furthermore, no less dubious regarding this matter is [to ascertain] whether heavenly bodies have any jurisdiction and power over a human soul, in such a way that the natural endowment of each of us, our moral character, is dependent on the force and the intercession of the stars, [to the point that] in general no one can be other than he or she actually is. As regards the latter point, here it seems opportune to state what follows.

XII Since the soul is something impassive, it is impossible for it to be affected from without, still less can it be affected by the heavens or another body. Heaven and soul indeed are not homogeneous; on the contrary, they differ from each other more than one genre differs from another. The former is corporeal, the latter spiritual; mobile the former, immobile the soul; heaven is finite in duration, the soul on the contrary is infinite, eternal and perpetually living: *by nature a body can be acted upon only by another body*, as is written in the first book of *On generation and corruption*.[85] This is why it is impossible that the soul undergoes an essential change, i.e. such that a single substance alters its innate faculties under the influence of the heavens.

XIII. What is more, there is an immense variety of human natures and characters, either because the birth of each human being occurs under a different configuration of the heavens or because she/he leads her/his life under a different heaven and in a different country. This may be established more than sufficiently by the consensus of nearly all the sages and also by the evidence of everyday experience.

XIV. For this reason, one should admit that the heavens can somehow act on our souls. I say that this is the case, but not as though the heavens, in accordance with its proper force, immediately and directly could perform an aggression on our souls, in order to impose a form on them and to forge and reforge them over again. But rather in the sense that [the heavens], by their own virtue and according to their different conformations, in different times and different places, are capable of disposing, altering and modifying these elementary bodies, in any possible way and at different times. From those [bodies], in some way, some traces of these affections overflow into our souls, due to the extremely strong bond with which they are held together with our bodies.

XV. On that basis, one should not believe that due to this natural bond [between body and soul] souls could be subjected to change (which is excluded by the very notion of *impassive*). The action and the operation of the soul is specific and proper to it alone, while the means and the instruments by which it performs its functions – such as the innate warmth and the congenital *spiritus* – could be variously affected [by material qualities]. Indeed, if the latter are altered, then the soul too performs its operation in a different manner. Consider the example of the jaundiced, who perceive all things distorted in taste and colour by bile, though these things are actually real, whereas the power of the soul or that of its faculties remains unaffected and original. This is why Aristotle claimed that an old man could have the same sight as a young man, if he had a young man's eyes,[86] precisely because it is not the soul that gets old, but the body.

XVI. At this point it is necessary to be cautious and specify that the soul's functions are not a mere and equal consequence of the body's *temperament*,[87] in such a way that they occur in every circumstance according to the way the body is, on the account of the latter's bond with the soul. One ought instead to believe that, since the part of the soul by which we live and have sensations cannot be separated from the actions of the body, being wholly and intimately implanted in the bodily organs, this occurs because it also imitates the general state of the body. In effect, in general we feed or have sensation according to the state in which the body is. Instead, moral habits and character, which both depend upon the part of the soul which shares the mind and the reason, are not so deeply immersed in the corporeal matter that they cannot [perform] deeds that are much clearer and much more free from the contamination of the body, or pursue other paths than those the body would impel them to follow.

XVII. In effect it is not true that those *habits* (as is well known, some are called *ethical* and some *dianoethical*) are what they are only due to the heavens (as Plato seemed to believe at the end of the *Timaeus*, when he, inter alia, declared that *the evil becomes evil because of the evil disposition of the body*[88]). Instead, they necessarily derive, for the most part, from education, science and the exercise they receive, despite being given a certain inclination and capacity by the conditions of the matter, in the manner just mentioned, namely in such a way that one can resist them by means of one's efforts, [an influence] which, with assiduous endeavour, can be deflected to the opposite side with the aid of the reason. This is why those who claim that if one was born to be a thief he cannot be anything but a thief, speak wrongly.

XVIII. On the other hand, if we now turn to the variable fortune of each human being, some believe that it is bestowed by the stars as if [they act] on the stage of the theatre of this life.[89] Some think otherwise. As to myself, if anything certain is to be said, I would agree that although the stars can to a great extent alter these inferior things according to their nature, they are scarcely capable of causing anything (still less necessitating) in the government of those highly inconstant events belonging to the realm of human fortune. If they can cause anything in this domain, I would say that it is only because events of such a kind are the consequence of a given corporeal quality or of a certain kind of moral habit. Namely, if as the result of a celestial influence one was born dull of wits, this tardiness, if not corrected, will prevent a brilliant career. In this case, in a sense, the stars can be said to have provoked the obscurity of such a one's name. In a similar way, we – illuminated by a celestial truth – cannot attribute the cause of events such as marriage, success in life, circumstances of death, etc., to the heavenly spheres, but rather to a much more powerful and divine cause. It can barely (or perhaps not at all) be conceived how the heavens could do this or something like it, since everything they do, indeed, is done by means of bodily qualities. Who – I ask – who of sound mind dares to attribute such events to these qualities, which are not the object of experience, except those depending on bodily matter.

XIX. And so we attribute many events to those higher creatures of God, though not everything. So that we seem to arrive at the following conclusion, as Cicero already did: just as the nature of the place has a certain relation to certain things and acts with a certain effect, while on other things it has no influence, so the conditioning of the stars, although effective for certain things (says Cicero[90]) is certainly not effective for all. And this is what we have established in the present about the influence of celestial bodies, which is commonly named physical fate.

XX. In relation to us [human beings] what may be considered as Fate is something superior to the power of heaven, [namely] what is called God's Providence. It includes not only an idle form of knowledge, by which God distinguishes all things with His gaze, but also His government, by which He protects and preserves the universe created by Him,[91] in the sense that He regulates each thing in the way that is most convenient to it. Moreover, as for all things that take place in humankind, He directs their succession in a firm and safe way and exerts His control on events.

XXI. Since this fate includes the knowledge that God has of all things and events, and also the deliberate action of God through which He is present in an effective way both in existing things and in those that happen in this life, we know for certain that nothing, even the slightest thing, escapes the knowledge that God has of human events and actions, and similarly that not everything (as in the case of the acts defined as criminal) happens because God wants it and still less because He is its author.

XXII. And I want this to be understood only in so far as things being done in [human] life are concerned, not those that exist. In fact, we all admit without hesitation that the essences and natures of all things that exist are created and preserved by God, while we know that no one of these things [would stand], if did not remain firm its *being*, through Him who is the source and the spring of each *being*, thanks to His universal presence. This was affirmed also with truth and religious sense by the Philosopher, when he said *that the order of everything and its good disposition is guarded by God*.[92]

XXIII. So, of all things, at least those that exist, some are such that God not only knows them but also makes them happen, while with regard to others He knows them only, not being the cause of them. And these are the many things that are placed in the will of a human being, and that – to use the expression of Aristotle – are generally *possible in an indefinite manner* or *likely to happen in one way or another*.[93] Of such a kind, first and foremost, are crimes of all kinds, whether slight or serious, private or public. To attribute their efficient, adjuvant or propulsive cause to fate, that is, to God's command, is impious and absolutely unacceptable in religion.

XXIV. So, while speaking of human actions, I judge rather a hyperbole that should not be taken literally the saying that: nothing comes to be, nothing moves, nothing happens, neither a speck rises nor a tuft floats, except what is prescribed and commanded by God. Unless it signifies that God has granted His own nature and His power to things one by one: for example, to a tuft so that it rises into the air for its lightness, or to the speck, to be carried up with violent motion, or to an animated being so that at will it can lift the speck or not.

XXV. Nevertheless, all human things are subject to this fate, that is to say, to divine providence and government, not because God acts on everything in the same way with His help and efficiency, but because, in certain cases He is the first to make things happen, and supports them and wants them to be. Whereas in other cases, such as those that are the effect of the action of the free human being, it is not He who accomplishes them, even if He could, but nor does He prevent them from happening, but lets them happen (even in the case of wicked deeds of e.g. Phalaris, Nero etc.[94]) under the guidance of His wise advice that goes beyond the understanding of all of us.

XXVI. But above all, and in particular, according to the common way of speaking, certain things are assigned to the administration of God (and therefore it is also said that they are fatal). They are those in which His action shines out in all evidence, since there are no sufficiently suitable means provided by secondary causes to favour that given thing [happening]. This is either because such things exhibit an extraordinary opportunity of circumstance and occasion, or because for other reasons they are sublime and of great importance for human life, or because for some reason they deserve a certain wonder on our part. It is in this way that we say that the emergence and alterations of empires are fatal; the punishments of crimes are fatal; marriages are fatal; the series and consequences of human counsels and actions are fatal; the fortune of every human being is fatal; the time and type of death is fatal; and all things similar to these.

XXVII. In this popular manner of speaking both the sense and the phrasing have a certain Stoic flavour. In fact, if someone says or does something foolish without thinking about it and without being aware of it and then a negative event follows, it is fate that is accused. *Thus was it fated* – they say – *it had to happen thus, it was God's will*, and other such nonsense, which by now has become very frequent. Thus, in the manner of the Stoics, they invest us with this indistinct necessity of all events, removing from a human agent any free will with which she/he was endowed by nature; against them, it is worth repeating what was famously said in the Odyssey:

> *It is from us, they say, that evils come, but they even of themselves, through their own blind folly, have sorrows beyond that which is ordained*[95]

XXVIII. It is true that there are, so to speak, fatal marriages. But fatal in what way? Perhaps in the sense that, just to provide some examples, it is necessary for Laius to marry Jocasta and Aegisthus Clytemnestra? If the causes of all these events or others of this kind are in fate, why then is David reproached by Nathan on divine order for having taken away Uriah's wife?[96] Why do we condemn *polygamy* in the holiest men of God because of the prescriptions of the divine precepts? Why was Laius ordered to abstain from marriage through the warning of an oracle? Why does the poet say of Aegisthus that he *seduced the wife of the son of Atreus against destiny*,[97] if such things happen *against destiny*[98] (and indeed they do happen this way) and against the will of God, and not merely by the will of a human agent who wants to commit those crimes? Therefore, let it be concluded that fate is not the cause of such things and of many other similar ones, which instead derive from the free will of a human agent.

XXIX. None the less, if someone insists on this point, then one could accept the proposition 'marriages are fatal', namely they take place through God who disposes them, i.e. in an indefinite sense, and not universally and distinctly. And there are indeed many factors that make a proposition a particular one. Even more, there is almost no marriage (or if there is, it is extremely rare) that is fatal, in the sense that God drags someone to marry – so to say – by force, or to marry someone or someone else, since in these matters to some extent the dominating factor is the freedom of the human will. However, I believe that a marriage may be called fatal since, if it is legitimate and honest, God Himself is the author of this supreme conjunction. He approves it, supports it, offers the opportunity to act, dispenses success, confirms the wills etc. However, as far as matrimonial affairs are concerned, many things happen that may be beyond or against God's will, but that He, even when he does not want them, none the less tolerates and allows them to happen. In fact, He can prevent anything, but He does not. And in this way, we have a fatal thing from which any Stoic fatality is absent.

XXX. Moreover, all people of sound mind recognize that the fatal revolutions of empires, which are like the penalties of crimes (and we all know from experience that are evenly inflicted by decree and command of God) do not happen according to the numerical harmonies or dissonances of the Platonists, and not without a violent cause, or just of old age, as if they collapsed spontaneously, but happen through God who wants them and causes them. Just as God embraces the whole duration of this world in a certain number of years, so He also wants the individual centuries and eras of the individual empires to be confined within well-defined terms (since even the parts of a defined totality should be defined).[99]

XXXI. Throughout almost all the fifth book of the *Politics*,[100] Aristotle maintains that the causes of the mutations of kingdoms are to be found in the cases of fortune of single persons, in their customs, in their acts of will, in their various initiatives. It circumscribes them more or less in categories such as offences, honour, fear, contempt, the excessive wealth of a few and the extreme poverty of many.

XXXII. None the less, in such a matter divine providence claims the main role for itself. In fact, even if God does not want anyone to sin, since human beings do evil spontaneously, He in accordance with His infinite wisdom takes advantage of the crimes of human beings – as though they were secondary causes or intermediary instruments – for the benefit of what He Himself does. In fact, though Helen's most base abduction was the cause of the expedition of the Greeks and of the destruction of Troy, on this war – which had been undertaken because of only one woman – in a truthful and authoritative way it has been written in the tragedy of Euripides that *this was a matter of God and it is not opportune to accuse mortals of it*.[101] But not in the sense that, when God wanted to overthrow the empire of Troy and establish from its ruins the empire of the Romans, then Paris in person came up as an author and fomenter of adultery, but in the sense that [God], as though the opportunity had been presented to Him and without Him explicitly wanting it, had taken advantage of it to destroy the empire of Priam in a manner that is His own.

XXXIII. In this way even private punishments are fatal, in the sense that God, unbeknownst to human beings and often in a wondrous manner, reveals the crimes of the dissolute, offering them the opportunity to confess spontaneously, either by probing their souls with the stings of conscience, or often by condemning the guilty by means of miracles and even by destining them to their well-deserved punishments.

XXXIV. In life, a human being (inasmuch he is a human being and a member of this civil society and also a *political animal*, and not because he/she is a citizen of the divine city, which is the object of the special care of God) can suffer more or less favourable or adverse events, especially if they are evaluated in terms of the lack or the enjoyment of external goods (e.g. honours, wealth, friends and the like), and on the basis of the positive or negative success of his/her desires, decisions and actions. Since all this is believed to depend on Fate or Providence and on divine will, it is opportune that this point too should be understood with discernment. Here too, indeed, we need to be careful – thinking and speaking unwisely – not to imprudently admit a form of Stoic *destiny*, as engraved in the diamond, for every case of luck that necessarily ensues in the life of each of us.

XXXV. At this point, it is necessary to uphold a precept that urges us to insist on what is required of us, because of the task we are committed to: the event must be referred to God and from Him we must expect a fortunate outcome, whatever that may be. On the basis of this precept, it seems that every cause of human destiny, without exception, must be referred to God alone as its author.

XXXVI. But in the meantime all of us in our lives appreciate and consider true proverbs such as these: *man is God to man; man is wolf to man.*[102] And no one will deny the truth of the sentence that I believe to be Cicero's own, from the second book *On Duties*, where he concludes in this way a prolonged discourse on a matter that, as he says, offers no reason for doubt. He says: *as we get great benefits from the cooperation and consent of men, so there is no plague so detestable that does not come to man by another man.* And shortly afterwards he adds to this reflection a very important precept: *therefore* – he says – *there is no doubt about this point, that men benefit and harm each other, so I affirm that the task of virtue is to join men each other and [by this union] lead them to favour their own advantage.*[103]

XXXVII. From these two fundamental points (no one will question them) put together it follows, in the question of the causes *of successes and failures*, as the Greeks call them, that is, of those things we experience in daily life (in which many things happen without God and against God), that the origin of many of them is not to be imputed entirely to God as their sole author. Instead, it sometimes happens that by far the most important part is to be imputed to single persons, whether they are good or evil. It is evident how powerful their consent is. And I wonder, what envy cannot do among people? What hatred, whether open or hidden, and also fear, perfidy, perverse emulation, self-love, suspicion, avarice, and many other vices of this kind? Certainly enough, in this kind of event, for these factors to be assigned the primary role, the secondary one and even the third.

XXXVIII. This is the role that fate seems to have in these things, since God, who regulates everything by His providence, lets people proceed to a certain point and do what they want to do for the benefit or to the detriment of others. He also grants, to a limited extent, that events correspond to their desires. However, whenever it seems right to His supreme wisdom, by means of an extraordinary action He himself infringes or sustains human efforts in amazing manners: either by putting obstacles in the way or by suggesting very happy opportunities that hasten the realization of the endeavour. And He does so because He Himself is the only ruler of human will, who knows how to steer in the direction He wants or how to divert it from the path it has undertaken. And all this with a form of command not at all like that of a master, but of a political kind, i.e. more tempered;[104] and in fact, it is not God that forces one to want something, if we remain within the sphere of human things, that is, while speaking in philosophical terms. In this sense [it can be said that] at times the fortune of human beings is fatal only to the extent that God sets the goals of human efforts, goals – we ought to specify – not Stoic, namely inevitable and immutable, but different in different cases and in accordance with human decisions and actions. This explains the truth of the proverb: *each one is the blacksmith of his fortune*, and the other one: *everyone reaps what he has sown*,[105] that is, things go well or not with everyone in the same way that every human being behaves both towards God and towards other people. In this way, we get rid of any Stoic necessity and providence is saved, and the freedom of human agents, as the Philosopher acknowledges it, also remains firm, and there is room for consultation and deliberation on what is to be done.

XXXIX. This is how people speak of the life and death of human beings: the time and manner of everyone's death is predetermined. It is prescribed as if it were written in a will. And as regards this term, however much effort and trouble one may take, he or she will never be able to overcome it or change it. And with regard to the manner of death, no one will ever in any way be able to avoid it or escape it, even if it were to be the most scandalous. So, they say that everyone who dies has fulfilled his or her fate or has been called by God from this life, as though God had simply wanted each of us to die at a given moment and by a given type of death. This is a manner of speaking that is certainly unworthy of a Christian, and yet is the most common in people's mouths.

XL. That being so, this idea has put down roots deeply in the souls of the plebeians, with the consequence that it has made room for what the ancient philosophers have called the *lazy argument*, meaning that all action becomes pointless. For example, if you are fated to be cured of this disease or not to be cured, whether you bring in a physician or not you will either be cured or not.[106] One of these two [contrary] outcomes is fatal, as many Stoics have said, and as now many other people are repeating. Accordingly, it does not matter whether you summon a physician or not. Therefore, it will be inevitable to ban medicine from humankind forever, since everything is governed by the fates. It will also follow that – for example – some human beings will inevitably be sent to the gallows, with God who wants and orders that a given person be a thief. Nothing is more impious than such discourses.[107]

XLI. So, in order not to decree that God is the cause of sin and also to leave some room for physicians, whose value, as we read, *is equal to that of many others put together*,[108] let this be our conclusion on the life and death of human beings: God, as He is the Lord of all things, so He is of life and death as well. In every single moment He can put an end to someone's life or extend it, but He does not immediately use this power of His. In fact, He created nature, to which He entrusted everything as to a minister, reserving for Himself the role of helping it according to His own ways, in different manners in different cases.

XLII. Human life consists in the conjunction of body and soul. The bond that holds them together is something which is like a middle term between the body and the spirit, that is, the innate warmth combined with the spirit supported by it; once the spirit has dissipated and the heat has been exhausted, due to disease or other causes, that bond is broken and then the soul is separated from the body. That's what death is all about. And since death does not happen in any other way than when, as a result of the failure of this conjunction, the innate heat is destroyed, and since the causes that can destroy this innate heat are already present in elementary nature, then the causes of death have to be sought in the conditions that already exist, which in fact exist to serve the will and resolution of their author.

XLIII. In the series of current conditions there is nearly an infinity of causes that can bring us death. To counteract them, we are given medicine and the work of physicians, with the warning that often, if you do not use medicine properly, not only do you fail to do the patients good, but even risk harming them; but if you use the art of medicine correctly, you will restore them to health. That is why it is opportune that we all admit that the life and death of many (though not all) is in the power of the medical science and that – as we all claim – capable physicians heal while the incompetent ones cause more damage. And how then can we attribute every law of life and death (living and dying not in absolute terms, but at a given moment and in a given manner) to fatality?

XLIV. Often, however, in medicine, as Celsus put it very well, although what must be done is definitively established, none the less its consequences are not,[109] so that often what follows [after the cure] disappoints the hopes of the physicians, even when they do exactly what their art prescribes. And only when this occurs do the causes of the lack of success become manifest: either a defect in the art itself – who has ever been able to discern all the arcana of nature? – or the virulence of the disease, which proves to be superior to any force of medicine.

XLV. And it is in these cases that the power of divine providence is often manifested. For when God, by a particular decision of His, wants to call someone from this world to Himself, He does so through the secondary causes and as the Lord of nature. Then He makes the causes of illness stronger and deeper, so that they resist the action of medicines; or He diminishes the strength of medicines themselves and limits their efficacy, so that they do not do what they would usually do, until death takes possession of the sick person. Hence, we can understand that the death of certain people is fatal in the sense that often a given person dies because God wants her or him and disposes of her or him, and then it happens that (albeit not inevitably, since the divine will can always be bent by prayers) that person dies. And if it is so (and often it is so), the sick person will not be freed from the disease, whether he or she avails him- or herself of the help of the physician or not. And medicine has nothing to do with such cases, unless something is done that abuses the rules of this art or to test the strength of the disease.

XLVI. God is not the cause of death in all cases and without distinction, I mean a death of this or that kind. Otherwise, even those whom the Greeks call *murderers by their own hands* would merely submit to the command of God while ignominiously taking their own lives. They themselves are the cause of their own death, voluntarily. And the others who die when they reach extreme old age, even though they die according to the laws imposed on nature by divine decree, could indeed have died much earlier if they had not behaved prudently in life or had not accepted the help of physicians. In fact, it is not out of necessity that their life is prolonged to that limit.

XLVII. And therefore the above-mentioned 'lazy argument', as Cicero calls it (he introduces and criticizes it, but does not fully explain *the reason for its falsehood*, in which the true refutation of the sophism consists, according to Aristotle) is not valid. In fact this assumption, which holds that one of the two is fatal – to treat or not to treat – is false if understood *in universal terms or as necessary*. It is certainly true in some cases that by fate one does not cure or likewise that by fate one does cure, but this is thanks to medicine. So we read in the Sacred Scriptures of Hezekiah:[110] although the prolongation of this king's life [to a given term] was fatally settled, however, in order to restore his health and to heal his tumour, a poultice of figs was prepared. For God, the creator of nature, wants to be efficacious also with regard to the health of the body, that is, through intermediaries, which are always proportionate [to the effect], even if He could [do the same] with His word alone. On these things what was said before is not true, since the deaths of many are voluntary, those of many others depend on other causes that are destructive, even without there being an order from God.

XLVIII. From all this it is correct to conclude that, as the inevitability of dying is the same for all, but not dying at a given moment or in a given manner, or if such an inevitability exists in certain cases, it is certainly not similar to the first. In this way it is clear that many of the propositions often used about what is fatal, being indefinite, should not be considered as being universal and always necessary in the same way, since divine providence is present in reality in a very variable way and therefore not all things are subject to fate in the same way, but some in one way and some in another. Some things are governed by fate in such a way as to happen of necessity and without variation; others are not necessary, but incline more towards one or the other of the two alternatives, and even that fatally. Others happen by fate, in such a way as to be completely at the mercy of their own inclination and freedom to do one thing and its opposite indifferently. In the same way many by fate submit themselves to the common course of nature. Finally, others are affected by the divine forces in a singular and peculiar way, that is to say, beyond the secondary causes, and these things are called miraculous.

XLIX. In general we must conceive of fate in such a way that, ruling out the necessity of human events on account of the contingency and mobility inherent in things, we leave to each thing what is its own and hence we reserve for human will the integral freedom it enjoys. We must also uphold that potentiality in things, thanks to which some things can happen even if they do not actually happen. It was this potentiality that the Megarians wanted to take out of the way, reproached by Aristotle in Book VIII of the *Metaphysics*.[111] Nor are these conclusions contradicted (as the philosophers mistakenly thought) by the fact that God, in His perfect wisdom, has a certain foreknowledge of all the things that will happen, even those that will happen after many centuries. In this He never is mistaken and this is more than true.

L. In fact, the certainty of divine foreknowledge does not confer any necessity on events, since events do not depend on prediction and, on the contrary, the precognition is a consequence of the events themselves and of their condition. Therefore, when the future thing is contingent and ready to happen in one way or another, God foresees it as such, that is, that it will happen in a contingent way, so that, although it is future, it will still have the same power to happen in another way and, before it happens, it remains in suspension. God, however, even in this doubtful state of affairs, is most certain of the event; this is proved by divination, which has always and everywhere been held in high esteem.

LI. And it is not a problem that, according to Aristotle's *On interpretation*,[112] future contingencies do not present a definite truth (because the state of the propositions always follows that of things themselves, so that if things are doubtful the truth of the [relative] propositions will also be doubtful). In God, indeed, this *axiom* is not valid, since for Him nothing is uncertain and nothing is future, since all those things that for us are future, even by many centuries, to Him are present. For He does not live in time like us, but in eternity, *in the instant*, which is permanent and forever the same.[113]

LII. Therefore, to use the most learned words of some learned men, the word 'foresee' is not appropriate for the almightiness of God, unless we presume to measure the intelligence of the highest majesty with our impaired intelligence.[114] That 'foreseeing' is just for us, since [for us] the future exists. But God, for whom there is no future, strictly speaking does not foresee, but in the simplest manner He sees what is present. And all things are ever present before Him, all are in actuality nothing in potentiality, there is no time in Him, but He is the Lord of time, [He is] before any principle, albeit unknown to us, and in Him there is no before and no after.

LIII. So let it be established that future contingencies cannot be known to us, even if they are known to God, before they happen to us. And therefore, not only what is future in a contingent manner is not known in a determinate way, but its truth is not certain before it happens. Therefore, when at school we teach that there is no determined truth of future contingencies, that is, in the human mind or by human judgement, this should not be understood as if the cause of this uncertainty was that this truth is not determined with respect to us or that it eludes our knowledge (as in the other case when we ask ourselves if the number of stars is even or odd, where neither is definitely true in the sense that this number is unknown to us, although one of the alternatives must definitely be true). Instead, in this case the truth is not determined because things are still in a state of uncertainty. Truth, in fact, does not depend on human knowledge, but on things themselves.

LIV. In general, let the conclusion of all these questions be the following: in human affairs God knows everything that is, that has been and that the future will bring. However, with regard to actions and other things that happen in this life, He does not want them all to happen in the same way, nor when they occur, does He act as the [direct] author of all that is done, not even in the case of all those things that, by mutual consent, we admit to being primarily fatal. However, all things are subject to fate, but each in its own way and diversely, thus preserving potentiality in what comes to pass. This is what may be said in this matter, especially if it is dealt with philosophically.

The end.

Conclusion

The writers considered in the previous pages belonged to the academic milieu of a circumscribed area – the German-speaking region situated between the Vistula and Upper Bavaria / Lower Saxony – over a relatively short period of time, namely the decades around 1600. With the only partial exception of Hermann Conring, all these authors could be considered 'minor'. In effect, names such as those of Philipp Scherb, Ernst Soner, Cornelius Martini, Henning Arnisaeus and Franz Tidike say very little to anyone who is not a specialist in the Reformed academic philosophy of the time. Moreover, these professors did not work in the capitals of German Reformation, like Wittenberg and Heidelberg, but in medium-sized cities such as Altdorf, Leipzig, Toruń, Gdansk and Helmstedt in which – even taking into account the considerable mobility characterizing the academic population of teachers and students at the time – the radius of influence of the academic institutions was regional or at most interregional. In this process, the impulse of the powerful movement of renewal of school education promoted by Ramus and followers was a decisive factor because it stimulated his opponents, the 'Aristotelians', to clarify their stance and then to submit the legacy of the Stagirite to an overall revision for the contribution it could make to this particular task. And I would say that this generation of academics, obviously with different results depending on the different intellectual temperaments and the particular local conditions, carried it out successfully, somehow laying the foundations of the modern *Schulphilosophie*. As we have seen, some of these figures, such as Scherb and Martini, had the makings of pioneering intellectual leaders.

In this context, 'Aristotelianism' is certainly not the name of a philosophical doctrine or of a set of doctrines, especially because in many cases it is arguable that the philosophical outcomes can in any way be qualified as Aristotelian (we have seen some examples in Conring's political thought, in the idea of philosophy as a 'scientific' and 'analytical' kind of knowledge, and of metaphysics becoming the most general of these sectorial disciplines, etc.). As we have suggested, it is instead, at best, a 'paradigm' with all the plurality of meanings that this term contains, and therefore also the label we give to a compromise, not devoid of ambiguous points and inevitably tentative and provisional.

There is one point, however, that I would like to highlight. In scholarship on early modern Aristotelianism, this orientation is often described as substantially 'antinomic', referring by this to an antinomy between its 'secular' variant, largely of Italian origin, i.e. sceptical about the possibility of bringing Aristotle and Christianity into agreement on major philosophical themes (the nature and destiny of soul, the origin of the cosmos and God's causality, the possibility of human freedom etc.); and that, largely of Iberian origin, which instead addresses the possibility of a composition between the two. This interpretation is obviously strengthened by considering the growing importance in the sixteenth century of confessional debates, which could be roughly described as pivoting on the antagonism between Catholic 'rationalism' and Protestant 'fideism'.[1] However, the writers and the texts examined here tell quite a different story. We have seen that, in the milieux and in the authors studied, the possibility or impossibility of keeping Aristotle and the principles of sacred doctrine together is not at issue, as ultimately all the participants in this collective effort take it for granted that this can and must be done. The hypothesis of an Aristotle explicitly oriented towards 'atheism' (*à la* Pomponazzi, to recall a famous stereotype), hostile on principle to the teachings of Holy Writ, is generally not taken seriously. And, as we have seen, the authors dealt with are inspired as much by Zabarella and Cesalpino as by Fonseca and Pereira, without measuring them by a confessional, religious or theological yardstick, but only by the hermeneutical contribution that they can make to understanding the doctrines of the Stagirite or philosophical truth as such. Likewise, the limits of the 'pagan' Aristotle are an obvious and discounted fact, which is not even worth dwelling too much on since they are the limits common to all philosophers, the limits of philosophy itself, i.e. the discourse that explains human experience by means of *logos* alone, without really coming up against higher principles of non-human origin. I think I am not mistaken in saying that more or less all the figures presented here would have recognized themselves in the famous formula *vera philosophia cum vera theologia nusquam pugnat*.[2]

The history of academic Peripateticism in the decades around 1600 is instead a story that brings to the fore a common and unifying ideal: namely, the conviction that philosophy, of which Aristotle is the most authoritative teacher, is irreplaceable in the education of young people. Beyond the sociological and intellectual aspects highlighted by Hotson, this is the sense – and the most frequently evoked feature – of the opposition to Ramism, which all Aristotelians believe 'mutilates' philosophy and ends up eliminating it or reducing it to something else. Or, in other words, if one takes the words seriously Ramist doctrine is not a philosophy. A similar meaning must be attributed to the omnipresent leitmotif of the 'acroamatic' Aristotle, which expresses nothing but the need for the truthful, consistent and thematically 'homogeneous' presentation of a given sector of knowledge as the foundation of an intellectually serious education, an education based on the knowledge of reality and not on the mere ability to master terms and discourses (highlighting the latent nominalism of the Ramists and its pernicious effects in pedagogy). Of course, the objection can be made that the claim of Lutherans and Calvinists to an 'integral' philosophy, especially in logic and metaphysics, was bent to the purpose of not lagging too far behind the hated Catholics. One has to study Zabarella and Suarez not to be left without arguments in the confessional debates on the real presence, existence and possible location of Purgatory and on other papist fantasies. However, I believe such an argument is misleading and does not do full justice to the protagonists of this common intellectual enterprise. Indeed, one should not overlook the simple fact that this philosophy was taught not only to future pastors and theologians, but also to future doctors, judges, administrators, diplomats and anyone who aspired to responsibility of any kind at urban, regional, national or even European level.

Since the 1970s, especially in the studies of Wolfgang Reinhard and Heinz Schilling, the so-called 'confessionalization' paradigm has been established as the key to understanding the epoch between the Peace of Augsburg and the outbreak of the Thirty Years' War.[3] However, what I attempt to analyse here is a process that tends instead to indicate the limits in the spread of the confessional factor or of other territorial idiosyncrasies. It is the process of circulation of ideas and the collective commitment to building a modern *paideia*. In this, an important role was attributed to classical philosophy, as expounded by Aristotle and his interpreters of every age, and hence deemed to have an objectively universal validity.

Several cases could have been studied in which the 'acroamatic' ideal did inspire the construction of academic disciplines. Here I have confined myself to the examples of metaphysics – which had a particularly troubled process of 'disciplinization', albeit also substantially immune to confessional influences – and of politics and ethics, which perhaps best illustrate how this process took place in the sometimes ambivalent confrontation with the Aristotelian heritage and the fruitful dialogue with the culture of the time. Inspired by the part historic, part legendary model of Aristotle as the educator of Alexander the Great, the sixteenth- and seventeenth-century professor of philosophy of Aristotelian persuasion addresses the leaders of tomorrow and provides them with the necessary preparation to perform their roles. To be a member of any elite it is important, for example, to know how to articulate a syllogism, recognize a fallacy and reveal a contradiction, but also to explain *per causas* a certain state of affairs, or to know how to recognize *virtutes* and *vitia* in one's own behaviour and that of others. It is similarly crucial to be able to distinguish between rightful and degenerate forms of government, between prudent rulers and demagogues, in short a series of – if I may say so – theoretical practices essential in any programme of secondary or higher education. Making philosophy a system of discipline was not a simple or risk-free operation, but through their efforts a generation of relatively obscure Aristotelians assured it a certain and widespread influence on the mindset of the European elites of early modernity.

Of course, nothing is forever. As said, the compromise reached was necessarily temporary and new times were pounding at the gate. The famous humanist and theologian Gerardus Vossius (1577–1649), Conring's former professor at Leiden, in a posthumous work advises his reader not to restrict himself to studying the doctrine of a single school, even if it were the most prestigious.[4] But in fact, the system of academic disciplines he proposes is nothing more than Aristotelian, at most integrated with those fields of knowledge that the Stagirite and his disciples had no time to deal with. However, Vossius had not been so ambiguous in the work *On philosophical sects* published together with the previous one and most likely revealing his true thoughts. While addressing the greatest praise to Aristotle among all the ancient thinkers for the progress he has made in philosophy,[5] he argues that the Peripatetic school, important as it is, is nothing more than a *sect* among others. Is it not better then – he asks – to overcome this sectarian logic and become followers of the 'eclectic' school? This, indeed, is the only sect which in reality is not a sect, because its concern is not with the *verba magistri*, but with truth itself, as it is attained by the senses and reason.[6] This a proto-enlightenment motif, which not incidentally was taken up a century later by the erudite author of the *Historia critica philosophiae*. In conclusion let us read Vossius' words:

> If we follow this [eclectic] sect we will no longer end up being Ionic or Italic or Eleatic, Platonic or Peripatetic, Stoic or Epicurean; Sceptical or followers of any other sect; but of all. Let us choose therefore the flowers of all the sects and let us make of them a crown for our head. This crown, the more it will obtain of truth and goodness, the more it will be beautiful and perfumed, and the less it will rot.[7]

Notes

Preface

1. *Aristotle and the Renaissance* (Cambridge, MA, 1983).
2. *Subverting Aristotle: Religion, History, and Philosophy in Early Modern Science* (Baltimore, 2014).
3. Silvia Fazzo, 'L'aristotelismo come tradizione esegetica', *Paradigmi*, 62 (2004), 367–84.
4. Cees Leijenhorst and Christoph Lüthy, 'The Erosion of Aristotelianism Confessional Physics in Early Modern Germany and the Dutch Republic', in Cees Leijenhorst, Christoph Lüthy and Johannes M.M.H. Thijssen, eds, *The Dynamic of Aristotelian Natural Philosophy from Antiquity to the Seventeenth Century* (Leiden/Boston/Cologne, 2002), 375–411.
5. See n. 2.

Chapter 1

1. Félix Ravaisson, *Essai sur la Métaphysique d'Aristote*, vol. I (Paris, 1837), 229. See the last note of this chapter.
2. Enrico Berti, *Aristotele: dalla dialettica alla filosofia prima* (2nd edn, Milan 2004), 143, draws attention to the following: *Phys.*, IV, 10; *Metaph.*, XIII, 1; *Nich. Eth.*, I, 13 and VI, 4; *Eud. Eth.*, I, 8 and II, 1; *Pol.* I, 5, III, 6, VII.
3. Quintilian mentions Aristotle's afternoon courses in rhetoric in *Inst. Or.*, III, 14; see also Strabo, *Geogr.*, XIV, 1, 48.
4. Berti (*Aristotele*, 148), following Düring, points out that the term *akroatika* was probably coined by Andronicus of Rhodes, the alleged editor of Aristotle's works and a contemporary of Cicero. Aulus Gellius then adopted it from Andronicus.
5. First, the Aldine *editio princeps* of 1495–8 and that of Erasmus, published in Basle in 1539.
6. Plutarch, *Vita Sullae* (26) and Strabo (XIII, I, 54). This evidence was collected by Ingemar Düring, *Aristotle in the Ancient Biographical Tradition* (Gothenburg, 1957). The Aldine *princeps* of Plutarch's *Lives* is dated 1519, although the text had been circulating for some time in Latin translations, notably that of Campano, 1470. The *princeps* of Strabo was published in 1519. Aulus Gellius was also widely available in

printed form, the first edition (by Johannes Andreas) dating to 1469, the *giuntina* to 1513, the *aldina* to 1516 and the *parisina* to 1519.

7 [These books] 'sunt extra id opus, in quo tunc versatur', See Aristotle, *Aristotelis de republica libri VIII interprete et enarratore Io. Ginesio Sepulveda Cordubensi* (Paris, 1558), 80v–81r. This is consistent with the passage in *Pol.* I, 5 (in Sepúlveda's division of chapters, Ch. 3), 1254a 33–4, where Aristotle employs the comparative form (*exôterikôtera*), no technical sense is assigned to this term: 'though his question seems to belong to a different genre (alienior esse)', 8v.

8 Ibid., 81r.

9 Ibid.

10 The programmatic nature of this preface has been stressed by Alejandro Coroleu, 'A Philological Analysis of Juan Ginés de Sepúlveda's Latin Translations of Aristotle and Alexander of Aphrodisias', *Euphrosyne*, 23 (1995), 175–95; see also id., 'The Fortuna of Juan Ginés de Sepúlveda's Translations of Aristotle and Alexander of Aphrodisias', *Journal of the Warburg and the Courtauld Institutes*, 59 (1996), 325–32.

11 *Aristotelis de republica, Praefatio ad Philippum*: 'Tamen ut [Aristotle] res tractat obscuras et vulgo ignotas, sic verbis necessario utitur novis aut populo inauditis, caeterisque doctis etiam hominibus inusitatis. Et quod veteres etiam annotarunt, obscuritatis interdum affectat, ne philosophia contemnatur, si tardis aut pigris hominibus optimarum rerum cognitio sine labore contingat. Et dubias orationes ex industria facit, quae in varios sensus trahi possint.'

An antecedent of this reading might be the well-known *Oratio de causis obscuritatis Aristotelis et de illarum remediis* (Valencia, 1554), by the humanist Juan Pedro Nuñes (Nunnesius, 1529–1602), a pupil and follower of Ramus but also an advocate of a renewed and 'methodical' Aristotelianism, which he endeavoured to introduce into the University of Valencia (see Wilhelm Risse, *Die Logik der Neuzeit* (Stuttgart/Bad Cannstatt, 1964–70), 2 vols, vol. 1, 164–5). Nuñes refers explicitly to Aristotle's effort of presenting philosophy in an unclear way (*studium obscurandae philosophiae*), actually a result from his exaggerated precision in the use of words (*singularis verborum proprietate*), so that – as all interpreters of the Stagirite admit – a superficial and occasional reading of his texts cannot provide a sufficient understanding of them. On the reformed Aristotelianism of Valencia, see Charles H. Lohr, 'Metaphysics', in Charles B. Schmitt, Quentin Skinner, Eckhard Kessler and Jill Kraye, eds, *The Cambridge History of Renaissance Philosophy* (Cambridge, 1988), 537–638, esp. 609–11.

12 *Francisci Patricii discussionum peripateticarum tomi IV* (Basel, 1581; 1st edn 1571), I, 6, 64.

13 Ibid., 72.

14 Ibid., 71, with a reference to *Eth. Eud.*, I, 8, 1217b 22–3, where *exôterikoi logoi* are distinguished from those *kata philosophian*.

15 Ibid., 68. On the importance of *De mundo* as the potential source of an Aristotelian doctrine about providence in fifteenth-century philosophy, see Jill Kraye, 'Aristotle's God and the Authenticity of De Mundo: An Early Modern Controversy', *Journal of the History of Philosophy*, 28/3 (1990), 339-58.

16 *Discussionum peripateticarum*, 68: 'Hoc autem significatu exotericum nil aliud refert, quam logicum, dialecticum, probabile. Philosophicum vero nil aliud itidem significat, quam demonstrative, scientifice, ex rebus per se, essentialibus, intrinsecis rei.'

17 Ibid., 73: 'Concludendum itaque secunda significatione exotericum idem significare, quod extraneum, alienum, vanum, dialecticum, logicum, ἔνδοξον, καθόλου, contraposite ad proprium, intrinsecum, essentiale, scientificum, demonstrativum, analyticum, philosophicum et ad veritatem dictum.'

18 As confirmed by Patrizi's concluding reference to *De gen. an.*, II, 8, 748a 8-13, where the 'universal and empty' discourses (although in Aristotle there is actually no allusion to dialectics) are contrasted with those resulting 'from special/proper principles' (*ek tôn oikeiôn archôn*).

19 Here a brief reference should suffice to the further evolution of Patrizi's interpretation of Plato's and Aristotle's esoterism, as detected in certain texts of the appendix to the *Nova de universis philosophia* (Ferrara, 1591: *Plato et Aristoteles mystici et exoterici*). On the *Appendix* see Erna Banić-Pajnić, 'Petrić's View of Plato and Aristotle According to the Appendix of *Nova de universis philosophia*', in Erna Banić-Pajnić, Laura Blažetić, Mihaela Girardi-Karšulin, Ivan Kordić and Ivica Martinović, eds, *Philosophical Topics: Interpreting Tradition and Modernity* (Zagreb, 2004), 9-34; on Aristotle in Patrizi see Maria Muccillo, 'La vita e le opere di Aristotele nelle Discussiones peripateticae di Francesco Patrizi da Cherso', *Rinascimento*, 21 (1981), 53-119; id., 'Dall'ordine dei libri all'ordine della realtà: ordine e metodo nella filosofia di Francesco Patrizi', in Tomáš Nejeschleba and Paul Richard Blum, eds, *Francesco Patrizi Philosopher of the Renaissance: Proceedings from The Centre for Renaissance Texts Conference, 24-26 April 2014* (Olomouc, 2015), 9-61, esp. 31-44; Michael J. Wilmott, ' "Aristoteles Exotericus, Acroamaticus, Mysticus": Two Interpretations of the Typological Classification of the "Corpus Aristotelicum" by Francesco Patrizi da Cherso', *Nouvelles de la République des Lettres*, 2 (1985), 67-95.

20 In *Opera logica* (Venice, 1578), *De natura logicae* represents the *ouverture* of the sylloge.

21 This theory is sustained by Antonino Poppi, *La dottrina della scienza in Giacomo Zabarella* (Padua, 1972).

22 *De natura logicae*, II, 12, 51-2.

23 Ibid., 49: 'Sequitur secundo loco usus artis dialecticae, quae probabilibus argumentis quodlibet problema confirmare docet, huiusmodi enim rationes faciles ac populares sunt et opinionem quandam in animo gignunt rei postea demonstrandae,

nostrumque animum praeparant ad vim demonstrationis, quae firmam rei scientiam pariat, percipiendam.'

24 *De dialogo liber* (Venice, 1562; Italian translation by Franco Pignatti, Rome, 1993).
25 Marta Spranzi, *The Art of Dialectic Between Dialogue and Rhetoric: The Aristotelian Tradition* (Amsterdam/Philadelphia, 2011), 137–54.
26 *De dialogo*, 1r and 5r–v; see *Ammonius* in *Aristotelis categorias commentarius*, ed. A Busse, in *Commentaria in Aristotelem Graeca*, vol. 4 (Berlin 1895), 4, 18–27.
27 *De dialogo*, 6r.
28 Ibid. As to *Nich. Eth.* I, 13, the term 'exoteric' could allude not to the *Eudemus*, i.e. a dialogue, but to *De anima*, which is undoubtedly a scientific treatise.
29 *De dialogo*, 6r.
30 Ibid., 7r.
31 Esp. *Top.*, I, 2, 101a 34–6.
32 The biographical document with most information about him is the funeral oration declaimed on 13 November 1587 by the humanist Francesco Ciceri, alluding to the fact that, thanks to *De sermonibus*, Ferrari's name was already well known 'north of the Alps' (*Francisci Cicerei epistularum libri XII et orationes quattuor*, 2 vols (Milan, 1782), vol. II, 240). Ciceri praised Ferrari by saying that 'ita bene graece loquebatur ac scribebat, ac si Athenis et natus et enutritus fuisset' (237), possibly alluding to the practice of lecturing in Greek (as Silvia Fazzo assumes: 'Philology and Philosophy on the Margin of Early Printed Editions of the Ancient Greek Commentators on Aristotle, with Special Reference to Copies Held in the Biblioteca Nazionale Braidense, Milan', in Constance Blackwell and Sachiko Kusukawa, eds, *Philosophy in the Sixteenth and Seventeenth Centuries: Conversations with Aristotle* (Aldershot 1999), 48–75). His philosophical orientation raises no doubts, since Ciceri himself called him *peripateticorum nostrae aetatis princeps* (222). Ciceri also recalls the inscription engraved on a bust of him: *philosopho aristotelico ac medico, graecis latinisque litteris egregie eruditus*. See also Girolamo Tiraboschi, *Storia della letteratura italiana* (Milan, 1833), vol. IV, 39–41. It should also be mentioned that Ferrari owes part of his posthumous fame (in Jakob Thomasius and, from the latter, in Leibniz) for having been associated with Marcantonio Maioragio (alias Anton Maria Conti) by Mario Nizolio in the final stage of the latter's famous polemic against 'pseudo-philosophers' and masters of 'dialectics and metaphysics'. More precisely, according to the author of *De veris principiis* (1553), it was Ferrari in person who instilled in Maioragio a preference for a version of Aristotelian philosophy drenched in Scholasticism. Needless to say, this was a fairly crass accusation, levelled when the polemic between Nizolio and Maioragio had degenerated. On the dispute Nizolio–Maioragio and its later echoes in Leibniz see Cristina Marras and Giovanna Varani, 'I dibattiti rinascimentali su retorica e dialettica nella "Prefazione al Nizolio" di Leibniz", *Studi Filosofici*, 27 (2004), 183–216.

33 *Octaviani Ferrarii Hieronymi F[ilii] mediolanensis de sermonibus exotericis liber* (Venice, 1575). Quotations here are from the Frankfurt edition of 1606, on which see below p. 26–7.
34 *De sermonibus*, 35.
35 Ibid., 41. The entire argument against Sepúlveda is on pp. 35–53.
36 Ibid., 50.
37 Ibid., 53.
38 If it were not too remote from the topic under discussion, it would be interesting to take into consideration Ferrari's controversy with the Florentine Bartolomeo Cavalcanti (1502–62), a political writer and a commentator on the *Rhetoric*, on the subject of moral virtue. Ibid., 131–3.
39 Ibid., 54: 'dummodo nos audiat, ad rem nihil interest, aditu prohibetur nemo'.
40 Ibid., 54–6.
41 Ibid., 56–7. Incidentally, certain scholars have recently questioned the convention crediting Andronicus with the 'editing' of Aristotle's work, and in particular of *Metaphysics*. On this aspect, see the instructive studies of Silvia Fazzo on the parallel 'emergence' of Aristotle's *Metaphysics* and 'metaphysics' as a science during the imperial age. Among other essays of this author, see 'L'emergenza della "Metafisica" di Aristotele in età romana', in Silvia Gastaldi and Cesare Zizza, eds, *Da Stagira a Roma: Prospettive aristoteliche tra storia e filosofia* (Pisa, 2017), 155–83.
42 *De sermonibus*, 59.
43 Ibid., 63.
44 Ibid., 64.
45 Ibid., 68.
46 Ibid., 70–2.
47 Ibid., 77. This is why they should be considered as dialecticians rather than as true philosophers; ibid., 72–3.
48 Ibid., 94.
49 Ibid., 96. Horum prius αυτοπρόσωπον simul et ἀκροαματικὸν nominari ait, ob eam rem, quod in eis doctor, nempe is qui disciplinam tradit alii, cum iusto et legitimo auditore solus cum solo sermonem habet; sic tamen ut qui audit, tamquam si persona muta sit, nihil nec roget nec respondeat. Posterius autem quodque contrarie opponitur superiori διαλογικὸν et ἐξωτερικόν ea de causa appellatum, quod idem scriptor aliena persona ad communem utilitatem suscepta multorum partes unus agit.
50 Ibid., 98–9.
51 Ibid., 102. As usual Ferrari prefers a word-by-word translation, which is worth quoting: 'Exotericas orationes dicit ad discrimen acroamaticarum et demonstrativarum, ex probabilibus et persuadibilibus profectas [τοὺς ἐξ ἐνδόξων καὶ πιθανῶν ὁρμημένους]. Dictum est autem in categoriis exotericas rationes neque

demonstrativas, neque ad legitimos auditores dictas fuisse, sed ad multitidinem ex persuadibilibus profectas.'

52 Ibid.: 'Primum, exotericas orationes confici ex probabilibus; alterum, illas neque demonstrativas esse, neque veris et legitimis auditoribus tradi; tertium, constare ex iis, quae ad persuadendum multitudinem sunt accomodata.'

53 *De disciplina encyclio* (Venice, 1569), printed just after the *De sermonibus exotericis* in the Frankfurt edition.

54 *De sermonibus*, 111–12.

55 Ibid., 141.

56 Ibid., 155. See also 165–6 for Ferrari's polemical remarks against Aquinas on this point.

57 Ibid., 107–66.

58 Ibid., 166.

59 Ibid., 213–15.

60 A similar view (with reference to the interpretation of *Poet.* 1447b 9–10) is attributed to Sigonio, Tasso and Speroni by Spranzi, *The Art of Dialectic*, 134–41.

61 *De sermonibus*, 182.

62 Up to p. 190 there is a rather technical discussion on the extension of the attributes *de inesse*, in which Ferrari argues with Themistius, jumping to the conclusion: even terms that are opposed as contrary (e.g. straight/curved, even/odd) belong to the *genus suppositum* (respectively: 'line' and 'number'), though they are not predicable of any species of that *genus*. On the importance of this discussion *de inesse* in the debate between the adversaries and followers of Ramus, see Chapter 2.

63 Ibid., 189–90: 'Itaque ex iis, quae in eodem genere sint, non extra illud, demonstrationem fieri prorsus necesse est. Ex quibus etiam patet, ea, quae rem vere consequuntur, non modo vera esse, sed et per se et intra idem genus cohiberi, non extra illud vagari.'

64 Ibid., 190. On Renaissance debate on *endoxa*, see Ch. 6 of Spranzi, *The Art of Dialectic*.

65 Ibid., 193.

66 Ibid., 192.

67 Ibid., 201.

68 Ibid., 204–7.

69 Ibid., 196.

70 Ibid., 198: 'infirma notitia; exoterica minime sunt de rebus, etiam si de iis esse videantur'.

71 *Top.*, I, 2, 101a 36–7: *pros ta prôta tôn peri ekastên epistêmên*.

72 *De sermonibus*, 225.

73 *Oratio III*, 231. Ciceri, in all likelihood referring to a malicious criticism addressed at the time to Ferrari, wondered why such an acute philosopher 'gathered so few listeners'. In the answer we recognize the ideals of *De sermonibus*:

Never he did seek the favour (*ambire*) of the listeners, though it is a very common habit. In the first place his practice was to determine the exact words of the Stagirite, comparing the Greek and the Latin sources and amending the new books in the light of the ancient ones; in short, he did nothing that was appropriate to a popular interpreter. And we know that the man who behaves thus cannot expect numerous listeners.... This supreme Peripatetic could not be satisfied with anything that was vulgar or popular. He was well aware that philosophy is content with few judges and purposely shies away from the multitude.

74 See Wolfgang Mährle, *Academia Norica: Wissenschaft und Bildung an der Nürnberger Hohen Schule in Altdorf (1575–1623)* (Stuttgart, 2000), 185–260. It is worth noting that in Altdorf the terminology exoteric/acroamatic had been adopted prior to this reform, since it originally corresponded to the basic division of the disciplines following the neo-Sturmian programme set up by Freige (see the *ratio studiorum* of the Altdorf *Semiuniversitas* as presented in his *Paedagogus* (Basel, 1582), in the dichotomic table at the beginning of the work). The distinction derives directly from Ramus's *Professio regia* (Basel, 1576), edited by Freige himself, where it is used to make a distinction between preparatory studies in the field of grammar, languages and rhetoric and advanced studies in mathematics, physics and ethics. It is also interesting to note that the students on the elementary and advanced courses were respectively labelled 'exoteric' and 'acroamatic' (Frederick J. Stopp, *The Emblems of the Altdorf Academy: Medals and Medal Orations 1577–1626* (London, 1974), 20–9).

75 Martin Mulsow,'*Die whare peripatetische Philosophie in Deutschland*: Melchior Goldast, Philipp Scherb und die akroamatische Tradition der Alten', in Helwig Schmidt-Glintzer, ed. *Fordern und Bewahren. Studien zur europäischen Kulturgeschichte der frühen Neuzeit* (Wiesbaden, 1996), 49–78. More synthetically, id. 'Ambiguities of the *Prisca Sapientia* in Late Renaissance Humanism', *Journal of the History of the Ideas*, 65/1 (2004), 1–13, esp. 9–12.

76 See n. 32.

77 *Endoxa paradoxa, de differentiis analytices et dialectices, auctore Ph. Scherbio, ea in Acad. Altorfina disputando tueri conabitur M. Georg. Gallus* (Altdorf, 1589).

78 Ibid.

> CXII Ex hac autem adumbrata veteris Dialectices et Analytices imagine, facile iam licet cernere, miserrimum naufragium optimorum in Peripato institutorum. Nam ut nihil de aliis dogmatibus dicam, quae tam erudito seculo, si nobis placet, e manibus nostris elapsa sunt, videmus quam praeclara illa sit Dialectica, quae nuper a novis sapientibus introducta est. Primum enim, quod palmarium illis est, penitus ab eis tollitur (o Ilium, o patria!) λόγος διδασκαλικός, id est, ratio docendi evertitur per Doctores, ratio sciendi per scientes, ratio Philosophandi per

Philosophos: negans enim apodixin, negat λόγον τῆς διδασκαλίας, negat φιλοσόφεμα, negat scientiam rerum, negat denique definitionem perfectam, quae sola thesi terminorum ab apodixi Aristotelica differt.

CXIII Cur igitur non aperte ἀκαταληψίαν profitemur et recta in Pyrrhoniorum castra concedimus? Cur non Physici, Medici, Politici, quisque suam artem definit, si nullius rei veram et continentem causam tenet?

79 *Clavis philosophiae peripateticae aristotelicae, hoc est Octaviani Ferrarii, Hieronymi F[ilii] Mediolanensis De sermonibus exotericis, liber unus, et De disciplina encyclio, liber alter, nunc primum in Germania editi ex Bibliotheca Melchioris Haiminsfeldii Goldasti, cum eiusdem De Cryptica veterum Philosophorum disciplina epistola ad Rodolphum Goclenium Philosophum Marpurgensem*, 1506 (sic). Formerly Goldast had published a dissertation *De Aristotelis libri acroamaticis et exotericis* (Altdorf, 1597).

80 On the mentioned oddities and on the overall meaning of Goldast's editorial operation see esp. 66–9 and 75 of Mulsow's essay.

81 *Clavis*, 4–6 and 15. Two other significant topics of the letter are the intentional and – of course – commendable *obscuritas* of Paracelsus (21, in a patriotic spirit: Paracelsus was Swiss like Scherb and Goldast) and the envy of the organization of the Jesuit schools (22: they make a strict selection of their students, we admit *oves et boves*).

82 Mulsow, 'Die whare peripatetische Philosophie', 75.

83 *Clavis*, 30–3.

84 *Clavis philosophiae peripateticae, sive Disputationum philosophicarum, quibus universa doctrina logica, physica, ethica et politica artificiosissima methodo proponitur et declaratur, liber singularis, in academia Altorfina conscriptus a Philippo Scherbio, . . . Accessere quaestiones logicae Flamini Nobilii* (Frankfurt, 1625). In actual fact, Nobili's *Quaestiones* precede the Altdorfian section, which has a separate numbering. On this edition see Mulsow, 'Die whare peripatetische Philosophie', 70.

85 *Isagoge in lectionem Aristotelis, hoc est hypotyposis totius philosophiae Aristotelis* (Nuremberg, 1605).

86 *Isagoge in lectionem Aristotelis, hoc est hypotyposis totius philosophiae Aristotelis . . . . Olim a Michaele Piccarto Professore Organico Altdorffino concinnata, nunc iis partibus, quibus deficiebat, aucta et notis plurimis altera vice illustrata, atque ad usum in Theologiam applicata a Johanne Conrado Dürrio SS. Theologiae et Philosophiae Morali in Academia Altdorffina Publico Professore. Praemissa est Epistola viri Hermanni Conringii, continens judicium de isto libello, ejusdemque iterata editione* (Altdorf, 1660). The Altdorf Lutheran theologian Johan Konrad Dürr enriches Piccart's text with, inter alia, long explanatory notes and a *Disputatio proemialis de origine, natura et progressu philosophiae aristotelicae*. In this edition it is easy to discern a, so to speak, confessional evolution of the acroamatic/exoteric topic:

according to Dürr, Scherb and Piccart reformed Aristotelian philosophy by disentangling it from theology. Dürr insists that the mingling and confusion of the two was characteristic of mediaeval scholasticism, actually fostering heresies. Piccart's work could have been an influential source on Aristotelian thought in the ulterior development of German philosophy, see Francesco V. Tommasi, 'Michael Piccart, Kant e i termini primi. Il trascendentale nel rapporto tra filosofia e linguaggio', *Archivio di Filosofia*, 73 (2005), 369–90. On Conring, see Chapter 4.

87 *Marii Nizolii de veris principis et vera ratione philosophandi contra pseudophilosophos libri IV* (Frankfurt 1670). In the *Dissertatio* it is written: 'Acroamaticus est in quo omnia demonstrantur, Exotericus in quo quaedam sine demonstratione dicuntur, confermantur tamen congruentiis quibusdam et rationis topicis, vel etiam demonstratoriis, sed non nisi topice propositis; illustrantur exemplis et similitudinibus. Tale dicendi genus dogmaticum quidem seu philosophicum est, acroamaticum tamen non est, is est, non rigorosissimum, non exactissimum.' On this point, see John Whipple's entry 'Leibniz's Exoteric Philosophy' in *The Stanford Encyclopedia of Philosophy* (Summer 2013 Edition), Edward N. Zalta, ed., https://web.archive.org/web/20131202064741/https://plato.stanford.edu/archives/sum2013/entries/leibniz-exoteric/

88 An alternative to the elimination of dialectics from philosophy is to assign dialectics the role of a ladder – to eliminate after using it – to the science of truth. This is exactly the solution arrived at by Félix Ravaisson during the Romantic era, interpreting the acroamatic/exoteric dichotomy as based on that between 'probable' dialectic (understood as a logic 'qui prend son point de départ dans l'apparence, dans l'opinion' and consisting in the clash of contradictory hypotheses) and truth-yielding demonstration (*Essai sur la* Métaphysique, 232–3). Ravaisson is aware that this dichotomy derives from the Neoplatonic commentators of Aristotle (Ammonius and Simplicius, 220–3) and that it was revived in the Renaissance tradition (he makes scattered references to Gian Francesco Pico, Patrizi and Scaligero). Within the perspective of his (Neoplatonizing) spiritualism, this amounts to saying that dialectics performs a preliminary work of survey and examination, in order to cut away (*retrancher*) all controversy and then die out (*expirer*) as such, stepping aside and making way for the 'intuition immediate par l'esprit' (*Essai sur la* Métaphysique, 243–4).

Chapter 2

1 Ulrich L. Leinsle, *Das Ding und die Methode: Methodische Konstitution und Gegenstand der frühen protestantischen Metaphysik* (Augsburg, 1985), vol. I, 21.
2 As to Ong, see *Ramus, Method and the Decay of Dialogue: From the Art of Discourse to the Art of Reason* (Chicago 1958; 2nd edn, Chicago 2004). According to Bruyère

(*Méthode et dialectique dans l'œuvre de la Ramée*, Paris 1984) *Introduction*, IV, the keystone of Ramus's thought is 'le concept de dialectique, enraciné dans un platonisme originel', which is further developed by Descartes and Port-Royal. See also Risse, *Die Logik der Neuzeit*, vol. 1, 126: 'Ramus begründet seine Dialektik zunächst metaphysisch durch die platonische Ideenlehre'; Cesare Vasoli, *La dialettica e la retorica dell'Umanesimo. 'Invenzione' e 'metodo' nella cultura del XV e XVI secolo* (Milan 1968), 340–3, talks about Ramus's Neoplatonic inspirations – not specifically philosophical, actually; Guido Oldrini, *La disputa del metodo nel Rinascimento: Indagini su Ramo e sul ramismo* (Florence, 1997), esp. Ch. IV: in the footsteps of Bruyère as to the focus on method, while stressing the theoretical limitations of Ramism. On the alleged Platonism of Ramus see also Leinsle, *Das Ding*, 24.

3   Hotson, *Commonplace Learning: Ramism and Its German Ramifications, 1543–1630* (Oxford, 2007).
4   Leinsle, *Das Ding*, vol. 1, 30.
5   See the discussion on this point in Ong, *Ramus*, 45–6, 172–4, with reference to the information reported by Johann Freige, Ramus' first biographer, who held that Ramus defended the assertion that: *omne quod Aristoteles scripsit est commentitium* (on Freige see Chapter 1, n. 77).
6   *Die Logik der Neuzeit*, 154–6. Bruyère is of a different opinion (*Méthode et dialectique*, 119): the revision consisted merely of a '*change de langage*' in a concept dominated by the suggestion of the Platonic dialogues, primarily the *Philebus*. For a well-balanced discussion of the topic, see Hotson, *Commonplace Learning*, 43–4.
7   The reference to Freige is made by Erland Sellberg (see the entry: Petrus Ramus', *The Stanford Encyclopedia of Philosophy* (Summer 2016 Edition), Edward N. Zalta, ed. https://plato.stanford.edu/archives/sum2016/entries/ramus/). The *Defensio* was published in Lausanne in 1571. See the following passage, remarkably insolent, where Ramus's attempts to convince Schegk to embrace his view about logic, as being the least prejudiced and the closest to the spirit of Aristotle's thought: 'Mitte stomachum et iracundiam, mitte anticipatas de Aristotele scriptis opiniones, Aristotelis animam in Aristotelis principiis ac legibus suspice, de corporis Aristotelei membris omnia complectere, quae ad illius anima usum facultatem, vitam, sensum, rationemque facient: tum dialecticam nostra in argumentorum inventione, in enunciati, syllogismi, methodi iudicio et dispositione laudabis et P. Ramum aristoteleum esse percipies', 224–5.
8   In addition to Leinsle's book, see the classic works of Max Wundt, *Die deutsche Schulmetaphysik des 17. Jahrhunderts* (Tübingen, 1939), and Walter Sparn, *Wiederkehr der Metaphysik: Die ontologische Frage in der lutherischen Theologie des frühen 17. Jahrhunderts* (Stuttgart, 1976).
9   Basel, 1569, col. 26.
10 Ibid., col. 29.

11 Ibid., cols 24–6.
12 Ibid., col. 30.
13 Ibid., col. 41.
14 Ibid., cols. 66–74. In the *Defensio* (70–1) Ramus returns to the three laws, now considered universal principles of logic, surpassing – and rendering futile – the Aristotelian distinction between analytic and dialectic ways of reasoning. Ramus discusses the three laws on different occasions; as a benchmark we can take that in the third part of the *Scholae in liberales artes*, the *Scholae dialecticae* (in turn mindful of *Animadversiones aristotelicae*, see Bruyère, *Méthode et dialectique*, 25–6) cols 354–441. There is a plain presentation also in the *Defensio*, 70–1. For a discussion of the 'laws' see Ong, *Ramus*, 258–63, Risse, *Die Logik der Neuzeit*, 156–8, Bruyère, *Méthode et dialectique*, 267–75, Oldrini, *La disputa*, 85–120, and also Hotson's remarks (*Commonplace Learning*, 44–5) on the difference between the meaning and role of these principles in Aristotle on the one hand (= rules of the demonstrative reasoning) and Ramus on the other (= laws, methods for the ordering of disciplines).
15 *P. Ramii regii professoris scholarum metaphysicarum libri quatuordecim* (Paris, 1566), *Praefatio*: 'hic [Aristotle] scientiam cogitarit a logica diversam omnium causarum, sed praesertim primae, seu omnis entis quatenus est ens, sed praecipue primi'.
16 Ibid.: 'Quare cum dico in quatuordecim libris nil nisi logicum ab Aristotele confundi, non dico ab Aristotele sciente et prudente contra logicas Aristotelis leges confundi, sed huc tamen re vera ac veritate philosophum contra philosophiae suae decreta delapsum esse.'
17 *Defensio*, 40, with a reference to *Scholae metaphysicae*.
18 *Praefatio* to *Scholae metaphysicae*.
19 Risse differentiated strict Ramists, Philippo-Ramists (trying to reconcile Ramus's logic with Melanchthon's), semi-Ramists or 'systematic' (like Keckermann, assembling a syncretic logic out of Aristotelian and Ramist elements), *Die Logik der Neuziet*, 163. On these denominations see Hotson, *Commonplace Learning*, Chs 3 and 4.
20 The first two chapters of Hotson's *Commonplace Learning* provide an extensive and precise description of the various phases ('generations') of this phenomenon.
21 Altdorf, 1590. This work was reprinted in 1644 in Johann Paul Felwinger's sylloge *Philosophia Altdorfina* (Nuremberg, 1644), 10–46, from which I quote. On Felwinger see Chapter 3, n. 8.
22 Mährle, *Academia Norica*, on Scherb, 215–17; on Freige, 235–43.
23 *Dissertatio*, 10.
24 Ibid., 11–13.
25 Ibid., 16. See Zabarella's *Opera logica* (Venice, 1578): 'Res omnes in genera duo dividuntur ab Aristotele', 1–4. Zabarella reworked the well-known passage of *Nic.*

Eth., 1139b 19–24. It seems that a substantial boost to the spread of Zabarella's thought in Germany was provided by the quarto edition of his works (Frankfurt, 1594), with the important and famous preface by Johann Ludwig Hawenreuter. On this see the essays by Ian Maclean, 'Mediations of Zabarella in Northern Germany, 1586–1623', 173–98, and Sachiko Kusukawa, 'Mediations of Zabarella in Northern Europe: The Preface of Johann Ludwig Hawenreuter', 199–213, both in Gregorio Piaia, ed., *La presenza dell'aristotelismo padovano nella filosofia della prima modernità: Atti del Colloquio internazionale in memoria di Charles B. Schmitt (Padova, 4–6 settembre 2000)* (Padua, 2002). Maclean convincingly argues (183) that the intention to curb the spread of Ramism was already immanent in other transalpine editions of Zabarella's work, like that of Frankfurt 1586 (or 1587) promoted by Giulio Pace.

26 *Dissertatio*, 26.
27 Ibid., 25–6:

> Cuius est agere de uno, modisque omnibus unitatis et identitatis ... eius quoque est agere de ente, cuius unum est quasi πάθος (convertuntur tamen inter se ens et unum). Nimirum scientia de ente eiusque omnibus divisionibus erit quoque tua. At qui agit de ente, agit de primo ente, sive de Deo, ut fieri debet in vocabulis ab uno, auctore ipse hoste tuo Aristotele. Ergo ages quoque de Deo. Ergo theologia quoque tota tua est. Iam quia axiomata illa: 'De quovis ente vera est affirmatio aut negatio', 'Non contingit idem simul affirmare et negare', in ente tuo insunt, etiam haec axiomata propria tua erunt, id est, habitus qui νοῦς dicitur, ad te pertinebit. Et quid multis moror? Habitus, qui σοφία ἁπλῶς vocatur, compositus ex intellectu et scientia, tibi quoque addicendus est, si modo oceanus causarum, in philosophiam Aristotelis, ut tu ais, effusus, tui quoque regni est. Ecquid beo te? Etiam amplius quid quaeris? Certe volebam eodem iure te quoque introducere in possessionem mathematicarum disciplinarum. Sed credo tibi hoc quidem temporis satis esse; fortassis ipsemet iam metuis ne tanta imperii magnitudo ruinam rebus tuis minetur.

28 Ibid., 26.
29 Ibid.
30 Ibid.
31 Ibid., 57–69.
32 Ibid., 28: 'optimus noster praeceptor, Jacobus Zabarella ὁ Μακαρίτης'.
33 See *Dissertatio*, Chs X and XI.
34 Ibid., 32: 'fit ut tunc quidem Dialecticorum finem dicamus victoriam, non quidem ambitionis aut pecuniae studio'.
35 See Ch. 3. See also the parts of Piccart's *Isagoge in lectionem Aristotelis* (Chs 26–30) devoted to the metaphysics. On this see Mährle, *Academia Norica*, 382–4.

36 Hotson, *Commonplace Learning*, 137–9, referring to the *epistola dedicatoria* to the *Contemplatio peripatetica de locatione et loco* of 1598 (in *Opera omnia*, Geneva, 1614), vol. I, col. 1766–7), of which Scherb is one of the two dedicatees. Keckermann makes a reference to Scherb's distinction between the exoteric and acroamatic books of Aristotle (1769–70), which was to be brandished against Ramus's followers too since they were unaware of the distinction (see the *Dissertatio* introducing the *Praecognita Logica*, in *Opera omnia*, vol. I, 82 B–H). Another Aristotelian thinker who turned out to be decisive for Keckermann's default from Ramism was Daniel Claepius. It was during his private lessons that the young Keckermann learnt Zabarella's ideas (Ibid., 135 D–E). For a detailed presentation and analysis of Keckermann's anti-Ramist polemics during his stay in Heidelberg, see Kees Meerhoff, 'Bartholomew Keckermann and the Anti-Ramist Tradition at Heidelberg', in Christoph Strohm, Joseph S. Freedman and Herman J. Selderhuis, eds, *Späthumanismus und reformierte Konfession: Theologie, Jurisprudenz und Philosophie in Heidelberg an der Wende zum 17. Jahrhunderts* (Tübingen, 2006), 169–206.
37 Hotson, *Commonplace Learning*, 136–55.
38 Ibid., 155–65.
39 *Opera omnia*, vol. I, col. 119 A–D (= *Praecognita logica*, II, 3).
40 Ibid., col. 83 C (= *Praecognita logica*):

> An tantum de rebus secundum species sint disciplinae conformandae, non autem secundum genus seu an disciplina eiusmodi constituenda sit, quae tractet de re seu ente qua res est, deque illis quae rebus naturalibus, rebus mathematicis, rebus ethicis communiter insunt non tamquam argumenta logica, sed tamquam reales et positivae affectiones ac modi, ut est essentia, existentia, bonitas, perfectio, finitudo, relatio ad primum ens seu Deum et ab eo dependentia.

41 Ibid., cols 163–4.
42 Ibid., cols 16G–17A. See also 163–4.
43 With his last forces, see Hotson, *Commonplace Learning*, 158–9. *Systema compendiosum totius metaphysicae* in *Opera omnia*, vol. I, cols 2013A–2014F.
44 Ibid., col. 2015 B.
45 Ibid., col. 2035 B.
46 *Metaphysicae systema methodicum* (Steinfurt, 1606).
47 *Systema compendiosum*, col. 2024 E–H.
48 Ibid., col. 2040 E–G. On this point, allow me to refer to Danilo Facca, *Bartłomiej Keckermann i filozofia* (Warsaw, 2006), 145–51, see also Hotson, *Commonplace Learning*, 154, n. 127.
49 Ibid., 157.
50 Lohr, 'Metaphysics', 632–3.
51 Meerhoff, 'Bartholomew Keckermann', 197–8.

52 Leinsle, *Das Ding*, 204.
53 Riccardo Pozzo, *Adversus Ramistas: Kontroversen über die Natur der Logik am Ende der Renaissance* (Basel, 2012), 52–62. On other aspects of the affirmation of Aristotelianism over Ramism in Helmstedt, see Chapter 4 of this book.
54 Pozzo, *Adversus Ramistas*, 68–90, describes in detail the development and chronology of this polemic between the Ramist circle, including Friedrich Beurhaus, Konrad Hoddäus, Heizo Buscher and Anton Nothold (with the addition of Kaspar Pfaffrad, a collaborator of the famous Daniel Hoffman) and Martini, who is the common target of their critiques.
55 Lemgo, 1596, pages not numbered. On Nothold's stance on the distinction between dialectics and metaphysics see Pozzo, *Adversus Ramistas*, 154–8.
56 Ibid., b1-2 (*Brevis et necessaria ramistarum ad duo capita dedicationis responsio*).
57 Nothold recalls a famous definition originally formulated by Lucian of Samosata and later approved by Melanchthon: *Ars est ordo* (σύστημα) *certarum propositionum exercitatione cognitarum, ad finem utile in vita*, *De Rameae institutionis principiis*, B. On the importance of this formula see Leinsle, *Das Ding*, 18.
58 Ibid., Chs 5–6. The reference is to *Vita Alexandri*, Ch. 7.
59 On this issue see Riccardo Pozzo, 'Res considerata and Modus considerandi rem: Averroes, Aquinas, Jacobo Zabarella and Cornelius Martini on Reduplication', *Medioevo*, 24 (1998), 151–76.
60 *De Rameae institutionis*, Ch. XX *Quod ens qua ens lib. 4 Metaph. cap. 1 non ut Cornelius sentit specificative sub sola natura entis sit accipiendum*. Ch. XXI *Quod ens, qua ens reduplicative, id est, pro omni ente accipiendum sit, juxta sententia Rami*.
61 Ibid., Ch. XV: *Quod viri doctissimi de subiecto logicae idem* [*scil*. than Ramus] *docuerint*.
62 Ibid., Ch. XXI *Quod ens . . . 3. Ex antiquiorum consensu* (I5-6).
63 Ibid., Ch. XXII *Quod capite 2 libri 4 Metaphysicorum Aristotelis sententia sit ens qua ens non solum Metaphysicae, sed etiam Dialecticae et Sophisticae subiectum esse*.
64 Ibid., Ch. XXIV *De non ente, ubi respondetur ad magistri Martini thesin 21* (m1).
65 Ibid. (m2).
66 Ibid., Chs XXVI–XIX.
67 Max Wundt, *Die deutsche Schulmetaphysik*, 6 and 98–103. On Martini see also Gino Roncaglia, *Palaestra rationis: Discussioni su natura della copula e modalità nella 'Scolastica' tedesca del XVII secolo* (Florence, 1996), 57–8, n. 7. See also the praise addressed to Martini by his pupil Henning Arnisaeus, cited in n. 73 to this chapter.
68 Leinsle, *Das Ding*, 206–8.
69 Martini completed this assignment in the *Adversus ramistas disputatio de subiecto et fine logicae*, published in 1596 in Hanover and Lemgo.
70 *Metaphysica commentatio compendiose, succinte et perspicue comprehendens universam Metaphysices doctrinam* (Strasbourg, 1605; another edition was published the same year in Wittenberg).

71 *Metaphysica, brevibus quidem sed methodice conscripta* (Jena, 1622; also published in Helmstedt in the same year). On this see Wundt, *Die deutsche Schulmetaphysik*, 99–100.
72 Leinsle, *Das Ding*, 207–8. The dedication of the *tractatus* to Martini is dated April 1603. In it Arnisaeus addresses his teacher with these words: 'Tu enim, quod quidem ego sciam, primus in Germaniae Academiis, metaphysicae veram faciem reddidisti, quae ab aliis prorsus abolita, a nonnullis futilibus nugis deturpata, ab omnibus certe neglectim habita erat' (A3). Aside from the obvious polemics with the Ramists, Arnisaeus defends the key points of Martini's conception (the subject of metaphysics is the real being and its properties/affections; metaphysics considers and evaluates the principles of all sciences without subordinating them), placing them within the context of mediaeval and modern Scholastic philosophy. A later publication by Arnisaeus, the *Epitome Metaphysices* (1606), contains no reference at all to Martini.
73 *Disputationum metaphysicarum prima ... praeside clarissimo acutissimoque viro M. Cornelio Martino Andvverpio, respondebit Iacobus Lampius Schermbecensi Calendiis Augusti* (Helmstedt, 1604); *Disputatio metaphysica secunda de subiecto metaphysicae ad quam praeside M. Cornelio Martino ... respondebit ad XI Calen[darum] Septembr[is] Ioannes Canutus Coldorphus Danus* (Helmstedt, 1604). These texts are worth reading for the limpid synthesis they offer of Martini's thought; for instance *thesis* 39 in the second one, on the 'analogy of intrinsic attribution'.
74 If I'm not mistaken the only references are in the preface (*nebulae Ramisticae*, A4r), plus a reference on p. 44 to a passage of the *Scholae metaphysicae*.
75 Jean-François Courtine, *Suarez et le système de la métaphysique* (Paris, 1990), 416. However, it is likely that Martini had already taken Suarez's thought into consideration, since the Spaniard is quoted in the texts mentioned in n. 73 to this chapter.
76 Here we do not go into the other polemics Martini was involved in, first with Daniel Hoffmann and then with Balthasar Meisner. Against them he defended the legitimacy of the use of logic and philosophy in theology. This episode has been extensively studied by German historians. For the second of these polemics see Sparn, *Wiederkehr der Metaphysik*.
77 *Metaphysica, brevibus quidem sed methodice conscripta*, 31–2: 'Ubi datur scibile, ibi quoque dari debet, certe potest, scientia.'
78 Ibid., 18–40.
79 Ibid., 31.
80 Ibid., 47.
81 Ibid., 36.
82 The 1605 edition also included the *res* and the *aliquis* (250), albeit with the proviso that they are less important and were added to the list of transcendentals beginning with the Arabs.

83 Ibid., 87–8. On the meaning of the introduction of the disjunctive transcendentals, as urged by Scotus, see Lohr, 'Metaphysics', 627.

84 *Metaphysica, brevibus quidem sed methodice conscripta*, respectively 33–64 and 64–86. On this see Riccardo Pozzo, 'Cornelius Martini sull'oggetto della metafisica', *Medioevo*, 34 (2009), 305–14.

85 *Metaphysica, brevibus quidem sed methodice conscripta*, 64–5. See Franco Riva, *Analogia e univocità in Tommaso de Vio 'Gaetano'* (Milan, 1995), 51–63.

86 *Metaphysica, brevibus quidem sed methodice conscripta*, 68: 'Haec autem sunt entia rationis, quae rebus non ex sua natura conveniunt, sed quatenus intellectui repraesentantur, vel ex eo, quod intellectus circa illa negociatur.'

87 Ibid., 69: 'ut facilius illos disponere, inter sese componere, a sese disiungere et de iis argumentari possit intellectus'.

88 Ibid., 82: 'aequaliter quoque et indifferenter iis [i.e. to lower beings] attribui non potest, sed tali ordine, ut prius fit absolute in substantia, deinde in accidente cum habitudine ad substantiam'.

89 Ibid., 85.

90 Lohr, 'Metaphysics', 614.

91 *Metaphysica*, 91.

92 I, 5, 38, quoted by Martini on pp. 107–10.

93 See the *Metaphysica in usum quaestionum in philosophia ac theologia adornata et applicata* by Jan Makowski (Maccovius) (Leiden, 1650; actually drafted about twenty years earlier) with subsequent editions edited by Adrian Heereboord; see also Alsted's 'methodical' *Metaphysica* (Herborn, 1613).

94 See esp. Courtine, *Suarez*.

95 Actually a *farragines scientiarum*, as Hotson put it, *Commonplace Learning*, 254–72.

96 On the evolution of the understanding of metaphysics in the academic centres of the territorial principalities during the epoch of the so-called confessionalization, i.e. after the promulgation of the *Formula concordiae* (1577), see the incisive reconstruction of Lohr, 'Metaphysics', 620–38.

97 See again Lohr, 'Metaphysics', 604–20.

98 Aristotle, *Metaph.*, Book A.

Chapter 3

1 *Philosophie in Deutschland zwischen Reformation und Aufklärung 1550–1650* (Berlin 1988), 352–66, esp. 353–9. This work drew inspiration from the nineteenth-century interpretation of Otto Fock's *Socinianismus nach seiner Stellung in Gesammtentwicklung des christliches Geistes, nach seinem historischen Verlauf und nach seinem Lehrbegriff dargestellt* (Kiel, 1847). On the Aristotelian and Paduan

inspiration of Socinian thought see Emanuela Scribano, 'Aristotele contro Platone in Fausto Sozzini', *Rinascimento*, 46 (2006), 73–92.

2 On Soner's life see Richard Falckenberg, 'Soner, Ernst', *Allgemeine Deutsche Biographie*, 34 (1892), 622–3, https://www.deutsche-biographie.de/pnd117751944 html#adbcontent; Johann Jakob Brucker, *Historia critica philosophiae, a mundi incunabulis ad nostram usque aetatem deducta*, 4 vols (Leipzig, 1742–4), vol. 3 (1743), 312–16; Philipp Knijff and Sibbe Jan Visser, *Bibliographia Sociniana: A Bibliographical Reference Tool for the Study of Dutch Socinianism and Antitrinitarianism* (Hilversum Amsterdam, 2004). Ralf Bröer, 'Antiparacelsismus und radikale Reformation: Ernst Soner (1573–1612) und der Socinianizmus in Altdorf', *Odrodzenie i Reformacja w Polsce*, 48 (2004), 117–47.

3 See for instance Wollgast, *Philosophie*, 386, on Crell's rejection of Aristotelian philosophy, in contention with Cesalpino and Soner. Also Zbigniew Ogonowski, *Socjnianizm a Oświecenie. Studia nad myślą filozoficzno-religijną arian w Polsce XVII wieku* (Warsaw, 1966), 2–3 and Ch. IV.

4 Wollgast, *Philosophie*, 365.

5 Ogonowski, *Socjnianizm a Oświecenie*, 452.

6 Ibid., Ch. IV. For some time Socinian 'rationalism' has been under reappraisal, underscoring its diversity from post-Cartesian and seventeenth-century rationalism in general. See Ogonowski, *Socjnianizm a Oświecenie*, Ch. VIII; id., 'Le rationalisme dans la doctrine des sociniens', in *Movimenti ereticali in Italia e in Polonia nei secoli XVI–XVII: Atti del convegno Italo-Polacco, Firenze 22–24 settembre 1971* (Florence, 1974), 141–57. More recently, Filippo Mignini, 'Spinoza e i sociniani', in Mariangela Priarolo and Emanuela Scribano eds *Fausto Sozzini e la filosofia in Europa: Atti del Convegno (Siena 25–27 novembre 2004)*, in (Siena 2005), 137–78, 175–8; Elisa Angelini, 'Introduzione', in Johannes Ludwig Wolzogen, *Annotationes in meditationes metaphysicas Renati Des Cartis* (Rome, 2012), VII–LXXV; id., 'Un commento eccentrico: Hans Ludwig Wolzogen e la lettura sociniana delle Meditationes de prima philosophia', in Mariangela Priarolo and Emanuela Scribano, eds, *Le ragioni degli altri: Dissidenza religiosa e filosofia in età moderna* (Venice, 2017), 81–100.

7 The famous *Historia Crypto-Socinismi Altorfinae quondam Academiae infesti arcana* (Leipzig, 1729).

8 See *Ernesti Soneri professori Norici Philosophi et Medici olim celeberrimi in libros XII metaphysicos Aristotelis commentarius editus a m. Johanne Paulo Felwinger norimbergensi, politicae, metaphysicae et logicae Altdorphi Professore Publico* (Jena, 1657), *Praefatio*, mentioned by Zeltner, *Historia Crypto-Socinismi*, 38–9. In this preface, Felwinger (on him, see Roncaglia, *Palaestra rationis*, 65–70) explains how he came to the difficult decision of publishing Soner's commentary largely because it was already circulating among students in a version to which *mixtae* matters of philosophy and theology had been added (e.g. *de visione Dei beatifica, de corporum*

nostrorum in resurrectione alietate, de corporibus sive materia angelorum). Aside from this consideration, he acknowledges Soner's value as a commentator: 'Since he explained Aristotle's text in a plain and authentic way (*perspicue et genuine*) winning a victory over almost all other interpreters.' It should also be noted that Friedrich Samuel Bock (*Historia antitrinitariorum, maxime socinianismi et socinianorum . . . Tomi primi, pars II* [Königsberg/Leipzig, 1776], 900–1) mentioned a second *emendatior* edition of the *Commentarius* dated 1666. A discussion of possible alterations by Felwinger can be read in Eric Achermann, 'Ratio und oratio mentalis: Zum Verhältnis von Aristotelismus und Sozinianismus am Beispiel der Philosophie Ernst Soners', in Hanspeter Marti, Karin Marti-Weissenbach, eds, *Nürbergs Hochschule in Altdorf: Beiträge zur frühneuzeitlichen Wissenschafts- und Bildungsgeschichte* (Cologne/Weimar/Vienna, 2014), 98–158, 129–30, n. 109, stressing that a comparison of the manuscript version with the 1657 print is yet to be made. From a quick look at the two texts I got the impression that they are practically identical.

9 *Historia Crypto-Socinismi*, 39: 'Idem Ruarus, vir perspicacissimus aeque ac callidissimus, ne ignem gladio foderet, eiusdem operis [Soner's commentaries], ceu deliberatum fuerat, magnopere formidavit, eamque adeo pro virili repressit.'

10 Ibid., 40. See *Georgii Richteri JC eiusque familiarium epistolae selectiores* (Nuremberg, 1662), 391–2. Ruar to Richter from Strasbourg, May 1616:

> De Commentario Soneri τοῦ μακαρίτου in Aristotelis Metaphysica propediem edendo per – mihi – gratum, quod scribis fuit. Verumtamen cum optimi viri fama, propter opiniones quasdam philosophicas, hoc tempore praeter aequum laborare ceperit, cavendum erit, ne levi occasione crabrones irritentur. Nollem equidem alienae manus iniuriam ad castrandum tanti viri laborem, imo nec ad castigandum accedere, sed tamen, cum nonnulla, quantum memini, satis ibi periculose et, si mihi iudicium hic sumere debeam, paulo magis peripatetice quam Christiane disputentur, invidiae declinandae optimum mihi videretur, si praefatione modesta scopus authoris detegeretur, qui, ut nos scimus, minime fuit religionis Christianae dogmata convellere, quod perversi quidam illius voluntatis interpretes autumant, sed ostendere quid et quantum de summis rerum causis, ipsoque primo ente, naturae lumine, Philosophorum Coryphaeo Aristoteli constiterit, aut nobis in illius vestigio haerentibus constare possit.

11 This affair was narrated by Ruar in a letter to Johann Huswedel, which can be read in Zeltner, *Historia Crypto-Socinismi*, 42–5. Based on the same letter, Bock too refers to the episode (*Historia antitrinitariorum*, 715) while insisting on Soner's subtle and 'fraudulent' apologetic strategy.

12 I infer this date from the fact that their correspondence took place between the end of 1618 and the beginning of 1619. Moreover De Bert declares that he has before

him a printer's proof of the commentary on the *Metaphysics*. It seems plausible that Richter procured it for De Bert while the latter was still in the Netherlands, namely before moving to Paris in 1619 at the summons of the king of France.

13 Richter, *Epistulae*, 158. The fragment quoted in the text is part of a longer passage:

> Vidi, ornatissime Richtere, specimen typographicum Commentariorum Soneri in libros Aristotelis Metaphysicos, fuitque iucunda mihi eius partis inspectio. Probo autem consilium tuum in divulgando tam insigni opere. Lustravi, enim, ut scis, totum, neque id indiligenter, tum ob argumenti praestantiam, tum ob Soneri, quem iuvenem hic novi, famam, tum ob Scherbii memoriam, cuius tanquam Praeceptoris vestigiis insistere Sonerum opinio fuit. *Sed miror praeposterum quorundam iudicium, adferentium Photiniani erroris fundamenta Metaphysicis istis contineri. Neque enim id magis in hac doctrina verum est quam in logica, rhetorica, poesi. Et revocantur istiusmodi officiis bona ingenia ab honestis sapientiae studiis. Fit enim ut verum fugiant, dum falsum vitare student. Certe non magis Socini infaustis erroribus patrocinatur metaphysica Aristotelis, quam ad metaphysicas subtilitates explicandas faciunt ineptiae Photinianorum; nihil enim habent commune.* Quocirca recte facies, si commentarios illos edi cures. Vale.

To my knowledge, the most comprehensive work to date on the relationship between theology and philosophy in Soner is Achermann's ('Ratio und oratio mentalis'). This is based on an analysis of all the relevant passages in Soner, taking into special consideration the legacy of the mediaeval and modern scholastics. Despite starting from different premises, Achermann too is very prudent, not to say sceptical, about attributing a Socinian character to Soner's 'philosophy and method' (ibid., 156), which appears to converge with the evaluation advanced here. It should also be noted that Achermann (135) is critical of the testimony of one of Leibniz's correspondents, Joachim Friedrich Feller, when he asserts that *in hoc libro* [the commentary on the *Metaphysics*] [Soner] *disseminavit opiniones quasdam minus probas*, and consistently with this assessment considers Richter's *excusatio* to De Bert unconvincing.

14 As mentioned, the commentary published by Felwinger does contain some *quaestiones mixtae*, like that on demons and the condition of the soul after death at Book XII, 8; I would consider the hypothesis that they were not originally included in the commentary and that it was Felwinger himself who inserted them, in order to overexpose its 'Socinian' elements and emphasize its heretical nature. It was probably these *quaestiones* that Richter alluded to in his funeral speech in honour of Soner. See Henning Witte, *Memoriae medicorum nostri saeculi clarissimorum renovatae decas prima [-secunda]* (Frankfurt, 1676), 31–2: it seems that it was Soner's Polish pupils, well known in the Altdorf community, who urged him to comment on the *Metaphysics*: 'Admirandum quoque illud et mysticum Metaphysicorum opus summis

saepe viris frustra tentatum, rogantibus generosis quibusdam e primaria nobilitate polonica iuvenibus, quibus ad epulum istud philosophicum velut umbrae alii postea accesserunt.' As indicated in the manuscript, Soner began the commentary on 14 February 1609.

15 Richter, *Epistulae*, 579: 'De Pellegrino in Metaphys. nihil audis, nemo edet? An solus Scherbius eum audivit, vix est ut credam, non superare aliquos apud vos, qui eundem et audiverint et habeant. O utinam habere possim! Gryphes, crede mihi, non ita aurum suum custodiunt, ut ille suum Pellegrinum.' This letter is also quoted by Matthew T. Gaetano, 'Renaissance Thomism at the University of Padua, 1465–1583', PhD dissertation (University of Pennsylvania, 2013), 156, https://repository.upenn.edu/edissertations/865/, and I wish to express my gratitude to the author for having made his valuable study available to me. More on Scherb's activity in Altdorf in Chapter 2.

16 *Isagoge in lectionem Aristotelis*, 169.

17 *Commentarius in 12 Libros Metaphysicorum Aristotelis, dictus Anno 1609*, ms. UER 714 (University Library of Erlangen, Nuremberg), 53–4: 'Accepimus enim a Praeceptore nostro Scherbio, Thomam Peregrinum, quo ipse usus est Praeceptore, vidisse duo instrumenta musicae, etc.'. On p. 15 Soner called Pellegrini 'the most acute of all metaphysicians'.

18 This expression recurs in Gaetano's study (n. 15), which provides an extensive, well-documented and clear presentation of the situation at the University of Padua. Gaetano's research comes after those of Antonino Poppi, focused on the teaching of theology at Padua and collected in the volume *Ricerche sulla teologia e la scienza nella Scuola padovana del Cinque e Seicento* (Catanzaro, 2001).

19 On this see Jill Kraye, 'Alexander of Aphrodisias, Gianfrancesco Beati, and the Problem of *Metaphysics α*', in John Monfasani and Ronald G. Musto, eds, *Renaissance Society and Culture: Essays in Honor of Eugene F. Rice, Jr.* (New York, 1991), 137–60.

20 Gaetano, 'Renaissance Thomism', 153–5. Gaetano recalls in particular the opinion of Francesco Piccolomini, one of the most famous professors at Padua, and also that of the great eighteenth-century historian of philosophy Johann Jacob Brucker (*Historia critica philosophiae*, vol. 4, 1, 3), who argued that it was through Pellegrini that Scherb imported to Germany a model of Aristotelianism 'purified' from the remnants of scholasticism. On testimonies by Scherb himself, and also by the famous Giulio Pace who attended Pellegrini's lectures as well, see Gaetano, 155.

21 Gaetano, 'Renaissance Thomism', 226–38.

22 Ibid., 236: 'Theology has no place in these lectures'.

23 Ibid., 235–6.

24 Ibid., 226.

25 For Soner too, the beginning of Book VII represents a caesura with the books preceding it: 'Constitutis hucusque omnibus, quibus animus auditoris tanquam

paideia instruendus erat, nunc tandem in hoc libro rem ipsam aggreditur, et de ente agit, quod non per accidens nec rationis est, sed certis de causis in hoc universo continetur, et quidem ut ens est, eius principia et causas investigat.' In this case (as is typical for the Altdorfers) the category of *paideia* is understood as preliminary and general questions. These are to be treated with the dialectical method, whereas the 'subject in itself' (*res ipsa*) requires a specialist approach, more precisely, an 'analytic' one. *Commentarius*, 353.

26 Milan, *Biblioteca Ambrosiana*, Dn 398 inf., 1v–221v, containing the *reportationes* of twenty-nine lessons (*Incipit*: 'Reverendi Magistri Thomae Pellegrini in primum de prima philosophia', 1v). The first seven are introductory, while the real commentary starts in the eighth. As Pellegrini recalls (5r), it was Averroes who maintained that the real beginning of the *Metaphysics* is the seventh book.

27 The question of the arrangement of the individual books of the *Metaphysics* is addressed in 26r–30r, i.e. the final section of the introduction.

28 Ibid., 2v:

> Subiectum ergo duplex, aliud adequatum aliud principale, principale adhuc duplex, aliud perfectionis, aliud attributionis. Notandum insuper quod in subiecto sit terminus respectivus. Sciendum quod diversa respicit diversa etiam nomina sortitur, nam comparari potest ad scientiam ipsam, idest habitum scientiae et potest comparari ad ea de quibus pertractatur in scientia tamquam superius ad sua inferiora. Et ultimo ad passiones ipsas. Si enim ad passiones comparatur, vere et proprie subiectum dicitur. Haec enim est ratio subiecti ut alia dicantur de illo et subiciatur aliis.

29 Ibid., 3v:

> Si quaeruntur principia entis ut ens, ergo ens ut ens est erit subiectum; in quarto vero metaph. texto secundo manifeste dicit quod substantia est subiectum: cum dixerit ens esse subiectum, addit quod quando sermo est multiplex, proprie vero et ubique primi est scientia, et ex quo alia pendent et propter quod alia dicuntur. Ergo si hoc est substantia, substantiarum principia oportet et causas habere philosophum ipsum. Primo dicitur principia entis modo vero principia substantiae.

30 Ibid., 3v–4r:

> Hoc clarius docet in septimo et in principio 12, ubi dicit substantia[e] theoria est. Nam substantiarum principia et causae quaeruntur. In texto vero secundo (et hoc notandum) assignans differentiam inter naturalem, mathematicam et divinam scientiam et dividens substantiam penes subiecta et obiecta, dicit scientia naturalis versatur circa mobilia et inseparabilia, mathematica circa immobi[4r]lia sed inseparabilia, prima vero circa immobilia separabilia, quod etiam repetebat in

secundo phys. texto 71, ubi docuerit quod naturalis debet per omnes causas demonstrare, loquendo de efficiente et tenetur physicus omnia considerare quantum mota movent.... Haec [scientia] quidem circa immobile, alia vero circa mobile quidem incorruptibile autem, quaedam autem circa mobilia et corruptibilia. Prima est metaphysica, secunda mathematica, tertia physica. Ecce igitur quod Aristoteles manifeste assignans subiectum huius scientiae dicit quod sunt substantiae abstractae immobiles.

31 Ibid., 4r:

Ex quo loco satis clare habetur quantum dissentiant ab Aristotele illi qui fingunt duplex genus abstractorum, quaedam enim, inquiunt, sunt abstracta per essentiam, ut deus et intelligentiae. Haec enim secundum esse suum non habent esse cum motu nec [sunt] in materia. Quaedam enim sunt abstracta per indifferentiam, quae quidem sunt communia. Abstrahit et materialibus et appellantur haec abstracta non per essentiam sed per indifferentiam, quia indifferenter possunt inesse in materialibus et immaterialibus entibus, ut ens, unum, actus, potentia et reliquae, quae dicit Aristoteles in metaph. Et ideo cum dicimus, inquiunt isti, quod scientia haec est de abstractis, non intelligimus quod universa scientia sit de abstractis per essentiam, quia verum est principaliter et per partem, sed non tantum, sed dicimus esse de abstractis [per essentiam, partim] per indifferentiam, quia agit de immaterialibus ut puta de intelligibilibus, et de uno ed de actu et de potentia et de aliis transcendentibus, quae communia sunt tum materialibus tum immaterialibus. Sed ex verbis Aristotelis manifeste patet horum error. Nam Aristoteles docet quod scientia haec sit de abstractis per differentiam quam habent a naturali et mathematica et dicit quod ab aliis differt, quia tractat de abstractis immobilibus aeternis, quorum meminit abstractorum certe de abstractis per essentiam. In brackets I put words to be omitted according to me.

32 Ibid., 9v:

Dico igitur quod ens multiplex est et quae multiplicia sunt in duplici sunt differentia, quaedam aequivoca pura, quaedam ab uno et ad unum. Quae ab uno et ad unum talis naturae sunt (et notate hoc, ex hoc enim patebit solutio quaestionis) quod nihil aliud significant nisi ea de quibus dicuntur, nec dicunt individualem naturam distinctam ab illis de quibus praedicantur. Ut ens ipsum si fuerit nomen ab uno ad unum non dicet nec significabit immediate aliquam naturam distinctam a speciebus entis. Immediate namque descendit in cetera genera et immediate significabit substantiam, qualitatem et qualitatem etc. Nec est par ratio de animali, ut dicitur de homine et de leone, et de iis quae ab uno ad unum dicuntur. Non enim significat unam naturam commune, qua mediante postea de speciebus predicentur, sed immediate de speciebus predicantur et immediate species ipsas significant. Declaro per Alexandrum et per Aristotelem.

33 Ibid., 10r:

> Si quis quaerat a nobis, cum dicitur ens est subiectum in metaphysica, quid intelligitur per ens, non naturam commune indifferentem ad substantiam, quantitatem, qualitatem etc. distinctam, quia esset nomen univocum, sed significat immediate substantiam, qualitatem etc. Ideo idem est dicere ens est subiectum in metaphysica quod dicere subiectum est substantia, quantitas, qualitas, etc., quae ad substantiam refferuntur. Declaro omnia per Aristotelem quarto metaph. textu octavo [suprascriptum: secundo]. Et hoc habetis contra graecos et Boetium, qui in Predicamentis collocant ea quae ab uno et ad unum dicuntur inter aequivoca, quod est contra Aristotelem qui dicit quod non aequivoce dicuntur.

Just after, 10v:

> Unum primo significat, cetera per attributionem ad ipsum unum. Quid est illud unum quod primo nomen sani significatur? Animal sanum, igitur sanum primo dicitur de animali, cetera autem quae sana dicuntur, non dicuntur sana seipsis, nec per suas quidditates, sed per attributionem ad ipsum animal, medicina igitur sana quia est causa sanitatis in animali, exercitium sanum quia confermat sanitatem in animali, urina sana quia indicat sanitatem animalis. Dempto scilicet animali non amplius sanum, demptis his, adhuc animal sanum dici potest. Sic de ente dicendum, nam ens primo significat substantiam, caetera per attributionem ad ipsam substantiam nec proprie dicuntur entia, sed aliquid entis, ut in VII metaph: qualitas est ens quia est dispositio substantiae ... et adeo se extendit hoc nomen ens, quod negationes etiam entia dicuntur, quia negant quae a substantia dicuntur. Et dicit Aristoteles sicut omnium sanorum una est scientia, ita et omnium quae ad substantiam refferuntur una erit scientia.

34 See *Sancti Thomae de Aquino sententia libri Metaphysicae, proemium*, in *Corpus thomisticum*: http://www.corpusthomisticum.org
35 Enrico Berti, 'Introduzione', in Aristotele, *Metafisica*, text, translation and notes by Enrico Berti (Bari/Rome, 2017), XV–XVI.
36 *Metaph.*, IV, 2, 1003a 33–b15.
37 *Sententia libri Metaphysicae*, lib. 4, lectio 1, no. 8: 'Et illud dicitur analogice praedicari, idest proportionaliter, prout unumquodque secundum suam habitudinem ad illud unum refertur'.
38 *Alexandri Aphrodisiensis in Aristotelis metaphysica commentaria* (ed. M. Hayduck), in *Commentaria in Aristotelem Graeca*, vol. 1 (Berlin 1891), 240–2.
39 Ibid., 241, 18–21.

40 A work that has been most helpful in the reconstruction of these passages is Maddalena Bonelli, *Alessandro di Afrodisia e la metafisica come scienza dimostrativa* (Naples, 2001), 81–130.
41 Although in some passages (*In metaphysica*, 246, 2–5) Alexander seems to allude to the pre-eminence of the ontological dimension over the theological one, since 'under' (*hypo*) the universal philosophy of the being as being there is 'a certain first philosophy' devoted to the first substances, it is not clear what kind of subordination is intended.
42 Ibid., 246, 9–13.
43 Ibid., 244, 16–20.
44 Ibid., 266, 9–11.
45 Ibid., 668, 3–5.
46 Currently considered 'the traditional interpretation', in recent decades a debate about its correctness has arisen among Aristotle scholars, triggered by various essays by Sarah Broadie, Aryeh Kosman and, above all, Enrico Berti. A synthesis of this discussion can be found in Alberto Ross, 'The Causality of the Prime Mover in *Metaphysics Λ*', in Christoph Horn, ed., *Aristotle's* Metaphysics Lambda: *New Essays* (Boston/Berlin, 2016), 207–27, esp. 207–11.
47 As regards Aquinas and with reference to the traditional interpretation see Stephen L. Bock, 'La causalità del motore immobile nel commento di Tommaso d'Aquino a *Metafisica XII*', *Humanitas*, 66/4 (2011), 644–66.
48 Milan, *Biblioteca Ambrosiana*, ms. D. 400 inf. (during 1563), f. 210v: 'Vidimus in lectione precedenti quod Aristoteles non tantum vult primum motorem movere sub rationem finis, sed etiam efficientis. Hoc idem videtur Alexandro et Averroi.'
49 *Commentarius*, 1–18.
50 Ibid., 1: 'Si enim substantia simpliciter dicitur primum ens respectu accidentium, quod ceterae omnes entis praedicationes ad illam referantur, multo magis prima substantia erit simpliciter primum ens, quia ab ea non minus dependent reliquae substantiae in existendo, quam accidentia a subiecto; . . . sublata prima substantia caetera omnia sublatum iri, cum omnia ab ea habeant esse, I de coelo.'
51 On this topic, see Chapter 2.
52 *Commentarius*, 5.
53 Ibid., 4–5.
54 Ibid., 5.
55 Ibid., 7.
56 Ibid.:

> Denique etiam illud nunc liquet, falsum esse quod dicunt doctrinam de deo, quae habetur, in XII libro veluti honorariam accessisse huic scientiae, ne cogeretur Aristoteles propter imperfectam istam cognitionem, quam lumine mentis humanae assequi potuerat, peculiarem scientiam constituere. Si enim primum

analogatum entis est Deus et huius est scientia primo, merito quaecumque intellectus humanus de Dei natura, ut sic loquar, cognita habere potest proprio lumine, huc tanquam in locum propriissimum congerenda fuerunt.

57 Ibid.
58 Ibid., 14.
59 Ibid. and 17.
60 Ibid., 17–18. See also 216.
61 Ibid., 7: 'Quare etsi concedatur esse conceptum quendam formalem in mente, communem omnibus entibus, quatenus scilicet omne ens est, ei tamen extra in rebus nullus conceptus obiectivus realis respondet, sed fictus ab intellecto nostro.'
62 Ibid., 116: 'hanc doctrinam non esse scientiam constitutam, sed eius constitutionem sed inventionem'.
63 Soner claims that the formula of *Eth. Nic.*, I, 4 has the same meaning as that of *Metaph.*, IV, 2, and in general seems to consider the abbreviated form *ab uno* as equivalent to the one with two members (*ab uno et ad unum*). Not without reason, when he uses the whole formula, the καὶ of the original is translated by him as *seu*, in order to make the two members equivalent, although they actually transmit two different meanings.
64 *Commentarius*, 219–20. These are examples borrowed from Cesalpino. See *Andreae Caesalpini aretini, Quaestionum peripateticarum libri V* (2nd edn, Venice, 1593), I, 4, 10v.
65 Ibid., 219–20.
66 Ibid., 220.
67 Ibid., 220–1: 'de his quae sunt ab uno, illa tantum considerantur, quae genus illud traxit communia a primo, relinquantur autem, quae sunt propria generis, v.g. physici. Quia vero communes istae affectiones nulli communi naturae competunt, sed immediate primo, et per primum reliquis, omnem difficultatem vitari, si primum consideretur et quae primi propria sunt'.
68 I omit the discussion on this matter, which embraces standard themes of the sixteenth-century tradition of commentary on the *Metaphysics*, such as the question of the 'subordination' of sciences to the first one or the question of the latter's capacity to 'descend' to the *ultimae species*. The discussion (and usually refutation) of Antonio Bernardi della Mirandola (see *Commentarius*, 86) became a routine point in this debate. Perhaps the most famous criticism earned by *Mirandulanus* was that of Francisco Suarez in his *Disputationes* (I, II, 2). See above p. 22 on Ferrari's thoughts on this point.
69 *Commentarius*, 222–3.
70 Ibid., 224–5: 'Nec video cur ipse cum Suarez improbet ac nugatorium appellet Fonsecae conceptum tertium, qui est partim distinctus, partim confusus, qualis est quando, dum concipitur primum analogatum distincte, cetera simul confuse

concipiuntur.... Conceptus tamen distinctus primi analogi sub hac ratione, ut est analogum, eminenter et virtute includit conceptus analogatorum: quemadmodum conceptus Patris, ut patris, includitur conceptum filii, etsi non distinctum.'

71 Ibid., 225. The reference is to *Henningi Arnisaei Halherstadiensis Epitome Metaphysices* (Frankfurt am Main, 1606), where Fonseca's solution is criticized on pp. 39–40.
72 *Commentarius*, 225–39.
73 Ibid., 229.
74 Ibid.
75 Ibid., 230: 'Hinc est quod theologi et philosophi dicunt: quaecunque sunt in Deo esse ipsam essentiam Dei, quia realiter nihil est ab ente distinctum, ut ens est. Esset enim non ens. Ens autem, ut ens est et primum ens, demonstratum est in prolegomenis, quod sint idem et quod primum ens sit Deus.'
76 E.g. 'good' conveys a 'convenience according to the existence', deriving from the fact that all things desire (*appetunt*) the first being and 'try to resemble' It 'in order to acquire from It more entity or to perfect their own'. Ibid.
77 Ibid., 230–1. For Cesalpino see *Quaestiones Peripateticae*, II, 6, 36r.
78 Ibid., II, 1, 26r.
79 *Commentarius*, 231. See also 271: for the first being to be 'principle' does not imply that a real relation or a real causality actually occurs *in Itself*.
80 Ibid., 231.
81 Ibid., 232: 'Et quemadmodum nulla est necessitas in centro, cur hac versus, potius quam illac emanet, ita etiam, cur Deus hanc potius quam illam virtutem exserat, nisi se iam ad alteram voluntate sua obstrinxerit.'
82 Ibid., 355.
83 Ibid., 357.
84 Ibid., 360.
85 *Commentarius*, 235, 341.
86 Ibid., 370–1: 'Quemadmodum qui regem excipit, licet simul omnem eius comitatum excipiat, primo tamen regis curam habet et principaliter denominatur hospes regis, non servorum.'
87 Piccart, *Isagoge in lectionem Aristotelis*, 169: 'Atque hoc Thomas Peregrinus illustravit simili: qui regem aut principem aliquem convivio excipit omnem simul eius comitatum et sic consequenter etiam minimos quoque, qui in comitatu eius sunt, convivio excipit; quia itaque primus philosophus tractat de Deo tamquam de rege entium, consequenter etiam de reliquis entibus omnibus gradatim tractabit.'
88 *Commentarius*, 573:

> Hic liber fastigium est huius scientiae, et principalis scopus totius operis metaphysici, in quo iam proprius accedit ad naturam substantiarum abstractarum et immobilium explicandam. Quaecumque enim hactenus

> disputata sunt, omnia eo pertinent, ut ducant nos sensim ex profunda mentis nostra caligine ad clarissimam lucem harum substantiarum, ad quarum cognitionem alioqui mens nostra se habet ut oculi noctuae ad splendorem solis. Et si quid unquam humanum praestitit ingenium, istius summam et quasi apicem in hoc libro contemplari licet, in quo eousque omnium saniorum consensu progressus est philosophus, ut viribus humanis ultra non licuerit.

89 Ibid., 574.
90 Ibid., 298:

> Finis et apex philosophiae aristotelicae: summa, quatenus Deus solus et primo est, eatenus omnia potest et sic omnia ab eo fluunt. Esse enim aliorum est ab eo, quod solum ex se est et maxime est. Quatenus autem est intelligens, omnia scit, quia omnia sunt ab ipso et in ipso, et ipse et per ipsum nos intelligimus. Omnis enim intellectio a primo intellectu, quemadmodum omnis entis a primo ente. Quatenus autem optimum est, ab omnibus appetitur.

91 See n. 46 in this chapter.
92 *Commentarius*, 631. Soner compares this type of philosophical problem *de Deo* to the difficult questions evoked by the Stagirite at the beginning of the *De divinatione per somnum*, while explaining that one recurs to divine causality in the absence of better explanations.
93 The same question might be raised about all God's attributes (ibid., 636–7):

> Quamobrem etsi nulla prorsus ratione assequi possimus qualiter ipsa [= bodily parts] Deo competant et quomodo ab eo procedant ad extra ut ipse nihil intus patiatur, non tamen idcirco statuendum est vere et proprie Deo illa inesse, quando saltem sunt sufficientes rationes pro parte negativa, quae cogant credere talia in Deo esse non posse. Nemo potest cogitatione assequi quei fieri possit ut aliqua substantia, quae magnitudinem aut materiam nullam habeat, et tamen credimus, aut potius scimus ex certissimis rationibus, Deum esse substantiam incorpoream, quia in absurda inevitabilia incideremus necessario, si ei corpus aut quantitatem aliquam tribueremus. Cur idem in caeteris Dei attributis non faciamus, etsi modum intelligere nequeamus?

It is plausible that here Soner is disputing Taurellus' stance, i.e. the attempt to build a *positive* Christian philosophy. See below p. 90 on Crell regarding the same issue.
94 See Charles B. Schmitt, *Gianfrancesco Pico della Mirandola (1469–1533) and His Critique of Aristotle* (The Hague, 1967). See also Pierre Gassendi, *Exercitationes paradoxicae adversus aristoteleos*, in *Opera* (Lyon, 1658), vol. 3, esp. 131: why is there so little metaphysics in the *Metaphysics*?
95 On the original meaning of 'first philosophy' for Aristotle see Berti, 'Introduzione', XXXI–XXXIII. The essentially theological orientation of Aristotle's *Metaphysics* is

sustained by leading twentieth-century scholars of Aristotle, such as Jaeger and Ross, who on this basis – though with different reasons – both consider it a failure in philosophical terms.

96 E.g. *In Aristotelis metaphysica*, 693, 31, 694, 16 and also 695, 37–40, where the first cause moves the universe incessantly as an 'unattainable' good. As to the real Alexander of Aphrodisias and his school, the concept of the presence of desire of (objective genitive) the Prime Mover in the prime mobile can be found in the *Quaestiones* (*Commentaria in Aristotelem Graeca, Supplementum Aristotelicum: Quaestiones, De fato, De mixtione*, ed. I. Bruns (Berlin, 1892), II.2, *Quaestio* I, 25, 40, 8–17).

97 See for example passages such as that on p. 614 of Soner's *Commentarius*:

> Merito igitur primum omnium principium substantia est et non tantum intelligens, sed sui ipsius intelligentia. Quatenus enim est, et quidem perfectissimus ac solum ens, omnia potest et omnibus esse distribuit, non faciendo aliquod laboriose, ut artifices, sed tantum essendo, quod summe est perfectionis. Quatenus autem haec eius substantia est intellectio et intellectionem sequitur appetitus, eatenus omnibus rebus perfectionis (i.e. sui) desiderium indit . . . . Item quatenus nihil melius est in mundo, aut extra mundum, sed ipse est optimum simpliciter, eatenus est etiam ab omnibus appetibilis, appetitu sui ipsius praesentia omnibus inexistente, et propter dependentiam ab ipso, qui est intellectio principium appetitus. Ita ut, stante hac doctrina aristotelica, omnia pulcherrime ad eius simplicitatem, maiestatem et principatum conspirent.

98 Ibid., 620–2.

99 Ibid., 621–2:

> His addi possunt, quae Alexander, I de anima cap. De vi impulsoria scribit non omne movens secundum unam rationem et eodem modo movere. Quaedam enim ea ratione dicuntur movere, non quia ab ipsis motus, sed quia secundum ipsa, quemadmodum anima et natura dicuntur movere, non quod efficienter impellant, quemadmodum aliquis trudit lapidem, sed quia secundum ipsa sit motus . . . Appetitus enim est ex eius [= the First Intelligence] assistentia. Idcirco dicitur etiam efficere, quamvis non revera faciat, cum fieri non possit, ut sit activus, aut factivus intellectus . . . . Neque igitur in ipso neque ab ipso tamquam impellente est motus, sed secundum ipsum, ut ait Alexander. Quare movet ut appetibile, sed non simpliciter quemadmodum movet appetitum, verum ita movet ut appetens simul ab eo habeat esse et appetitus sive dependentia ab ipso. Ob quam causam dicitur efficiens, licet proprie ratio efficientis tribui ei nequeat, quod recte concludunt rationes initio propositae, et ea quae supra dicta sunt.

It seems to me that, once again, the demonstration – rather contorted, to be honest – is adopted in order to prove God's causality, preserving at the same time His immutability. In the first book of his treatise Alexander was trying to explain how intellect and imagination can cause motions in the body without being its direct 'movers'. See the chapter *De impulsu ac vi impulsoria* in *Alexandri aphrodisei enarratio de anima ex Aristotelis institutione, interprete Hieronymo Donato Patritio Veneto* (Brescia, 1495).

100 *Commentarius*, 640.
101 Ibid., 642.
102 Ibid., 646:
Cum itaque res hoc modo se habeat, manifestum esse potest Deum non solum esse causam finalem rerum (quod ab omnibus conceditur: omnia enim repetunt suum principium, a quo sunt) sed etiam ita esse causam, quae totum esse largiatur primitus omnibus. Et propter hoc dicitur causa efficiens improprie, quia efficientis principii est facere aliquid in aliquo, quod praeexistit. Deus autem simul est auctor illius in quo, i.e. materiae et facit sine motu et mutatione. Idcirco dicitur efficiens per emainationem, non per factionem.
103 Ibid., 646–7.
104 Ibid., 631–9.
105 Ibid., 635:
Et quemadmodum dependentia haec in tempore nihil eius essentiam mutavit, ita etiam in principio Dei interno, si pro volitione aut voluntate accipiatur, nihil fuit mutatum.... Non vero alius est Deus nunc, cum mundus ab eo promanavit, et alius fuit ante mundum secundum essentiam. Ergo nec secundum voluntatem est alius ante, alius postea.... Quemadmodum enim nunc sine interna sui mutatione uni se communicat, alteri se subtrahit, unde generationes et corruptiones rerum existunt, ita etiam universum a se emanare sivit, cum antea non emanaret, sine ulla mutatione.
106 Ibid., 639.
107 *Commentarius*, 637.
108 Ibid., 638: 'Ita possumus quodammodo intelligere quomodo aliquid sit separabile et secundum essentiam suam separatum ab omnibus, cum interim illa ab hoc sint inseparabilia; et quomodo aliquid non mutetur, cum tamen multa ab ipso fluant mutabilia.'
109 Ibid.: 'Quod de voluntate dicitur, id de caeteris affectibus multo magis dicendum est, nullum istorum esse in Deo, omnes autem incipere extra ipsum ut eum tangant immutabiliter. Non enim viveret vitam beatissimam, si odio, ira, misericordia, tamquam perturbationum fluctibus agitaretur.'
Every attempt to rupture God's absolute unity can be refuted in a similar way, 660: 'Omnis igitur distinctio oritur extra Deum, in quanto, non in Deo.' Achermann

('Ratio und oratio mentalis', 140) rightly emphasizes that Soner works with a 'radically metaphysical concept of God' as absolute unity and immutability, albeit without Antitrinitarian leanings but rather as a classical topic discussed in scholastic theology and philosophy (144–5). The same topic returns in the first part of the public oration *De vita contemplativa*, given by Soner before the academic body of Altdorf in December 1609 (*Ernesti Soneri orationes duae* (Altdorf, 1610)).
110 *Commentarius*, 670–689. See Ogonowski, *Socynianizm a Oświecenie*, 201–16 (references to the *Commentarius* are instead absent in Ogonowski's most recent work *Socynianizm: Dzieje, Poglądy, Oddziaływanie* (Warsaw, 2015)); Wollgast, *Philosophie*, 393–7.
111 *Commentarius*, 672.
112 Ibid., 689.
113 Achermann ('Ratio und oratio mentalis', 132) does not see such a connection either.
114 It is relevant to cite a polemic passage taken from Taurellus' *De rerum aeternitate ... metaphysyces universalis partes quatuor in quibus placita Aristotelis, Vallesii, Piccolominei, Caesalpini, Societatis Conimbricensis, aliorumque discutiuntur, examinantur atque refutantur* (Marburg, 1604). Taurellus' words correctly expound the point of view of his Peripatetic colleagues. As to the theory of the resurrection of the body, Taurellus – in dispute with them – vindicates its fully philosophical character, holding that:

> puerilis profecto philosophia est, si nihil sapias aliud, praeter id quod tibi ob oculos ponitur. Mentis ergo potius quam sensuum iudicio, res haec est discutienda. He then continues: Sintne peracto huiusce mundi cursu resurrectura corpora, quaestio est, quam plerique peripateticorum negant. Censent enim tale quiddam hoc esse, quod credendum modo sit, cum nullis possit philosophicis exquiri rationibus. Mentem hi forte suam viresque suas amussim esse putant, qua theologicae quaestiones a philosophicis discernantur. Καὶ τοῦτο μέγα λίαν αἴτημα. Postulant hi quod nullo certe possit iure stabiliri. His response: Haud ego quidem adeo simplex et timidus sum, quin audeam profiteri philosophicum id esse quod philosophicis potuerim assequi rationibus. Sed ut id quod assequi non possim, philosophicum esse negem, tantum mihi neque audaciae est neque arrogantiae. Quare igitur quaestio haec philosophica non est? Hanc Aristoteles non discussit. Quod de mea caeterorumque non stupidorum philosophorum mente dixi, de Aristotelica etiam affero. Non quid nesciverit Aristoteles spectandum hic est, sed quid sciverit. At nullus unquam fuit philosophus, qui de corporum humanorum resurrectione quicquam sciverit, quin et huiusce rei veritas divinitus fuit revelata.

The conclusion is: 'Credo equidem, sed quot et quanticumque modo fuerint omnes, plurima tamen potuerunt nescire, quae philosophica sunt.'
Resurrection is hence something known by revelation, which can also now be known *per philosophiam*. The entire discourse should be contextualized within

Taurellus' theory of the three stages of human knowledge (Edenic, *post lapsum, post incarnationem*) developed in the previous pages: Christ's incarnation establishes a new situation, also opening new fields for philosophical knowledge: *De rerum aeternitate praefatio ad lectorem*, 16–17. As regards the theory of the sleep of the souls, Taurellus argues that it is entirely reasonable to conceive such a state of suspension for souls, since they cannot perform their functions before the final reunification with their bodies (18). Notwithstanding their philosophical divergences, personal relations between Soner and Taurellus must have been intense and cordial: Magnus Daniel Omeis, prosopographer of Altdorf University, recalls the loving care with which Soner attended Taurellus throughout the illness that eventually led to his death in 1606 (*Gloria Academiae Altdorfinae* [Altdorf, 1683], 65).

115 See for instance Ogonowski, *Socynianizm a Oświecenie*, 162–4.
116 Ibid., 352.
117 Ibid., 196.
118 Ibid., 235.
119 'Ratio und oratio mentalis', 156.
120 In general, when Soner compares the theories of the two, he prefers those of the Angelic Doctor to those of the Subtle Doctor. In the commentary there are numerous references to the Iberian scholastic philosophers. Soner himself declares that 'nowadays the Scholastics are those with the most followers' (*Commentarius*, 671). If I'm not mistaken, in only one passage is Soner ironic about the *prolixissimae nugae Scholasticorum* (ibid., 668) regarding the question of the *principium individuationis*, which in turn seems an allusion rather to Mediaeval than to Modern scholastic philosophy.
121 *Johannis Volkelii Misnici De vera religione libri quinque, quibus praefixus est Johannis Crellii Francii liber de Deo et eius attributis* (Raków, 1630). See p. 28 for a reference to the beginning of the second book of Cesalpino's *Quaestiones peripateticae*.
122 In the meantime, see the essay by the author of the future edition: Roberto Torzini, 'Filosofia e teologia nel *De Deo* di Crell', in Mariangela Priarolo and Emanuela Scribano, eds, *Le ragioni degli altri: Dissidenza religiosa e filosofia in età moderna* (Venice, 2017), 63–80.
123 *Socjnianizm a Oświecenie*, especially Ch. IV.2 entitled 'Ernst Soner – Cesalpinizujący Socynianin' ['A Cesalpinasing Socinian']).
124 See *De deo*, 28: 'they' maintain that the Primary Being is a kind of intellect which is: non practicum, qui consilio agat aut praeter se quippiam consideret, sive efficere velit, sed qui in seipso tantum contemplando perpetuo sit occupatus; imo nil aliud sit, quam sui ipsius contemplatio sive intellectio. Itaque non quia is ita apud se decernat ac velit, sed ipso hac de re ne cogitante quidem, necessario hoc universum

ab ipso manare. Modum vero eius rei hunc esse volunt. Deum, inquiunt, finis ac boni rationis habere. Bonum autem omne desiderabile esse seu appetibile. Appetibili posito necessario ponitur etiam id quod appetat.

125 Worthy of notice, there is a singular analogy between the titles of two of their works: on one hand, Taurellus' *Synopsis Aristotelis metaphysices ad normam Christianae religionis explicatae, emendatae et completae* (Hanau, 1596. This edition is extremely rare; I saw the text transcribed and commented by Jacob Wilhelm Feuerlein in his *Taurellus defensus* [from the charge of atheism], Nuremberg, 1734) and Crell's *Ethica Aristotelica ad Sacrarum Litterarum normam emendata* (Cosmopolis [= Amsterdam], 1681), on the other. On the 'Christian philosophy' of Taurellus, 'the first German philosopher', see now Walter Sparn, 'Aristotelismus in Altdorf: Ein vorläufige Profil', in Hanns Christof Brennecke, Dirk Niefanger and Werner Wilhelm Schnabel, eds, *Akademie und Universität Altdorf: Studien zur Hochschulgeschichte Nürbergs* (Cologne/Weimar/Vienna, 2011). In this context it would be interesting to reappraise the role of another Altdorf philosopher, Michael Piccart. Sparn (ibid., 133, n. 42) reports that Piccart re-edited the two works *de mundo* and *de coelo* where Taurellus argues against Piccolomini. This information is also provided by Pierre Bayle's *Dictionnaire* (entry *Taurellus*), but unfortunately I was not be able to find this edition.

126 *De deo*, 35: 'Reliquum ergo est ut alio modo a primo ente astra ac caetera omnia pendeant, quam ut a fine; et Deus sit agens practicum, quod nimirum certo consilio ac fine, quem sibi proponat, alia extra se producat entia.' It is important to stress (as Torzini did, 'Filosofia e teologia', 76) that Aquinas in the *Summa Theologiae* also took into consideration the possibility that God is a practical intellect, but then ruled it out. It would be intriguing to compare Crell's solution with the conclusion of Taurellus in the *Synopsis metaphysices*, where, in the context of a critique of traditional Aristotelian 'theology', he declared that God is an *agens voluntarius* (78) and that His action *ad extra* consists in a *praxis* (95–6).

127 Crell, *De Deo*, 296. As to Soner, see above with reference to the passage of the *Commentarius* on p. 636.

128 *De deo*, Ch. 21, for example 140.

129 Ibid., 138.

130 See Alexander of Aphrodisia's *De fato* in *Supplementum Aristotelicum, Commentaria in Aristotelem Graeca*, ed. I. Bruns, II, 2 (Berlin, 1892), 182, 24.

131 There is an interesting reference to the Molinist theory of the *scientia media*, apropos divine omniscience, ibid., 215.

132 *De deo*, 28: 'Est autem illa [the opinion of Cesalpino's supporters] ex Aristotelis dictis ita concinnata ut ipsius omnino esse videatur.' And 38: 'Satis hucusque ostendimus Aristotelicam, seu ex Aristotelicis hypothesibus extructam, de prima huius universi causa rerumque aeternitate sententiam, consistere nullo modo potest.'

133 See Giovanni Santinello, 'Jakob Thomasius (1622–1684): *Schediasma historicum*', in id., ed., *Models of the History of Philosophy: From Its Origins in the Renaissance to the 'Historia Philosophica'* (Dordrecht 1993 [1st Italian edn Brescia, 1981]), 409–42, esp. 428–9 and 433–4.

Chapter 4

1 See Valentina Lepri, *Layered Wisdom: Early Modern Collections of Political Precepts* (Padua, 2015), which focuses on the collective dimension and the 'open' character of these works.
2 This stance is expressed by the recent editor of the *Politica*: Justus Lipsius, *Politica: Six Books of Politics or Political Instruction*, with translation and introduction by Jan Waszink (Assen, 2004).
3 *Iusti Lipsi politicorum sive civilis doctrinae libri sex* (Leiden, 1589). On the *prudentia* in Lipsius, see Diana Stanciu, 'Prudence in Lipsius's *Monita et Exempla Politica*: Stoic Virtue, Aristotelian Virtue or Not a Virtue at All?', in Eric De Bom, Marijke Janssens, Toon Van Houdt and Jan Papy, eds, *(Un)masking the Realities of Power: Justus Lipsius and the Dynamics of Political Writing in Early Modern Europe* (Leiden/Boston, 2011), 233–62.
4 *Gabrielis Naudaei Parisiensis Bibliographia politica in qua plerique omnes ad civilem prudentiam scriptores, qua recensentur, qua diiudicantur* (Wittenberg, 1641; 1st edn Venice 1633, also edited by Conring in 1673), 39: 'quidquid enim postea vel a Justo Lipsio, vel a Timplero, aut Keckermanno superadditum est, styli potius, aut facilioris methodi occasione, quam rerum novitate commendatur'. On p. 123, while expressing a similar judgement, Timpler is accompanied by 'Moldenarius et Goclenius', probably an error of recall since these three authors are recorded in sequence in the physiognomy section of the catalogue of Naudé library (Estelle Boeuf, *La bibliothèque parisienne de Gabriel Naudé en 1630* [Geneva, 2007], 284). On the *Bibliographia politica* see Anette Syndikus, 'Philologie und Universalismus: Gabriel Naudés enzyklopädische Schriften und ihre Rezeption im deutschsprachigen Raum', in Denis Thouard, Friedrich Vollhardt and Fosca Mariani Zini, eds, *Philologie als Wissensmodell / La philologie comme modèle de savoir* (Berlin/New York, 2010), 309–43.
5 On p. 6 in the 1610 edition, on p. 8 in the 1614 one, with reference to the 'goal' of politics.
6 Timpler calls Althusius 'amicus i collega olim meus' (*Politica* in *Philosophiae practicae systema*, 14) and refers to him in the section on the *collegia* (46–7).
7 See nn. 19 and 20 to this chapter.
8 *Philosophiae practicae pars tertia et ultima complectens politicam integram libris V pertractatam* (Hanau, 1611), in: *Philosophiae practicae systema methodicum in tres*

partes digestum, . . . pars prima (1608); *pars altera . . . oeconomica* (1610). Hereafter *Politica*.

9   *Politica, Epistola*. In what follows Timpler compares himself both to the craftsmen, who make new works out of material they were provided with, and to bees, taking pollen from several flowers in order to produce the best honey.

10 An extensive monograph on Timpler is Joseph S. Freedman, *European Academic Philosophy in the Late Sixteenth and Early Seventeenth Centuries: The Life, Significance, and Philosophy of Clemens Timpler (1563/4–1624)* (Hildesheim/Zurich/New York, 1988), 2 vols. On Timpler's Aristotelianism, vol. I, 162–84, on politics, 363–86.

11 *Metaph.*, I, 1 providing a general description of how human knowledge goes beyond the empirical level towards generalizations; *Nich. Eth.*, I, 1, on the superiority of politics over other 'practical sciences'.

12 *Politica*, 1: 'Politica est ars, quae tradit modum bene constituendi et administrandi rempublicam.'

13 *Politica, Epistola*: 'magistratui politico ad bene imperandum'.

14 See the 'precepts' expounded on pp. 198–200, 220–1 and 224–7.

15 See for example *Politica*, III, I, fifth question (208–11): 'An virtus moralis sit necessaria magistratui ad rectam officii sui functionem?'

16 In the fourth book of his *Philosophiae practicae systema methodicum*, 387.

17 The three main editions were issued in 1603 (Herborn), 1610 (Groningen) and 1614 (Herborn); the most substantial changes occurred between the first and the second. Except for one instance, I will quote from the Groningen edition.

18 Ibid.: 'Selegi illa tantum, quae huic scientiae et disciplinae essentialia et homogeneas mihi esse videbantur.'

19 *Johannes Althusius und die Entwicklung der naturrechtlichen Staatstheorie* (Breslau, 1880).

20 See, among many others, the following studies: Thomas O. Hueglin, *Early Modern Concepts for a Late Modern World: Althusius on Community and Federalism* (Waterloo, Ont., 1999) and Francesco Ingravalle and Corrado Malandrino, *Il lessico della Politica di Johannes Althusius* (Florence, 2005).

21 *Politica methodice digesta, Praefatio*.

22 Ibid.

23 Ibid.: 'Contrarium ego cum paucis aliis statuo, adeo nimirum haec [= maiestas] corpori symbiotico consociationis universalis propria esse.'

24 Ibid.

25 Ibid., 116: 'Vinculum hujus corporis et consociationis est consensus et inter membra Reipublicae fides data et accepta ultro citroque; hoc est, promissio tacita vel expressa de communicandis rebus et operis mutuis, auxilio, consilio et iuribus iisdem communibus, prout utilitas et necessitas vitae socialis universalis in regno postulaverit.'

26 *Dicaeologica libri tres, totum et universum ius, quo utimur, methodice complectens* (Herborn, 1617). Here I use the second edition, Frankfurt 1649, I, 8, 1, 21: 'Placito et consensu suo coniunguntur, qui communione utilitatis, commodorum et incommodorum certorum, auxilii et consilii, unum quasi corpus constituunt.'
27 *Politica methodice digesta*, 383–401 (*de consiliariis summi magistratus*).
28 Ibid., 43.
29 Ibid., 312–17.
30 Ibid., 381.
31 Ibid., 318–24.
32 Ibid., 386: 'Consiliarii sunt, qui fidi, rerum hominumque periti, salutaria suggerunt, et velut periti nautae in tempestatibus maris clavum regere iuvant, sed tamen absque potestate, imperio et iurisdictione.'
33 His famous book *El Concejo, y consejeros del príncipe*, published in 1559, was swiftly translated into Latin and other modern languages. See Simonetta Scandellari, 'El "Consejo y Consejeros del Príncipe": algunos aspectos de la literatura política española del siglo XVI', *Res Publica*, 15 (2005), 49–75.
34 *Politica methodice digesta*, 210.
35 Ibid., 214.
36 Ibid., 209.
37 See, for instance, ibid., 224, on the limits of the magistrate's power resulting from his 'contract' with the consociates. As to the magistrate's consultation in major state affairs see, for instance, p. 395.
38 Ibid., 265–6 and 383–5. See. *Nich. Eth.*, VI, 5.
39 *Praefatio*.
40 *Systema disciplinae politicae* (Hanau, 1608; other editions: Hanau, 1607, 1613, 1616 and Frankfurt, 1625).
41 Ibid., 21.
42 See also 19–20: 'Cum in humana societate magis ac magis crevisset hominum malitia, ita ut una civitas inhiaret alterius civitatis bonis et homo ab homine sibi metueret, tamquam ab hoste, tum etiam civitates hoc discrimine a pagis sortita sunt, ut fossis, muris et vallis cingerentur.' The following passages reveal that Keckermann was inspired by Lambert Daneau's *Politices Christianae libri septem* (Geneva, 1596). This is not the only difference with the Aristotelian model: in the *Apparatus practicus* p. 68 (full title in n. 45 to this chapter), *obligatio* and *consensus* granted by individuals and families to laws and to the Prince are cited as 'efficient causes' of the political community. Also worth noting is the distinction between communities such as families and clans, which are *ex natura*, and those *ex instituto*, such as villages, towns, provinces, kingdoms, and also *sodalitates et collegia*. The latter suggest an influence of the ideas of Althusius.
43 *Systema*, 145–64.

44 A complete bibliography of Keckermann's works in Joseph S. Freedman, 'The Career and Writings of Bartholomew Keckermann (d. 1609)', *Proceedings of the American Philosophical Society*, 143 (1997), 305-64. For an explanation and defence of the Peripatetic classification of academic disciplines see Keckermann's *Praecognita philosophica* (Hanau, 1607), Book I, Ch. 2.
45 *Apparatus practicus sive idea methodica et plena totius philosophiae practicae nempe ethicae, oeconomicae et politicaem* (Hanau, 1609).
46 Ibid., 5:

> *Colligere locos communes est unus ex praecipuis effectis artis logicae, atque adeo e fructibus doctrinae logicae de methodo . . .; siquidem hoc est inter praecipua logicae artis exercitia, quod mirifice conducit 1. ad rem quamlibet explicandam; 2. Ad tractandas controversias et probandas conclusiones in utramque partem; 3. Ad solide iudicandum de rebus atque adeo ad consilia dextre danda, et denique ad memoriam firmandam*

47 Ibid., 15-16.
48 *Nich. Eth.*, VI, 1, 1139 a1.
49 *Disputationes practicae* (Hanau, 1612).
50 There is extensive literature available on the practice of disputations in early modern times, starting with the seminal Ewald Horn, *Die Disputationen und Promotionen an den Deutschen Universitäten vornehmlich seit dem 16. Jahrhundert* (Leipzig, 1893; repr. Wiesbaden, 1968); more recently Hanspeter Marti, *Philosophischen Dissertationem deutscher Universitäten 1660-1750: eine Auswahlbibliographie* (Munich, 1982); Ku-ming (Kevin) Chang, 'From Oral Disputation to Written Text: The Transformation of the Dissertation in Early Modern Europe', *History of Universities*, 19/2 (2004), 129-87; Donald Felipe, 'Ways of Disputing and *Principia* in 17th Century German Disputation Handbooks', in Marion Gindhart and Ursula Kundert, eds, *Disputatio 1200-1800: Form, Funktion und Wirkung eines Leitmediums Universitärer Wissenkultur* (Berlin/New York, 2010), 33-61.
51 *Discursus politici de consilio, consiliario et concilio sive consultatione, ingenii in politicis acuendi gratia conscripti ab Andrea Rey a Naglowice et in celebri Gymnasio Dantiscano ad disputandum extraordinario propositi, sub praesidio Cl. Viri Bartholomaei Keckermanni Philosophiae professoris ad diem Iulii 21 anno 1607* (Hanau, 1612), in *Disputationes practicae*, 430-567.
52 *Discursus*, 430: 'Quae materia in politicis instar principii est, a quo pendet omnis non disciplina tantum politica, sed et huius scopus, procuratio dico publicae salutis.'
53 *Discursus*, 438 (*Praefatio*):

> At vero si consilia Romanorum, qualia partim a Livio, partim a Dione et aliis gravissimis historicis descripta sunt, conferantur cum iis quae ab annis centum in Hispania, Italia et huius parte Republica Veneta, Gallia, Germania, Anglia,

Polonia, aliisque regnis, sive ad pacem sive ad bellum inventa susceptaque a Comineo, Guicciardino, Sleidano, recentioribus itemque Gallicae historiae autoribus, Meterano itemque aliis ex parte annotantur, fatendum fuerit aetatem hanc inveniendi promto acumine et iudicandi exquisita dexteritate antiquitatem non tantum aemulari, sed et superare. And 439: Nullo umquam mundi saeculo plures libri vel scripti et editi, vel lecti sunt quam hoc nostro, non in aliis tantum scientiis et artibus, sed etiam in politica, tam togata quam bellica.

Leaving aside Rej's historiosophical (and millenarian-influenced) remarks on the 'world's ageing', as to the mentioned authors: *Comineus* is Philippe de Commynes (1447–1511), author of *Memoires contenans l'Histoire des Roys Louis XI et Charles VIII depuis l'an 1464, jusque en 1498*, translated into Latin by Johannes Sleidanus and published in 1540 as *De rebus gestis etc.*; Guicciardini is the author of the famous *Ricordi* as well as the *Storie fiorentine*; Johann Sleidan is remembered for his *De statu religionis et rei publicae Carolo quinto Caesare commentarii* and also for *De quatuor summis imperiis, babylonico, persico, graeco et romano*; as to those who wrote about the recent affairs in France, Rej himself on p. 446 refers to François de la Noue, author of a *Discours politiques et militaires* and of *Observations sur l'histoire de Guicciardini*, while Emanuel van Meteren wrote a history of the war between the Provinces and Spain. In general, as to the contemporary writers mentioned by Rej in the *Discursus*, these include, *inter alios*, Althusius, Richter, Gregoire, Machiavelli, Mariana, Arniseus, Gentillet, Guevara, de Chasseneuze, James I Stuart, Lenccius, Mittendorp, Lipsius, Bodin, Ceriol, Mikołaj Rej, Frycz-Modrzewski, Botero, Daneau, Case, P. Camerarius, Ribadeneira, Laueterbeck, Hyppolitus a Collibus, Gentili, Scaligero, Francesco Patrizi of Siena, Schutz, Castellani and Contarini.

54 *Discursus, Praefatio*, 439–40: 'Bonum consilium esse nullo modo potest, quo ad id quidem pervenitur quod sit bonum, non autem qua ratione decuit, inquit maximus Philosophorum lib. 6 Eth. c. 9 [*sic*]. Plus est ubique scientiae quam conscientiae et plenus est mundus sapientiae ut ebrii vino, quod concoquere recte, inque bonum succum convertere non possunt.' Rej cites the passage of *Nich. Eth.*, VI, 10, 1142b 24–6 in Périon's Latin version (*Aristotelis ad Nicomachum filium de moribus, quae ethica nominantur, Libri decem, Ioachimo Perionio Benedictino Cormoeriaceno interprete*, Paris, 1542), 55r. Worth noting that it was the Byzantine commentator Eustratius of Nicaea (ed. Heylbut, *Commentaria in Aristotelem Graeca*, XX, 360, 5–21) who interpreted this passage of Aristotle as maintaining that it is an evil kind of deliberation to aim at a good end by wicked means.
55 *Discursus, Praefatio*, 442–5.
56 Ibid., 448.
57 Ibid., 449. Rej declares that none of the about forty 'political' authors, whose work he studied 'consilii capiendi praecepta ac regulas in politicis praescriberet, praeter unum Leonem Imperatorem, cui ob hoc etiam immortales gratias debet posteritas'. On

pp. 450–2 Rej provides seventeen rules for offering good counsel taken from Leo's treatise.
58 *Discursus*, 452 and 453.
59 Ibid., 453–4.
60 Ibid., 454.
61 Ibid., 446.
62 Ibid., 452–3.
63 Ibid., 498–503.
64 Ibid., 502: 'Quod ad eloquentiam attinet, ea in consiliario quatenus consiliarius est, non ita requiritur, sed quatenus idem ille, qui consiliarius est, vel legati munus suscipit, vel simile aliud officium. Consilium purae mentis opus est, non affectuum, non linguae, et logicae magis quam rhetoricae proprium. Paucis iisque siccis et nudis verbis optima consilia proponuntur, quando sine verborum ornamentis ac figuris promuntur.'
65 See Horst Dreitzel, *Protestantischer Aristotelismus und absoluter Staat: Die Politica des Henning Arnisaeus (ca. 1575–1636)* (Wiesbaden, 1970); id., 'Reason of State and the Crisis of Political Aristotelianism: An Essay on the Development of Seventeenth Century Political Philosophy', *History of European Ideas*, 28/3 (2002), 163–87; Artemio Enzo Baldini, ed., *Aristotelismo politico e ragion di Stato: Atti del convegno internazionale di Torino 11–13 febbraio 1993* (Florence, 1995); and Henning Ottmann, 'Protestantische Schulphilosophie in Deutschland: Arnisaeus und Conring', in Christoph Horn and Ada Neschke-Hentschke, eds, *Politischer Aristotelismus: Die Rezeption der aristotelischen 'Politik' von der Antike bis zum 19. Jahrhundert* (Stuttgart, 2008), 218–31. Among numerous works by the late Merio Scattola on the topic, see the most recent 'Politica architectonica: L'aristotelismo politico nel dibattito politico tedesco della prima età moderna', *Res Publica*, 19/1 (2016), 15–33 (with some criticism of Dreitzel's Luther-centric perspective).
66 Enrico Nuzzo, 'Crisi dell'aristotelismo politico e ragion di Stato: Alcune preliminari considerazioni metodologiche e storiografiche', in Artemio Enzo Baldini, ed., *Aristotelismo politico e ragion di Stato: Atti del convegno internazionale di Torino 11–13 febbraio 1993* (Florence, 1995), 43.
67 Ibid., 45.
68 Ibid.
69 See also Enrico Berti's considerations in the last chapter of his *Aristotele nel '900* (Bari/Rome, 1993), which I consider valuable also for the characterization of early modern Aristotelianism.
70 Horst Dreitzel, 'Aristoteles' Politik im Denken Hermann Conrings', in Francesco Fagiani and Gabriella Valera, eds, *Categorie del reale e storiografia: Aspetti di continuità e trasformazione nell'Europa moderna* (Milan, 1986), 33–59.
71 The role of the political Aristotelianism in this context has been analysed by Horst Dreitzel, 'Die "Staatsräson" und die Krise des politischen Aristotelismus: zur

Entwicklung der politischen Philosophie in Deutschland im 17. Jahrhundert', in Artemio Enzo Baldini, ed., *Aristotelismo politico e ragion di Stato: Atti del convegno internazionale di Torino 11–13 febbraio 1993* (Florence, 1995), 129–56. The formula *arcana imperii*, which Lipsius took from Tacitus, became famous following the influential work by the jurist Arnold Clapmar (active in Altdorf in 1600–4): *De arcanis rerumpublicarum libri sex* (Bremen, 1605).

72 'Nec finis unicus politici est status conservatio, sed felicitas civilis societatis, quae revera absolvitur exercitatione virtutis cum rerum sufficientia coniuncta.' Quoted in Dreitzel, 'Reason of State and the Crisis of Political Aristotelianism', 174.

73 First edn, Helmstedt, 1662. On the lengthy incubation of the work (eleven years!) see Conring's introductory letter to the *benevolent reader*.

74 Ibid.

75 Relevant to this topic are Conring's words in *Hermanni Conringii Aristotelis laudatio: Orationes duae* (Helmstedt, 1633), *Oratio altera*, where he states that, at the time, the term *civilis prudentia* was misused by the jurists, who related it to the study of the local and ephemeral forms of positive law, whereas genuine *prudentia* is none other than the ethical and political doctrine established in antiquity by Aristotle. The same topic is addressed in the *Praefatio* to Tacitus' *Germania* edited by Conring himself (*C. Cornelii Taciti de moribus Germanorum liber* [Helmstedt, 1652], 15), arguing that current German public law, both positive and common, should be carefully differentiated from *prudentia civilis*, the former being concerned with the particular and the latter with the universal.

76 *Neostoicism and the Early Modern State* (Cambridge, 1982), 161–5.

77 The term can, in fact, be found in the most diverse contexts. An excellent example of the 'migration' of this concept is furnished by the seventeenth-century success beyond the Alps of a somewhat singular book, Cardano's *Proxeneta*. Published as *Arcana Politica sive de prudentia civilis* (Leiden 1627, 1635 and 1656, Geneva 1630, Helmstedt 1668 [2nd edn], Leipzig 1673 [2nd edn]), the work actually deals with the difficult art of surviving and maintaining one's identity and dignity in the snare-laden milieux of the social and political elites.

78 This text is included in Conring's posthumous collected works with the title: *Dissertationum politicarum Hermanni Conringi, disputatio I, de natura ac optimis auctoribus civilis prudentiae ad diem IX Januarii 1639 defensa, respondente Friderico Strubio Bocnemensi*, in *Opera*, 7 vols (Brunswick, 1730), vol. 3, 1–16.

79 *Disputatio*, 3 (III): 'Est autem prudentia, ut recte docetur lib. VI Ethicorum ab Aristotele, habitus ille mentis, qui occupatur circa id, quod ex re est aut abs re est civili hominum societati.'

80 Ibid., 11 (XXVII).

81 *De prudentiae civilis optimis auctoribus dissertatio ... praeside Gebhardo Theodoro Meier, publico eruditorum examini subiiciet Georg. Joann. Völger hannoveranus*

(Helmstedt, 1659). As one can guess from the future verb, this is a publication preceding the public discussion. Often the author refers to Conring himself (e.g. thesis XV: ὁ πάνυ *Conringius Praeceptor noster venerandus*).

82 Ibid., th. XVI.
83 Ibid., th. XVII.
84 Ibid.
85 Viotti is recalled as the author of a tract *De demonstratione* (Paris, 1560), on which see Neal W. Gilbert, *Renaissance Concepts of Method* (New York/London, 1960), 152–7.
86 Ibid., th. XIX.
87 Ibid., th. XXV.
88 *Eth. Nic.*, I, 1, 1094b 20, 7, 1098b 26–32. See also the considerations at the end of this chapter.
89 *Commonplace Learning*, Ch. 1, 3–36.
90 On Conring's life and works see the collected essays edited by Michael Stolleis, *Hermann Conring (1606–1681): Beiträge zu Leben und Werke* (Berlin, 1983). For biographical information, see Constantin Fasolt, *The Limits of History* (Chicago, 2004), 50–89.
91 Cited in n. 73. The *Oratio altera* is preceded by a letter to the Arminian Caspar Barlaeus (1584–1648), one of Conring's professors at Leiden. The words referred to here come from this letter.
92 Fasolt, *The Limits*, 67.
93 *Oratio altera*:

> Nec tamen in verba eius iurandum est scientiae assectatori, aut in solidae eruditionis titulo collocandum placita huius intelligere. Hic enim non cultus est, sed manis quaedam superstitio, nulli magis quam Aristoteli ipsi invisa quondam atque improbata. Non sane mystes Licei est qui magistri callet sententias, sed qui acri iudicio suas illas reddidit. Tantum scilicet sapimus quantum iudicio nostro sumus assecuti; quae vero auctoritati solum alicuius innititur cognitio, agerit illa[m] quidem eruditionis speciem, nihil tamen aliud quam speciem atque inanem umbram. Igitur id satis fuerit si Aristotelem principis loco in eruditis habeamus, non qui dictator fit (neque enim dictaturam admittit res litteraria), sed qui primo loco sententiam dicat, a qua inferioris subselli hominibus non facile sit recedendum. Utinam vero isthoc ille apud omnes loco esset! Nunc etiam in laudatoribus eius invenias qui quemvis potius alium et consulunt et audiunt quam hunc quem ipsi principem confitentur. Alii magno quidem illum in honore habent, in reliquo tamen eruditissimorum ordine tantum collocant et multa quidem neque inania eius admirantur, non tamen eum qua parte maximus est suspiciunt. Sed illos fortassis ipsa Aristotelis magnitudo deterret propiusque vetat accedere, nescio tamen an non et illa se submittat tandem, si quotidiano usu familiaris reddatur. Operae certo pretium videtur, cum possis, ipsum potius principem adire ac sequi, quam sequioris illos cum prudentiae tum auctoritatis

homines. Horum vero bona quidem mens aequum sane est ut erigatur, quo autem sunt errore imbuti eximendus ille est est tollendus; interest enim publicae rei ut Aristotelis principatus innotescat plurimis et ab obrectationibus vindicetur.

On these *orationes* see also the information provided in volume V of Conring's *Opera, praefatio*, XIII. The *orationes* are reproduced on pp. 726–59. The topic of *libertas philosophandi* returns in Meier-Völger's *Dissertatio de prudentia civili* (Chs V–VI), along with an attack on 'sectarian' philosophy (*Philosophia enim non est Stoica, aut Platonica, aut Epicurea, aut Aristotelica, sed quaecumque ab his sectis recte dicta sunt*) and praise of 'eclectic' philosophy, as championed by Potamo of Alexandria in antiquity and subsequently defended by no few Fathers of the Church. This issue refers here to the *De philosophia et philosophorum sectis* (The Hague, 1658) of Gerardus Vossius, a Dutch humanist who was Conring's professor (see Conclusion).

94 See Chapter 2.
95 It would be desirable to clarify the relation – and eventually the clash – between this universalism of a philosophical origin, and the claimed primacy of traditional German law over the universalistic pretension advanced by the supporters of Roman-Imperial power, whom Conring opposed. This problem is addressed for example in a *Disputatio* published in the eighteenth-century collection of Conring's papers (*De natura ac optimis auctoribus civilis prudentiae, ad diem IX Januarii 1639 defensa, respondente Friderico Strubio, Bocnemensi* in *Opera*, vol. III, p. 5, th. X) very similar in content to that cited in n. 18. From this perspective Conring's thought was convincingly presented by Fasolt in the essay 'A Question of Right: Hermann Conring's New Discourse on the Roman-German Emperor', *Sixteenth Century Journal*, 28/3 (1997), 739–58; see also Alberto Jori, *Hermann Conring (1606–1681): Der Begründer der deutschen Rechtsgeschichte* (Tübingen, 2006).
96 In these parts Conring probably had in mind Daniel Heinsius' oration *De politica sapientia* (Leiden, 1614), on which see Paul van Heck, '*Cymbalum Politicorum, Consultor Dolosus*: Two Dutch Academics on Niccolò Machiavelli', in Toon van Houdt, Jan L. de Jong, Zoran Kwak, Marijke Spies and Marc van Vaeck, eds, *On the Edge of Truth and Honesty: Principles and Strategies of Fraud and Deceit in the Early Modern Period* (Leiden/Boston 2002), 48–63. Also noteworthy is Heinsius' effective formula, referring to Philip of Macedon: 'nihil Florentia hoc tempore docet, quod non ante Macedonia invenerit' (from the *Oratio de civili sapientia*).
97 *Oratio altera*: 'Unde factum, ut quantumvis arcana sua haud perinde pia haberet Lyceum, non corruperit tamen vulgi mores . . ., contra quam Melio Diagorae et Epicuro accidit, cuius disciplinam moratae olim urbes eiecerunt.'
98 ΑΡΙΣΤΟΤΕΛΟΥΣ ΠΟΛΙΤΙΚΩΝ ΤΑ ΣΩΖΩΜΕΝΑ. *Aristotelis Politicorum libri superstites, editio nova. Cura Hermanni Conringii cum eiusdem Introductione et Emendationibus* (Helmstedt, 1656), from which I quote. It is reproduced in the *Opera*, vol. 3, 457–90; the Latin and Greek versions are printed side by side in double columns on pp. 491–717.

99   *Aristotelis Politicorum libri superstites, Benevolo Lectori.*
100 Ibid., b 1–2.
101 On Conring's 'empirism', see Fasolt, *The Limits*, 206–7.
102 *Aristotelis Politicorum libri superstites, Benevolo Lectori,* b 2–3.
103 Ibid., b 3.
104 Ibid., the *Introductio* on pp. 557–652. The idea of filling this gap by writing this type of introduction had already been put forward by Heinsius.
105 Ibid., 557–9.
106 These appear to be original hypotheses on the part of Heinsius, as nothing similar can be found in Casaubon's remarks on Diogenes. On the fifteenth-, sixteenth- and seventeenth-century editions and translations of the *Lives and Opinions of Eminent Philosophers*, see Ilario Tolomio, 'The "Historia Philosophica" in the Sixteenth and Seventeenth Century', in Giovanni Santinello, ed., *Models of the History of Philosophy, I: From Its Origins in the Renaissance to the 'Historia Philosophica'* (Dordrecht, 1993; 1st Italian ed. Brescia 1981), 154–60 (Ch. 5: 'Editions of Diogenes Laertius in the Fifteenth to Seventeenth Centuries'). However, Heinsius–Conring's conjecture was not accepted by the leading seventeenth-century commentator on Diogenes, Giles Menage (*De vitis, dogmatibus et apophthegmatibus clarorum philosophorum libri X* [Amsterdam, 1692], vol. II, 194), who merely approves Muret's remark that the seventh book of the *Politics* should actually be the fourth.
107 *Introductio*, 578. It seems to me that Conring consistently bears in mind Daniel Heinsius' *De politica sapientia oratio*; in effect, the Dutch humanist argued that Aristotle's *Politics* should have consisted of twelve books, like Plato's *Laws*.
108 *Introductio*, 580.
109 Ibid., 583: 'Sua omnia vaferrimus hic nequitiae doctor dissimulato plagio ex Aristotele fortasse transcripsit, eo tamen discrimine, quod hic impie ac imprudenter omni principi commendet, quae nonnisi Dominis ac Tyrannis convenire longe rectius ac prudentius scripserat ante Aristoteles.'
110 Ibid., 582.
111 Ibid., 585–8.
112 Ibid., 593: 'Ceterum quomodo ergo pertinet haec tractatio ad Politicum, si nihil in ea de republica agitur.'
113 Ibid., 593: 'Quemadmodum igitur quemlibet artificum oportet cognitionem aliquam habere sui subiecti circa quod occupatur, ita necessum est ut Politicus noscat materiam civitatis. Non potest autem illa pernosci, nisi cognitis simplicissimis civitatis partibus.'
114 Ibid., 594. Conring declares his disagreement with Duns Scotus. The opposite statement (a 'science' is not concerned with its own principles) was usually associated with the name of Averroes, here explicitly recalled by Conring, and that of Zabarella.

115 Ibid.
116 Ibid., 600.
117 Conring again refers (612) to Heinsius, who in certain notes placed at the end of his edition, translation and paraphrase of the *Politics* (Leiden, 1621, 1042) in turn referred to several conclusions taken from the *Questiones Politicae* of Antonio Scaini (1524–1612): 'Post tertium, inquit [Scaini], statim sequuntur septimus et octavus, deinde quartus, qui sic erit sextus. Ac deinceps quintus. sextus est postremus, et octavo ideo ponendus loco.' Conring admits that these words inspired him as a young scholar, stimulating him to further investigation of the daring hypothesis of the change in order of the books of the *Politics*.
118 *Introductio*, 605.
119 Ibid., 625: 'nihil de administratione civitatis optimae, nihil de eius magistratibus, nihil de iudiciis, nihil de consiliis'.
120 Ibid., 645.
121 The preface (*Benevolo lectori*) explains that this work preceded the *De civili prudentia* of 1562 and was an abridged version of the same, drafted as far back as 1549 to meet the needs of certain 'selected' students. Needless to say, here again is the distinction between the more precise exposition of the 'acroamatic' *De civili prudentia*, and the 'exoteric' approach of the present book.
122 Fasolt, *The Limits*, 72–89.
123 See the references in n. 96. On Conring as counsellor see Fasolt, *The Limits*, 77–88.
124 *Politicae Succinctae, ex Aristotele potissimum erutae ac ad praesentem Imperii Romani statum multis in locis accommodatae libri II quorum synopsin praefixa tabella exhibet* (Jena, 1551). Numerous editions followed in the ensuing years.
125 At 197–8.
126 Ibid., 81–3. Not surprisingly, starting from such premises Conring argues for the tendential autonomy of ethics from politics, *pace Aristotelis*, ibid., 98.
127 Ibid., 95–6: 'coiisse autem primum homines in civilem coetum, sive per potentiam aliis inferendae sive arcendae aliorum potentium iniuriae'.
128 *Michaelis Piccarti ... argumenta librorum politicorum Aristotelis cum praefatione de naevis istius operis aristotelici* (Helmstedt, 1715).
129 *Praefatio* (unnumbered pages).
130 Ibid.:

> Omnia Aristotelis ratiocinia vel generaliora nimis esse hic loci vel nimis theoretica ad praxin vel parum vel nihil conferentia vel sine Aristotele in vulgus nota. Licet nonnumquam ad specialiora descendat, omnia tamen a nostris temporibus esse alienissima, iisque praeter doctrinam de Tyrannide vix aliquid applicari posse; disputationi scholasticae eum magis inservire, quam ut iudicium politicum formare et expolire queat, cuius cultura lectione scriptorum pragmaticorum et usus maxime sit instituenda. [Writers such as Grotius,

Pufendorf, Bacon, Bodin etc.] concludunt opus illud obscurissimum, imperfectissimum, a nostris temporibus alienissimum, in Monarchiis non tantum, sed etiam in ceteris rerumpublicarum generibus ob principia sua fundamentalia eorumque errores periculosissimum iure meritorque excludi ab academiarum cathedris. In omnibus fere academiis Germaniae valere iussum esse illum autorem tamquam publicis praelectionibus parum aptum, ob monstrosam proceritatem, malam partium cohaerentiam exiguumque fructum, quem iuvenis ex illius tractatione capere posset. Breviorem monent patere viam ad politica praecepta haurienda ex iis scriptoribus, qui praesentis saeculi genio rem omnem accomodassent, pragmatice regulas prudentiae pertractarent, sub vividis exemplis earum usum demonstrarent et iactis ex iure naturae honestatis et utilitatis fundamentis, reliquam disciplinae oeconomiam superstruerent.

131 Ibid.: 'Maxime enim monente illustri Puffendorfio prae oculis instituta graecarum suarum civitatum habuisse Aristotelem earumque libertatem cumprimis aestimasse, quem gravem esse defectum disciplinae universi generis humani usui inserviturae.'
132 Ibid.: 'de regno paucissima tradens pro democratia graeco more acerrime pugnat, omnia ad rempublicam componat et ideam monarchae atque monarchiae vel ut impossibilem tecte repraesentet vel colubrina calliditate atque arcana deductione eius horrorem incutiat, dum flagitia dominationis et Tyrannidis artes apertius et copiosius explanat'.
133 Ibid.: 'cum homo animal a natura sit ad turbas excitandas aptissimus multaeque rationes istud principium [i.e. that human being is naturally 'political'] destruant ab Hobbesio, Puffendorfio, Thomasio, Gundlingio observatae'.

Chapter 5

1 See Michael G. Müller, *Zweite Reformation und ständische Autonomie im Königlichen Presussen: Danzig, Elbing und Thorn in der Epoche Konfessionalisierung (1557-1660)* (Berlin, 1997), 77–110. Stanisław Tync, *Dzieje Gimnazjum Toruńskiego (1568–1772)*, 2 vols (Toruń 1928 and 1949) is still paramount for Tidike's milieu in Toruń and in general for the history of the Gymnasium.
2 Allow me to refer to Danilo Facca, 'Franz Tidike i kultura renesansowego platonizmu', *Odrodzenie i Reformacja w Polsce*, 51 (2007), 94–120. On the teaching of philosophy see Stanisław Salmonowicz, 'Nauczanie filozofii w Toruńskim Gimnazjum Akademickim (1568–1793): Organizacja, wykładowcy, podręczniki', in Lech Szczucki, ed., *Nauczanie filozofii w Polsce w XV–XVIII wieku* (Warsaw, 1978), 137–96, esp. 158–60. More recently Tomasz Dreikopel has provided detailed information on Tidike's life and activity, in particular: 'Życie i działalność naukowa Franciszka Tidicaeusa (1554–1617), fizyka miejskiego i profesora Gimnazjum

Akademickiego w Toruniu', *Rocznik Toruński*, 32 (2005), 23–50 and id., *Recepcja poglądów etycznych Arystotelesa w Isagoge Ethica i Aristotelis de virtutibus libellus Franciszka Tidicaeusa* (Olsztyn, 2010).

3 The long title, as was the style of the time, runs as follows:

> *Aristotelis de virtutibus libellus graece et latine, versione in latinum nova et accurata, graeco textui ad unguem respondente et commentariis eruditis, atque iucundis in singula capitula illustratus. Isagoge Ethica, introductio in disciplinam moralem practicam, qua per compendium causae pleraeque omnes vitiorum humanorum, tum eorundem medelae, ordine et erudite proponuntur, explicantur et confirmantur tam philosophicis quam sacrarum literarum rationibus evidentissimis. Reliqua quae huc accesserunt, versa pagina lectori subiiciet* [at the next page are listed:] *Disputatio de fato et rebus fatalibus; De summo bono seu felicitate humana disputatio; Quaestio ethica et politica utrum honestum constet natura an vero tantum opinione; Themata disputationis de voluptate et dolore. Autore Francisco Tidicaeo Dantiscano, philosoph[o] ac medicinae doctore et Reip[ublicae] Thoruniens[is] in Boruss[ia] Phys[ico] ordinario. Lipsiae 1609.*

The *epistola dedicatoria* is dated July 1608. The *Isagoge* begins on p. 241 under the expanded title: *Isagoge ethica, id est introductio, etc.* [as above], *in usum studiosorum ethices, ad morum et vitae rectitudinem graviter contendentium. Olim illa quidem publice praelecta, in celebri Academia Lipsensi, nunc vero de novo elaborata, ac non paucis salutaribus, neque adeo apud Ethicos scriptores ubique obviis praeceptionibus atque monitis expolita, aucta atque ad publicam editionem adornata, autore Francisco Tidicaeo, etc. anno 1609.* The four *disputationes* are separately numbered.

4 This author, a professor at Pisa university, wrote a short treatise *De fato*, left in manuscript (allow me to refer to my essay 'Il "De fato" di Simone Porzio: nota storico critica', *Archiwum Historii Filozofii i Myśli Społecznej*, 47 (2002), 95–102), and a few dense pages in his published works on the same topic: *An homo bonus vel malus volens fiat* (Florence, 1551) and *De rerum naturalium principiis* (Naples, 1553). On this neo-Aristotelian *de fato et providentia* literature see now Rita Ramberti, *Il problema del libero arbitrio nel pensiero di Pietro Pomponazzi: La dottrina del* De fato – *spunti di critica filosofica e teologica nel Cinquecento* (Florence, 2007), esp. Ch. 3. Guy Guldentops, 'L'anti-fatalisme de Julius Sirenus', in Pieter d'Hoine and Gerd Van Riel, eds, *Fate, Providence and Moral Responsibility in Ancient, Medieval and Early Modern Thought: Studies in Honour of Carlos Steel* (Leuven, 2014), 653–76.

5 An overview of this literature, providing a lot of information, albeit not always pertinent: Peter Friedrich Arpe, *Theatrum fati sive notitia scriptorum de providentia, fortuna et fato* (Rotterdam, 1712), who does not mention Tidike.

6 Dreikopel, *Recepcja poglądów etycznych*, 83–152. On Tidike's ethical works see also Tync, *Dzieje Gimnazjum Toruńskiego*, 45–7.

7 More precisely: the disputation on fate was held and published in Leipzig; that on the supreme good was published in Toruń; that on the concept of honesty appears hitherto unpublished; that on pleasure and pain had been discussed in Leipzig, but not published. As was the practice at the time, these were printed in limited edition and published either before or after the public disputation. In effect, I have found no trace of the previous editions to which Tidike refers in the title. On the practice of disputation see the works quoted above, Chapter 4, n. 50.

8 *De virtutibus, epistola dedicatoria.*

9 Ibid., 1–2.

10 Ibid., 2. Tidike claims that Alexandre Chamaillard is generally attributed the merit of having rediscovered the small work (in the Paris edition of 1538), although he seems to have some doubts about it. In effect, apart from the fifteenth-century translations (on which see Schmitt in the article referenced at the end of this note), there was a Latin version by the humanist and philosopher from Nola, Ambrogio Leone (Venice, 1525), whereas the translation most popular at the time was provided by Simon Grynaeus (Basel, 1539), not to mention that by the humanist Andrés Laguna from Segovia (Cologne, 1543). See Dreikopel, *Recepcja poglądów etycznych*, 83–5. On the success of the *De virtutibus*, which was appreciated as a useful synthesis of ancient ethics, see: Charles B. Schmitt, 'Etyka Arystotelesa w XVI wieku. Rozważania wstępne', *Odrodzenie i Reformacja w Polsce*, 24 (1979), 21–41, esp. 34–41). On p. 41 Schmitt mentions Tidike's version, but not his commentary.

11 *De virtutibus*, 2.

12 Ibid., 2–3.

13 Ibid., 238–9.

14 A number of hypotheses (dated first century BC or AD, a work expressing a Platonic-Aristotelian concordism, influenced by Stoicism) were suggested by one of the nineteenth-century editors, Franz Susemihl, taken up by Eduard Zeller. See: Harris Rackham, 'Introduction', in Aristotle, *The Athenian Constitution, Eudemian Ethics, On Virtues and Vices* (London/Cambridge, 1935), 485. In the context of this rediscovery of an ethics of virtue, Epicurus himself is defended from the charge of being 'Epicurean': *De virtutibus libellus*, 128–9, 484–7.

15 Ibid., 7. See Cicero, *De officiis*, I, 27. It was the Stoic Panaetius who transferred the concept of *decorum* from rhetoric to ethics.

16 As emerges from the very first sentence of the *De virtutibus* (ibid., 4). In Tidike's translation: 'laude digna quidem sunt ea, quae bona et honesta sunt (gr.: *ta kala*), vituperio autem, quae mala, foeda et turpia (gr.: *ta aischra*)'.

17 *De virtutibus libellus*, 16–17. See *Rhet.*, 1, 5, 1361a 30.

18 II, 6, 1106b 36 – 1107a 1. Tidike adopts the variant ὡρισμένη with subscribed iota and referred to the 'mean'. It could be derived from Aspasius' *scholia* (ed. Heylbut in

Commentaria in Aristotelem Graeca, XIX, 1, 48, 13), whereas modern editions omit the iota, referring the term to 'virtue'.

19 Ibid., 19–20: 'Virtus proprissime accepta, nimirum quando de sola humana virtute loquimur, sit nihil alius quam firmum propositum et constans voluntas, quae diuturna assuetudine contracta et confirmata sit, ac penitus inoleverit, recte et laudabiliter vivendi, secundum dictamen rectae rationis nobiscum nascentis, quam propterea legem naturae appellamus, agendique nil nisi quod rectae rationi, cuius omnes participes sumus, conveniens est atque consonum.'

20 See the *Quaestio* (included in the sylloge, see n. 80 to this chapter) *utrum honestum natura constet an vero tantum opinione*, where *conscientia* is defined as *nobis naturaliter insitum et nobiscum natum honestorum et turpium evidens discrimen*, 45. At the beginning of the *Isagoge ethica* (243–4) too, while quoting Cicero, *De fin.*, 3, Tidike speaks of a moral order 'imprinted' in nature as a whole by its *conditor* and reflected inside the human *mens*.

21 *Isagoge ethica*, 248–50. This is why (281): 'ethnici tamen sapientiores et saniores recte de hac re [= on the divine law as a guide in morality] senserunt, disseruerunt et docuerunt alios, ita ut potuerunt. Nam ipsorum philosophia quae fuit, ipsorum etiam fuit theologia'.

22 Ibid., 279–83.

23 This is a standard topic in studies on Melanchthon. See a recent reappraisal, with reference to essential bibliography, in Jan Rohls, 'Zwischen Stoizimus und Aristotelismus: Lutherische und reformierte Ethik im Zeitalter der Orthodoxie', in Sabrina Ebbersmeyer and Eckhard Kessler, eds, *Ethik – Wissenschaft oder Lebenskunst? Modelle der Normenbegründung von der Antike bis zu Frühen Neuzeit* (Berlin, 2007), 267–91. On the motive of the 'common notions' (*koinai ènnoiai*), the God's Law / Law of Nature dichotomy and on Melanchthon's interpretation of Rom 2.14, with regard to the emerging German scholastics of the sixteenth century, see Kees Meerhoff, 'Some XVIth-Century Readings of Aristotle's Ethics', in Günter Frank and Andreas Speer, eds, *Der Aristotelismus in der Frühen Neuzeit – Kontinuität oder Wiederneignung?* (Wiesbaden, 2007), 291–324, in particular 295–6.

24 *Isagoge ethica*, 273; pp. 273–9 contain a long and gloomy tirade against the insidious work of the devil on human moral capacities.

25 *De virtutibus*, 23.

26 Ibid., 24. See also *Isagoge Ethica*, 318–19.

27 *De virtutibus*, 23.

28 *Nic. Eth.*, VI, 6 and 8–9, the famous example of the practical syllogism in Ch. 8, 1141b 18–21.

29 *De virtutibus*, 36: 'omnibus virtutibus hoc commune est, moderari scilicet cupiditatem eius, quod maxime libet'.

30 Ibid., 50. The full text of this analogy is:

> Ut propterea altera animae bipartita distinctio, quae Aristoteli usitata est, a qua etiam Sacrae Literae non abhorrent, longe videatur esse commodior et opportunior, qua simpliciter ratio recta et appetitus sibi opponuntur. Ratio tamquam dominus et id quod praeest, appetitus ut subditus et servus, cuius est moderamen rationis acceptare, admittere et morigerum esse. Per appetitum autem intelligitur totus affectum cupiditatumque militaris exercitus, sive illis castra in medio ventre, circa cor, statuas, sive in imo circa epar designes, perinde est. Sunt omnes affectus et cupiditates τοῦ ὀρεκτικοῦ, facultatis appetentis, cuius gubernatio penes rationis est. Haes est agens et imperans, illa vero patiens, ut cui a ratione tamquam in materiam sive subiectum virtutis forma et effigies imprimi debet, sicut cera inditur figura sigilli.

See also *Isagoge*, 245–6, referring to *Nic. Eth.*, I, 12, 1102b 29–1103a 3 (to be compared with I, 6, 1098a 3–5): this doctrine, according to Tidike, is implicit in all the best writers, such as in Ovid (*Video meliora . . .*) and the Apostle ('flesh' and spirit are ruled by different laws). On the topical role of Medea's famous sentence on ethical discussion within the Reformation and in particular in Melanchthon see Risto Saarinen, *Weakness of Will in Renaissance and Reformation Thought* (Oxford, 2011), esp. Ch. 3.3. See also ibid., 142 on the dualism – in the spirit of a 'commonplace Platonism' – of the soul powers (or parts), actually immanent in the Melanchthonian perspective on morality and projected on Aristotle in the case of Camerarius. According to Saarinen, it basically consists in a 'voluntarist' – rather irrationalist – option assumed by these two Reformers, who 'locate the will in the realm of affects and passions in distinction from the cognitive soul' (ibid., 146).

31 See for instance the passage on pp. 250–1 of the *Isagoge* on conscience as an instance, which is separate and superior compared to the other parts of the soul.

32 See *Isagoge Ethica*, 312–17. On *continentia* as the virtue par excellence see for example 318: 'tot enim sunt continentiae quot virtutis species, singulis enim speciebus virtutis singulae species continentiae proportionis similitudine respondent'.

33 Ibid., 319: 'Quae felicitas etsi secundum Aristotelis doctrinam sit quidam conflatum ex omnis generis bonis . . . tum animae, ut virtutum intellectualium et moralium, tum corporis, ut sanitatis, pulchritudinis, roboris, etc., tum externorum, ut divitiarum, amicorum, gloriae, etc., et tamen potissimum et fundamentaliter in virtutis actionibus posita atque sita est . . ., ut Stoici illam solam ad vitam bene beateque degendam satis esse statuerunt.'

34 See the title of the book cited in n. 23 to this chapter (*Ethik – Wissenschaft oder Lebenskunst?*) and also Juliusz Domański, *La philosophie, théorie ou manière de vivre? Les Controverses de l'Antiquité à la Renaissance* (Fribourg/Paris, 1996), with a preface by Pierre Hadot, who famously investigated the historical recurrence of the conception of philosophy as a way of life.

35 *Isagoge*, 244–5:

> Finis igitur Ethicae est virtus, ita ut Ethica virtutem efficiat quasi, fabrefaciat, producat, generet, non simpliciter (nam virtutis species seu honestatis ratio sese ipsa iam constat, ab ipso omnis boni summo autore egressa, et in hac rerum natura ab ipso conditam, effusa quasi et implantata ac insita) sed in hoc vel isto homine, ut in singulis hominibus virtutem fabricetur.... Ex quo constat Ethicen, quoad hoc, similem esse artium reliquarum, quibus omnibus hoc est commune, ut ex ratione officii sui certam quandam formam introducant in certum quoddam subiectum. Sic Ethica virtutis habitum tanquam formam imprimit et introducit in hominem tanquam subiectum suum; est enim, quoad animam, et quidem quoad alteram animae partem, subiectum ipsius virtutis, siquidem altera animae pars per Ethicam doctrinam virtute instruitur et informatur.... Facile enim mens videt et intelligit, naturali etiam instinctu, quid in vita fieri oporteat, recto autem mentis consilio reluctatur appetitus, sua natura effrenis, indomitus, ita ut impetum frangere ac domare omnium difficillimum vitae opus sit.

36 Ibid., 247.
37 Ibid., 282–3.
38 Ibid., 283: 'Altera vero parte virtutes suas etiam appetitui praescribit, quas virtutes morales vocamus. Hae sunt: liberalitas, temperantia, iustitia, fortitudo, veracitas, comitas, amicitia.' These virtues correspond to those presented in the *De virtutibus*.
39 Ibid., 298: 'vitiorum correctrix philosophia moralis, quam ethicam dicimus'.
40 Ibid., 299.
41 Ibid., 299–305. Tidike quotes Galen's *De corrigendis animi vitiis*, better known as *De cognoscendis curandisque animi morbis*. This title in vol. 5 (1–57) of Kühn's edition. The Περὶ διαγνώσεως καὶ θεραπείας τῶν ἐν ἑκάστου ψυχῇ ἰδίων παθῶν was edited at Helmstedt by Johannes Caselius in 1592 under the title *Galeni aureolus libellus quomodo quis et dinoscat et sanet proprios animi sui affectus*.
42 *Isagoge*, 305–9.
43 Ibid., 321: 'Ideoque, ut perpetuus stimulus sit animis nostris penitus infixus et quasi oculis nostris continue observans, qui calcaris instar numquam non admoneat nos officii, excitetque acriter et efficaciter ad exercendum ea quae ex sapientum doctrina et praeceptis hausimus, accepimus atque arripuimus.'
44 Ibid., 322.
45 Tidike quotes Vives's *Satellitium*. See *Ioannis Lodovici Vivis Valentini exercitationes animi in Deum . . . Satellitium animi sive Symbola* (Paris, 1551) (letter dedicatory to the King of Portugal of 1535). It is worth noting that in his *De vera sapientia* (colophon: Bruges, 1524) on pp. 224–5, nn. 118–19, Vives too divides the soul into two parts, the rational and the brutish, seat of passions. Vives also addresses the question of *amor sui*, 239–40, nn. 231–7.

46 *Apophtegmatum opus* (Paris, 1533, new edition by Paolo Manuzio in Venice, 1577). More probably Tidike is alluding to a scholastic adaptation of the work. The Toruń city library (Księżnica Miejska) conserves the following edition: *Argutissima quaeque Apophtegmata ex Erasmi Roterodami opere selecta, inque communes locos redacta, in commodum iuventutis, praesertim Goslarianae. Per Antonium Corvinum* ([Magdeburg], 1534). See Stanisław Tync, *Najdawniejsze ustawy Gimnazjum Toruńskiego* (Toruń, 1925), 155.

47 ΓΝΟΜΟΛΟΓΙΑ ΕΛΛΕΝΙΚΟΛΑΤΙΝΗ, Ἐκ ἰωάννου τοῦ στοβαῖου ἐκλογῶν παραινετικῶν συγκομισθεῖσα. *Gnomologia geaecolatina hoc est, insigniores et vetustiores sententiae philosophorum, poetarum, oratorum et historicorum, ex magno Anthologio Ioannis Stobaei excerptae et in locos supra bis centum digestae* (Basel [1557]). It should be noted that Stobaeus' *sententiae* had been printed several times in the Renaissance together with the Pseudo-Aristotelian *De virtutibus*, see Schmitt, *Etyka Arystotelesa*, 36, n. 70.

48 The first edition of this work is: *Regulae vitae: Virtutum omnium methodicae descriptiones in Academia Rostochiana propositae a Davide Chytraeo, collectae per Petrum Sickium Rensourgensem* (Wittenberg, 1555). This work is composed of a series of maxims arranged in the order of the Decalogue and illustrated by examples taken from the ancient authors. It is recommended from as far back as the 1568 statutes of the Toruń gymnasium along with Erasmus' *Apophtegmata*. See Tync, *Najdawniejsze ustawy*, 9.

49 *Isagoge*, 315–16.

50 Ibid., 327–8.

51 Ibid., 329.

52 Ibid., 330: 'Est ergo praeteritorum etiam leviorum errorum reminiscentia magnus magister ad disciplinam meliorum morum.' Here Tidike quotes a passage on the evening examination of conscience taken from the Pythagorean *Carmina aurea*, frequently employed in the moralistic-parenetic literature of the time. See, for instance, Crell, *Ethica aristotelica*, 30. Lastly, I would mention the way the issue of the conscience is developed in the *Disputatio de summo bono*, included in the sylloge: the peace of the conscience coincides with the highest good and with *eudaimonia*, which is hence more a state (*diathésis, kataskeue*) than an activity. It seems to me that in these passages Tidike explicitly stresses the distance of his Platonic–Stoic–Christian conception from that of Aristotle. *Disputatio de summo bono*, 29–30.

53 *Isagoge*, 332–7.

54 *Isagoge*, 336–7, on the providential function of adversities (including calumnies) for human moral improvement. This topic also occurs in Tidike's *Microcosmus* (Leipzig, 1615), on pp. 202–4, in the discussion of *similitudo* and *conformitas* between human beings and God/Christ. See *De imitando Christo, contemnendisque mundi vanitatibus libellus authore Thoma Kempisio, interprete Sebastiano Castellione* (Basel, 1563). On

the translations of this work and its popularity in the Reformation, and more specifically on the various operations performed on the text to adapt it to Protestant sensibility and dogmatic principles, see Maximilian von Habsburg, *Catholic and Protestant Translations of the* Imitatio Christi, *1425–1650: From Late Medieval Classic to Early Modern Bestseller* (Farnham, 2011), Chs 6 and 7.

55 See Donald Sinnema, 'The Discipline of Ethics in Early Reformed Orthodoxy', *Calvin Theological Journal*, 28 (1993), 10–44.

56 There is a conspicuous literature on the history of the concept of *conscientia* in the Reformation and the Protestant area. See the recent monograph by Benjamin T.G. Mayes, *Counsel and Conscience: Lutheran Casuistry and Moral Reasoning after the Reformation* (Göttingen, 2011), which, among other things, draws attention to the importance of the Melanchthonian definition of conscience as a *syllogismus practicus*, as a starting point for the emergence and ulterior evolution of Reformed and Lutheran casuistry. An extensive presentation of the subject, in its moral, legal and theological aspects, can be read in Merio Scattola, 'Gewissen und Gerechtigkeit in den Beichtbüchernder Früher Neuzeit', *Journal of Early Modern Christianity*, 2/2 (2015), 117–58.

57 *Alexandri Aphrodisei Problematum libri duo Theodoro Gaza interprete*, in: *Aristotelis opera cum Averrois commentariis*, Venetiis apud Iunctas 1562, vol. VII, 180v:

> Quod si praeter rem [patientem atque] efficientem aptitudo quoque rei patientis causam affectus [Tidike: effectus] adhibeat, fieri potest ut nos quoque, si animum pietate muniamus, si corpus victu sobrio tueamur, si spretis opibus magnis, contenti paucis degamus, labe humana immunes, quoad humanis viribus licet, evadamus, dum scilicet occasionem rei efficienti nullam suggerimus, qua agere quicquam valeat in rem patientem, sive daemon infestus sit, sive sydus, sive quodlibet aliud, quod extrinsecus causam afferat nostri erroris vel vitii.

58 *Epistola Dedicatoria*: 'libellum ethicum'.
59 See n. 7 to this chapter.
60 In his *De theriaca* (Toruń, 1607), on pp. 120–1. Tidike adds this eulogy of Simoni almost as if to apologize for the criticism he addresses to the Italian immediately afterwards regarding the point at issue, the *sympathia et antipathia rerum*. While in Leipzig Simoni never succeeded in obtaining the much-desired chair of medicine (see Cantimori's article cited in the following note, 451), despite being widely appreciated for his knowledge in this field, as Tidike's words confirm. However, while praising Simoni's learning and intellectual brilliance, Tidike expresses serious reservations about his master's morality, i.e. on his incontinence in general and in particular *in venereis*: for him 'adultery was like a game and a diversion', *De virtutibus*, 189–90.

61 Tidike was in Leipzig from 1573 to 1577, Simoni arrived there in 1569 and stayed till 1581. On Simoni in general see Claudio Madonia, 'Simone Simoni da Lucca', *Rinascimento*, 20 (1980), 161–97. On his Leipzig period see Delio Cantimori, 'Un

italiano contemporaneo di Bruno a Lipsia', *Studi Germanici*, 3/4–5 (1938), 445–66. On the overall reform of Leipzig University proposed by the Italian, 'a man of the Elector of Saxony', on the opposition and tension it generated within the local academic milieu, where the Melanchthonian inspiration of Camerarius senior was still alive, see Frank Ludwig, 'Dr. Simon Simonius in Leipzig. Ein Beitrag zur Geschichte der Universität von 1570 bis 1580', *Neues Archiv für Sächsische Geschichte*, 30 (1909), 209–90.

62 *Ethicorum Aristotelis Nichomachiorum explicatio accuratissima Ioachimi Camerarii Pabergensis* (Frankfurt, 1578, 1st edn 1570, last 1583), 96–100. Also, 14, on the theory of the *imago Dei*, the essential theological foundation of all these considerations. On Camerarius' *Explicatio* and his philosophical (more than Melanchthon's) approach to ethics, see Saarinen, *Weakness of Will*, 142–51.

63 On Simoni's thought see Cantimori (*Un italiano contemporaneo*, 455–6), although his appraisal of the Lucchese is closely dependent on his conception of the interplay between Reformation, humanism and 'critical' thought. A preferable approach in Domenico Caccamo, *Eretici italiani in Moravia, Polonia e Transilvania* (Florence, 1970), 131–45, who detects in Simoni 'an intellectualist attitude which led him to transfer to theology problems and methods borrowed from the Paduan philosophical tradition' (131) and who also refers to the most famous book published by Simoni, *De vera nobilitate* (Leipzig, 1572). Caccamo returns to this work in his essay, 'Commento al *De vera nobilitate*', in *Simone Simoni, filosofo e medico nel '500*, ed. Mariano Verdigi (Lucca, 1997), 137–41. On Simoni's literary production see Claudio Madonia, 'Simone Simoni', in André Séguenny, ed., *Bibliotheca Dissidentium IX: Répertoire des non-conformistes religieux des seizième et dix-septième siècles*, vol. 9 (Baden-Baden, 1988), 25–110).

64 *Simonis Simonii lucensis . . . Antischegkianorum liber unus* (Basel, 1570) 119–32. The definition of Vimercato at 126.

65 *Simonis Simonii lucensis, philosophiae in Gymnasio Genevensi professoris, in libros Aristotelis Περὶ τῶν αἰσθητερίων καὶ τῶν αἰσθητῶν* (Geneva, 1566), *Epistola*, with extensive information on his university studies.

66 *Antischegkianorum*, 127.

67 A subject of lively debate, see Guldentops, 'L'anti-fatalisme de Jules Sirenius'.

68 It is an attempt to employ philosophical reason in theology, though in turn pivoting on a notion of God alien to Aristotle and to philosophy. It has recently been suggested that the nub of this 'theological' notion is the 'self-limitation' of God. See Ramberti, *Il problema del libero arbitrio*, 129–31, developing a suggestion of Martin L. Pine (*Pietro Pomponazzi: Radical Philosopher of the Renaissance*, Padua, 1986).

69 Published in Venice in 1563. On Sirenio, besides the article cited in nn. 4 and 68 to this chapter, see Giancarlo Zanier, 'Noterelle pomponazziane', *Giornale Critico della Filosofia Italiana*, 10 (1979), 211–25, esp. 211–17.

70 ΦΙΤΟΛΟΓΙΑ *generalis* (Leipzig [1582]), Chs 11–18. Ch. 16 on the biblical (*apud Moysen*) origin of this notion, Ch. 18 on its compatibility with Melanchthon's thought.
71 Facca, *Franz Tidike*, 100–3.
72 *Isagoge ethica*, 266–70 and *passim*. As regard parents, this topic had been discussed by Simoni in *De vera nobilitate* and its conclusions (the decisive contribution made to 'nobility' by being well-born) seems sufficiently close to those proposed by Tidike in these pages.
73 Ibid., 289–98.
74 Cic., *De fato*, XIII, 29–30.
75 *In Iatromastigas, de recto et salutari usui, de abusu item multiplici atque nefario, nobilissimae ac salutiferae artis medicinae, libellus* (Toruń, 1592), where the arrogance of the ignorant – including the sick and their relatives – regarding such an important matter as human health is attacked with sarcasm. The part on pp. 141–9 anticipates the issues of the final section of the *Disputatio*. On theological fate (= God as the 'first physician'), see 29–32.
76 *Johannis Beverovicii epistolica questio de vitae termino, fatali an mobili cum doctorum responsis* (Dordrecht, 1634).
77 On Melanchthon's 'Lutheran' natural philosophy see Sachiko Kusukawa, *The Transformation of Natural Philosophy: The Case of Philip Melanchthon* (Cambridge, 1995). On the marriage between ethics and natural philosophy see Dino Bellucci, 'Natural Philosophy and Ethics in Melanchthon', in Jill Kraye and Risto Saarinen, eds, *Moral Philosophy at the Threshold of Modernity* (Dordrecht, 2005), 235–54; Günter Frank, 'Melanchthon – der "Ethiker der Reformation"', in Günter Frank and Felix Mundt, eds, *Der Philosoph Melanchthon* (Berlin/Boston, 2012), 45–75.
78 See Melanchthon, *Initia scientiae physicae*, col. 197: 'Ita iam physica dimittit studiosum, tum ad medicorum doctrinam, tum ad ethicen'.
79 See Tync, *Najdawniejsze ustawy*, where Melanchthon's *De anima* is mentioned several times as the text adopted for the teaching of natural philosophy.
80 The text of the *disputatio* is included in the sylloge cited in n. 3 (*Aristotelis de virtutibus libellus*), together with three other *disputationes* with separate numbering (*De fato*: a1r–a3v and 1–23; *De summo bono*: 24–30; *De voluptate et dolore*: 31–6, *Quaestio ethica et politica utrum honestum natura constet an vero tantum opinione*: 37–48). The exemplars of this publication are still rare, the translation was conducted on that of the Herzog August Bibliothek of Wolfenbüttel, sign. M: Lg 402 (1). Tidike's text is often elliptical and sometimes unclear, therefore in the translation I used insertions of words or groups of words that should assist in its understanding.
81 *Tusc. Disp.*, V, 10, 31.
82 See Cic., *De nat. deor.*, I, 38–40, referring to Chrysippus' doctrines.
83 Tidike actually quotes from *Noct.*, VII, 2.
84 Melanchthon, *Initia doctrinae physicae*, cols 331–5.

85 *De gen. et corr.*, I, 7, 323b 33–324a 1.
86 *De an.*, I, 4, 408b 22–3.
87 A reference to Galen's famous treatise *Quod animi mores corporis temperamenta sequantur*.
88 *Tim.*, 86d–e.
89 Melanchthon, *Initia doctrinae physicae*, col. 189.
90 *De fato*, IV, 8.
91 See Melanchthon, *Initia doctrinae physicae*, col. 203: 'Usitatum est vocare providentiam, et cognitionem, qua Deus omnis cernit et prospicit, et gubernationem, qua naturam universam servat.'
92 Ps. Aristotle, *De mundo*, 391b 11–13. Tidike patently still considers this text as authentically Aristotelian.
93 This syntagma appears several times in *De int.*, 9. As to ἐνδεχόμηνα ἀόριστα see *An. pr.*, I, 13, 32 b4–13.
94 Melanchthon, *Initia doctrinae physicae*, col. 192.
95 *Od.*, I, 33–4.
96 2 Sam. 11–12.
97 *Od.*, I, 35–6.
98 Melanchthon, *Initia doctrinae physicae*, col. 331.
99 Ibid., col. 330.
100 The book in which Aristotle deals with constitutional changes.
101 Euripides, *Ciclopes*, v. 285.
102 See Desiderius Erasmus, *Adagiorum chiliades* (Basel, 1539), 47–9.
103 *De Off.*, II, 16–17.
104 See Arist., *Pol.* I, 7, 1255b 16–20.
105 This is the last sentence of the answer given by the Oracle of Delphi to Battus of Thera on the expediency of establishing a colony in Cyrene in Libya (see Book IV, Chs 150–61 of Herodotus' *Histories*). The sentence can be read in the *Scolia* to Pindar (to *Pyth.* IV, 10) with the variant ἔρξει instead of ῥέζει.
106 Cic., *De fato*, 28–9.
107 See Tidike, *In Iatromastigas*, 29–32 and 141–9.
108 See Plato, *Laws*, 730d.
109 The sentence is taken from Celsus's *De medicina* (VII, 12, 4), published in several editions in the course of the sixteenth century.
110 Is. 38.
111 Actually in Book IX, Ch. 3.
112 *De int.*, 9.
113 See Boethius, *De cons. Phil.*, V, sixth prose.
114 *Iulii Caesaris Scaligeri exotericarum exercitationum libri XV* (Frankfurt, 1576), 365, 8, 1126–7.

Conclusion

1 Martin's broad reference to Pierre Bayle's interpretation of Renaissance Aristotelianism is exemplary of this trend, see *Subverting Aristotle*, 170-6.
2 Richard A. Muller, '*Vera Philosophia cum sacra Theologia nusquam pugnat*: Keckermann on Philosophy, Theology and the Problem of Double Truth', *The Sixteenth Century Journal*, 15/3 (1984), 341-65.
3 Among the numerous works on the topic, see the following collective work: Heinz Schilling, ed., *Die reformierte Konfessionalisierung in Deutschland – Das Problem der 'Zweiten Reformation'. Wissenschaftliches Symposium des Vereins für Reformationsgeschichte* (Gütersloh, 1986).
4 *De philosophia et philosophorum sectis libri II* (The Hague, 1658), 11.
5 *De philosophicis sectis*, 82-5.
6 Ibid., 109-17.
7 Ibid., 117.

Bibliography

Primary sources

Alexander of Aphrodisias, *In Aristotelis metaphysica commentaria*, ed. M. Hayduck, in *Commentaria in Aristotelem Graeca*, vol. 1 (Berlin, 1891).
Alexander of Aphrodisias, *Enarratio de anima ex Aristotelis institutione, interprete Hieronymo Donato Patritio Veneto* (Brescia, 1495).
Alexander of Aphrodisias, *De fato*, ed. I. Bruns, in *Supplementum Aristotelicum, Commentaria in Aristotelem Graeca*, vol. 2 (Berlin, 1892).
Alexander of Aphrodisias, *Problematum libri duo Theodoro Gaza interprete*, in *Aristotelis opera cum Averrois commentariis*, vol. 7 (Venice, 1562).
Alsted, Johann H., *Metaphysica* (Herborn, 1613).
Althusius, Johannes, *Dicaeologica libri tres, totum et universum ius, quo utimur, methodice complectens* (Herborn, 1617).
Althusius, Johannes, *Politica metodice digesta atque exemplis sacris et profanis illustrata* (Herborn, 1603 and 1614).
Ammonius, *In Aristotelis categorias commentarius*, ed. A. Busse, in *Commentaria in Aristotelem Graeca*, vol. 4 (Berlin, 1895).
Aquinas, Thomas, *Sententia libri Metaphysicae* in *Corpus Thomisticum*. Available online: http://www.corpusthomisticum.org.
Aristotle, *Ad Nicomachum filium de moribus, quae ethica nominantur, Libri decem, Ioachimo Perionio Benedictino Cormoeriaceno interprete ... commentarii eiusdem in eosdem libros* (Paris, 1542).
Aristotle, *ΑΡΙΣΤΟΤΕΛΟΥ ΠΟΛΙΤΙΚΩΝ bib. Q. Aristotelis Politicorum libri VIII cum perpetua Danielis Heinsii in omnes libro paraphrasis* (Leiden, 1621).
Aristotle, *Aristotelis de republica libri VIII interprete et enarratore Io. Ginesio Sepulveda* (Paris, 1558).
Aristotle, *Aristotelous Politikôn ta Sôzômena. Aristotelis Politicorum libri superstites, editio nova. Cura Hermanni Conringii cum eiusdem Introductione et Emendationibus* (Helmstedt, 1656).
Arnisaeus, Henning, *De constitutione et partibus metaphysicae tractatus* (Frankfurt am der Oder, 1606).
Arnisaeus, Henning, *Epitome Metaphysices* (Frankfurt, 1606).
Arpe, Peter F., *Theatrum fati sive notitia scriptorum de providentia, fortuna et fato* (Rotterdam, 1712).
Beverovicius, Johannes, *Epistolica quaestio de vitae termino, fatali an mobili* (Dordrecht, 1634).

Bock, Friedrich S., *Historia antitrinitariorum, maxime socinianismi et socinianorum*, 2 vols (Königsberg/Leipzig, 1776–84).
Bodin, Jean, *Les Six Livres de la République* (Paris, 1576).
Brucker, Johann Jakob, *Historia critica philosophiae, a mundi incunabulis ad nostram usque aetatem deducta*, 4 vols (Leipzig, 1742–4).
Camerarius, Joachim (senior), *Ethicorum Aristotelis Nichomachiorum explicatio accuratissima* (Frankfurt, 1578).
Cardano, Gerolamo, *Arcana Politica sive de prudentia civilis liber singularis* (Leiden, 1635).
Cellarius, Balthasar, *Politicae Succinctae ex Aristotele libri II* (Jena, 1551).
Ceriol, Fadrique Furió, *El Concejo, y consejeros del príncipe* (Antwerp, 1559).
Cesalpino, Andrea, *Quaestionum peripateticarum libri V* (2nd edn, Venice, 1593).
Chytraeus, David, *Regulae vitae* (Wittenberg, 1555).
Ciceri, Francesco, *Epistularum libri XII et orationes quattuor*, 2 vols (Milan, 1782).
Clapmar, Arnold, *De arcanis rerumpublicarum libri sex* (Bremen, 1605).
Conring, Hermann, *Aristotelis laudatio: Orationes duae* (Helmstedt, 1633).
Conring, Hermann, *De civili prudentia liber unus quo prudentiae politicae, cum universalis philosophicae, tum singularis pragmaticae, omnis propaedia acroamatice traditur* (Helmstedt, 1662).
Conring, Hermann, *Opera*, vols 1–7 (Brunswick, 1730).
Crell, Johannes, *Ethica Aristotelica ad Sacrarum Litterarum normam emendata* (Cosmopolis [= Amsterdam], 1681).
Crell, Johannes, *Johannis Volkelii Misnici De vera religione libri quinque, quibus praefixus est Johannis Crellii Francii liber de Deo et eius attributis* (Raków, 1630).
Daneau, Lambert, *Ethices Christianae libri tres* (Geneva, 1577).
Daneau, Lambert, *Politices Christianae libri septem* (Geneva, 1596).
Diogenes Laertius, *De vitis, dogmatibus et apophthegmatibus clarorum philosophorum libri X . . . seorsum excusas Aeg. Menagii in Diogenem observationes auctiores habet volumen II* (Amsterdam, 1692).
Erasmus, Desiderius, *Adagiorum chiliades* (Basel, 1539).
Erasmus, Desiderius, *Apophtegmatum opus* (Paris, 1533).
Erasmus, Desiderius, *Argutissima quaeque Apophtegmata ex Erasmi Roterodami opere selecta, inque communes locos redacta, in commodum iuventutis, praesertim Goslarianae. Per Antonium Corvinum* ([Magdeburg], 1534).
Eustratii et Michaelis et anonyma in Ethica Nichomachea commentaria, ed. G. Heylbut, in *Commentaria in Aristotelem Graeca*, vol. XX (Berlin, 1892).
Felwinger, Johann Paul, *Philosophia Altdorfina* (Nuremberg, 1644).
Ferrari, Ottaviano, *Clavis philosophiae peripateticae aristotelicae, hoc est Octaviani Ferrarii, Hieronymi F[ilii] Mediolanensis De sermonibus exotericis, liber unus, et De disciplina encyclio, liber alter, nunc primum in Germania editi ex Bibliotheca Melchioris Haiminsfeldii Goldasti, cum eiusdem De Cryptica veterum Philosophorum disciplina epistola ad Rodolphum Goclenium* ([Frankfurt], 1506 (sic)).

Ferrari, Ottaviano, *De disciplina encyclio* (Venice, 1569).
Ferrari, Ottaviano, *De origine Romanorum* (Pavia, 1589).
Ferrari, Ottaviano, *De sermonibus exotericis liber* (Venice, 1575).
Freige, Johann T., *Paedagogus* (Basel, 1582).
Galen, *Galeni aureolus libellus quomodo quis et dinoscat et sanet proprios animi sui affectus, ex emendatione accurata* Johannis Caselii (Helmstedt, 1592).
Gassendi, Pierre, *Exercitationes paradoxicae adversus aristoteleos*, in *Opera*, 6 vols, vol. 3 (Lyon, 1658).
Goldast, Melchior, *De Aristotelis libri acroamaticis et exotericis* (Altdorf, 1597).
Heinsius, Daniel, *De politica sapientia oratio* (Leiden, 1614).
Keckermann, Bartholomäus, *Apparatus practicus sive idea methodica et plena totius philosophiae practicae nempe ethicae, oeconomicae et politicae* (Hanau, 1609).
Keckermann, Bartholomäus, *Disputationes practicae nempe ethicae, oeconomicae, politicae* (Hanau, 1612).
Keckermann, Bartholomäus, *Opera omnia*, 2 vols (Geneva, 1614).
Keckermann, Bartholomäus, *Praecognita Philosophica* (Hanau, 1607).
Keckermann, Bartholomäus, *Systema disciplinae politicae* (Hanau, 1608).
Kempis, Thomas à, *De imitando Christo, contemnendisque mundi vanitatibus libellus authore Thoma Kempisio, interprete Sebastiano Castellione* (Basel, 1563).
Lipsius, Justus, *Politicorum sive civilis doctrinae libri sex* (Leiden, 1589) (see: *Politica: Six Books of Politics or Political Instruction*, ed. Jan Waszink, Assen, 2004).
Makowski, Jan, *Metaphysica in usum quaestionum in philosophia ac theologia adornata et applicata* (Leiden, 1650).
Martini, Cornelius, *Adversus ramistas disputatio de subiecto et fine logicae* (Hanau/Lemgo, 1596).
Martini, Cornelius, *Disputationum metaphysicarum prima ... secunda* (Helmstedt, 1604).
Martini, Cornelius, *Metaphysica commentatio compendiose, succinte et perspicue comprehendens universam Metaphysices doctrinam* (Strasbourg, 1605).
Martini, Cornelius, *Metaphysica, brevibus quidem sed methodice conscripta* (Jena, 1622).
Meier, Ghebardt T., see: Völger.
Melanchthon, Philip, *Initia doctrina physicae*, in *Corpus Reformatorum*, vol. XIII (Halle, 1846).
Menage, Giles, see Diogenes Laertius.
Naudé, Gabriel, *Bibliographia politica* (Wittenberg, 1641).
Nizolio, Mario, *De veris principis et vera ratione philosophandi contra pseudophilosophos libri IV* (Frankfurt, 1670).
Nothold, Anton, *De Rameae institutionis principiis et natura logicae* (Lemgo, 1596).
Núñez, Pedro Juan, *Oratio de causis obscuritatis Aristotelis et de illarum remediis* (Valencia, 1554).
Omeis, Magnus Daniel, *Gloria Academiae Altdorfinae* (Altdorf, 1683).
Patrizi, Francesco, *Discussionum peripateticarum tomi IV* (Basel, 1581; 1st edn 1571).

Patrizi, Francesco, *Nova de universis philosophia* (Ferrara, 1591).
Pellegrini, Tommaso, *In metaphysicam Aristotelis*, Milan, *Biblioteca Ambrosiana*, MS. Dn 398 inf., ff. 1v–221v; MS. D. 400 inf. (course from 1563).
Périon, Joachim, see: Aristotle, *Ad Nicomachum filium de moribus*.
Piccart, Michael, *Argumenta librorum politicorum Aristotelis cum praefatione de naevis istius operis aristotelici* (Helmstedt, 1715).
Piccart, Michael, *Isagoge in lectionem Aristotelis, hoc est hypotyposis totius philosophiae Aristotelis* (Nuremberg, 1605; 2nd edn, Altdorf, 1660).
Ramus, Petrus, *Defensio pro Aristotele adversus Jacobum Schecium* (Lausanne, 1571).
Ramus, Petrus, *Professio regia* (Basel, 1576).
Ramus, Petrus, *Scholae in liberales artes* (Basel, 1569).
Ramus, Petrus, *Scholarum metaphysicarum libri quatuordecim, in totidem metaphysicos libros Aristotelis* (Paris, 1566).
Rej, Andrzej, 'Discursus politici de consilio, consiliario et concilio sive consultatione', in Bartholomäus Keckermann, *Disputationes practicae nempe ethicae, oeconomicae, politicae* (Hanau, 1612).
Richter, Georg, *Epistolae selectiores ad viros nobilissimos clarissimosque* (Nuremberg, 1662).
Scaligero, Giulio Cesare, *Exotericarum exercitationum libri XV* (Frankfurt, 1576).
Scherb, Philipp, *Clavis philosophiae peripateticae, sive Disputationum philosophicarum quibus universa doctrina logica, physica, ethica et politica artificiosissima methodo proponitur et declaratur, liber singularis, in academia Altorfina conscriptus a Philippo Scherbio, . . . Accessere quaestiones logicae Flamini Nobilii* (Frankfurt, 1625).
Scherb, Philipp, *Dissertatio pro philosophia peripatetica adversus ramistas* (Altdorf, 1590).
Scherb, Philipp, *Endoxa paradoxa, de differentiis analytices et dialectices* (Altdorf, 1589).
Scherb, Philipp, see also Aristotle, *Aristotelous Politikôn ta Sôzômena* and Tacitus, *De moribus Germanorum liber*.
Sepúlveda, Juan Ginés see: Aristotle, *Aristotelis de republica libri VIII*.
Sigonio, Carlo, *De dialogo liber* (Venice, 1562); Italian transl. by Franco Pignatti (Rome, 1993).
Simoni, Simone, *Antischegkianorum liber unus* (Basel, 1570).
Simoni, Simone, *In libros Aristotelis Περὶ τῶν αἰσθητερίων καὶ τῶν αἰσθητῶν, hoc est de sensuum instrumentis et de iis quae sub sensum cadunt* (Geneva, 1566).
Simoni, Simone, *De vera nobilitate* (Leipzig, 1572).
Sirenio, Giulio, *De fato libri novem* (Venice, 1563).
Soner, Ernst, *Commentarius in 12 Libros Metaphysicorum Aristotelis, dictus Anno 1609*, ms. UER 714 (University Library of Erlangen, Nuremberg).
Soner, Ernst, *In libros XII metaphysicos Aristotelis commentarius* (Jena, 1657).
Soner, Ernst, *Orationes duae* (Altdorf, 1610).
Stobaeus, Johannes, ΓΝΟΜΟΛΟΓΙΑ ΕΛΛΕΝΙΚΟΛΑΤΙΝΗ (Ἐκ Ἰωάννου τοῦ στοβαίου ἐκλογῶν παραινετικῶν συγκομισθεῖσα). *Gnomologia geaecolatina . . . per Michaelem Neandrum Soraviensem* (Basel, [1557]).

Tacitus, Publius Cornelius, Conring, Hermann, *De moribus Germanorum liber* [...] *ex recensione H. Conringi* (Helmstedt, 1652).

Taurellus, Nicolaus, *Alpes Caesae* (Frankfurt, 1597).

Taurellus, Nicolaus, ΚΟΣΜΟΛΟΓΙΑ, *hoc est physicarum et metaphysicarum discussionum: de mundo libri duo adversus Franciscum Piccolominaeum* (Amberg, 1603).

Taurellus, Nicolaus, ΟΥΡΑΝΟΛΟΓΙΑ, *hoc est physicarum et metaphysicarum discussionum: de coelo libri duo adversus Franciscum Piccolominaeum* (Amberg, 1603).

Taurellus, Nicolaus, *De rerum aeternitate ... metaphysyces universalis partes quatuor* (Marburg, 1604).

Taurellus, Nicolaus, *Synopsis Aristotelis metaphysices ad normam Christianae religionis explicatae, emendatae et completae* (Hanau, 1596), in Jakob W. Feuerlein, *Taurellus defensus. Dissertatio apologetica pro Nic. Taurello Philosopho* (Nuremberg, 1734).

Tidicaeus, Franciscus, *Aristotelis de virtutibus libellus graece et latine, versione in latinum nova et accurata, graeco textui ad unguem respondente et commentariis eruditis, atque iucundis in singula capitula illustratus. Isagoge Ethica, introductio in disciplinam moralem practicam.* [...] *Disputatio de fato et rebus fatalibus; De summo bono seu felicitate humana disputatio; Quaestio ethica et politica utrum honestum constet natura an vero tantum opinione; Themata disputationis de voluptate et dolore. Autore Francisco Tidicaeo Dantiscano* (Leipzig, 1609).

Tidicaeus, Franciscus, *Disputatio de fato*, see *Aristotelis de virtutibus libellus*.

Tidicaeus, Franciscus, *Fitologia generalis* (Leipzig, [1582]).

Tidicaeus, Franciscus, *In Iatromastigas, de recto et salutari usui, de abusu item multiplici atque nefario, nobilissimae ac salutiferae artis medicinae, libellus* (Toruń, 1592).

Tidicaeus, Franciscus, *Microcosmus, hoc est descriptio hominis et mundi parallelos* (Leipzig, 1615).

Tidicaeus, Franciscus, *De theriaca et eius multiplici utiitate ac recta conficiendi ratione* (Toruń, 1607).

Timpler, Clemens, *Metaphysicae systema methodicum* (Steinfurt, 1606).

Timpler, Clemens, *Philosophiae practicae systema methodicum in tres partes digestum* (Hanau, 1610–12).

Viotti, Bartolomeo, *De demonstratione libri quinque* (Paris, 1560).

Vives, Juan Luis, *Exercitationes animi in Deum. Eiusdem ad veram sapientiam introductio. Satellitium animi sive Symbola* (Paris, 1551).

Völger, Georg Johann, *De prudentiae civilis optimis auctoribus dissertatio ... praeside Gebhardo Theodoro Meier* (Helmstedt, 1659).

Vossius, Gerardus J., *De philosophia et philosophorum sectis* (The Hague, 1658).

Witte, Henning, *Memoriae medicorum nostri saeculi clarissimorum renovatae decas prima [-secunda]* (Frankfurt, 1676).

Zabarella, Jacopo, *Opera logica* (Venice, 1578).

Zeltner, Gustav Georg, *Historia Crypto-Socinismi Altorfinae quondam Academiae infesti arcana* (Leipzig, 1729).

Literature

Achermann, Eric, 'Ratio und oratio mentalis: Zum Verhältnis von Aristotelismus und Sozinianismus am Beispiel der Philosophie Ernst Soners', in Hanspeter Marti and Karin Marti-Weissenbach, eds, *Nürbergs Hochschule in Altdorf. Beiträge zur frühneuzeitlichen Wissenschafts- und Bildungsgeschichte* (Cologne/Weimar/Vienna, 2014), 98–158.

Angelini, Elisa, 'Un commento eccentrico: Hans Ludwig Wolzogen e la lettura sociniana delle Meditationes de prima philosophia', in Mariangela Priarolo and Emanuela Scribano, eds, *Le ragioni degli altri: Dissidenza religiosa e filosofia in età moderna* (Venice, 2017), 81–100.

Angelini, Elisa, 'Introduzione', in Johann Ludwig Wolzogen, *Annotationes in meditationes metaphysicas Renati Cartesii* (Florence, 2012), VII–LXXV.

Baldini, Artemio Enzo, ed., *Aristotelismo politico e ragion di Stato: Atti del convegno internazionale di Torino, 11–13 febbraio 1993* (Florence, 1995).

Banić-Pajnić, Erna, 'Petrić's View of Plato and Aristotle According to the Appendix of Nova de universis philosophia', in Erna Banić-Pajnić, Laura Blažetić, Mihaela Girardi-Karšulin, Ivan Kordić and Ivica Martinović, eds, *Philosophical Topics: Interpreting Tradition and Modernity* (Zagreb, 2004), 9–34.

Bellucci, Dino, 'Natural Philosophy and Ethics in Melanchthon', in Jill Kraye and Risto Saarinen, eds, *Moral Philosophy at the Threshold of Modernity* (Dordrecht, 2005), 235–54.

Berti, Enrico, *Aristotele nel '900* (Bari/Rome, 1993, repr. 2008).

Berti, Enrico, *Aristotele: dalla dialettica alla filosofia prima* (2nd edn, Milan, 2004).

Berti, Enrico, 'Introduzione', to Aristotele, *Metafisica*, text, translation and notes by Enrico Berti (Bari/Rome, 2017), V–XXXIII.

Bock, Stephen L., 'La causalità del motore immobile nel commento di Tommaso d'Aquino a Metafisica XII', *Humanitas*, 66/4 (2011), 644–66.

Boeuf, Estelle, *La bibliothèque parisienne de Gabriel Naudé en 1630* (Geneva, 2007).

Bonelli, Maddalena, *Alessandro di Afrodisia e la metafisica come scienza dimostrativa* (Naples, 2001).

Bröer, Ralf, 'Antiparacelsismus und radikale Reformation: Ernst Soner (1573–1612) und der Socinianizmus in Altdorf', *Odrodzenie i Reformacja w Polsce*, 48 (2004), 117–47.

Bruyère, Nelly, *Méthode et dialectique dans l'œuvre de la Ramée* (Paris, 1984).

Caccamo, Domenico, 'Commento al De vera nobilitate', in Mariano Verdigi, ed., *Simone Simoni, filosofo e medico nel '500* (Lucca, 1997), 137–41.

Caccamo, Domenico, *Eretici italiani in Moravia, Polonia e Transilvania* (Florence, 1970).

Cantimori, Delio, 'Un italiano contemporaneo di Bruno a Lipsia', *Studi Germanici*, 3/4–5 (1938), 445–66.

Chang, Ku-ming (Kevin), 'From Oral Disputation to Written Text: The Transformation of the Dissertation in Early Modern Europe', *History of Universities*, 19/2 (2004), 129–87.

Coroleu, Alejandro, 'The Fortuna of Juan Ginés de Sepúlveda's Translations of Aristotle and Alexander of Aphrodisias', *Journal of the Warburg and the Courtauld Institutes*, 59 (1996), 325-32.
Coroleu, Alejandro, 'A Philological Analysis of Juan Ginés de Sepúlveda's Latin Translations of Aristotle and Alexander of Aphrodisias', *Euphrosyne*, 23 (1995), 175-95.
Courtine, Jean-François, *Suarez et le système de la métaphysique* (Paris, 1990).
Domański, Juliusz, *La philosophie, théorie ou manière de vivre? Les Controverses de l'Antiquité à la Renaissance* (Fribourg/Paris, 1996).
Dreikopel, Tomasz, *Recepcja poglądów etycznych Arystotelesa w 'Isagoge Ethica' i 'Aristotelis de virtutibus libellus' Franciszka Tidicaeusa* (Olsztyn, 2010).
Dreikopel, Tomasz, 'Życie i działalność naukowa Franciszka Tidicaeusa (1554-1617), fizyka miejskiego i profesora Gimnazjum Akademickiego w Toruniu', *Rocznik Toruński*, 32 (2005), 23-50.
Dreitzel, Horst, 'Aristoteles' Politik im Denken Hermann Conrings', in Francesco Fagiani and Gabriella Valera, eds, *Categorie del reale e storiografia, Aspetti di continuità e trasformazione nell'Europa moderna* (Milan, 1986), 33-59.
Dreitzel, Horst, *Protestantischer Aristotelismus und absoluter Staat. Die* Politica *des Henning Arnisaeus (ca. 1575-1636)* (Wiesbaden, 1970).
Dreitzel, Horst, 'Reason of State and the Crisis of Political Aristotelianism: An Essay on the Development of 17th Century Political Philosophy', *History of European Ideas*, 28/3 (2002), 163-87.
Dreitzel, Horst, 'Die "Staatsräson" und die Krise des politischen Aristotelismus: zur Entwicklungder politischen Philosophie in Deutschland im 17. Jahrhundert', in Artemio Enzo Baldini, *Aristotelismo politico e ragion di Stato: Atti del convegno internazionale di Torino, 11-13 febbraio 1993* (Florence, 1995), 129-56.
Düring, Ingemar, *Aristotle in the Ancient Biographical Tradition* (Gothenburg, 1957).
Facca, Danilo, *Bartłomiej Keckermann i filozofia* (Warsaw, 2006).
Facca, Danilo 'Il "De fato" di Simone Porzio: nota storico critica', *Archiwum Historii Filozofii i Myśli Społecznej*, 47 (2002), 95-102.
Facca, Danilo, 'Franz Tidike i kultura renesansowego neoplatonizmu', *Odrodzenie i Reformacja w Polsce*, 51 (2007), 94-120.
Falckenberg, Richard, 'Soner, Ernst', *Allgemeine Deutsche Biographie*, 34 (1892), 622-3 Available online: https://www.deutsche-biographie.de/pnd117751944.html#adbcontent
Fasolt, Constantin, *The Limits of History* (Chicago, 2004).
Fasolt, Constantin, 'A Question of Right: Hermann Conring's New Discourse on the Roman-German Emperor', *Sixteenth Century Journal*, 28/3 (1997), 739-58.
Fazzo, Silvia, 'L'aristotelismo come tradizione esegetica', *Paradigmi*, 62 (2004), 367-84.
Fazzo, Silvia, 'L'emergenza della Metafisica di Aristotele in età romana', in Silvia Gastaldi and Cesare Zizza, eds, *Da Stagira a Roma: Prospettive aristoteliche tra storia e filosofia* (Pisa, 2017), 155-83.

Fazzo, Silvia, 'Philology and Philosophy on the Margin of Early Printed Editions of the Ancient Greek Commentators on Aristotle, with Special Reference to Copies Held in the Biblioteca Nazionale Braidense, Milan', in Constance Blackwell and Sachiko Kusukawa, eds, *Philosophy in the Sixteenth and Seventeenth Centuries: Conversations with Aristotle* (Aldershot, 1999), 48–75.

Felipe, Donald, 'Ways of Disputing and *Principia* in 17th Century German Disputation Handbooks', in Marion Gindhart and Ursula Kundert, eds, *Disputatio 1200–1800: Form, Funktion und Wirkung eines Leitmediums Universitärer Wissenkultur* (Berlin/New York, 2010), 33–61.

Fock, Otto, *Socinianismus nach seiner Stellung in Gesammtentwicklung des christliches Geistes, nach seinem historischen Verlauf und nach seinem Lehrbegriff dargestellt* (Kiel, 1847).

Frank, Günter, 'Melanchthon – der "Ethiker der Reformation"', in Günter Frank and Felix Mundt, eds, *Der Philosoph Melanchthon* (Berlin/Boston, 2012), 45–75.

Freedman, Joseph S., 'The Career and Writings of Bartholomew Keckermann (d. 1609)', *Proceedings of the American Philosophical Society*, 143 (1997), 305–64.

Freedman, Joseph S., *European Academic Philosophy in the Late Sixteenth and Early Seventeenth Centuries. The Life, Significance, and Philosophy of Clemens Timpler (1563/4–1624)*, 2 vols (Hildesheim/Zurich/New York, 1988).

Gaetano, Matthew T., 'Renaissance Thomism at the University of Padua, 1465–1583' (PhD dissertation, University of Pennsylvania, 2013). Available online: https://repository.upenn.edu/edissertations/865/

Gierke, Otto von, *Johannes Althusius und die Entwicklung der naturrechtlichen Staatstheorie* (Breslau, 1880).

Gilbert, Neal W., *Renaissance Concepts of Method* (New York/London, 1960).

Guldentops, Guy, 'L'anti-fatalisme de Julius Sirenius', in Pieter d'Hoine and Gerd Van Riel, eds, *Fate, Providence and Moral Responsibility in Ancient, Medieval and Early Modern Thought: Studies in Honour of Carlos Steel* (Leuven, 2014), 653–76.

Habsburg, Maximilian von, *Catholic and Protestant Translations of the* Imitatio Christi, *1425–1650: From Late Medieval Classic to Early Modern Bestseller* (Farnham, 2011).

Heck, Paul van, '*Cymbalum Politicorum, Consultor Dolosus*: Two Dutch Academics on Niccolò Machiavelli', in Toon van Houdt, Jan L. de Jong, Zoran Kwak, Marijke Spies and Marc van Vaeck, eds, *On the Edge of Truth and Honesty: Principles and Strategies of Fraud and Deceit in the Early Modern Period* (Leiden/Boston, 2002), 48–63.

Horn, Ewald, *Die Disputationen und Promotionen an den Deutschen Universitäten vornehmlich seit dem 16. Jahrhundert* (Leipzig, 1893).

Hotson, Howard, *Commonplace Learning: Ramism and Its German Ramifications, 1543–1630* (Oxford, 2007).

Hueglin, Thomas O., *Early Modern Concepts for a Late Modern World: Althusius on Community and Federalism* (Waterloo, Ont., 1999).

Ingravalle, Francesco and Corrado Malandrino, *Il lessico della Politica di Johannes Althusius* (Florence, 2005).

Jori, Alberto, *Hermann Conring (1606–1681): Der Begründer der deutschen Rechtsgeschichte* (Tübingen, 2006).

Knijff, Philipp and Sibbe Jan Visser, *Bibliographia Sociniana: A Bibliographical Reference Tool for the Study of Dutch Socinianism and Antitrinitarianism* (Hilversum Amsterdam, 2004).

Kraye, Jill, 'Alexander of Aphrodisias, Gianfrancesco Beati, and the Problem of *Metaphysics α*', in John Monfasani and Ronald G. Musto, eds, *Renaissance Society and Culture: Essays in Honor of Eugene F. Rice, Jr.* (New York, 1991), 137–60.

Kraye, Jill, 'Aristotle God's and the Authenticity of De Mundo: An Early Modern Controversy', *Journal of the History of Philosophy*, 28/3 (1990), 339–58.

Kusukawa, Sachiko, 'Mediations of Zabarella in Northern Europe: The Preface of Johann Ludwig Hawenreuter', in Gregorio Piaia, ed., *La presenza dell'aristotelismo padovano nella filosofia della prima modernità: Atti del Colloquio internazionale in memoria di Charles B. Schmitt (Padova, 4–6 settembre 2000)* (Padua, 2002), 199–213.

Kusukawa, Sachiko, *The Transformation of Natural Philosophy: The Case of Philip Melanchthon* (Cambridge, 1995).

Leijenhorst, Cees and Christoph Lüthy, 'The Erosion of Aristotelianism: Confessional Physics in Early Modern Germany and the Dutch Republic', in Cees Leijenhorst, Christoph Lüthy and Johannes M.M.H. Thijssen, eds, *The Dynamic of Aristotelian Natural Philosophy from Antiquity to the Seventeenth Century* (Leiden/Boston/Cologne, 2002), 375–411.

Leinsle, Ulrich L., *Das Ding und die Methode: Methodische Konstitution und Gegenstand der frühen protestantischen Metaphysik*, 2 vols (Augsburg, 1985).

Lepri, Valentina, *Layered Wisdom: Early Modern Collections of Political Precepts* (Padua, 2015).

Lohr, Charles H., 'Metaphysics', in Charles B. Schmitt, Quentin Skinner, Eckhard Kessler and Jill Kraye, eds, *The Cambridge History of Renaissance Philosophy* (Cambridge, 1988), 537–638.

Ludwig, Frank, 'Dr. Simon Simonius in Leipzig. Ein Beitrag zur Geschichte der Universität von 1570 bis 1580', *Neues Archiv für Sächsische Geschichte*, 30 (1909), 209–90.

Maclean, Ian, 'Mediations of Zabarella in Northern Germany, 1586–1623', in Gregorio Piaia, ed., *La presenza dell'aristotelismo padovano nella filosofia della prima modernità: Atti del Colloquio internazionale in memoria di Charles B. Schmitt (Padova, 4–6 settembre 2000)* (Padua, 2002), 173–98.

Madonia, Claudio, 'Simone Simoni', in André Séguenny, ed., *Bibliotheca Dissidentium IX: Répertoire des non-conformistes religieux des seizième et dix-septième siècles*, vol. 9 (Baden-Baden, 1988), 25–110.

Madonia, Claudio, 'Simone Simoni da Lucca', *Rinascimento*, 20 (1980), 161–97.

Mährle, Wolfgang, *Academia Norica: Wissenschaft und Bildung an der Nürnberger Hohen Schule in Altdorf (1575–1623)* (Stuttgart, 2000).

Marras, Cristina and Giovanna Varani, 'I dibattiti rinascimentali su retorica e dialettica nella 'Prefazione al Nizolio' di Leibniz', *Studi Filosofici*, 27 (2004), 183–216.

Marti, Hanspeter, *Philosophischen Dissertationem deutscher Universitäten 1660–1750: eine Auswahlbibliographie*, Karin Marti, ed. (Munich, 1982).

Martin, Craig, *Subverting Aristotle: Religion, History, and Philosophy in Early Modern Science* (Baltimore, 2014).

Mayes, Benjamin T.G., *Counsel and Conscience: Lutheran Casuistry and Moral Reasoning After the Reformation* (Göttingen, 2011).

Meerhoff, Kees, 'Bartholomew Keckermann and the Anti-Ramist Tradition at Heidelberg', in Christoph Strohm, Joseph S. Freedman and Herman J. Selderhuis, eds, *Späthumanismus und reformierte Konfession: Theologie, Jurisprudenz und Philosophie in Heidelberg an der Wende zum 17. Jahrhunderts* (Tübingen 2006), 169–206.

Meerhoff, Kees, 'Some XVIth-Century Readings of Aristotle's Ethics', in Günter Frank, and Andreas Speer, eds, *Der Aristotelismus in der Frühen Neuzeit: Kontinuität oder Wiederneignung?* (Wiesbaden, 2007), 291–324.

Mignini, Filippo, 'Spinoza e i sociniani', in Mariangela Priarolo and Emanuela Scribano, eds, *Fausto Sozzini e la filosofia in Europa: Atti del Convegno (Siena, 25–27 novembre 2004)* (Siena, 2005), 137–78.

Muccillo, Maria, 'Dall'ordine dei libri all'ordine della realtà: ordine e metodo nella filosofia di Francesco Patrizi', in Tomáš Nejeschleba and Paul Richard Blum, eds, *Francesco Patrizi, Philosopher of the Renaissance: Proceedings from The Centre for Renaissance Texts Conference, 24–26 April 2014* (Olomouc, 2015), 9–61.

Muccillo, Maria, 'La vita e le opere di Aristotele nelle Discussione peripatericae di Francesco Patrizi da Cherso', *Rinascimento*, 21 (1981), 53–119.

Müller, Michael G., *Zweite Reformation und ständische Autonomie im Königlichen Presussen. Danzig, Elbing und Thorn in der Epoche Konfessionalisierung (1557–1660)* (Berlin, 1997).

Muller, Richard A., '*Vera Philosophia cum sacra Theologia nusquam pugnat*: Keckermann on Philosophy, Theology, and the Problem of Double Truth', *The Sixteenth Century Journal*, 15/3 (1984), 341–65.

Mulsow, Martin, 'Ambiguity of the *Prisca Sapientia* in the Late Renaissance Humanism', *Journal of the History of the Ideas*, 65/1 (2004), 1–13.

Mulsow, Martin, '*Die whare peripatetische Philosophie in Deutschland*: Melchior Goldast, Philipp Scherb und die akroamatische Tradition der Alten', in Helwig Schmidt-Glintzer, ed., *Fordern und Bewahren: Studien zur europäischen Kulturgeschichte der frühen Neuzeit* (Wiesbaden, 1996), 49–78.

Nuzzo, Enrico, 'Crisi dell'aristotelismo politico e ragion di Stato: Alcune preliminari considerazioni metodologiche e storiografiche', in Artemio Enzo Baldini, ed., *Aristotelismo politico e ragion di Stato: Atti del convegno internazionale di Torino, 11–13 febbraio 1993* (Florence, 1995), 11–52.

Oestreich, Gerhard, *Neostoicism and the Early Modern State* (Cambridge, 1982).

Ogonowski, Zbigniew, 'Le rationalisme dans la doctrine des sociniens', in *Movimenti ereticali in Italia e in Polonia nei secoli XVI–XVII: Atti del convegno Italo-Polacco, Firenze 22–24 settembre 1971* (Florence, 1974), 141–57.

Ogonowski, Zbigniew, *Socynianizm: Dzieje, Poglądy, Oddziaływani* (Warsaw, 2015).
Ogonowski, Zbigniew, *Socynianizm a Oświecenie: Studia nad myślą filozoficzno-religijną arian w Polsce XVII wieku* (Warsaw, 1966).
Oldrini, Guido, *La disputa del metodo nel Rinascimento: Indagini su Ramo e sul ramismo* (Florence, 1997).
Ong, Walter G., *Ramus, Method, and the Decay of Dialogue: From the Art of Discourse to the Art of Reason* (Cambridge, MA, 1958; 2nd edn Chicago, 2004).
Ottmann, Henning, 'Protestantische Schulphilosophie in Deutschland: Arnisaeus und Conring', in Christoph Horn and Ada Neschke-Hentschke, eds, *Politischer Aristotelismus: Die Rezeption der aristotelischen 'Politik' von der Antike bis zum 19. Jahrhundert* (Stuttgart, 2008), 218–31.
Piaia, Gregorio, ed., *La presenza dell'aristotelismo padovano nella filosofia della prima modernità: Atti del Colloquio internazionale in memoria di Charles B. Schmitt (Padova, 4–6 settembre 2000)* (Padua, 2002).
Pine, Martin L., *Pietro Pomponazzi: Radical Philosopher of the Renaissance* (Padua, 1986).
Poppi, Antonino, *La dottrina della scienza in Giacomo Zabarella* (Padua, 1972).
Poppi, Antonino, *Ricerche sulla teologia e la scienza nella Scuola padovana del Cinque e Seicento* (Catanzaro, 2001).
Pozzo, Riccardo, *Adversus Ramistas: Kontroversen über die Natur der Logik am Ende der Renaissance* (Basel, 2012).
Pozzo, Riccardo, 'Cornelius Martini sull'oggetto della metafisica', *Medioevo*, 34 (2009), 305–14.
Pozzo, Riccardo, 'Res considerata and Modus considerandi rem: Averroes, Aquinas, Jacobo Zabarella, and Cornelius Martini on Reduplication', *Medioevo*, 24 (1998), 151–76.
Rackham, Harris, 'Introduction', in Aristotle, *The Athenian Constitution, Eudemian Ethics, On Virtues and Vices* (London/Cambridge, MA, 1935), 484–7.
Ramberti, Rita, *Il problema del libero arbitrio nel pensiero di Pietro Pomponazzi: La dottrina del De fato – spunti di critica filosofica e teologica nel Cinquecento* (Florence, 2007).
Ravaisson, Félix, *Essai sur la Métaphysique d'Aristote*, vol. I (Paris, 1837).
Risse, Wilhelm, *Die Logik der Neuzeit, 1500–1640*, 2 vols (Stuttgart/Bad Cannstatt, 1964–70).
Riva, Franco, *Analogia e univocità in Tommaso de Vio 'Gaetano'* (Milan, 1995).
Rohls, Jan, 'Zwischen Stoizimus und Aristotelismus: Lutherische und reformierte Ethik im Zeitalter der Orthodoxie', in S. Ebbersmeyer and E. Kessler, eds, *Ethik – Wissenschaft oder Lebenskunst? Modelle der Normenbegründung von der Antike bis zu Frühen Neuzeit* (Berlin, 2007), 267–91.
Roncaglia, Gino, *Palaestra rationis: Discussioni su natura della copula e modalità nella 'Scolastica' tedesca del XVII secolo* (Florence, 1996).
Ross, Alberto, 'The Causality of the Prime Mover in Metaphysics Λ', in Christoph Horn, ed., *Aristotle's* Metaphysics Lambda: *New Essays* (Boston/Berlin, 2016), 207–27.

Saarinen, Risto, *Weakness of Will in Renaissance and Reformation Thought* (Oxford, 2011).

Salmonowicz, Stanisław, 'Nauczanie filozofii w Toruńskim Gimnazjum Akademickim (1568–1793). Organizacja, wykładowcy, podręczniki', in Lech Szczucki, ed., *Nauczanie filozofii w Polsce w XV–XVIII wieku* (Warsaw, 1978), 137–96.

Santinello, Giovanni, 'Jakob Thomasius (1622–1684): *Schediasma historicum*', in id., ed., *Models of the History of Philosophy, I: From Its Origins in the Renaissance to the 'Historia Philosophica'* (Dordrecht, 1993; 1st Italian edn Brescia, 1981), 409–41.

Scandellari, Simonetta, 'El "Concejo y Consejeros del Príncipe": algunos aspectos de la literatura política española del siglo XVI', *Res Publica*, 15 (2005), 49–75.

Scattola, Merio, 'Gewissen und Gerechtigkeit in den Beichtbüchernder Früher Neuzeit', *Journal of Early Modern Christianity*, 2/2 (2015), 117–58.

Scattola, Merio, 'Politica architectonica: L'aristotelismo politico nel dibattito politico tedesco della prima età moderna', *Res Publica*, 19/1 (2016), 15–33.

Schilling, Heinz, ed., *Die reformierte Konfessionalisierung in Deutschland – Das Problem der 'Zweiten Reformation': Wissenschaftliches Symposium des Vereins für Reformationsgeschichte* (Gütersloh, 1986).

Schmitt, Charles B., *Aristotle and the Renaissance* (Cambridge, MA, 1983).

Schmitt, Charles B., 'Etyka Arystotelesa w XVI wieku: Rozważania wstępne', *Odrodzenie i Reformacja w Polsce*, 24 (1979), 21–41.

Schmitt, Charles B., *Gianfrancesco Pico della Mirandola (1469–1533) and His Critique of Aristotle* (The Hague, 1967).

Scribano, Emanuela, 'Aristotele contro Platone in Fausto Sozzini', *Rinascimento*, 46 (2006), 73–92.

Sellberg, Erland, entry: 'Petrus Ramus', *The Stanford Encyclopedia of Philosophy* (Summer 2016 Edition), ed. Edward N. Zalta. Available online: https://plato.stanford.edu/archives/sum2016/entries/ramus/

Sinnema, Donald, 'The Discipline of Ethics in Early Reformed Orthodoxy', *Calvin Theological Journal*, 28 (1993), 10–44.

Sparn, Walter, 'Aristotelismus in Altdorf: Ein vorläufiges Profil', in Hanns Christoph Brennecke, Dirk Niefanger and Werner Wilhelm Schnabel, eds, *Akademie und Universität Altdorf: Studien zur Hochschulgeschichte Nürbergs* (Cologne/Weimar/Vienna, 2011), 121–50.

Sparn, Walter, *Wiederkehr der Metaphysik: Die ontologische Frage in der lutherischen Theologie des frühen 17. Jahrhunderts* (Stuttgart, 1976).

Spranzi, Marta, *The Art of Dialectic Between Dialogue and Rhetoric: The Aristotelian Tradition* (Amsterdam/Philadelphia, 2011).

Stanciu, Diana, 'Prudence in Lipsius's *Monita et Exempla Politica*: Stoic Virtue, Aristotelian Virtue or Not a Virtue at All?', in Eric De Bom, Marijke Janssens, Toon Van Houdt and Jan Papy, eds, *(Un)masking the Realities of Power: Justus Lipsius and the Dynamics of Political Writing in Early Modern Europe* (Leiden/Boston, 2011), 233–62.

Stolleis, Michael, ed., *Hermann Conring (1606-1681): Beiträge zu Leben und Werke* (Berlin, 1983).

Stopp, Frederick J., *The Emblems of the Altdorf Academy: Medals and Medal Orations 1577-1626* (London, 1974), 20-9.

Syndikus, Anette, 'Philologie und Universalismus: Gabriel Naudés enzyklopädische Schriften und ihre Rezeption im deutschsprachigen Raum', in Denis Thouard, Friedrich Vollhardt and Fosca Mariani Zini, eds, *Philologie als Wissensmodell / La philologie comme modèle de savoir* (Berlin/New York, 2010), 309-43.

Tiraboschi, Girolamo, *Storia della letteratura italiana* (Milan, 1833).

Tolomio, Ilario, 'The "Historia Philosophica" in the Sixteenth and Seventeenth Century, Ch. 5: Edition of Diogenes Laertius in the Fifteenth to Seventeenth Centuries', in Giovanni Santinello, ed., *Models of the History of Philosophy, I: From Its Origins in the Renaissance to the 'Historia Philosophica'* (Dordrecht, 1993), 154-60.

Tommasi, Francesco V., 'Michael Piccart, Kant e i termini primi: Il trascendentale nel rapporto tra filosofia e linguaggio', *Archivio di Filosofia*, 73 (2005), 369-90.

Torzini, Roberto, 'Filosofia e teologia nel De Deo di Crell', in Mariangela Priarolo and Emanuela Scribano, eds, *Le ragioni degli altri: Dissidenza religiosa e filosofia in età moderna* (Venice, 2017), 63-80.

Tync, Stanisław, *Dzieje Gimnazjum Toruńskiego (1568-1772)*, 2 vols (Toruń, 1928-49).

Tync, Stanisław, *Najdawniejsze ustawy Gimnazjum Toruńskiego* (Toruń, 1925).

Vasoli, Cesare, *La dialettica e la retorica dell'Umanesimo: 'Invenzione' e 'Metodo' nella cultura del XV e XVI secolo* (Milan, 1968).

Whipple, John, entry: 'Leibniz's Exoteric Philosophy' in *The Stanford Encyclopedia of Philosophy* (Summer 2013 Edition), ed. Edward N. Zalta. Available online: https://web.archive.org/web/20131202064741/https://plato.stanford.edu/archives/sum2013/entries/leibniz-exoteric/

Wilmott, Michael J., ' "Aristoteles Exotericus, Acroamaticus, Mysticus": Two Interpretations of the Typological Classification of the "Corpus Aristotelicum" by Francesco Patrizi da Cherso', *Nouvelles de la République des Lettres*, 2 (1985), 67-95.

Wollgast, Siegfried, *Philosophie in Deutschland zwischen Reformation und Aufklärung 1550-1650* (Berlin, 1988).

Wundt, Max, *Die deutsche Schulmetaphysik des 17. Jahrhunderts* (Tübingen, 1939).

Zanier, Giancarlo, 'Noterelle pomponazziane', *Giornale Critico della Filosofia Italiana*, 10 (1979), 211-25.

Index

Achermann, Eric 87, 192 n.8, 193 n.13, 203 n.109, 204 n.113
Acquario, Mattia 48
acroamatic
   in antiquity 3–5
   in Ferrari 13–24
   in Germany
      Conring 113–14, 119–29, 181 n.74
      Scherb and Goldast 24–9
   in Renaissance thought 6–13, 173
   in Tidike 138–9 , 182 n.86
Aegisthus 148, 163
Aesop 143
affectiones entis 43, 69
   in Martini 49–51
   in Soner 72–7, 189 n.72
Albert the Great 70
Alexander of Aphrodisias 12, 16, 26, 36, 176 n.10
   commentary on *Metaphysics* 7, 63, 65–70, 74, 81, 87, 194 n.19, 198 n.41, 202 n.96
   De anima 203 n.99
   De fato 90, 137, 153
   Ps. Alexander
      Commentary on *Metaphysics* 63, 68–9, 81
      Problems 144
Alexander the Great 4, 5, 6, 119, 123, 174
Alsted, Johann Heinrich 53, 79, 144, 190 n.93
Altdorf 42, 123–4, 181 n.74, 182 n.86, 213 n.71
   and Scherb 24, 27–9, 38
   and Soner 56–62, 193 n.14, 204 n.109, 205 n.114
   theology 87–9, 206 n.125
Althusius, Johannes (Johann Althaus) 96–7, 100–4, 111, 207 n.6, 209 n.42, 211 n.53
Ames, William 144
Ammirato, Scipione 102

Ammonius Hermiae 8, 10, 12, 17, 21, 70, 183 n.88
Anabaptists 136
analogy
   in Martini 50–2, 189 n.73
   in Pellegrini 67
   in Soner 71–5, 78–80, 87
   in Tidike 137
analytic-analitycal 10, 19–26, 43, 114–15, 171, 185 n.14, 195 n.26
Andronicus of Rhodes 15–16, 21, 27, 175 n.4, 179 n.41
Angelini, Elisa 191 n.6
Antitrinitarians 56–60, 88, 136, 155, 204 n.109
apodictic 10, 17, 40, 42, 131; *see also* demonstration
appetitus Dei 79, 81–2, 202 n.97, n.99
arcana imperii 93, 102, 111, 123, 130, 213 n.71
Arians, *see* Antitrinitarians
Aristotle (the Philosopher, the Stagirite)
   his adversaries 7–11, 25, 33–8, 45–7
   his authority vi–ix, 22, 45, 117–18, 128, 132, 136, 214 n.93
   Categories 12, 17
   Eudemian Ethics 6, 138
   Eudemus 14, 178 n.28
   his library 15, 35, 36
   Metaphysics 40, 48, 63, 66–72, 90, 137, 179 n.41, 195 n.26, n.27, 199 n.68, 201 n.94, 201 n.95
      Metaphysics book
         Alpha (I) 98
         Alpha elatton (II) 79
         eta (VIII), 169
         gamma (IV) 46, 67
         lambda (XII), 65, 68–9, 72, 78–88
      Ramus on 36–7, 52
   Neoplatonic commentators of 5, 10, 21, 122, 124, 183 n.88

Nicomachean Ethics 14, 124
   his obscurity 7, 36, 176 n.11
On Divination in Sleep 80
On Generation and Corruption 159
On the Heavens 13
On Interpretation 137, 169
On Soul 81, 178 n.28
Organon 35
Physics 9, 78, 84, 122
Politics, 6–7, 14, 93–4, 148, 164
   Conring on 121–33,
      216 n.106, n.107, 217 n.117
   Keckermann on 105
Posterior Analytics 28–9, 49, 63
   Conring on 115, 125
   Ferrari on 18, 21, 25
   Ramus on 36
   Zabarella on 11
Prior Analytics 11, 19
Ps. Aristotle, *On the Universe* 138,
      177 n.15, 228 n.92
Rhetoric 139, 179 n.38
Sophistical Refutations 11
Topics 31
Aristotelianism, political 93–133
Armenians 8
Arminians 58
Arnisaeus, Henning 47, 70, 74–5, 111, 171,
      188 n.67, 189 n.72
Arpe, Peter Friedrich 155
Aspasius 220 n.18
atheism 85, 120, 172, 206 n.125
Atreus 163
Augustine of Ippona, Saint 105, 142
Averroes 11, 26, 63, 66, 69–70, 74, 81,
      195 n.26, 216 n.114
   Averroism 11, 55, 85, 151

Bacon, Francis 40, 218 n.130
Baerle, Caspar van (Barlaeus, Caspar)
      214 n.91
Baldini, Artemio Enzo 212 n.65,
      213 n.71
Banić-Pajnić, Erna 177 n.19
Bartholin, Caspar (Thrasibulus
      Philalethes) 47
Basel 56
Bathsheba 148
Battus of Thera 228 n.105

Bayle, Pierre 57, 85, 87, 206 n.125, 229 n.1
Beato, Gianfrancesco 62
Bellucci, Dino 227 n.77
Bernardi della Mirandola, Antonio
      199 n.68
Bert, Pieter de (Petrus Bertius)) 60, 192,
      193 n.12, 13
Berti, Enrico 175 n.2, n.4, 197 n.35,
      198 n.46, 201 n.95
Beurhaus, Friedrich 188
Beverwijck, Johan van (Johannes
      Beverovicius) 188 n.54
Beza, Theodore 101, 151
Bible, Holy Writ
   and ethics 139–42
   and theology 57, 79–80, 102, 172
Biblioteca Ambrosiana x, 14, 195 n.26,
      198 n.48
Blackwell, Constance W.T. 178 n.32
Blažetić, Laura 177 n.19
Blum, Paul Richard 177 n.19
Bock, Friedrich Samuel 192 n.8, n.11
Bock, Stephen L. 198 n.47
Bodin, Jean 93, 95, 133
   Althusius on 100–1
   Conring on 119
   Keckermann on 104, 211 n.53
   Piccart on 218 n.130
body politic 100–2, 104
Boeckler, Johann Heinrich 132
Boeuf, Estelle 207 n.4
Boethius, Anicius Manlius Severinus 66,
      228 n.113
Bohemian Brethren 136
Bologna 24
Bonelli, Maddalena 198 n.40
Botero, Giovanni 102, 211 n.53
Brennecke, Hanns Christoph 206 n.125
Broadie, Sarah 198 n.40
Bröer, Ralf 191 n.2
Brucker, Johann Jakob 85, 174, 191 n.2,
      194 n.20
Bruno, Giordano 24, 27, 85
Bruns, Ivo 202 n.96, 206 n.130
Bruyère, Nelly 34
Buscher, Heizo 188, 54

Caccamo, Domenico 226 n.63
Calixt, Georg 117

Calvinism 24, 97 , 136, 173
    political Calvinism 96, 100–1, 103
Camerarius, Joachim the Elder 150–1, 155,
    222 n.30, 226 n.61, n.62
Camerarius, Phillip 211 n.53
Campano, Giovanni Antonio 175 n.6
Canobiana, scuola 13
Cantimori, Delio 225 n.60, n.61, 226 n.63
Cardano, Girolamo 213 n.77
Casaubon, Isaac 216, n.106
Case, John 104
Caselius, Johannes 46–7, 118, 223 n.41
Casmann, Otho 98, 104
Cassius Dio 210 n.53
Castellani, Vincenzo 211 n.53
Castellion, Sébastien 144, 224 n.54
casuistry 144, 225 n.56
categories 53, 66–71, 137
Cavalcanti, Bartolomeo 22, 179 n.38
Cellarius, Balthasar 128
Ceriol, Fadrique Furió 103, 211 n.53
Cesalpino, Andrea 57, 61–2, 70, 74–7,
    84–9, 172, 191 n.2, 199 n.64
Chaldeans 8
    Chaldean Oracles 7
Chamaillard, Alexandre 138, 220 n.10
Chang, Ku-ming (Kevin) 210 n.50
Charpentier, Jacques (Jacobus
    Carpentarius) 34
Chasseneuz, Barthélemy de 211 n.53
Cheke, John 107
Chemnitz, Martin 45
Christian philosophy 64, 69, 82, 85–90
    Chrysippus 154, 157, 40
    and ethics 140, 143–4 224 n.52
    and Hermeticism 24
    and natural philosophy 37, 55–7, 153
    in Soner 79–89
    in Taurellus 89–90, 201 n.93, 206 n.125
Chytraeus, David 45, 143
Ciceri, Francesco 178 n.32, 190 n.73
Cicero 4, 6, 8, 12, 16–17, 21–3, 28, 35, 104,
    114, 136, 141, 147
    On Duties 139
    On the Ends of Good and Evil 4, 16
    On Fate 148
    On the Nature of the Gods 158
    Tusculan Disputations 157
civil society 111–13, 124, 131

Claepius, Daniel 187 n.36
Clapmar, Arnold 213 n.71
Cleary, Helen x
Clement of Alexandria 16
Clytemnestra 148, 163
Coldorphus, Johannes Canutus 189 n.73
Colli, Hyppolit von (Hyppolitus a
    Collibus) 211 n.53
commonplaces 95, 105, 110
Commynes, Philippe de (Philippus
    Comineus) 211 n.53
concept, formal and objective 49–51, 71,
    74
confessionalisation vii, 110, 155–6, 172–3,
    182 n.86, 190 n.96
Conring, Hermann 28, 207 n.4, 213 n.75,
    215 n.96
    on acroamatic doctrines 114–15,
        124–5, 128–9, 216, n.114
    on Aristotle's authority viii, 117–18,
        131–3, 213 n.75, 215 n.95
    on Aristotle's *Politics* 94, 109–33,
        216 n.106,
        217 n.117, n.123, n.126
conscience 140–4, 154, 164, 222 n.30,
    224 n.52, 225 n.56
constitution 111, 123–7
Contarini, Gasparo 211 n.53
continence (*enkrateia*) 141
contingency 64, 86, 89, 119, 129, 150,
    169–70
    contingent/necessary 41, 43, 49, 75
Coroleu, Alejandro 176 n.10
Council of Trent 53
counsel (advise), counsellor 94–115
Courtine, Jean-François 189 n.75
creation 69, 75, 82–3, 86
Crell, Johann 56–7, 88–90, 201 n.93,
    224 n.52
Cremonini, Cesare 62, 85
Cyrene 228 n.105

Daneau, Lambert 101, 104, 144, 211 n.53
David, King of Israel 148, 163
De Bom, Eric 207 n.3
Deism 55, 57, 85
demons 60, 79, 84–6, 193
demonstration 9–11, 13, 17–21, 26–9, 40,
    55, 155, 177 n.16

in metaphysics and theology 50, 79
in practical sciences 114–15, 123–4, 130–1
Descartes, René 184
determinism 147, 150, 157–8, 170
De Vio, Tommaso (Gaetanus) 48–9, 50–1, 74
dialectics 13, 22, 25, 29, 108, 177 n.18, 183 n.88, 188 n.55, 195 n.25
    dialectical reasoning 10, 17, 25, 114–15, 124, 155
Diogenes Laertius 5–6, 121–2, 216 n.106
disciplines
    instrumental 45, 58
    practical 12, 29, 43, 45, 93–4, 99, 105–6, 110–15, 118–19, 124–5, 129–33, 142; *see* ethics, politics
    theoretical 12, 25, 39, 43; *see* metaphysics, physics
disputations 138, 210 n.50
Domański, Juliusz x, 222 n.34
Donato, Girolamo 203 n.99
Dreikopel, Tomasz 218 n.2, 219 n.6, 220 n.10
Dreitzel, Horst 111, 212 n.65, n.70, n.71, 213 n.72
Dremierre, Dorota x
Duns Scotus 70, 216 n.114
Düring, Ingemar 175 n.6
Dürr, Johann Konrad 182 n.86

Ebbersmeyer, Sabrina 221 n.23
Egyptians 8, 15
Elbląg 135
Emden 96–7
encyclopaedia 22–3, 45
endoxa 17, 25, 41, 180 n.64
ens commune 47, 49, 66, 71–2, 74–5
Erasmus of Rotterdam 143–4, 175 n.5, 224 n.48
Erythraeus, Valentin 24
ethics
    and philosophy 137–45
    and religion 140–1
Etruscans 8
Eurypides 164
Eustratius of Nicaea 12, 18, 211 n.54
exoteric 183 n.88

in Altdorf 24–6, 181 n.74, 182 n.86, 183 n.87
in antiquity 3–5, 178 n.28
in Conring 114–15, 123, 127, 217 n.121
in Ferrari 13–21
in Goldast 28–9
in the Renaissance 5–13
in Tidike 138

Fagiani, Francesco 212 n.70
Falckenberg, Richard 191 n.2
Fasolt, Constantin 214 n.90, 215 n.95, 216 n.101, 217 n.123
fate 137, 145–55, 156–70, 227 n.75
Fathers of the Church 215 n.93
Fazzo, Silvia 175 n.3, 178 n.32, 179 n.41
federalism 100, 104
Felipe, Donald 210 n.50
Feller, Joachim Friedrich 193 n.13
Felwinger, Johann Paul 58, 60, 70, 191 n.8, 192 n.8, 193 n.14
Ferrari, Ottaviano 5, 13–29 178 n.32, 179 n.51, 180 n.62, n.73
First (primary, unmoved) Mover 69, 78, 81, 198 n.46, 202 n.96
Fonseca, Pedro da 47–8, 53, 69, 74–5, 172, 200 n.71
Formula concordiae 190 n.96
Frank, Günter 221 n.23, 227 n.77
Frank Ludwig 226 n.61
Freedman, Joseph S. 187 n.36, 208 n.9, 210 n.44
freedom in human agency 147, 149, 154, 159, 163, 166, 168–70, 172
Freige, Johann Thomas (Fregius) 24, 35, 38, 181 n.74, 184 n.5, n.7
Frycz-Modrzewski, Andrzej
futura contingentia 56, 107, 147, 150, 158, 169–70

Gaetano, Matthew T. 63–5, 190 n.85, 194 n.15, n.20
Galen 35, 115, 137, 143, 153, 223 n.41, 228 n.87
Gassendi, Pierre 80, 201 n.94
Gastaldi, Silvia 179 n.41
Gdansk 33, 96–7, 104–5, 117, 135–6, 171
Gellius, Aulus 4–6, 8, 123, 143, 158, 12, 175 n.4, n.6

Gentillet, Innocent 102, 211 n.53
Gentili, Alberico 211, 53
Genua (Marco Antonio Passeri) 11, 151
German law 111, 213 n.75, 215 n.95
Gesner, Conrad 122
Gheeraerdst, Andreas (Hyperius, Andreas Gerhard) 144
Gierke, Otto von 100
Giffen, Hubert van (Hubertus Giphanius) 122, 126-7
Gilbert, Neal Ward 214 n.85
Gindhart, Marion 210 n.50
Girardi-Karšulin, Mihaela 177 n.19
Goclenius, Rudolph (the younger?) 27
Goclenius, Rudolph the elder 98, 144, 207 n.4
Goldast, Melchior 26-8, 182 n.79, n.81
Gospel 55, 57
Gouveia, Antonio de 34
Gregoire, Pierre (Tolosanus) 99, 104, 211 n.53
Gregory of Nyssa 59
Grotius, Hugo 117, 133, 217 n.130
Grynaeus, Simon 220 n.10
Guevara, Antonio de 211 n.53
Guicciardini, Francesco 211 n.53
Guldentrops, Guy 202 n.4
Gundling, Nicolaus Hieronymus 132
Gymnasium Illustre or *Academicum* 96, 98, 104, 135-6

Habsburg, Maximilian von 225 n.54
Hadot, Pierre 222 n.34
Harnack, Adolf von 57
Hawenreuter, Johann Ludwig 186 n.25
Hayduck, Michael 197 n.38
Heck, Paul van 215 n.96
Heereboord, Adrian 190 n.93
Heidelberg 117, 155-6, 171, 187 n.36
Heinsius, Daniel 120-3, 126-7, 215 n.96, 216 n.104, n.106, n.107, 217 n.117
Helen of Troy 148
Helmstedt 33, 46, 116-18, 171, 188 n.53
　and Conring 28, 111, 113, 128, 131
　and Martini 45-7, 52
Herborn 96
Hermeticism 7-8, 11, 23-8, 37

heterodoxy 58, 60-1, 85-8; *see* Antitrinitarians
Heylbut, Gustav 211 n.54, 220 n.18
Hezekiah 168
Hobbes, Thomas 93, 130, 132-3
Hoddaeus, Konrad 188 n.54
Hoffmann, Caspar 61
Hoffmann, Daniel 188 n.54, 189 n.76
Hoine, Pieter d' 219 n.4
Horn, Christoph 198 n.46, 212 n.65
Horn, Ewald 210 n.50
Hornejus, Konrad 117
Hotman, François 101
Hotson, Howard 34, 116, 172, 184 n.3, n.6, 185 n.14, n.19, n.20, 187 n.36, n.37, n.43, n.48, 190 n.95
Houdt, Toon van 207 n.3, 215 n.96
Hueglin, Thomas O. 208 n.20
humanists vii, 23, 35, 57, 87, 81, 88, 90, 109, 117, 136, 226 n.63
　Dutch 94, 97, 123
　German 47, 155-6
　Italian 13, 62-3, 116
　Spanish 15, 63, 103
humanist dialectics 29
Huswedel, Johann 192 n.11

Ingravalle, Francesco 208 n.20
imago Dei 150, 226 n.62
irenism 156

James IV Stuart, King of England 211 n.53
Janssens, Marijke 133 n.3
Javelli, Giovanni Crisostomo 48
Jesuits 53
Jocasta 148, 163
John of Jandun 70
Jong, Jan L. de 215 n.96
Jori, Alberto 215 n.95
jurisprudence 128

Keckermann, Bartholomaeus 144
　criticizes Ramus 38, 42-4, 185 n.19, 187 n.36
　on metaphysics 45 52-3
　on politics 95-8, 104-9, 209 n.42
Kempis, Thomas à 224 n.54
Kessler, Eckhard 176 n.11, 221 n.23

Knijff, Philipp 191 n.2
Kondracka, Ewa x
Kordić, Ivan 177 n.19
Kosman, Aryeh 198 n.46
Kraye, Jill 176 n.11, 177 n.15, 194 n.19,
    227 n.77
Kühn, Karl Gottlob 223 n.41
Kundert, Ursula 210 n.50
Kusukawa, Sachiko 178 n.32, 186 n.26,
    227 n.77
Kwak, Zoran 215 n.96

Laguna, Andrés 220 n.10
Laius 148, 163
Lampius, Iacobus 189 n.73
Laskowska, Anna x
Lauterbeck, Georg 211 n.53
Law of Nature
    as a political concept 93, 124, 130,
        132
    as source of morality 140,
        221 n.21, n.23
    legitimation of political power 101, 105,
        110–11
Leibniz, Gottfried Wilhelm von 24, 28,
    90, 178 n.32, 183 n.87,
    193 n.13
Leiden 22, 56, 60, 117, 174, 214 n.90
Leijenhorst, Cees 175 n.4
Leinsle, Ulrich L. 34, 47, 52, 183 n.1,
    184 n.2, n.4, 188 n.52, n.57,
    188 n.68, 189 n.72
Leipzig 117, 137–8, 145, 150–1, 155–6, 171,
    220 n.7, 225 n.60, n.61,
    226 n.61
Leo VI, Byzantine Emperor 107
Leone, Ambrogio 220 n.10
Lepri, Valentina x, 207 n.1
Lipsius, Justus 93–7, 104, 111, 113,
    207 n.2, n.3, 211 n.53,
    213 n.71
Lithuania 135
Livius, Titus 210 n.53
Loch, Marcin x
logic 11, 26, 29, 36–41, 44–7, 49, 78, 105–6,
    108–9, 185 n.14, n.19,
    189 n.76
    as dialectics 13
    Ramist 39–41, 44

Lohr, Charles H. 176 n.11, 187 n.50,
    190 n.83, n.90, n.96, n.97
Lucian of Samosata 13, 188 n.57
Ludwig, Frank 226 n.61
Luther, Martin 53, 95, 212 n.65
    Lutherans 24, 45, 47, 53, 59, 155, 225 n.56
        Gnesio-Lutherans 45
    Lutheran metaphysics 47
Lüthy, Christoph 175 n.4
Lyceum 3–4, 118, 123, 215 n.97

Machiavelli, Niccoló 102, 119–20, 123, 130,
    211 n.53
    Machiavellianism 99, 109, 119–20, 123
Maclean, Ian 186 n.25
Madonia, Claudio 225 n.61
Magi 8
magistrate 97, 99, 101–5, 209 n.37
Mährle, Wolfgang 181 n.73
Maioragio, Marcantonio (Anton Maria
    Conti) 178 n.32
Makowski, Jan (Johannes Macovius) 52,
    190 n.93
Malandrino, Corrado 208 n.20
Manuzio, Paolo 13, 223 n.46
Marburg 26–8
Mariana, Juan de 211 n.53
Mariani Zini, Fosca 207 n.4
Marras, Cristina 178 n.32
Marti, Hanspeter 192 n.8
Marti-Weissenbach, K. 192 n.8, 210 n.50
Martin, Craig vii
Martini, Cornelius 43, 45–53, 171,
    188 n.54, n.64, n.69,
    189 n.72, n.75, m. 76
Martini, Jakob 44, 53
Martinović, Ivica 177 n.19
Mayes, Benjamin T.G. 225 n.56
Mazurek, Sławomir x
Medea 222 n.31
Meerhoff, Kees 187 n.36, 187 n.51,
    221 n.23
Megarians 150, 169
Meier, Gebhart Theodor 213 n.81,
    215 n.93
Meisner, Balthasar 189 n.76
Melanchthon, Philipp 95, 140, 142, 150,
    188 n.57, 185 n.19
    and Aristotelianism 116–17, 121

his influence 25, 45–6, 116, 155,
221 n.23, 222 n.30, 225 n.56,
226 n.61, 227 n.77
as *praeceptor Germaniae* 35, 45–8, 53,
135–6, 152–3, 226 n.62
and Tidike 155, 227 n.70, n.78
Memnius, Gaius 20
Menage, Giles 216 n.106
metabasis es allo genos 51
metaphysics
and analogy, unity of 42, 52, 67–69,
73–4
as architectonic 33, 36, 40–2, 45, 52, 74,
199 n.68
as a discipline 42–3, 51–3, 173,
179 n.41
Luther's rejection of 53
its method 40–1, 50–1
in Protestant Germany 33–4, 38, 40,
47–53, 155, 171, 190 n.96
Ramus and Ramist critique of 34–8,
46–7, 178 n.32, 201 n.94
scholastic 62, 87
its subject/object 6, 36–7, 43–5, 48–50,
53, 61, 63–5, 70–84
as theology 36–7, 44, 56–7, 63–4, 67–8,
74, 78, 81–4, 87, 118,
201 n.95
as universal science 14, 17, 22–3, 42, 46
Meteren, Emanuel van 211 n.53
method
in Conring 113–15, 127–8
demonstrative, *see* demonstration,
analytic
in Keckermann 43
in Ramus 34–9, 100
in Scherb 41–2
of teaching 10, 15–17, 23, 26, 28, 98,
178 n.11
Michael of Ephesus, *see* pseudo-Alexander
63
Mignini, Filippo 191 n.6
Milan x, 13, 22
Mittendorp, Rheinold von 211 n.53
modus considerandi 46, 48–9
Moldenauer, Christian (Moldenarius)
207 n.4
Monfasani, John 194 n.19
Montecatini, Antonio 122

Montesquieu, Charles-Louis de Secondat,
baron de 100
Muccillo, Maria 177 n.19
Muller, Richard A. 229 n.2
Mulsow, Martin 26–7, 181 n.75,
182 n.80, n.82, n.84
Mundt, Felix 227 n.77
Muret, Marc-Antoine 126, 216 n.106
Musto, Ronald G. 194 n.19
Müller, Michael G. 218 n.1

Nathan 163
natural law 93, 115, 130–2
Naudé, Gabriel 95, 207 n.4
necessity
in events 148, 150, 158, 163, 166, 168–9
in God's action 76, 86
in practical reasoning 129
Nejeschleba, Tomáš 177 n.19
Neleus of Scepsis 15
Neo-Stoicism, *see* Lipsius
Nero, Roman Emperor 162
Neschke-Hentschke, Ada 212 n.65
Niefanger, Dirk 206 n.125
Nifo, Agostino 70
Nizolio, Mario 24, 28, 178 n.32
Noah 8
Nobili, Flaminio 27
nobility 226 n.63, 227 n.72
nominalism 25, 34, 72, 173
Nothold, Anton 46–7, 188 n.54, n.57
notions
common 221 n.23
primary and secondary 41, 43, 49–51
Noue, François de la 211 n.53
Nuñes, Juan Pedro (Petrus Nunnesius)
176 n.11
Nuremberg 33, 56
Nuzzo, Enrico 212, n.66

Oestreich, Gerhard 112
Ogonowski, Zbigniew x, 56–7, 61, 87–8,
191 n.3, n.5, n.6, 204 n.110,
205 n.115
Oldrini, Guido 184 n.2, 185 n.14
Ong, Walter G. 34, 183 n.2, 184 n.5, 185 n.14
Orpheus 8
Ottman, Hennig 212 n.65
Ovid 222 n.30

Pace, Giulio 186 n.25, 194 n.20
Pacuvius 143
Padua 11–13, 41–2, 65, 78, 114, n.20,
        190 n.1, 226 n.63
    Altdorfians at 24, 39, 56, 61, 88
    metaphysics in 61–5, 194 n.18
paedia, paideia 18–23, 173, 195 n.25
Panaetius 220 n.15
pantheism 57
Papists 47, 155, 173
Pappus of Alexandria 130
Papy, Jan 207 n.3
Paracelsus (Theophrastus von
        Hohenheim) 24, 182 n.81
Paris (in France) 34, 193 n.12
Paris (of Troy) 148, 164
Patrizi, Francesco (humanist) 211 n.53
Patrizi, Francesco (philosopher) viii, 15,
        24, 27, 80, 177 n.19,
        183 n.88
    Discussiones peripateticae 7–10
    Nova de universis philosophia 177 n.19
Paul, Saint 86
Pavia 13
Pellegrini, Tommaso 38, 42, 61–70, 72, 74,
        77–8, 81, 87, 194 n.17, n.20,
        195 n.26
Pendasio, Federico 70, 85
Pereira, Benedict 48, 53, 172
Peressin, Roberto x
Périon, Joachim 211 n.54
Perkins, William 144
Peripatetic
    school 4, 16, 26, 120, 174
    tradition 3, 7, 52, 63–4, 94, 133, 117
Peter of Spain 34
Pfaffrad, Kaspar 188 n.54
Phalaris 162
Philip II of Macedonia 119, 176 n.11,
        215 n.96
Phillipism 45
philology 22–3, 62, 64, 81, 109 116–17
Philoponus 8, 10, 17, 21, 124
Phocilydes 143
Photinians, *see* Antitrinitarians
physiology 155
Piccart, Michael 61–2, 123, 131–2,
        183 n.86, 206 n.125
    on Goldast 27–8

on metaphysics 42, 61, 77, 155,
        186 n.35
Piccolomini, Francesco 24, 89, 151,
        194 n.20, 206 n.125
Pindar 228 n.105
Pine, Martin 226 n.68
Pisa 13, 27, 219 n.4
Piso, Marcus Pupius 4
Plato
    Epinomis 22
    Laws 126, 228 n.108
    Philebus 36, 184 n.6
    Republic 36
    Timaeus 161
Platonism 57, 184 n.2, 222 n.30
Plutarch 4–8, 12, 35, 46, 139, 175 n.6
Pocock, John 110
Polansdorf, Amandus Polanus von 144
Polish Commonwealth 95–6, 101, 135–6
politics
    as an acroamatic learning 17, 113–15,
        120, 123–4
    as an exoteric learning 4, 8, 123
    and jurisprudence 100–1, 111, 119, 128,
        208 n.11, 213 n.75, 215 n.95
    modern theory of 101–3, 109–10, 120,
        127–8, 131–3, 217 n.126
    and *prudentia* 93–4, 98–9, 111–15, 125
Pomerania 105, 135
Pomponazzi, Pietro 7, 85, 137, 152, 172
Poppi, Antonino 177 n.21, 194 n.18
Port-Royal 184
Porzio, Simone 137
Potamo of Alexandria 215 n.93
Pozzo, Riccardo 188 n.53, n.54, n.55,
        190 n.84
practical syllogism 114, 141, 174, 221 n.28
praxeology 99
precepts 41, 94, 97–9, 112, 143, 207 n.1
prescience of God 150
Priam 148, 164
Priarolo, Mariangela 191 n.6, 205 n.122
Protestant
    confessions 136
    schools 33, 47, 53, 95–6
providence 56, 147–9, 151–5, 161–2, 164–8
prudence 25, 141–2, 149
    prudentia civilis 94–109, 112–15,
        125–30

Prussia, Royal 135
psychopannychia 85
Pufendorf, Samuel 132–3, 218 n.130
purgatory 47, 85, 173
Pythagoras 8, 15, 143, 224 n.52

quatenus, in quantum, see also *modus considerandi* 46, 48
Quintilian 175

Rackham, Harris 220 n.14
Raków 57, 88
Ramberti, Rita 219 n.4
Ramus, Petrus 25, 33–8, 52–3, 183 n.2, 184 n.7, 185 n.14
    Ramus' three laws 36–7, 51–2, 185 n.14
    Scherb on 39–42
Ramism 24, 26, 35, 38, 42–3, 53, 116, 186 n.25, 187 n.36
    Phillipo-Ramism 185 n.19
    semi-Ramism 185 n.19, 187 n.36
rationalism 55–7, 80, 172, 191 n.6
Ravaisson, Félix 183 n.88
reason of state 93–4, 104, 107, 109–12
Reformed schools 24, 33, 45, 98, 116, 135–44, 155
Renaissance viii, 3–4, 27, 35, 37, 70, 102, 106, 109, 111, 115, 120, 124–30, 138, 183 n.88
Renan, Ernest 85
Rej, Andrzej 106–8, 211 n.53, n.54, n.57
Rej, Mikołaj 106, 211 n.53
rhetoric 7, 13, 16, 19–20, 24, 26, 29, 45, 108, 115, 175 n.3, 181 n.74
Ribadeneira, Pedro de 211 n.53
Richter, Georg 58, 60, 192 n.10, 193 n.13, n.14, 194 n.15, 211 n.53
Riedel, Manfred 110
Riel, Gerd Van 219 n.4
Risse, Wilhelm 35, 176 n.11, 184 n.2, 185 n.14, n.19
Riva, Franco 190 n.85
Rohls, Jan 221 n.23
Rome 24
Roncaglia, Gino 188 n.67, 191 n.8
Ross, Alberto 198 n.46
Ross, David 202 n.95
Ruar, Martin 58–60, 192 n.10, n.11

Saarinen, Risto 222 n.30, 226 n.62, 227 n.77
sacraments 151
Salamanca, school of 109
Salmonowicz, Stanisław 218 n.2
Santinello, Giovanni 207 n.133, 216 n.106
sapientia 6, 8, 14–15, 17, 40, 44, 53, 120, 148, 164–5, 169
    prisca 7, 22–5, 47
Saxony 117, 171
Scaini, Antonio 70, 217 n.117
Scaligero, Giulio Cesare 183 n.88, 211 n.53
Scandellari, Simonetta 209 n.33
Scattola, Merio 110, 212 n.65, 225 n.56
science of politics 93–133
scientia realis 47, 49, 51
Schegk, Jakob 35, 151, 184 n.7
Scherb, Philipp 51–2, 56, 60, 123, 171, 183 n.86, 194 n.20
    and Goldast 24–9, 182 n.81
    and Pellegrini 61–2, 81
    and Ramus 38–42, 187 n.36
Schilling, Heinz 173, 229 n.3
Schmidt-Glintzer, Helwig 181 n.75
Schmitt, Charles B. vii, 176 n.11, 201 n.94, 220 n.10, 224 n.47
Schnabel, Werner Wilhelm 206 n.125
scholastic philosophy
    mediaeval 70, 81, 151, 155, 183 n.86, 189 n.72, 205 n.120
    modern , 48, 52, 90, 152, 189 n.72, 205 n.120
    Iberian 62, 70, 72, 109, 172, 205 n.120
school teaching/learning 135–45, 227 n.79
    and acroamatic/exoteric distinction 3–5, 10–11, 19–24, 25–9, 119, 123
    in Conring 119–22
    in Keckermann 45–6
    of metaphysics 45–7, 53, 62–3
    of politics 95–6, 113–16, 128–32
    in Ramus 34–5, 38, 116
Schönborn, Johann Philipp von 121
Schoppe, Caspar 112
Schulphilosophie 29, 33, 69, 94–5, 111, 128, 171
Scribano, Emanuela 191 n.1, n.6, 205 n.122
Selderhuis, Herman.J. 187 n.36

Sellberg, Erland 184 n.7
Sepulveda, Juan Gines de
   criticized by Ferrari 14, 17, 20, 22
      by SIgonio 12
   on *Politics* 5–7, 122, 123, 127
   translator of the *Metaphysics* 63
Sgarbi, Marco x
Siegen 96
Sigonio, Carlo 12–13, 123, 180 n.60
Simoni, Simone 145, 151, 225 n.60, n.61, 226 n.63
Simplicius 8, 10, 13, 18, 70, 124, 183 n.88
Sinnema, Donald W. 225 n.55
Sirenio, Giulio 137, 152, 226 n.69
Skinner, Quentin 110, 176 n.11
Sleidanus, Johannes 211 n.53
Socinianism 55–9, 88
   crypto-Socinianism 58–60
Socrates 36–7, 112
Solon 143
Soner, Ernst 56–88, 171, 193 n.13, n.14, 194 n.17, 199 n.63, 201 n.92, n.93, 204 n.109, 205 n.114, n.120
Sophists 112
sovereignty 93, 100, 105, 111, 128, 132
Sozzini, Fausto 55–6, 60, 61
Sparn, Walter 184 n.8, 189 n.76, 206 n.125
Speer, Andreas 221 n.23
Sperone, Speroni 180 n.60
Spies, Marijke 215 n.96
Spinoza, Baruch 93, 133
Spranzi, Marta 178 n.25, 180 n.60
Stanciu, Diana 207 n.3
state 127–31
statecraft 128
Starzyński, Wojciech x
Steuco, Agostino 15
Steinfurt 96, 98
Stobaeus 143, 224 n.47
Stoics 40, 142, 146, 156, 158, 163, 166
Stolleis, Michael 214 n.90
Stopp, Frederick J. 214 n.74
Strabo 5, 16, 35, 175 n.3, n.6
Strigel, Viktorin 144
Stroband, Heinrich 135
Strohm, Christoph 187 n.36
Strubius, Fridericus 213 n.78, 215 n.95
Sturm, Johann 135, 181 n.74

Suarez, Francisco 48, 50, 52–3, 69, 74–5, 173, 189 n.75, 199 n.68
subordination
   logical 11, 22, 39, 189 n.72, 199 n.67
   ontological 198 n.41
substance, substances 37, 44, 50, 64–78, 155
Susemhil, Franz 220 n.14
Sylburg, Friedrich 121
syllogism, theory of 11, 17, 19, 106
   demonstrative 114
   dialectical 20
system 44, 45, 46, 95, 111, 174
Szczucki, Lech x, 218 n.2

Tacitus 213 n.71, n.75
Tasso, Torquato 180 n.60
Taurellus, Nicolaus 24, 42, 44, 61–2, 85–90, 201 n.93, 204 n.114, 206 n.125, 206 n.126
tautologies 37, 41, 52
Telesio, Bernardino 24
temperance 139, 141, 143
theism 77
Themistius 180 n.62
Theodor of Gaza
Theognis 143
theology
   rational or philosophical 36, 49, 52, 56–8, 64, 67, 76, 79–90, 155–6, 189 n.76, 193 n.13, 206 n.126, 226 n.63
   revealed 60, 64, 69, 85, 150–1, 155
Theophrastus 4, 15–16, 21
Thijssen, Johannes M.M.H. 175 n.4
Thomas Aquinas, Saint (the Angelic Doctor) 14, 62–4, 66–7, 69–70, 151
   Thomism 49, 62–4
Thomasius, Jakob 90, 132, 178, 207 n.133
Thouard, Denis 207 n.4
Tidike, Franz (Franciscus Tidicaeus) 136–45, 150–1, 220 n.7, n.10, 221 n.20, 222 n.30, 224 n.52, 225 n.60, n.61
Timpler, Clemens 71, 96–100, 207 n.4, 208 n.9
Tiraboschi, Girolamo 178 n.32
Tolomio, Ilario 216 n.106

Tolosanus, *see* Pierre Gregoire
Tomitano, Bernardino 11
Tommasi, Francesco V. 183 n.86
Toruń 135–6, 224 n.48
Torzini, Roberto 205 n.122
transcendentals 48–51, 69, 75, 189 n.82, 190 n.83
Transylvania 135
Tübingen 35, 155
Tync, Stanisław 218 n.1, 219 n.6, 224 n.46, n.48, 227 n.79
Tyrannion 15–16

univocity 50, 66–7, 71–4
Uriah 163

Vaeck, Marc van 215 n.96
Valera, Gabriella 212 n.70
Varani, Giovanna 178 n.32
Vasoli, Cesare 184 n.2
Verdigi, Mariano 226 n.63
Vermigli, Pietro Martire 144, 155
Vettori, Pietro 13, 116, 121–3, 127
Vielmi, Girolamo 62
Vimercato, Francesco 34, 85, 151, 226 n.64
Vindiciae contra tyrannos 101
virtue
    dianoethical 105, 108, 141, 143, 160
    ethical 108, 110, 120, 139–44, 179 n.38, 220 n.14, 222 n.32
    political, *see prudentia civilis*
Visser, Sibbe Jan 191 n.2
Vitruvius 23
Vives, Juan Luis 143, 223 n.45

Völger, Georg Johann 113–14, 121, 213 n.81
Völkel, Johann 205 n.121
Vollhardt, Friedrich 207 n.4
voluntarism 222 n.30
Voss, Gerhard Johannes 117, 174, 215 n.93

Waszink, Jan 207 n.2
Wilmott, Michael J. 177 n.19
Wipple, John 183 n.87
wisdom, *see sapientia*
Witte, Henning 193 n.14
Wittenberg 42, 117, 155, 156, 171
Wollgast, Siegfried 56, 57, 191 n.3, n.4, 204 n.110
Wolzogen, Johannes Ludwig 191 n.6
Wundt, Max 184 n.8, 188 n.67

Zabarella, Giacomo 11–13, 38–9, 41–2, 49, 52–3, 173, 185 n.25, 186 n.25, n.32, 187 n.36, 216 n.114
    his followers 46
Zalta, Edward N. 183 n.87
Zanchi, Girolamo 155
Zanier, Giancarlo 226 n.69
Zeller, Eduard 220 n.14
Zeltner, Georg Gustav 58–9, 191 n.8, 192 n.11
Zeno of Citium 157
Zimara, Marcantonio 151
Zizza, Cesare 179 n.41
Zwinger, Theodor 122

www.ingramcontent.com/pod-product-compliance
Lightning Source LLC
Chambersburg PA
CBHW072136290426
44111CB00012B/1886